History, Gender & Eighteenth-Century Literature

History, Gender &

Eighteenth-Century

Literature

Edited by Beth Fowkes Tobin

The University of Georgia Press

Athens and London

© 1994 by the University of Georgia Press
Athens, Georgia 30602
All rights reserved
Designed by Louise OFarrell
Set in 11.5/13 Garamond #3
by Tseng Information Systems, Inc.
Printed and bound by Thomson-Shore, Inc.
The paper in this book meets the guidelines for
permanence and durability of the Committee on
Production Guidelines for Book Longevity of the
Council on Library Resources.

Printed in the United States of America
98 97 96 95 94   C   5   4   3   2   1

Library of Congress Cataloging in Publication Data
History, gender, and eighteenth-century
literature / edited by Beth Fowkes Tobin.
p.
Includes bibliographical references and index.
ISBN 0-8203-1577-X (alk. paper)
1. English literature—18th century—History
and criticism. 2. Feminism and literature—
Great Britain—History—18th century.
3. Literature and history—Great Britain—
History—18th century. 4. Women and
literature—Great Britain—History—18th
century. 5. Authorship—Sex differences.
6. Sex role in literature. I. Tobin, Beth Fowkes.
PR448.F45H57   1994
820.9'005'082—dc20
                                    93-4161

British Library Cataloging in Publication Data available

🙰 *Contents*

Acknowledgments

I would like to thank the contributors of this volume for their cooperation, patience, and generosity. This book would not have been possible without the support and encouragement from the following: Ruth Perry, Nancy Armstrong, Judith Newton, Lillian Robinson, Susan Staves, and Nancy Holmes. I would also like to thank Cambridge University Press for permission to reprint portions of Dianne Dugaw's chapter on *Polly,* Yale University Press for permission to reprint portions of my book *Superintending the Poor,* and Macmillan and St. Martin's Press for permission to reprint selections from Jan Fergus's book on Jane Austen.

History, Gender & Eighteenth-Century Literature

Introduction:
Feminist Historical Criticism

✣ *Beth Fowkes Tobin*

The essays in this volume are at once feminist and historical, utilizing culture and history as well as gender as categories of analysis to explore literature. The texts under investigation range from the late seventeenth to the early nineteenth centuries, from popular and subliterary genres, such as conduct books and agricultural manuals, to "classics" by writers such as Henry Fielding, Frances Burney, and Jane Austen. Employing a wide range of historical approaches, including biographical, new historicist, and Marxist, these essays as a group make the case that an understanding of the economic, political, and cultural circumstances of women's and men's lived experience is vital to the task of literary criticism. These essays provide models that will encourage feminists to turn to history and culture in their analyses of literary texts and to regard with skepticism an essentialism that permeates too much of feminist literary criticism.[1]

Essentialism in Feminism

Among the many stages through which American feminist literary criticism has passed in the last two decades is the shift in the late seventies from a preoccupation with women's oppression and victimization to women's power and agency. Such books as *A Literature of Their Own* (1977) and *Communities of Women* (1978) celebrate women's creative capacity and productivity, despite the constraints placed upon them; *The Madwoman in the Attic* (1979) and *Women, Power and Subversion* (1981) examine women's ability to survive and subvert patriarchy. As Judith Newton notes, "power was discovered where only oppression had stood before, in masked forms and unlooked for places . . . in women's culture and in women's sphere."[2] Implicit in this movement to examine women's experience is the assumption that women are to be valued and that their actions, words, and thoughts are to be recovered and appreciated. Ordinary women's daily lives were investigated by social historians such as Nancy Cott and Barbara Epstein, and women's diaries, letters, and journals were recovered and published.[3] Literary critics argued that although women's writing tended to be less formal, more private, and more interpersonal than men's, it deserved to be recognized as art.

With this "recovery and cultivation of women's culture,"[4] feminists focused on women's writing and women's reading with an aim to define female experience, often basing their analyses on psychological definitions of what it means to be a woman.[5] To answer the question, "What does it mean for a woman, reading as a woman, to read literature written by a woman writing as a woman?," Patrocinio Schweickart, in her award-winning essay "Reading Ourselves: Toward a Feminist Theory of Reading," turns to psychological explanations that characterize women as having "more flexible ego boundaries" and as defining themselves "in terms of their affiliations and relationships with others," while men are characterized as defining "themselves through individuation and separation from others." Schweickart tells us that women "value relationships, and they are most concerned in their dealings with others to negotiate between opposing needs so that the relationship can be maintained" and that "men value autonomy, and they think of their interactions with others principally in terms of procedures for arbitrating conflicts between individual rights."[6] While this may very well be true of late twentieth-century American women and men, such psychologizing of women's experience implies an essentialism that, in assuming a universal and transhistorical human nature, is profoundly ahistorical and acultural. Feminist Marxist Catharine MacKinnon sees in this kind of feminist psychologizing a liberal humanist tradition that has never taken "social determination and the realities of power seriously enough" and therefore falls into the fallacy of construing "evidence of women's subordination as evidence of women's difference, elevating the body of women's oppression to the level of a universal, a category beyond history."[7]

Hélène Cixous warns feminists: "We have to be careful not to lapse smugly or blindly into an essentialist ideological interpretation." Arguing that "there is no 'destiny' no more than there is 'nature' or 'essence' as such," Cixous turns to history or "historiocultural" determinations to explain why women feel, think, and act as they do. "One can no more speak of 'woman' than of 'man' without being trapped within an ideological theater where the proliferation of representations, images, reflections, myths, identifications, transform, deform, constantly change everyone's Imaginary and invalidate in advance any conceptualization."[8]

This turning away from psychology and toward history is shared by feminists who, as Marxists or cultural materialists, tend to see "woman" and "femininity" as well as "man" and "masculinity" as social constructions. In their introduction to *Making a Difference*, Gayle Greene and Coppelia Kahn argue that feminist scholarship should take Simone de Beauvoir's statements that "one is not born, but rather becomes a woman" and that "it is civilization as a whole that produces this creature" as the central assumptions of historical, anthropological, and literary analyses of women's experience. Feminist scholarship, they argue, "undertakes to 'deconstruct' the social construction of gender and the cultural paradigms that support it."[9]

Taking Greene and Kahn's advice on how to do feminist scholarship, we can historicize and rephrase Schweickart's question: what does it mean for a late twentieth-century, American, white, middle-class, academic woman to read literature by an early nineteenth-century, upperclass, British woman? Or, what did it mean in the eighteenth century to be a working-class woman writing anonymously, without much monetary recompense, in a society that severely limited women's roles? And in what ways did these various women writers support or subvert the dominant social, political, and economic structures in Britain and the world economy?

These, it seems to me, are far more interesting questions, ones that focus on the variety and specificity of women's experiences.[10] Catharine Simpson sees in "presenting the differences among women" a new kind of feminist criticism, one she calls "herterogeneity." Herterogeneity sights the "differences among women that body and community, place and history, have bred, and often inbred."[11] More important, these are the questions that will lead us to a greater understanding of the historical locations of women's power and oppression, and that may, in turn, give us the insight and the ability needed to challenge the patriarchal conditions that construct gender. Patriarchy does not consist of one great monolith, as critics too often mistakenly portray it;[12] rather, patriarchy, like other hegemonic manifestations, "does not just passively exist as a form of dominance. It continually has to be renewed, recreated, defended, and modified." [13] Patriarchy, as Teresa Ebert has argued, "while seemingly universal," is "at any given moment . . . historically determined since it is formed in conjunction with a specific social formation and its dominating mode of production." [14] Because patriarchy is always in flux and constantly embattled, the conditions that shape women's lived experience are, too, constantly shifting. A working-class woman writing in 1740 lived, thought, and felt very differently from a middle-class woman in 1790. As feminists, we must recognize historical difference because with this understanding will come the recognition that as women, as writers, and as readers, we are constituted by our society, and upon this recognition depends our liberation. "To change the social, economic, and power relations among individuals and society," we have to interrogate "the ideological production and circulation of gender." [15] So that we may resist, as Lillian Robinson says, "a kind of idealism we become susceptible to when we explore the question of feminine consciousness," we must historicize our readings of literature and gender.[16]

But how do we go about following Fredric Jameson's edict "always historicize!"? [17] Historicizing involves more than an occasional reference in the course of a literary analysis to a historical fact contained in a huge social history such as Lawrence Stone's *The Family, Sex and Marriage in England, 1500–1800*. The aim of this volume of essays is to provide answers to the question of *how* to historicize our reading of literature and gender.

Historicizing Gender

In *Feminist Literary History,* Janet Todd, reviewing the Anglo-American tradition of feminist criticism, concludes that "the potential of the historical feminist approach has not yet been fulfilled, an approach that disrupts the canon and all readings and is informed by an apprehension of ideology as material and psychological." [18] Recently, however, American feminists have begun to focus on literature and its relation to ideology, specifically literature as it participates in the construction of gender. Nancy Armstrong's work on discourse and gender, Mary

Poovey's on the ideology of separate spheres, and Felicity Nussbaum's analysis of the construction of gendered subjectivities have profoundly revised our critical practice, while such work as Donna Landry's recovery and analysis of the poetry of women of the laboring classes and Elizabeth Brophy's detailing of women's material lives in the eighteenth century are invaluable sources for the recovery of women's lives and literary achievements.[19]

The essays in this volume, building on these important feminist literary histories, delineate the cultural construction and historical specificity of eighteenth-century ideas about women and men, their roles, and their "nature." Shawn Maurer, Kathryn Kirkpatrick, Beth Tobin, and Ruth Perry, using Marxist and neo-Marxist methods of analysis, examine ways in which texts create gendered subjectivities and promote the production of masculine and feminine spheres of activity. Mitzi Myers, Janice Thaddeus, and Jan Fergus use more traditional historical methods aimed at rediscovering women's lived experience, while Joseph Lew investigates economic forces that shape women's lives, and Susan Staves interrogates the legal foundations of women's powerlessness. Dianne Dugaw, Beth Kowaleski-Wallace, and Jill Campbell look at the representation of the body, violations of gender categories, and deviations from the sexual norms as ways to explore the cultural constructions of gender, race, and class in the eighteenth century.

Several of the essays deal explicitly with the social construction of gender. The new domestic woman, a product of the new capitalist social and economic relations, is the topic of Kirkpatrick's discussion of conduct books. She argues that conduct book writers represent women as private property, using capitalist terms of ownership—enclosure and improvement. Dugaw, Maurer, and Tobin investigate the formation of various types of masculinities, examining the aristocratic model of warrior-gentleman as well as tracing the newly emergent economic and affective masculinities of the middle classes. Dugaw argues that *Polly*, Gay's sequel to *The Beggar's Opera*, interrogates the European heroic ideal and exposes as its basis an enslaving will to empire. Gay's use of the female warrior figure upsets the heroic formula of male glory rewarded by female love. While Dugaw's analysis of *Polly* exposes the violence that inheres in aristocratic masculinity, Maurer demonstrates how early British periodicals promulgated a new discourse on bourgeois masculinity, a discourse that stressed affective ties that not only bound husband and wife in domestic harmony but also bound father and son in "sacred" friendship "as pleasurable as love." Examples of idealized father-son relations, based on the concept of a partnership, abound in the *Spectator*. Men have relationships of collaboration rather than competition in both the structural and the narrative levels of the periodical; the fictional joint authorship of the Spectator Club mirrors the real collaboration of Addison and Steele. Shifting to a late eighteenth-century version of middle-class masculinity, Tobin analyzes the new gender-inflected discourse on scientific agriculture and estate management. In the writings of such agriculturalists as Arthur Young, Tobin sees the construction of the new economic man, one who was posited in opposition to a profligate aristocracy and who possessed the middle-class skills in quantification, valuation, and management of land and labor, skills that were in the nineteenth century generalized and attributed to all males.

Perry, Campbell, and Kowaleski-Wallace deal with writers who portray deviations from the gendered ideal. In her examination of four utopian fictions, Perry uncovers the connection between the way in which intellectual women are represented and the reinscription of social relations of class, gender, and empire. If a narrative mocks an educated woman and assumes she violates the natural subordination of women to men, then that narrative invariably assumes the naturalness of economic exploitation of the lower classes and other races; whereas, a text that values intellectual women reimagines social relations, stressing the communal over hierarchical relations. Campbell suggests that Lady Mary Wortley Montagu's Turkish letters register her increasing awareness of the essential historicity of gender roles. Campbell argues that when Lady Mary describes cultural difference, she engages in the re-negotiation of her own country's rigid gender boundaries, enabling her to address the issue of female erotic passion, the expression of which would have constituted a violation of decorum in her own culture. Burney's passion for the Italian opera is Kowaleski-Wallace's topic. Seeking to explain Burney's fascination with the celebrated soprano Signori Agujari, who combined great talent with physical deformity, Kowaleski-Wallace argues that Burney presents opera as the "natural" location for an "elevated consciousness" that transcends the body, a site where the artist with her beautiful voice can transcend the sordid and vulgar body. For Burney, Agujari's opera career is analogous to her own struggle to establish herself as a professional woman writer, who, like the singer of Italian opera, is positioned on the margins of society.

While these essays focus on ideologies of gender and the intersection of class and gender, other essays use historical information about the period to formulate finely textured and historically specific readings of gender as it appears in literary and nonliterary texts. Using biographical information, diaries, and letters, Fergus examines the relationship between Austen's marginal economic status and her depiction of impoverished gentlewomen in *Emma,* while Thaddeus reexamines Mary Delany's two marriages and her negotiation of this incarcerating institution. Three essays stand out for their rigorous reconstruction of the historical context: Lew on the debate over the slave trade, Myers on Hannah More's battle to defend her Sunday schools, and Staves on the law's representation of rape. Lew demonstrates that *Mansfield Park* is full of allusions to the current debate on the international prohibition of the slave trade, arguing that Austen condemns the tyranny of the absentee landlord over the bodies of not only his slaves but also other forms of human property—the women in his household. Lew suggests that Fanny's "no" is an act of rebellion that carries with it the reference to other kinds of rebellions against landowners, and her refusal of Crawford's proposal signals her refusal to participate as a commodity in the trade in human bodies. While Lew notes Austen's leanings toward Evangelicalism and its powerful abolitionist position, Myers gives a full account of Anglican Evangelicalism and Hannah More's participation in that movement. In her meticulous reconstruction of the Blagdon controversy, Myers attempts a revaluation of More's life and writings that takes into account the cultural predicament of women in the late eighteenth century. By carefully recreating the context of one of More's many charitable projects, her establishment of Sunday schools, Myers argues that More is responsible for the construction of an ideology of benevolent female power that opened the public realm to female activity, signaling to women the possibility of meaningful action not only in religious and charitable causes but also in other more political forms of militancy. Also using historical detail to rethink a controversial topic, Staves explores Fielding's representation of attempted rape, seeking to explain by reference to contemporary legal theory, court records, and trial transcripts how attempted rape could be portrayed as a comic rather than as a serious or tragic action. In her review of cultural and legal definitions of rape, she uncovers assumptions about attempted rape as a measure of a woman's desirability. She also discovers that attempted rape was in the eyes of the law only a misdemeanor, and she notes that alleged rapists were usually not convicted, and that women's protestations of their own innocence and their accused attacker's guilt were usually not believed. Despite all-too-contemporary-sounding results, she argues that crime and sexuality have histories and that neither is a transhistorical constant.

Gender and Academia

Before urging you to read these essays, all of them fine examples of different historical approaches to gender and literature, I must say something about this book's emphasis on gender and where it fits into the current political debates in academia about gender studies as an alternative to feminist or women's studies. The movement in some institutions to replace women's studies programs with gender studies has been hotly contested, particularly by feminists who fear that gender studies will undermine the political agenda that feminists bring to bear on their work—to expose and to resist the oppression of women and to encourage women to work for political and social change. Some feminists fear that gender studies is a "cop-out," or worse, a subterfuge. Despite the declaration by the proponents of gender studies that it is a radical position signaled by its poststructuralist stance to language and representation, feminists suspect that gender studies will subsume and eventually erase the field of study—women's lives, women's texts, women's bodies—that feminist and women's studies programs have fought long and hard to legitimize. Soon departments of gender studies, some feminists fear, will be hiring men to study masculinity, and we will have white, middle-class males writing dissertations, albeit through the lens of poststructuralist techniques of analysis, on texts produced by white males, and such authors as Hemingway will again take a privileged position in the canon. In the worst scenario figured by feminist critics of gender studies, women, as researchers and subjects, will eventually be marginalized, even excluded from the discipline feminists have worked so hard to forge.[20]

The other side of this argument is that feminists, particularly those who see themselves as working within a tradition that focuses on recovering women's lives, work, and texts, accept uncritically the conventions of their disciplines, whether it be history, psychology, anthropology, or literature. Alice Jardine criticizes American feminists for naively accepting humanist assumptions about the existence of self and identity and for unself-consciously accepting metaphysical assumptions about the referentiality of language and the possibility of seeking the truth.

> The sex of the author, narrative destinies, images of women and gender stereotypes continue to be the touchstones of feminist literary criticism as it has developed, most particularly, in the United States. When the feminist critic turns to France, she learns that this bedrock of feminist inquiry has been increasingly and rapidly dislodged: there, in step with what are seen as the most important fictional texts of modernity, the "author" (and his intentionalities) has disappeared; the "narrative" has no teleology; "characters" are little more than proper name functions; the "image" as icon must be rendered unrecognizable; and the framework of sexual identity, recognized as intrinsic to all of those structures, is to be dismantled.[21]

Her book is an attempt to educate American feminists by reviewing the work of French feminists and deconstructionists and to appropriate from France a critical stance that will enable feminists to be truly radical in their rethinking of patriarchy and its phallogocentrisms.

In *Gender and the Politics of History,* Joan Scott also argues that a feminism that accepts its discipline's conventions can never be radical, and that no real change can occur until the phallogocentric assumptions that shape our world and determine the way in which we negotiate our way in it have been interrogated and resisted. She is critical of "herstory," histories of women's lives and descriptions of women's culture, because "it tends to isolate women as a specific and separate topic of history," and thus reinscribes patterns of difference and oppression.[22] Scott follows Natalie Zemon Davis's advice—"we should be interested in the history of both women and men," and "our goal is to understand the significance of the *sexes*"—[23] by calling for "a genuine historicization and deconstruction of the terms of sexual difference" (41), and by urging historians to use gender as a way to think about "how people construct meanings, about how difference (and therefore sexual difference) operates in the construction of meaning, and about how the complexities of contextual usages open the way for changes in meaning" (53).

This volume contains essays by scholars who are clearly working in the tradition of "herstory" (Myers, Thaddeus, and Fergus), and by others who are clearly in the gender studies camp (Dugaw, Maurer, and Kowaleski-Wallace), while yet others manage to dip into both (Perry and Lew). It seems to me that both perspectives must be maintained, for without an emphasis on real women—their lives, work, and art— the political agenda of feminism, its focus on power and oppression, could disappear in the proliferation of trendy studies on gender, and, likewise, without gender studies' insistence that we reflect on the assumptions that inform our work, feminist literary criticism could be in danger of participating in the reinscription of the social, political, and economic relations that feminists work to transform.

To avoid an ahistorical notion of "women" and "men" as transhistorical and universal categories, feminist literary critics need to use history and culture to complicate and problematize our understanding of gender. Feminists should use history and gender to create, as Scott says, a "double-edged analytical tool," [24] to cut through mystifying ideologies that smooth over contradictions and that appear to provide answers to questions, which, in reality, are evaded. Furthermore, feminist literary historians, as Catherine Belsey contends, can expose ideological constructs that masquerade as coherence and, in reality, function in the interest of those in power. [25]

Notes

1. See Diana Fuss's *Essentially Speaking: Feminism, Nature and Difference* (London: Routledge, 1989) for a provocative analysis of the theoretical implications of the attack on essentialism by "constructionists," who are concerned with "the *production* and *organization* of differences" and "reject the idea that any essential or natural givens precede the processes of social determination" (2–3). Fuss demonstrates that "essentialism and constructionism are deeply and inextricably co-implicated with each other" (xii). She urges feminists to resist an either/or position and to adopt a stance that will allow one to "work through" this debate.

2. Judith Lowder Newton, *Women, Power and Subversion: Social Strategies in British Fiction, 1778–1860* (New York: Methuen, 1981), xv.

3. See Nancy F. Cott, *The Bonds of Womanhood: Woman's Sphere in New England, 1780–1835* (New Haven: Yale University Press, 1977), and Barbara Leslie Epstein, *The Politics of Domesticity: Women, Evangelism, and Temperance in Nineteenth-Century America* (Middleton, Conn.: Wesleyan University Press, 1981). See also *Teaching Women's Literature from a Regional Perspective,* ed. Leonore Hoffmann and Deborah Rosenfelt (New York: MLA, 1982).

4. Patrocinio P. Schweickart, "Reading Ourselves: Toward a Feminist Theory of Reading," in *Gender and Reading,* ed. Elizabeth A. Flynn and Patrocinio P. Schweickart (Baltimore: Johns Hopkins University Press, 1986), 51.

5. See, for instance, the editorial policy of *Tulsa Studies in Women's Literature* and the introduction to Flynn and Schweickart's *Gender and Reading.*

6. Schweickart, "Reading Ourselves," 51–55. Here, Schweickart is relying on the work of Nancy Chodorow, which has too frequently been misused by feminists in making arguments about women's "nature." Chodorow's description of men and women's different styles of relating has often been taken out of context. Chodorow's argument is not at all that of an essentialist, but rather that of a Marxist who sees these styles of interaction as being determined by the economic conditions under which men and women live. She sees the kind of mothering that produces dependent women and independent men as a product of industrialized capitalism. "Women's mothering . . . is pivotal to the reproduction of the capitalist mode of production and the ideology which supports it." See Chodorow, "Mothering, Male Dominance, and Capitalism," in *Capitalist Patriarchy and the Case of Socialist Feminism,* ed. Zillah R. Eisenstein (New York: Monthly Review Press, 1979), 95.

7. Catharine MacKinnon, *Toward a Feminist Theory of the State* (Cambridge, Mass.: Harvard University Press, 1989), 52, 59.

8. Hélène Cixous, "Sorties: Out and Out: Attacks/Ways Out/Forays," in *The Newly Born Woman,* trans. Betsy Wing (Minneapolis: University of Minnesota Press, 1986), 81–83.

9. Gayle Greene and Coppelia Kahn, "Feminist Scholarship and the Social Construction of Woman," in *Making a Difference: Feminist Literary Criticism,* ed. Greene and Kahn (New York: Methuen, 1985), 2.

10. In *Discovering Women's History* (London: Pandora, 1983), Deirdre Beddoe urges historians to look at the specificity of women's lives: "Women have, at different times and in different circumstances, faced varying problems and have reacted to them in diverse ways. One cannot simply lift out of context women from medieval Europe, Puritan England and World War II America and treat them as some a-historical caste, transcending time and place, and sharing the same difficulties, pursuits and thought patterns" (7).

11. Catharine R. Simpson, "Woolf's Room, Our Project: The Building of

Feminist Criticism," in *Future Literary Theory,* ed. Ralph Cohen (New York: Routledge, 1989), 143.

12. See Nancy Armstrong's critique of Sandra M. Gilbert and Susan Gubar's ahistorical understanding of patriarchy in *Desire and Domestic Fiction* (New York: Oxford University Press, 1987): "Gilbert and Gubar virtually ignore the historical conditions that women have confronted as writers, and in so doing they ignore the place of women's writing in history. . . . So long as we assume that gender transcends history, we have no hope of understanding what role women played—for better or worse—in shaping the world we presently inhabit" (8).

13. Raymond Williams, *Marxism and Literature* (Oxford: Oxford University Press, 1977), 112.

14. Teresa Ebert, "The Romance of Patriarchy: Ideology, Subjectivity, and Postmodern Feminist Cultural Theory," *Cultural Critique* 10 (Fall 1988): 19–57. "Under capitalism, the kinship relations and exchange of women characterizing previous (agricultural) patriarchal societies are displaced by new class relations and commodity exchange, and the domestic economy—the 'production of life,' specifically subsistence goods and human life—is subsumed under the privileged, profit-making production of commodities in terms of wage labor—the 'production of things'—while domestic labor is literally 'de-valued' as non-wage labor," 19–20.

15. Ebert, "The Romance of Patriarchy," 19.

16. Lillian Robinson, "Dwelling in Decencies: Radical Criticism and the Feminist Perspective," in *Sex, Class, and Culture* (Bloomington: Indiana University Press, 1978), 8.

17. Fredric Jameson, *The Political Unconscious* (Ithaca: Cornell University Press, 1981), 9.

18. Janet Todd, *Feminist Literary History* (London: Routledge, 1988), 98. See also Marilyn L. Williamson, "Toward a Feminist Literary History," *Signs* 10 (1984): 136–47.

19. There is a growing number of excellent feminist literary histories of eighteenth-century literature. See, for instance, Mary Poovey, *The Proper Lady and the Woman Writer: Ideology as Style in the Works of Mary Wollstonecraft, Mary Shelley, and Jane Austen* (Chicago: University of Chicago Press, 1984); Nancy Armstrong, *Desire and Domestic Fiction, A Political History of the Novel* (New York: Oxford University Press, 1987); Ruth Salvaggio, *Enlightened Absence: Neoclassical Configurations of the Feminine* (Urbana: University of Illinois Press, 1988); Felicity Nussbaum, *The Autobiographical Subject: Gender and Ideology in Eighteenth-Century England* (Baltimore: Johns Hopkins University Press, 1989), and Nussbaum's special issue of *Eighteenth-Century Studies* 23 (1990), "The Politics of Difference"; Donna Landry, *The Muse of Resistance: Laboring-*

class Women's Poetry in Britain, 1739–1796 (Cambridge: Cambridge University Press, 1990); and Elizabeth Bergen Brophy, *Women's Lives and the Eighteenth-Century Novel* (Tampa: University of South Florida, 1991).

20. Tania Modleski argues that anti-essentialist feminists produce a kind of gynocidal feminism that endangers the feminist project of liberation from male dominance. See her *Feminism Without Women: Culture and Criticism in a "Postfeminist" Age* (New York: Routledge, 1991), 3–22.

21. Alice A. Jardine, *Gynesis: Configurations of Woman and Modernity* (Ithaca: Cornell University Press, 1985), 57.

22. Joan Wallach Scott, *Gender and the Politics of History* (New York: Columbia University Press, 1988), 20.

23. Natalie Zemon Davis, "Women's History in Transition: The European Case," *Feminist Studies* (1975–76) 3:90, quoted by Scott, 29.

24. Scott, *Gender and the Politics of History,* 9–10.

25. Catherine Belsey, *Critical Practice* (New York: Methuen, 1980), 57–58.

"As Sacred as Friendship, as Pleasurable as Love": Father-Son Relations in the *Tatler* and *Spectator*

🙊 *Shawn Lisa Maurer*

> The revolution in which the slogan "liberté, egalité, fraternité" was proclaimed began in 1789, but the alliance between the three elements was forged much earlier. Modern patriarchy is fraternal in form and the original contract is a fraternal pact.
>
> —Carole Pateman, *The Sexual Contract*

From Rae Blanchard in 1929 to Kathryn Shevelow in 1989,[1] critics have examined the ways in which Joseph Addison and Richard Steele's periodical publications, in particular the *Tatler* (1709–11) and the *Spectator* (1711–12), acted to influence and define their female audience in the process of constructing a new ideology of domestic femininity: "Through the work of their authoritative yet benign personae, these early periodicals established a definition of feminine nature, rewarded the behavior that adhered to this definition, and punished behaviors that did not." In particular, these texts "created a situation in which female readers were cast into these roles of daughters and wives in the act of reading the periodical 'properly.' "[2] In addition, such critics as Terry Eagleton and Michael Ketcham have attempted to analyze the ways in which the *Spectator* in particular generated an inclusive discursive realm, serving a variety of social and political uses.[3] In *The Function of Criticism,* Eagleton, following Jürgen Habermas,[4] argues for the early eighteenth-century periodicals' central place in bringing about a bourgeois "public sphere," a site of discourse that, by cutting across class and party lines, served to unify an English ruling bloc through culture.[5] Ketcham argues that in contrast to the dominant seventeenth-century model of society, which saw public and private, city and country, land and money as conflicting polarities, the newer eighteenth-century model, expressed within the *Spectator,* attempted to represent a unified and cohesive social order embodied within an intimate group—both the Spectator Club itself and the affective family—as secure against the self-interest and disorder of the outside world.

Although Ketcham's analysis does include some discussion of the family as an important part of the *Spectator*'s redefinition of social groups,[6] it is nevertheless notable that in the emphasis on inclusion and social definition, neither Eagleton nor Ketcham adequately addresses the part played by gender. In this article, I look at the intersection and interrelation of these two constructions—of a new domestic femininity, as well as of a nonpartisan, noncompetitive and familial masculinity— as they are manifested within the shift in narrative structure and situation from the *Tatler* to the *Spectator.* As a literary endeavor, the *Tatler* is defined fictionally as the production of one man—the "Lucubrations of Isaac Bickerstaff"—and is aimed in particular toward women. Bickerstaff announces in the *Tatler*'s first number: "I resolve also to have something which may be of Entertainment to the Fair Sex, in Honour of whom, I have invented the Title of this Paper." In contrast, the later periodical eidolon is an unnamed, anonymous "Spectator," whose voice sounds only within the confines of his (all-male) club. I argue that this shift creates a different model of intratextual relations, which is then manifested in the relations between text and reader. Just as Bickerstaff reconstitutes gossip and "tattle" into materials for the reformation of "manners and morals," so too does Mr. Spectator exploit the possibilities inherent within "spectatorship," as a theme, a process, and a rhetorical position. These shifts in narrative, as well as in authorial relations—the *Tatler* is primarily Steele's production, whereas Addison shared equal responsibility for the *Spectator*'s original 555 numbers[7]—allowed for the fuller development of a discourse about male homosocial relations.

Yet the ideology of male consolidation that is, I think, accurately described by Eagleton and Ketcham, depends in large part upon the creation and then effacement of a female "other"—a construct itself dependent upon a rigid separation between male and female qualities and appropriate behaviors. Unlike the earlier periodical productions of John Dunton, which often described male and female attributes, as well as sexual appetites, as relatively comparable, different in degree rather than in kind,[8] the *Tatler* promulgated an incommensurability of both bodies and spirits, declaring that "there is a sort of Sex in Souls" and that "the Soul of a Man and that of a Woman are made very unlike, according to the Employments for which they are designed," so that even "the Virtues have respectively a Masculine and a Feminine Cast."[9] As Shevelow has written, "Conflating souls, minds and virtues in order to assign gender opposition, Steele here was less concerned with situating gender within the framework of Christian doctrine than he was with reifying, by recourse to an essentialist argument, a notion of intrinsic gender opposition."[10] For a woman, reading the *Tatler* meant educating herself into that essentialist position, becoming a desirable object and thus desirable woman to the extent to which she internalized the periodical's pronouncements and narrative examples.

In concentrating on *women's* education, however, critics have overlooked the ideological construction of the *male* reader. For him, reading the *Tatler* meant identifying with Isaac Bickerstaff, as a character older, of the world, opinionated, and benevolently paternalistic in his dictates. Through Bickerstaff's functions as "a correspondent, a persona, [and a] figure of wise male behavior," Steele asserted his eidolon's "authority to articulate the periodical's moral standards and reformist sentiments."[11] The familial model for this interaction, best exemplified in the papers detailing the relationship between Bickerstaff—who is sixty-four—and his young half-sister Jenny Distaff, is that of a father to a daughter. As Shevelow has persuasively argued, this relationship takes *its* model and moral authority from the genre of father-daughter conduct literature, which, in the seventeenth and well into the eighteenth centuries, provided norms for female behavior and feminine gender identity. Jenny Distaff's "education," from a flighty, feisty, pleasure-loving young woman into the dedicated, loving, and obedient wife of "Tranquillus"—a trader whom Bickerstaff has chosen for her—serves as a model for the *Tatler*'s female readers, just as Bickerstaff's paternal, indeed patriarchal, attitudes and actions provide a paradigm for correct male behavior.[12]

For whether by direct example, as with Jenny Distaff, or through stories, often presented as responses to readers' queries, men are being taught to control women, to educate them into proper daughters, wives, and mothers. In the second number, a Bickerstaff-type figure mends the marriage of his beautiful but ill-natured niece by prescribing a "Cordial" that she must hold in her mouth when with her husband; that is, he makes her "good" by keeping her silent. Another man, by seeing through his wife's "little Arts"—her faking "Fits" and "Convulsions" to get her own way—turns her into a dutiful wife (No. 23). In a reworking of *The Taming of the Shrew,* still another man cures his wife's bad temper by dissimulating one of his own (No. 231). In all of these examples, as with Jenny Distaff, women are seen as both more open to, as well as more in need of, reform. Yet this contrast is also formulated as a result of inherent gender difference. In *Tatler* No. 139, Bickerstaff ruminates upon "the many Nights I have sat up for some Months past in the greatest Anxiety for the Good of my Neighbors and Contemporaries," noting that "it is no small Discouragement to me, to see how slow a Progress I make in the Reformation of the World." Although his tone is satirical by virtue of its exaggeration, the analysis that follows is wholly serious, when, to give women credit, he notes that they have indeed been better subjects than men, for women's "tender Hearts are much more susceptible of good Impressions, than the Minds of the other Sex." Women respond emotionally, men intellectually: although this perspective is hardly new to us, the sentimentalized configuration of that difference is worth noting, as is its explanation with reference to separate spheres: "Business and Ambition take up Men's Thoughts too much to leave Room for Philosophy: but if you speak to Women in a Style and Manner proper to approach them, they never fail to improve by your Counsel." Of course the "you" refers here exclusively to men: although men may be too busy to pay much attention to their own reformation, an integral part of their "Business" must be their attention to reforming women. In deference, therefore, to this greater receptivity in women, Bickerstaff writes that "I shall therefore for the future turn my Thoughts more particularly to their Service, and study the best Methods to adorn their Persons, and inform their Minds with the justest Methods to make them what Nature designed them, the most beauteous Objects of our Eyes, and the most agreeable Companions of our Lives."

A separation of spheres—women to the domestic realm, men to the

realm of economics and politics—is fundamental to the *Tatler*'s reforming process. Necessary as well is the narrative authority invested in
Bickerstaff, an authority Richard Steele, in the periodical's last number, claims has been lost or certainly compromised by his eidolon's
loss of anonymity.[13] It seems no coincidence, therefore, that the next
periodical persona—Mr. Spectator—is narratively distinguished by his
public *silence,* as well as by his position as an observer rather than a
worldly participant. Mr. Spectator's description of his own "neutrality"
encompasses both a personal and a party political level. His spectatorial
position not only enables him to know far more than he could ever have
practical experience of—he has been "a Speculative Statesman, Soldier,
Merchant and Artisan," and is, moreover, "well-versed in the Theory
of an Husband, or a Father"—but it also gives him the moral detach-
ment to "discern the Errors in the Oeconomy, Business, and Diversion
of others, better than those who are engaged in them; as Standers-by
discover Blots, which are apt to escape those who are in the Game."[14]
In addition, his statement of political disinterest—"I never espoused
any Party with Violence, and am resolved to observe an exact Neutrality between the Whigs and Tories" (No. 1)—becomes a model for
civic interaction in general. In *Spectator* No. 125, written by Addison,
Mr. Spectator comments that "there cannot a greater Judgment befal
a Country than such a dreadful Spirit of Division as rends a Government into two distinct People, and makes them greater Strangers and
more adverse to one another, than if they were actually two different
Nations." These divisions are as dangerous personally as they are civilly:
the "private Evils which they produce in the Heart of almost every
particular Person . . . is very fatal both to men's Morals and their Under-
standings; It sinks the Vertue of a Nation, and not only so, but destroys
even Common Sense."

The allegedly neutral and therefore emulatable position of Mr. Spectator is also enacted by the Spectator Club itself, particularly in the
characters of two of its members, the Tory squire Sir Roger de Coverly
and the Whig merchant Sir Andrew Freeport. In No. 126, Mr. Spectator uses the example of his two companions, who, although "of different
Principles," one "inclined to the *landed* and the other to the *moneyed*
Interest," nevertheless become a model for the kind of neutral association he had argued for in the previous number, an association of
detached merit rather than partisan interest. In both Sir Roger and Sir

Andrew, political "Humour" is "so moderate . . . that it proceeds no farther than to an agreeable Raillery, which very often diverts the rest of the Club." In the supposedly disinterested discourse of the public sphere, dissent becomes diversion; enemies are friends.

Yet as a model for human interaction, the Spectator Club is clearly a model for *male* interaction. Although in No. 34 the Spectator claims that "my Readers too have the Satisfaction to find, that there is no Rank or Degree among them who have not their Representative in this Club, and that there is always some Body present who will take Care of their respective Interests," it is notable that the "interests" of women are supposedly taken up by Will Honeycomb, an over-the-hill "ladies man," itself a stereotypical masculine "type" that had been thoroughly satirized in the *Tatler* and was to come in for its share of attack in the *Spectator* as well. So much for women's interests. In the Spectator Club, women's "interest" turns out to be sexual interest in women. [15]

The supposedly nonpartisan, apolitical stance of both the Spectator Club and the periodical itself—a stance that, as Eagleton and others [16] have pointed out, represents a definite political position—depends upon women's exclusion both from the club and from the realm of politics. Women can serve as the "common enemy," the "other," against whom, and in the name of whom, men of conflicting interests can unite. The articulation of an essentialist gender identity is a crucial part of this process, and in the pages of the *Spectator,* two things are represented as especially odious: the crossing of gender boundaries, in the form of women who dress as men, or men who act like women, and the involvement of women in party politics. Sempronia, who mingles her toilet with political talk (No. 45), is an example of the dangerous "Fopperies" that will be a consequence of the peace with France; in a slightly later number, Mr. Spectator's attack on women's use of patches to signify party affiliation unites the two elements when he writes that women should distinguish themselves as "tender Mothers and faithful Wives" rather than as "furious Partizans," for "Female Virtues are of a Domestick turn. The Family is the proper Province for Private Women to Shine in. If they must be showing their Zeal for the Publick, let it not be against those who are perhaps of the same Family, or at least of the same Religion or Nation, but against those who are the open, professed, undoubted Enemies of their Faith, Liberty, and Country" (No. 81).

If the *Tatler*'s guiding textual dynamic is enacted familially as that between fathers and daughters, developing into that between husbands and wives, I would argue that the *Spectator,* while still retaining elements of that dynamic, is more strongly dominated by a different relationship—the one between fathers and sons. This homosocial bond parallels, indeed epitomizes, the masculine consolidation, toleration, and nonpartisan spirit exemplified by and within the Spectator Club. The essentiality of gender difference discussed in relation to the *Tatler* and maintained throughout the *Spectator* constitutes the father-daughter, husband-wife relationship as one of permanent inequality, because it is based upon the fixed characteristic of sex. In the relationship between father and son, however, the inequality is only temporary, structured by disparities in age and experience. In *The Sexual Contract,* Carole Pateman argues that both Locke and Rousseau "agreed that the natural duty of parents to care for their children gave them rightful authority, but, they argued against Filmer, parental power was temporary." As Pateman notes, however, for Locke, "children" become "sons," for she continues: "Once out of their nonage, at the age of maturity, sons become as free as their fathers and, like them, must agree to be governed." Pateman cites Locke's *Second Treatise* for emphasis: "Thus we are *born Free,* as we are born Rational; . . . Age that brings one, brings with it the other too. And thus we see how *natural Freedom and Subjection to Parents* may consist together, and are both founded on the same principle. A *Child* is *Free* by his Father's Title, by his Father's Understanding, which is to govern him, till he hath it of his own." [17]

I wish to argue that the potential to see the father-son relation as only temporarily unequal is a phenomenon that gains increasing importance in the early eighteenth century, as England's shift from a rural, landed economy toward a commercial, trade-based system allowed for representations of new, noncompetitive relations between fathers and sons, as well as often between the oldest son and his brother or brothers. In *Tatler* No. 189, Bickerstaff contrasts desirably empathetic parent-child relations, in which parents "repeat their Lives in their Offspring; and their Concern for them is so near, that they feel all their Sufferings and Enjoyments as much as if they regarded their own proper Persons," with the brutishly competitive situation of "the common Race of 'Squires in this Kingdom [who] use their Sons as Persons that are waiting only for their Funerals, and Spies upon their Health and Happiness; as indeed they are by their own making them such." [18]

Under a mercantile system, however, all can, in theory, work and prosper simultaneously. Unlike the *Tatler,* where Bickerstaff's trading nephew is eclipsed in a woman's favor by his scholar and courtier brothers (No. 207), the *Spectator* is extremely explicit in its celebration of business and trade. Although Mr. Spectator expresses an extremely warm, almost filial fondness for the kindly but doddering Sir Roger de Coverly, it is clearly Sir Andrew Freeport who exemplifies desirable masculine and civic characteristics: he is a man of "indefatigable Industry, strong Reason, and great Experience"; he has a "natural unaffected Eloquence"; he is "richer than other Men" (No. 2). In *Spectator* No. 69, Addison writes that "there are not more useful Members in a Commonwealth than Merchants. They knit Mankind together in a mutual Intercourse of good Offices, distribute the Gifts of Nature, find Works for the Poor, add Wealth to the Rich, and Magnificence to the Great." Indeed, he sets up trading interests as comparable with, if not superior to, landed ones: "Trade, without enlarging the *British* Territories, has given us a kind of additional Empire: it has multiplied the Number of the Rich, made our Landed Estates infinitely more Valuable than they were formerly, and added to them an Accession of other Estates as Valuable as the Lands themselves." [19]

The *Tatler*'s, and more explicitly the *Spectator*'s representations of "commercial man" can thus become a way to rethink the very separation of gender and class. I agree with the historians Leonore Davidoff and Catherine Hall, when in *Family Fortunes: Men and Women of the English Middle Class, 1780–1850,* they argue that gender and class always operate together, that consciousness of class always takes a gendered form.[20] Their study attempts to dismantle traditional separations of public and private, to demonstrate how "middle-class men who sought to be 'someone,' to count as individuals because of their wealth, their power to command or their capacity to influence people, were, in fact, embedded in networks of familial and female support which underpinned their rise to public prominence." [21] Beginning in the late seventeenth century, England's mercantile expansion, the development of London as a center of international commerce, and the concomitant "birth of a consumer society" [22] contributed toward constituting trade, traders, and trading as essential components of contemporary discourse and debate. While the development of a coherent and solidified middle-class identity may have been a later eighteenth-century phenomenon, writers of the late seventeenth and early eighteenth centuries were certainly concerned with describing, as well as often promoting, behaviors and values—for both men and women—later to be termed "middle-class."

The process of tracing these shifts in notions of value and virtue is extremely problematic, for these changes were simultaneous rather than sequential, the categories themselves not unified and discrete but contradictory and fluid. What needs to be emphasized are the tensions and interactions among two different embodiments of exemplary masculinity: the gentleman of landed property, who could "claim the public virtue of disinterestedness," [23] and the "gentleman trader," who acts to reconfigure aristocratic benevolence and generosity in a new form. As texts written by men who span both worlds, the *Tatler* and particularly the *Spectator* can be read as barometers of the dialectical process of class consolidation. In the *Spectator,* the triumph of Whig economic and political interests is made possible by the denial of those interests within a social position construed as neutral and thus universally benevolent. The period's crucial issue—how to make commercial man virtuous man [24]—is enacted within the pages of the *Spectator* by developing a new ideology of commercial relations articulated in family terms, and a new ideology of familial relations described in economic terms. The process of "multiplying affinities" described by Samuel Clarke in his "Discourse of Natural Religion," first printed in 1706, expands the familial language of "natural affection" to encompass "the agreeing community of all mankind":

> Next to that natural *self-love,* or care of his own preservation, which
> every one necessarily has in the first place for himself; there is in all men
> a certain natural affection for their children and posterity, who have a
> dependence upon them; and for their near relations and friends, who
> have an intimacy with them. And because the nature of man is such,
> that they cannot live comfortably in independent families, without still
> further society and commerce with each other; therefore they natu-
> rally desire to increase their dependencies, by multiplying affinities,
> and to enlarge their friendships, by mutual good offices, and to estab-
> lish societies, by a communication of arts and labour: till by degrees the
> affection of single persons, becomes a friendship of families; and this
> enlarges itself to society of towns and cities and nations; and terminates
> in the agreeing community of all mankind. [25]

The conflation of economic and homosocial benevolence is best exemplified in the *Spectator*'s "*Cornelii,*" a family of "eminent Traders" in
which the personal relationships among father, sons and brothers are
depicted as entirely compatible with—indeed, a reason for the success of—their business interests: "their good Correspondence with each
other is useful to all that know them as well as to themselves: And their
Friendship, Good-will, and kind Offices, are disposed of joyntly as well
as their Fortune; so that no one ever obliged one of them, who had not
the Obligation multiplied in Returns from them all" (No. 192). This
Edenic portrait of masculine familial relations is celebrated by Addison
as a "sublime Pleasure, . . . as sacred as Friendship, as pleasurable as
Love, and as joyful as Religion." Although throughout these periodicals, *women* are most commonly the focus of spectatorial approbation,
here Addison tellingly writes that "it is the most beautiful Object the
Eyes of Man can behold, to see a Man of Worth and his Son live in an
entire unreserved Correspondence. The mutual Kindness and Affection
between them give an inexpressible Satisfaction to all who know them"
(No. 192).

As a way further to explicate this intersection of economics and
family, I want to modify the position taken by Albert O. Hirschman in
*The Passions and the Interests: Political Arguments for Capitalism Before Its Tri-
umph.*[26] Hirschman argues for a shift from the Augustinian perception
of three comparable passions—the desire for money and possessions,
the desire for power, and sexual desire—to a belief in the late seventeenth century that economic activity could emerge as a benign form of
"interest," rather than a destructive passion, which could itself serve to
counteract the tyrannical abuse of power. Although Hirschman's analysis is particularly helpful in understanding the early eighteenth-century
view of economic activity as personally benevolent and socially useful,
his emphasis on the relation between economics and politics ignores or
even erases the third "passion"—sexual lust. I believe that the ideology
of a domestic, benevolent, even "companionate" masculinity becomes a
way not of sublimating passions to interests but of integrating the two
within the context of the sentimental nuclear family.

And yet, the idealized view of the family implicit within its sentimental construction acts to mask areas of discomfiture and anxiety about
the family's proper roles and functions, in particular with regard to
the kinds of "expenditure" necessary to a developing consumer society.

When configured as detached from the spheres of business and especially politics, the family can vindicate production, consumption, and expenditure as integral to masculinity. Sexual desire, when channeled into marriage, produces the legitimate heirs who will both prosper from and participate in the father's material enterprise. Power, the most dangerous of passions according to Hirschman's conception, is achieved not by the aristocratic means of status or wealth, but through the benevolent and educative relation to one's (male) offspring: "It is not in the Power of all Men to leave illustrious Names or great Fortunes to their Posterity, but they can very much conduce to their having Industry, Probity, Valour, and Justice. It is in every Man's Power to leave his Son the Honour of descending from a virtuous Man, and add the Blessing of Heaven to whatever he leaves him" (*Spectator* No. 192). Thus the status of the "New Man" becomes increasingly defined by his ability to provide for his family, in material, social, and spiritual terms. He, in turn, becomes dependent upon that family unit to provide his raison d'être. This situation, however, comprises another site of anxiety, for to be dependent—even upon one's dependents—can prove psychologically threatening.

It becomes, then, part of emerging domesticity to define femininity in a way that distinguishes women's attributes, behaviors, even bodily responses from those of men. Women's enforced absence from the public realm becomes reinscribed as their necessary presence within the domestic sphere. And yet, it is a presence riddled with ambivalence. While the periodical's approbative attitude toward the marital relationship is epitomized by Mr. Spectator's claim to "make the Word *Wife* the most agreeable and delightful Name in Nature" (No. 490), in this text the ideal form of human relationship is represented not by husbands and wives but by fathers and sons.[27] The original but temporary inequality of the father and son is transformed in the interests of trade into a "partnership" between brothers, thus exemplifying the move, described by Pateman, from paternal or traditional patriarchy to fraternal patriarchy. To recast Freud's anthropological narrative, the brothers no longer need to kill the father, they just go into business with him.

The *Spectator* provides a compelling instance of such male bonding. We witness relationships of collaboration rather than competition on both structural and narrative levels. Structural examples range from the extra-fictional authorial collaboration of Addison and Steele to the fictional joint authorship of the Spectator Club; textual examples include numerous stories of cooperation among family members. Although both social historians and literary critics usually focus on bonds between husbands and wives, or on the general relations of parents to children, I believe that a consideration of male relations is equally important to an understanding of the ideology of the family. Begun in the *Tatler* and realized more fully in the *Spectator,* the discourse of masculinity best exemplified in the relation between fathers and sons served to educate male readers into their familial roles, which became simultaneously the expression of a class position.

The paternal characteristics that I am terming "sentimental" are not, of course, exclusive to the middle classes. Such attributes, however, become represented in a way that serves to mark them as fundamentally middle class, a form of "partnership" impossible within families in which inheritance was determined by "the need to keep together the estate upon which the standing of gentry families depended."[28] In contrast, partible inheritance, as well as the opportunity for sons to join their father in the family business,[29] permitted a form of economic affiliation that could also carry moral and emotional weight. The most extreme form of this father-son "partnership" is manifested in the type I shall call the "fraternal father." He, like the father in the Cornelii family, "lives with his Sons like their eldest Brother" (*Spectator* No. 192). It is therefore no accident that the exemplary Cornelii are a family of "eminent Traders," so that their benevolent familial relations have public implications, and can produce "Returns" that are both pecuniary and societal.

All of the "moral" characteristics associated with the exemplary sentimental father are made possible by changes in economic structures. A father's lack of filial partiality (*Tatler* No. 235)—emulating Noah rather than Jacob—is manifested materially in partible inheritance or business partnership rather than primogeniture; financial liberality (*Tatler* No. 60) can result from the fact that the son's learning to manage the family fortune is also in his father's interest; sympathy, empathy, and understanding (*Spectator* No. 263) are possible in part because father and son are functioning together within the same or a similar system. The "transplanted self-love" of *Spectator* No. 192 is in part transplanted self-interest. The idealized image of the "sentimental father," who protects, supports, advises, and understands his son or sons is thus a composite

151.5 49

portrait. Formed, on the one hand, in light of the middle-class fraternal ideal, he is also developed in contrast to the traditionally authoritative "patriarchal father": the king who decrees rather than discusses, has complete control over familial resources, and competes for those resources with his heir or heirs. Such a type is associated, as we shall see, primarily with the aristocracy and landed gentry. As in *Tatler* No. 189 cited above, the patriarchal father serves mainly to personify the negative aspects of aristocratic paternity: selfishness, profligacy, competitiveness, and insensitivity. Taking its motto from Terence—"My son should enjoy these things equally with me, or even more, because youth is more appropriate for these things"—*Spectator* No. 496 describes those fathers who unbecomingly pursue their own pleasures at the expense of their sons. Not only do these men provide a negative role model by failing to teach their sons "to resist the Impetuosity of growing Desires," but they also deplete the stock that should allow their offspring to live honorable lives: "Narrowness in their Circumstances has made many Youths to supply themselves as Debauchees, commence Cheats and Rascals." [30]

And yet, the *Spectator*'s portraits of such men are complemented, and conquered, by the presence of their opposite, the "fraternal father." Although the supposed egalitarianism implicit in this latter form of father-son relations is manifested less frequently than is, for example, the father's role of benevolent guardian to his son,[31] the fraternal ideal is both omnipresent and extremely important. In addition to promoting a critique of patriarchal attitudes, such an ideal can also buttress a belief in liberal individualism. In *The Sexual Contract,* Carole Pateman contends that by obscuring the part of the social contract that depends upon men's subordination of women, contract theory, far from being opposed to patriarchal right, reinscribes that right in a new configuration: "modern patriarchy is fraternal in form and the original contract is a fraternal pact." [32] Thus while the concept of a cooperative "fraternal fatherhood" might seem seductive in its promise of male relations apparently stripped of hierarchy and dominance, Pateman's analysis reminds us of such a concept's dark underside. In spite of Defoe's analogy between a trading partnership and a marriage, since both are "engaged in for better for worse, till the years expire," [33] in this period the only "true" contract, and therefore partnership, can exist between men.[34] And what makes possible that partnership, and the model of egalitarianism upon which it is based, is the subordination of women. In these new, increasingly middle-class representations of masculine virtue, modeled upon the relations between the sentimental father and his "towardly" son (*Spectator* No. 263), oppressive relations are reinscribed, albeit in new forms. Such "fraternal patriarchy" serves as both a basis for the capitalist endeavor, and as a means of perpetuating women's subordination and exploitation.

In the *Spectator,* the sentimental father is exemplary in large part because he combines patriarchal and fraternal roles. Such mentoring can cross both party lines[35] and class positions. *Spectator* No. 330 includes a letter from the eighteen-year-old "Son of a Merchant of the City of *London,*" who, after his father's death, is rescued from both aristocratic profligacy and professional oblivion by a country "Gentleman." The son, whose mother has already died, inherits a modest estate, but "without Friend or Guardian to instruct me in the Management or Enjoyment of it," soon encounters bad company and worse debt. Later, in an attempt at self-reformation, he begins to "study the Law," but, equally bereft of advice, fails to progress: "I trifled away a whole year in looking over a thousand intricacies without Friend to apply to in case of doubt." Good-hearted but ill-guided, our correspondent is delivered by a "relation," who, observing in him "a good inclination," carries him to his country seat. Under the "Favour and Patronage" of this virtuous man, the youth blossoms: his mentor has provided him with books, horses, and good conversation; inspired him with confidence, so that he feels "acceptable" wherever he goes; and most important, inclined him toward virtue. The youth writes that his patron has achieved such influence by blending superior knowledge, experience, and position with sympathetic understanding: "he has an Authority of a Father over me, founded upon the Love of a Brother." Indeed his letter is meant as both a tribute to his mentor, and an exhortation to other men in similar positions to follow such an example: "If a Gentleman of Figure in a County would make his Family a Pattern of Sobriety, good Sense, and Breeding, and would kindly endeavour to influence the Education and growing Prospects of the younger Gentry about him, I am apt to believe it would save him a great deal of stale Beer on a publick Occasion, and render him the Leader of his Country from their Gratitude to him, instead of being a Slave to their Riots and Tumults in order to be made their Representative."[36] Such commendable behavior, he writes, is desirable for all men who have achieved some kind of success, because it costs nothing and returns much: "others may gain Preferments and Fortunes from their Patrons, but I have, I hope, received from mine good Habits and Virtues."

While these representations of idealized paternal benevolence emphasize the father or guardian's concern for "the Virtue and Disposition of his Children, [rather] than their Advancement or Wealth" (*Spectator* No. 192), the commercial man is, nevertheless, a better father precisely because of his superior ability to be "liberal without the least expense of [his] own Fortune" (*Spectator* No. 348), to share his mobile resources with his sons rather than compete with them for limited ones. Similar to the process through which potentially dangerous masculine sexual desire is purified when directed toward a chaste spouse,[37] so too is wealth rendered virtuous only when attached to virtuous behavior, thus serving to moralize worldly success: "Good Habits are what will certainly improve a Man's Fortune and Reputation; but on the other Side, Affluence of Fortune will not as probably produce good Affections of the Mind" (*Spectator* No. 192).

In *Spectator* No. 240, the benevolent qualities of these relations are exemplified in a letter that tells the story of a trader saved from "criminal Pleasures, some Excesses, and a general loose Conduct" by "the handsome Behaviour of a learned, generous, and wealthy Man," of no relation, who takes the correspondent under his wing. Described, indeed, as a "good Angel," this man puts his "Friendship," "Advice," and money at the youth's disposal, giving him "the Use of any Part of his Fortune, to apply the Measures he should propose to me, for the Improvement of my own." A veritable sentimental son, the narrator reflects that "I assure you I cannot recollect the Goodness and Confusion of the good Man when he spoke to this Purpose to me without melting into Tears"; he is, however, able to put his gratitude into practice, not through direct returns to his mentor, who is far from needing them, but "by being ready to serve others to my utmost Ability, as far as is consistent with the Prudence" his mentor prescribes. Perhaps the correspondent's greatest gift from his mentor is not the "present Ease and Plenty of my Circumstances" made possible by the use of his money, but his having learned from him "the Government of my Passions, and the Regulation of my Desires."[38] It is this last quality that the young trader distinguishes with the title of "Heroick Virtue in common Life," and he asks the *Spectator* to furnish more such examples.

Spectator No. 248 extends the attributes of benevolent paternity to encompass possibilities for all men by comparing the worthy and public actions performed by those in "conspicuous Stations of Life" with the good works of the more common folk. Mr. Spectator points out that the former are in fact obliged by their "great Talents and high Birth" to "exert some noble Inclinations for the Service of the World" as part of their inheritance, for, if ignored, "such Advantages become Misfortunes, and Shade and Privacy are a more eligible Portion." Romanticizing noble behavior can thus obscure the "heroick" possibilities available to men "in lower Scenes of Life": "It is in every Man's Power in the World who is above meer Poverty, not only to do things worthy but heroick."[39] By practicing the "Self-Denial" that is the "great Foundation of civil Virtue," all men can be in a position to help others. Actions by those who "in the domestick Way of Life deny themselves many Advantages, to satisfy a generous Benevolence which they bear to their Friends oppressed with Distresses and Calamities," are thus juxtaposed with those "great and exalted Spirits [who] undertake the Pursuit of hazardous Actions for the Good of others, at the same time gratifying their Passion for Glory." It is not that the gentleman has less interest in helping other men, but that the commercial man has more resources with which to do so.

Two letters exemplify the number's most "sentimental" moments. The first concerns two brothers, and is structured by relations of both blood and inheritance. Lapirus, a younger son, has inherited from his father a "great Estate . . . by reason of the dissolute Behaviour of the First-born." "Shame and Contrition," however, have reformed the profligate brother; he became, according to Mr. Spectator, "as remarkable for his good Qualities as formerly for his Errors." Lapirus, now in the role of father, restores the succession in the following letter:

Honoured Brother,

I enclose to you the Deeds whereby my Father gave me this House and Land: Had he lived till now he would not have bestowed it in that Manner; he took it from the Man you were, and I restore it to the Man you are.

Witnessing Lapirus's mixture of fraternal and paternal generosity can, however, obscure the fact that his own position is diminished, if not outright destroyed, by his good deed, as it were. Thus while he might sign himself "Your affectionate Brother," his action reinscribes patriarchal

succession. The second letter, in contrast, presents an example of fraternal affection that may very well surpass any other portrait in the *Tatler*
or *Spectator* series. Implicitly categorized as a "love letter" by Mr. Spectator's comment that "I think there is more Spirit and true Gallantry in it
than in any Letter I have ever read from *Strephon* to *Phillis*," this missive
describes an encounter between two tradesmen, which Mr. Spectator
inserts "even in the mercantile honest Stile in which it was sent":

> Sir,
> I have heard of the Casualties which have involved you in extreme Dis-
> tress at this Time; and knowing you to be a Man of great Good-nature,
> Industry, and Probity, have resolved to stand by you. Be of good Chear,
> the Bearer brings with him five thousand Pounds, and has my Order to
> answer your drawing as much more on my Account. I did this in Haste,
> for Fear I should come too late for your Relief; but you may value your
> self with me to the Sum of fifty thousand Pounds; for I can very chear-
> fully run the Hazard of being so much less rich than I am now, to save an
> honest Man whom I love.

This narrative, described by Mr. Spectator as a "City Romance," re-
writes the *Tatler*'s earlier example of "Heroic Love in the City" (No.
213), in which the trader "Tom Trueman" wins his bride by saving her
father from ruin at the hands of a corrupt factor. Paradoxically, Trueman
is exemplary both because he rescues the father and because he forgoes
the economic benefits incurred by such deliverance.[40] In the *Spectator*
story, no woman is necessary to inspire male bonding. The increasing
consignment of women to an allegedly isolated domestic sphere positions them as the necessary centerpiece of the nuclear family in their
roles of wife and mother and, ironically, as the least important members of that intimate unit. In this period, as the sentimental father is
melded into the sentimental man, women's protective, nurturing, and
even moral qualities are shadowed by the greater possession of those
same characteristics by men.

    In what is perhaps the *Spectator*'s most damning portrait of paternal
relations gone awry, illegitimacy is configured as paternal betrayal. In
No. 203, women who give birth to illegitimate children are mentioned
solely in their child-bearing role, for their sexual behavior is never
noted; removed from judgment, they are neither condemned nor pitied.
It is as if they exist only as repositories for the seed of those "young

Patriarchs," who, "like heedless Spendthrifts that squander away their Estates before they are Masters of them, have raised up their whole stock of Children before Marriage." Not only do the men in this "Generation of Vermin" squander their resources, but they also misuse their time and energies. The consummate, as it were, bad businessmen, these men apply themselves with "indefatigable Diligence" to the wrong things. Extraordinarily inventive in pursuing their "vicious Amour[s]," they misapply their resources by channeling them improperly. As Mr. Spectator notes, they "might conquer their corrupt Inclinations with half the Pains they are at in gratifying them." The potent libertine, as he is represented in this text, betrays not his mistress but his legal wife, should he have one, and, most important, his progeny. Society itself, according to Mr. Spectator, colludes in such libertine behavior by using terminology that condemns the victims rather than the perpetrators: "And here I cannot but take notice of those depraved Notions which prevail among us, and which must have taken Rise from our natural Inclination to favour a Vice to which we are so very prone, namely, that *Bastardy* and *Cuckoldom* should be looked upon as Reproaches, and that the Ignominy which is only due to Lewdness and Falsehood, should fall in so unreasonable a manner upon the Persons who are Innocent."

Addison, through the persona of Mr. Spectator,[41] uses the voice of another to make his most powerful argument against the fathering of illegitimate children. He prints a letter written, not by a repentant father, but by a wronged son. In this most pathetic of epistles, we find represented all that the sentimental father shuns. Plagued by "continual Uneasiness" and "continual Anxiety," this far from prodigal son is both infantilized and feminized. Deprived of paternal "Tenderness . . . Love and Conversation," he is kept at "so vast a Distance" and treated so haughtily that he cannot express his feelings or communicate his situation to his father, nor can he "render him the Duties of a Son." Uneducated in any occupation or profession but that of "Gentleman," he is wholly dependent upon his father's doubtful "Assistance." In his own terms, he is "a Monster strangely sprung up in Nature, which every one is ashamed to own."

In this representation, reforming attention is focused not upon the wife or mother, who must be virginal before and chaste within marriage to ensure the "legitimacy" of her husband's heirs, but upon the chastity of the man himself, who must restrict the fulfillment of his appetites to the sphere of lawful marriage; status as father should follow, not precede, position as husband. The letter ends with the correspondent asking for Mr. Spectator's advice about his unhappy situation, with particular regard to the "part, I being unlawfully born, may claim of the Man's Affection who begot me, and how far in your Opinion I am to be thought his Son, or he acknowledged my Father." Although Mr. Spectator does not here respond directly, of course his implicit answer is that even if legal ties are absent, emotional, moral, and material obligations are very much present. By distinguishing the products of custom from supposedly natural "Affections," this text can criticize cultural norms at the same time as it reaffirms them. Just as Mr. Spectator's desire "to make the word *Wife* the most agreeable and delightful Name in Nature" (No. 490) elides nature and culture, instinct and law, so too does the construction of the "sentimental father" represent as intrinsic to all virtuous men attributes specific to a distinctive group at a particular historical moment.

I have argued that in the eighteenth century, the configuration of the family as the sphere of masculine virtue allows that family to justify men's pursuits of both passions and interests. Yet the shift into a "fraternal" representation of familial relations via a father and son "partnership"—an association seemingly cooperative, benevolent, and without hierarchies of power and dominance—erases the oppressive implications, for both men and women, of that new masculine role. As the sentimental father develops into the sentimental man, men (as sons) are being socialized to assume the role of the active producer as if their life depended on it, for indeed it does; and these sons are taught to sustain their position through the subordination and objectification of desirably "dependent" women. For despite the concept of a *"doux commerce,"*[42] mercantile relations are neither benevolent nor cooperative. Thus while the emerging ideology of a moral sentimental fatherhood made possible by commercial relations seems to be about good connections among certain men, this investment in sentimental masculinity can also reveal both the guilt and the human cost of these relations.

Notes

For their assistance with versions of this article, I am grateful to Julie Ellison, James Winn, Adela Pinch, Wendy Motooka, and Brittain Smith.

1. Rae Blanchard, "Richard Steele and the Status of Women," *Studies in Philology* 26 (1929): 325–55; Kathryn Shevelow, *Women and Print Culture: The Construction of Femininity in the Early Periodical* (London: Routledge, 1989).

2. Shevelow, *Women and Print Culture,* p. 140.

3. Terry Eagleton, *The Function of Criticism: From "The Spectator" to Post-Structuralism* (London: Verso, 1984); Michael G. Ketcham, *Transparent Designs: Reading, Performance and Form in the "Spectator" Papers* (Athens: University of Georgia Press, 1985).

4. Jürgen Habermas, *The Structural Transformation of the Public Sphere* (1962), trans. Thomas Burger (Cambridge: MIT Press, 1989).

5. Recent feminist analyses of the "public sphere" as a site for the construction of bourgeois individuality have emphasized the gendered quality of that construction. Exposing the "liberal fiction" of discursive universality by stressing its necessary, rather than just contingent, exclusion of women, such critics as Joan Landes and Nancy Fraser have used gender as a lens through which to refract the gendered bias and basis of Habermas's analysis. See Joan Landes, *Women and the Public Sphere in the Age of the French Revolution* (Ithaca: Cornell University Press, 1988), Introduction and 40–53; and Nancy Fraser, "What's Critical About Critical Theory? The Case of Habermas and Gender," *New German Critique,* no. 35 (Spring/Summer 1985): 97–131, reprinted in *Unruly Practices: Power, Discourse and Gender in Contemporary Social Theory* (Minneapolis: University of Minnesota Press, 1989), 113–33. Ironically, the analyses of both Habermas and Eagleton after him replicate the exclusionary practices present within the very texts they discuss.

6. See Ketcham, *Transparent Designs,* chapter 4, "The Family and Intimate Community."

7. Although in the *Tatler*'s last number (271) Steele credits Addison with "the finest strokes of wit and humour in all Mr. Bickerstaff's Lucubrations," in addition to help with specific "noble discourses," Joseph Otten states that Addison's actual share amounted to one-fifth: "He wrote 49 issues completely by himself and contributed a share in 22 other numbers" (*Joseph Addison* [Boston: Twayne, 1982], 69). Richmond Bond ascribes 47 complete papers to

Addison (*"The Tatler": The Making of a Literary Journal* [Harvard University Press, 1971], 20). Compare this with Donald Bond's assessment of Addison's share in the *Spectator:* Bond claims that of the original 555 numbers, Addison wrote 202 of the "independent essays" that contained no contributed letters, whereas Steele wrote 89; of papers made up wholly or in part of letters or contributed matter Addison wrote 49 and Steele 162 (*Spectator,* ed. and intro. Donald F. Bond, 5 vols. [Oxford: Clarendon Press, 1965], 1:lix).

8. I am thinking here of John Dunton's *Athenian Mercury* (1691–97) and *Night-Walker* (1696–97). For an analysis of the ways in which these texts' emphasis on marital chastity became the focus for a discussion of changing familial relations, see Shawn Lisa Maurer, "Chaste Heterosexuality in the Early English Periodical," *Restoration* 16, 1 (Spring 1992): 38–55.

9. *Tatler,* ed. and intro. Donald F. Bond, 3 vols. (Oxford: Clarendon Press, 1987), No. 172. All further references will be cited by issue number and included in the text.

10. Shevelow, *Women and Print Culture,* 100.

11. Ibid., 102.

12. Note that in Nos. 10, 33, 36, and 247, in which Jenny Distaff takes over while Bickerstaff is "out of town," she answers correspondence, as well as conducting discussions of love "in all its forms" (No. 36). Yet all of the numbers dealing with Jenny's marriage and marital situation—75, 79, 85, 104, and 143—are narrated by Bickerstaff.

13. Richmond Bond argues that there may have been additional motivations behind Steele's decision to end the *Tatler.* Although political compromise with the powerful Tory leader Sir Robert Harley, who had been a subject of Steele's satire some months earlier "cannot now be demonstrated to the point of full acceptance, . . . it seems plausible as a major factor in Steele's decision and perhaps as the strongest" (186). See also pages 59–69 for Bond's discussion of overt political issues within the *Tatler.*

14. *Spectator,* ed. Bond, No. 1. All further references will be cited by issue number and included in the text.

15. Also conspicuous, of course, is the absence of any representative of the poor or laboring classes—but such an omission is subject for another essay.

16. See also Edward Bloom and Lillian Bloom, *Joseph Addison's Sociable Animal: In the Market Place, on the Hustings, in the Pulpit* (Providence: Brown University Press, 1971), and especially Andrew Lee Elioseff's "Review Essay: Joseph Addison's Political Animal: Middle-Class Idealism in Crisis," in *Eighteenth-Century Studies* 6 (1973): 372–81.

17. Carole Pateman, *The Sexual Contract* (Stanford: Stanford University Press, 1988), 84; John Locke, *Two Treatises of Government,* ed. Peter Laslett (New York: Cambridge University Press, 1988), second treatise, section 60.

18. For an analysis of the gentry's greater employment of primogeniture in the seventeenth century, see Joan Thirsk, "Younger Brothers in the Seventeenth Century," in *The Rural Economy of England* (London: Hambledon Press, 1984), 335–57.

19. For additional, and comparably celebratory, representations of trade and traders, see *Spectator* Nos. 21, 108, 174, 232, 283, 348, and 549.

20. Leonore Davidoff and Catherine Hall, *Family Fortunes: Men and Women of the English Middle Class, 1780–1850* (Chicago: University of Chicago Press, 1987), 13.

21. Ibid.

22. See Neil McKendrick, John Brewer, and J. H. Plumb, *The Birth of a Consumer Society: The Commercialization of Eighteenth-Century England* (Bloomington: Indiana University Press, 1982).

23. John Barrell, *An Equal, Wide Survey: English Literature in History, 1730–1780* (London: Hutchinson, 1983), 22.

24. This implies, of course, its inverse: how to make virtuous man commercial man.

25. *British Moralists, 1650–1800,* ed. D. D. Raphael, 2 vols. (Oxford: Clarendon Press, 1969), 1:210.

26. Albert O. Hirschman, *The Passions and the Interests: Political Arguments for Capitalism Before Its Triumph* (Princeton: Princeton University Press, 1977). See part 1, "How the Interests Were Called Upon to Counteract the Passions."

27. While the ostensible focus of this article is the workings of sentiment in relations between men, feminist critiques of sentimental family ideology that emphasize its detrimental effect upon women, and especially wives, both underlie and make possible my own approach. In "Women and the Making of the Sentimental Family," Susan Moller Okin stresses the ironic fact that both doctrines of individual rights and ideologies of increased familial "affect" brought women only greater limitations. She contends that the "development—or idealizing—of the sentimental domestic family, much documented by historians in recent years," provided "a new rationale for the subordination of women" (*Philosophy and Public Affairs* 11, 1 [1981]: 65). Okin's discussion of family history thus challenges "the alleged connection between the growing idealization of families as private sanctuaries of sentiment, on the one hand, and an improvement in prevalent conceptions of and attitudes toward women, on the other" (74). Rather than ameliorating the situation of women, the conception of the family as "sentimental and domesticated" served instead "as *reinforcement* for the patriarchal relations between men and women that had been temporarily threatened by seventeenth-century individualism" (74). In contradiction to the assertions of historian Lawrence Stone (*The Family, Sex and Marriage in England, 1500–1800* [Harmondsworth: Penguin, 1977])

and Randolph Trumbach (*The Rise of the Egalitarian Family* [New York: Academic Press, 1978]), Okin cites three negative effects of sentimental family ideology: a stronger division than ever before between "women's spheres of dependence and domesticity" and the "outside world"; women's increasing characterization as "creatures of sentiment and love rather than of the rationality that was perceived as necessary for citizenship"; and, most important to this essay, "a greater intensifying of masculine authority and sentiment in both private and public spheres" (74). Moreover, Susan Staves's recent study, *Married Women's Separate Property in England, 1660–1833* (Cambridge: Harvard University Press, 1990), criticizes the very basis of sentimental familial relations as articulated by Stone and Trumbach. Staves writes that "both historians have succumbed to a bourgeois illusion that there can be a clear separation between, on the one hand, a public and economic sphere, and, on the other, a private domestic sphere of true feeling and personal authenticity. In this aspect of their work, they have accepted the very ideological formulation created by eighteenth-century advocates of domesticity" (223). While all parts of Staves's book are relevant to this topic, see in particular her concluding chapter, especially pages 221–28.

28. Keith Wrightson, *English Society, 1580–1680* (London: Hutchinson, 1982), 112.

29. Davidoff and Hall, *Family Fortunes,* 205–6.

30. *Tatler* No. 189 offers a very near example of such parental misrule in a branch of Bickerstaff's own family, where children's desires are sacrificed to those of their father rather than compatible with them. Unlike good fathers, who favorably "repeat their Lives in their Offspring," bad ones just keep perpetuating the same sins: "When one of the Family has, in the Pursuit of Foxes, and in the Entertainment of Clowns, ran out the Third Part of the Value of his Estate, such a Spendthrift has dressed up his eldest Son, and married what they call a Good Fortune, who has supported the Father as a Tyrant over them, during his Life, in the same House or Neighborhood: The Son in Succession has just taken the same Method to keep up his Dignity, till the Mortgages he has eat and drank himself into, have reduced him to the Necessity of sacrificing his Son also, in Imitation of his Progenitor."

But not only do decent sons suffer the faults of unprincipled fathers; the exigencies of landed inheritance can also create situations like that of "Ruricola" (*Spectator* No. 192), in which an admirable father is harnessed to a reprobate son. Although Ruricola's own life "was one continued Series of worthy Actions and gentleman-like Inclinations," he is to be succeeded by "the Booby his Heir," who is his father's opposite in every way. As "the Companion of drunken Clowns," this son "knows no Sense of Praise but in the Flattery he receives from his own Servants; his Pleasures are mean and inordinate, his Language base and filthy, his Behaviour rough and absurd."

31. Just as the reformist position of the *Spectator* is in many ways defined and motivated by the particular qualities of "spectatorship," so too does the rubric of "guardianship" inform the moral and political position of the *Guardian,* a periodical published by Steele, with help from Addison, from March 12 to October 1, 1713. The periodical's eidolon, Nestor Ironside, derives his epithet and his authority from his actual experience as guardian first to Marmaduke Lizard, the son and heir of his college friend, Sir Ambrose Lizard, and then to Marmaduke's own children.

32. Pateman, *The Sexual Contract,* 77.

33. Daniel Defoe, *The Compleat English Tradesman* (1728), in *The Novels and Miscellaneous Works of Daniel Defoe* (Oxford, 1841), vols. 17 and 18, ch. 33, p. 169.

34. Chapter 22 (213–27) of Defoe's *Compleat English Tradesman* deals in much detail with the relation of women to their husbands' business. In addition to criticizing those "gentlewomen" who marry traders but scorn their business, Defoe also commends those women who become knowledgeable, less for its own sake than for their ability to maintain that business for their children should they become widowed. Women's place in business thus becomes "natural"—in contrast to the "unnatural" widow who might "think herself above having children by a tradesman"—when it maintains the link between men: "I have known many a widow that would have thought it otherwise below her, has engaged herself in her husband's business, and carried it on, purely to bring her eldest son up to it, and has preserved it for him, and which has been an estate to him; whereas otherwise it must have been lost, and he would have had the world to seek for a new business" (218).

35. See the story of "Tom the Bounteous" in *Spectator* No. 346, who, although "so known a Tory," supports others on a collegial rather than a paternal level by "lend[ing] at the ordinary Interest, to give Men of less Fortune Opportunities of making greater Advantages."

36. Compare the dialogue between Sir Roger de Coverly and Sir Andrew Freeport in *Spectator* No. 174; in No. 330, however, wealth is to be found in guidance rather than in labor.

37. While this theme runs throughout these texts, see in particular *Tatler* No. 120, Addison's allegory of love and lust.

38. Compare the discussion of the "Rake" in *Tatler* No. 27: represented as "the most agreeable of all bad Characters," a Rake's "Faults proceed not from Choice or Inclination, but from strong Powers and Appetites, which are in Youth too violent for the Curb of Reason, good Sense, good Manners and good

Nature. . . . His Desires run away with him through the Strength and Force of a lively Imagination, which hurries him on to unlawful Pleasures, before Reason has Power to come to his Rescue." One could argue that in this depiction, "Reason" personifies the benevolent older guardian figure, whose timely intervention turns a bad young man good, or keeps a good one that way. In this sense, the "Rake" is in many ways a fatherless son.

39. See also *Tatler* No. 202: "I would have a Thing to be esteemed as Heroick which is great and uncommon in the Circumstances in the Man who performs it. Thus there would be no Virtue in human Life which every one of the Species would not have a Pretence to arrive at, and an Ardency to exert."

40. The story seems conventional enough at first: a young apprentice falls in love with his master's daughter; the love is reciprocated, but the family business is failing, due, the young man suspects, "to the ill Management of a Factor, in whom his Master had an entire Confidence." To remedy the situation, our hero goes on a "quest," absenting himself from his true love in order to spend the rest of his apprenticeship with the "Foreign Correspondent [and become] acquainted with all that concerned his Master." He learns his lessons so well that he is able to save his master ten thousand pounds. Soon afterward, Trueman inherits "a considerable Estate" from an uncle; he then returns to England and "demands" his beloved of her father. Along with his daughter, the generous and grateful merchant offers Trueman "the 10000 *l.* he had saved him, with the farther Proposal of resigning to him all his Business," but Trueman refuses both, and retires "into the Country with his Bride, contented with his own Fortune, though perfectly skill'd in the Methods of Improving it."

41. Steele had himself fathered an illegitimate child, but unlike the examples cited in this text, he did not disown her: "During his time in the Footguards [1694] Steele engaged in amorous adventures and received for his trouble a baby girl, born to Elizabeth Tonson, sister of Steele's future publisher. To his credit, he acknowledged the child and later brought her into his home" (Richard H. Dammers, *Richard Steele* [Boston: Twayne, 1982], 3).

42. Hirschman, *The Passions and the Interests,* 56–63.

The Anatomy of Heroism:
Gender Politics and Empire
in Gay's *Polly*

✖✖ *Dianne Dugaw*

John Gay wrote *Polly* fast on the heels of his unparalleled hit of 1728, *The Beggar's Opera.* From the start, this "Second Part of *The Beggar's Opera*" sparked dispute. Immediately banned, it remained unstaged for half a century. In our own time, however, *Polly* is more perplexing than controversial. Modern critics find the play neither serious nor provocative, probably because they fail to recognize the gender politics at its core. Indeed, Gay's *Polly* is a strenuous—if ultimately unsatisfying—satire that exposes the European heroic ideal as an ethos of slavery: an enslaving gender ideology and an enslaving will to empire that mutually construct each other. (Small wonder it was immediately banned and has remained obscure and misread for two and a half centuries.)

Gay based *Polly* on two conventional heroic models: (1) the Antony and Cleopatra story of John Dryden's *All for Love,* whose tragic pair he parodically recast as the pirate Macheath and the strumpet Jenny Diver; and (2) the female warrior motif of eighteenth-century balladry in which the heroine—in this case, Polly Peacham, a much-transformed Octavia—dresses as a man and ventures to war for the sake of her beloved. Through an ingenious deconstructing of these two motifs, one by the other, Gay dismantles the archetypal European heroic ideal of Love and Glory epitomized in *All for Love,* the ideal upon which the whole Western heroic tradition depends.

Polly exposes this heroic ideal as an ethos of slavery: an enslaving gender ideology and enslaving will to empire that construct and imply each

39

other. This ideal—whether for European men or women, for Antonys or Cleopatras—conquers and enslaves. Conquest of the "other" is a matter first of gender, and eventually—in the realm of empire—of race. For this reason, disguisings of gender and race are pivotal in Gay's play: Polly disguises her gender; Macheath disguises his race. Exposing these two masquerades, Gay orchestrates a fascinating exposure of vicious empire and failed love.

The satire of Gay's *Polly* actually extends well beyond Dryden's *All for Love,* its immediate target. For Gay undermines the basis for Dryden's tragedy, the Herculean dilemma, that traditional heroic conflict between "manly" glory and "womanly" love whose representations include—besides Antony and Cleopatra, and any number of tragic Restoration protagonists—such renowned pairings as Samson and Delilah, Paris and Helen, Odysseus and Circe, Aeneas and Dido. Bringing into a dismantling concurrence Polly's heroic romance quest with Macheath's Herculean dilemma, Gay's satire shows that European conquest, ethnocentrism, and empire are logical extensions of a gendered heroic ideal, which itself requires mutual conquest and delusion. Using the reversal of disguise, Gay exposes the seams of those gender categories that costume the two interlocking sides of European heroism: male and female, Mars and Venus.

But before I trace Gay's indictment of the heroic ideal, let me summarize the plot of this little-known ballad opera. *Polly* takes up the fortunes of Macheath and Polly shortly after the last curtain of *The Beggar's Opera,* when the heroic pair are separated by Macheath's transportation to the West Indies. Here Gay's sequel opens as Polly arrives in the New World in search of her man. Hers is the traditional heroic quest of ballad, romance, and comedy—a venturing heroism occasionally made available to women by the convention of gender disguise. She is, as we shall see, a female warrior.

When Macheath appears in act 2, there is no doubt that Gay has heroism on his mind. Just as Polly's story represents a conventional heroic paradigm, so does Macheath's as Gay retells *All for Love.* With his Cleopatra, Jenny Diver, Macheath has run away from the plantation where he was indentured. He now remains in his hideout disguised as "Morano," the "Neger" leader of a group of pirates. Act 2 centers on the "tragic" pair Macheath and Jenny—but with a difference. Gay retells the Antony and Cleopatra story from Octavia's point of view. If Polly enters act 1 as the traditionally venturing heroine of comedic romance, act 2 applies this conventional paradigm to Dryden's Octavia. How different this story looks when seen not with Antony at the center, as is usual, but from the perspective of a heroic and sympathetic Octavia, a venturing female warrior.

Act 2 undoes both heroic paradigms—Polly's comedic story and Macheath's tragic one—as a battlefield collision exposes our deluded allegiance to both. Macheath and his pirate band, plundering New World "Alexanders," meet in battle the victims of their unruly conquest, noble Native Americans on whose side we find the disguised Polly. Ironically, she is the only admirably "manly" European in the whole play. Macheath's blackface disguise makes him unrecognizable to Polly, who is equally unrecognizable in her men's clothes. Unwittingly she conquers him in battle: he looks nothing like the hero for whom she has ventured. After the destruction of her hero, Polly awakens—with her audience—to the failure of European heroism and leaves at play's end with her Indian allies, representatives of a redemptive New World otherness.

It was no accident that John Gay chose for the lead in *Polly* the female warrior, a conventionalized heroine of lower-class street-song. It was his well-known habit to create ironic mirrorings of low art and high, beggars and magistrates, pirates and kings, prostitutes and queens. Moreover, the female warrior herself, with explicit ambivalence, encompasses the terms of the heroic ideal that was Gay's target: those twin structural and thematic polestars of virtue, Love and Glory. As the female warrior enacts, and as Gay saw, these polestars reflect and irradiate an ideology of gender.

The female warrior sold as a "pop-song" fashion for over two hundred years and persists (albeit marginally) in Anglo-American folk tradition of our own day. Female warrior ballads tell the highly conventionalized story of a brave and virtuous woman who, separated from her beloved by "war's alarms" or the plotting of her cruel father, masquerades as a man and ventures to war for Love and for Glory. The female warrior ballads are success stories. Inevitably their transvestite heroine—a model of beauty and pluck—proves herself deserving in romance, able in war, and rewarded in both. A centuries-old cliche in British commercial songs, the motif governs some 120 separate ballads that circulated on cheap prints among the lower classes from about 1650 to 1850. The earliest such ballad in Anglo-American tradition is "Mary Ambree," which flourished as a "hit song" about 1600 and remained popular well into the eighteenth century. As for more recent female warriors—folksong versions of commercial ballads from the eighteenth and nineteenth centuries—"Jack Monroe," "Polly Oliver," "The Handsome Cabinboy," to name a few titles—are undoubtedly being sung somewhere in the English-speaking world at this very moment.[1]

As Gay recognized, the female warrior motif subverts the European heroic ideal of male glory—Mars—rewarded by female love—Venus. Based upon this gendered icon, the female warrior motif reverses the gender roles and collapses the opposition between male Glory and female Love, for the heroine plays out both ideals herself. "When Mars and Venus *conjunct* were, / 'tis thought that she was born"—so one ballad describes it (emphasis mine).[2] As the female warrior's commandeering of male identity suggests, heroism in this ethos depends upon gender.

The female warrior motif requires explicitly gendered conceptions of Love and Glory. Like Chaucer's Wife of Bath, the female warrior represents an encompassing conjunction of Venus and Mars.[3] Simultaneously a loving Venus and a heroic Mars, she ranges across both sides of a conspicuously bifurcated ideal as she plays out the conventional events of her narrative. Indeed, we recognize the female warrior as heroic precisely because we find in her story the familiar gendered terms of the heroic pattern. The motif retells the heroic quest of romance and comedy, a transposition of the disguised/returned-lover pattern that governs such ancient sagas as *The Odyssey* and whose archetypal structure shapes the whole Western romance tradition.[4]

In the female warrior motif we recognize the telltale heroic ingredients—however surprisingly they may be transposed: the loving heroine, the venturing hero in arms, the glory-and-love-rewarded ending. It is true that, quite unconventionally, the female warrior is the heroic center of her narrative, overstepping by way of her gender disguise her "women's portion"—the Venus hemisphere of the heroic paradigm. Nonetheless, she is an ideal woman in the conventional sense because she ventures all, indeed, even identity, for love. At the same time, the female warrior is celebrated in traditional ways for bearing arms—the glory side of the heroic paradigm, the side governed by Mars. One ballad heroine explicitly identifies in her story the two aspects of the Venus-Mars conjunction, "amor' and "arma":

> Come all you young virgins attend to my song,
> See how boldly I ventur'd my life for a man,
> I took up arms and a soldier did become.[5]

But, of course, the song's second line, "I ventur'd my life *for* a man" is a pun: the female warrior ventures *on behalf of* a man *as* a man. Such word-play demonstrates the oxymoronic dissembling at work in the motif, a dissembling that in some sense destabilizes the coded conventions of gender identity, for she is not a man.

While destabilizing gender categories, the female warrior also enacts and similarly exposes the conventions of a Western heroic ideal whose features intersect with those that construct and identify gender. The truth is, the European paradigm of Love and Glory is but heroized gender identity: Venus and Mars represent the separate categories of "woman" and "man" idealized.[6] Furthermore, the ideal of Love and Glory heroizes not only the conventions of gender attribution, but cross-gender reciprocity as well—that is, the relationship women and men are supposed to have with each other: men conquer empires to woo, win, and maintain women, who have conquered the hearts of men. Moreover, while Love is secondarily available to Mars, Glory is really not to Venus: "Arma *virum*que cano," as Virgil's epic so thunderously specifies (emphasis mine). In this gendered system, taking up arms re-quires that the female warrior venture as *"vir,"* which is precisely what her masquerade enables her to do. Dressed as a man, she plays the hero; playing the hero, she is taken for a man. Gender and heroism mutually construct each other. And this dissembling heroine commandeers both.

Thus, at one level the female warrior motif destabilizes this gender-heroism construct by making it a shifting and histrionic system. After all, she is not a man. Moreover, the motif reverses, conflates, and thus undermines the idealized reciprocity of women and men in relation to each other: who wins wars and who wins hearts. But, however provoca-tive the ballad female warrior's exploitation of the heroic ideal may be, it is in the main naively so. The satire one finds in ballads is equivocal, ambiguous, intermittent, surfacing by provocative implication rather than purposeful design. Fanciers of the female warrior were lower-class songmakers and their audiences, people who either did not hold up for scrutiny the motif's provocative deconstruction of gender and heroism, or—if they did—left us no record of their thoughts on the matter. But the female warrior motif's implied critique of the heroic ideal did not go unnoticed in the eighteenth century, as John Gay's *Polly* attests. If the ballad-makers could not or would not commandeer the subversiveness of the female warrior motif, John Gay did.[7]

The production history of *Polly* suggests that Gay's contemporaries recognized—as modern critics have not—that the play is deeply and seriously political. As I mentioned, *Polly* was banned before its opening night and remained unstaged for nearly half a century.[8] In December 1728 an official order, apparently from the prime minister, Robert Walpole, stopped the play in rehearsal shortly before its scheduled opening at Lincoln's Inn Fields. Immediately, Gay undertook to publish *Polly* by subscription, with the help of the young duchess of Queensbury, in whose company much of the play was written. Because of her open support of Gay and her direct involvement in this publication, the duchess and her husband were ousted from Court. A feisty woman, the duchess apparently felt no regrets, as her description of the incident testifies: "*I* was punished because Macheath was to be hanged; & Gay's morality vindicated—I told the L. Chamberlain *I thanked him*— it saved me trouble & Curtisies."[9] In a compassionate stroke of destiny, the duchess of Queensbury lived to see *Polly* finally staged in 1777, nearly fifty years after she so stalwartly stood by the play and its maker.

Twentieth-century critics find baffling this suppression of a play that they read as "innocent," "harmless," "simple," and "inoffensive."[10] *Polly* is perplexing. But then, Gay is perplexing in general. However engaging for a modern onlooker, he is often misread. What Bertrand Bronson has observed about *The Beggar's Opera* is true of Gay's work as a whole: "We incline to ignore its serious inclinations."[11] But this seems to have been less the case in his own time, as the suppression of *Polly* attests. Moreover, as early commentaries make clear, *The Beggar's Opera* and its sequel were read in political terms as indictments of "a system of corruption." The *Biographia Dramatica* states that "it was the political tendency of *The Beggar's Opera,* as exposing that system, not the pretended immoral tendency of that piece, that raised the Court clamour against [Gay]."[12] At the time *Polly* was suppressed, the courtier Lord Hervey described the banning as a decision of the prime minister, who found the play politically and personally offensive. Indeed, Hervey describes

Polly as "more abusive" than *The Beggar's Opera* and says that "Sir Robert Walpole resolved, rather than suffer himself to be produced for thirty nights together upon the stage in the person of a highwayman, to make use of his friend the Duke of Grafton's authority as Lord Chamberlain to put a stop to the representation of it." [13] Thus, contemporary perception stands at odds with modern readings of the play as "innocent politically." [14]

Infuriated by the suppression of *Polly,* Gay proceeded to publish it by subscription. Notorious by report, it was an instant moneymaker, quickly going into extra editions, a good many of them pirated. [15] Moreover, despite the fact that it was not put on until 1777, its influence was felt later in the century in ballad-opera-like pieces such as Sheridan's *The Camp,* whose masquerading Pollys and Nancys set off to find their heroines in the mode of Gay's Polly Peacham. Clearly, Gay's *Polly* has importance in the eighteenth century both as satire and as theater, striking a chord in its own era that modern criticism has yet to hear.

Unlike these later pieces, *Polly* is deeply satirical, for Gay is systematic, and fully self-conscious both in his unblinking exposure of the political "heroes" around him—the most conspicuous of them being Walpole—and in his indictment of the whole Western icon of heroism as Love and Glory. [16] The key to Gay's deconstructive reading of *All for Love* is his use of the female warrior motif to decenter Dryden's tragedy. As its title underscores, Gay's "Second Part of the Beggar's Opera" is entirely Polly Peacham's play, a feature that stymies the play's (mostly male) critics, who struggle to locate the central subject and sensibility where it "ought to be"—with Macheath. [17] But like all female warriors, Polly is the story's center and subject, and the play's events are seen from her perspective, a revealing decentering of the heroic Antony and Cleopatra story. This *All for Love* is the story of Octavia, the abandoned wife who ventures to Egypt for her faithless Antony. So ventures the dauntless Polly to the West Indies to find her Macheath, who—unknown to her—plays a captivated Antony to Jenny Diver's Cleopatra. Moreover, Gay further deconstructs this now-decentered paradigm by bringing his Octavia into the familiar arena of European epic not only from a margin now become center but also as a female warrior, that paradoxically dressed-up transformation of the heroic ideal who subverts her gendered model even as she plays it.

Polly's story—Gay's retelling of Octavia's quest for Antony—fits the narrative structure of the female warrior motif. Separated from Macheath, perhaps through her father's contrivance, Polly ventures to the Indies in search of her hero, characterizing her love quest in terms that eerily call up Shakespeare's *Hamlet:* "I love him, and like a troubled ghost shall never be at rest till I appear to him" (I.v.45–47).[18] Thus, Polly opens with the female warrior motif's conventional separation of lovers, develops the same tests of the heroine's love and prowess that send her in disguise ranging across the Venus/Mars division of the heroic ideal, and brings her to a final encounter and test of her hero. But as we shall see, Gay's *Polly* leads in the end not to a comic reunion of lovers, as the pattern prompts us to expect, but instead—in the vein of *Hamlet*—to a surprising and severing revenge.

The problem of slavery permeates Gay's play. At the outset it defines Polly's tests of love and of virtue; by play's end it will emerge as the European raison d'être, whether in love or in empire. As the first step in his anatomizing of European gender politics and colonialism as a single failed ethos, Gay threatens Polly with slavery *as a woman*—with sexual assault and exploitation.[19] (For this reason, Polly does not assume her male costume until the second act.) In act 1 the faithful Polly arrives in the New World in search of Macheath. Penniless, she finds employment on a plantation. Here Gay begins the forging of the gender-slavery link as Polly discovers that, hired as a servant to the mistress, she is in reality a slave to the master. Barring the door, the slave-owning Ducat claims her service: "A Kiss on those lips" (I.xi.33). Polly refuses. In the struggle that ensues, she and we awaken to her predicament, whose politics Gay maps in terms that gain in resonance and significance as the play proceeds: she is a slave.

> DUCAT. I shall humble these saucy airs of your [*sic*], Mrs. *Minx*. Is this language for a servant! from a slave!
> POLLY. Am I then betray'd and sold!
> DUCAT. Yes, hussy, that your [*sic*] are; and as legally my property, as any woman is her husband's, who sells her self in marriage. . . . Your fortune, your happiness depends upon your compliance. (I.xi.55–64)

Protesting her "vertue and integrity," Polly stands firm despite Ducat's threat to inflict upon her a more obvious slavery, "work in the fields among the planters." But a crisis without interrupts them as a servant rushes in with the alarm: "The whole country is in an uproar! The pyrates are all coming down upon us" (I.xii.105–6). In the midst of this "uproar" Polly escapes sexual slavery by running into the battle-ready countryside in male disguise. Thus, act 1 establishes as our point of reference and sympathy the courageous Polly, who refuses to act the slavish part of Ducat's concubine. As we shall see, Polly's resistance will in the acts to come contrast with the acquiescence of the willing slaves, Jenny and Macheath.

Act 2 opens with an ironic look at the necessary contingency on a man of a woman's heroic behavior. That is, the relationship of men and women constructed by the heroic ideal requires that a woman's final motivation must be love. Having donned her disguise, Polly observes with irony how Macheath's fate—life or death—rules her own. His death, she notes, would require her own according to the conventional heroic paradigm. This prescription for female heroism, it should be remarked, permeates the street ballads and other popular literature upon which Gay's Newgate satire feeds. Quite self-evidently, it dictates the self-immolation of Antony's tragic Cleopatra. A flippant Polly summarizes the requirements of her womanly role:

> When Papa 'peach'd him,
> If death had reach'd him,
> I then had only sigh'd, wept, and dy'd!
> (II.i.4–6)

But as she ponders further, the fact that he is not dead requires of her something a bit more complicated than "only" to sigh, weep, and die. When her man is "far from his home, and constant bride," a virtuous woman undertakes the conventional heroism of the female warrior. With simple dying not in order, Polly will venture to find Macheath, putting on the necessary guise: "With the habit, I must put on the courage and resolution of a man; for I am every where surrounded with dangers" (II.i.8–9).

Through the remainder of the play, Polly pretends to be a man, venturing *en travestie* into the Mars side of the heroic paradigm, where Gay explores this issue of "manly" heroism as it stands in relationship both to empire and to "womanly" love. These relationships are for Gay interconnected and deeply problematic. Ironically, the woman Polly emerges as an altogether exceptional "man"—conspicuously, the only admirably "manly" European in the play. Donning "courage and resolution" along with her trousers, she stands in sharp contrast to the representative "Alexanders" of her culture, the base and squabbling pirates who surround her.

At this point, Gay ushers onto the scene a ragtag group of underling pirates who immediately turn our attention to the glory side of the heroic paradigm. "Hacker" proclaims to his comrades: "Our profession is great, brothers. What can be more heroic than to have declar'd war with the whole world?" (II.ii.26–27). In short order Gay pushes to the forefront of this heroic realm the mythology of the Herculean dilemma and the politics of colonialism, the interconnected targets of his satire. The pirates complain about their chief, "Morano," who, unknown to them, is really Macheath in blackface disguise:

> HACKER. He is too much attach'd to his pleasures. That mistress of his is a clog to his ambition. She's an arrant *Cleopatra*.
> LAGUERRE. If it were not for her, the *Indies,* would be our own.
> (II.11.67–70)

Singing "Resolution is lull'd in her arms," these pirates then introduce the familiar outlines of the Herculean conflict: the love of siren woman blinds and emasculates the hero.[20]

In short order, however, Gay subverts the "manly" claims of these warring heroes and exposes in their greed the politics of European colonialism. Hacker concludes the pirates' paean to manly Glory: "after [your heroes] take to women, they have not good deeds to come. That inviegling gipsey, brothers, must be hawl'd from [Morano] by force. And then—the kingdom of *Mexico* shall be mine. My lot shall be the kingdom of *Mexico*" (II.ii.91–94). Thus, in an instant this ode to heroism metamorphoses into a petulant—and patently absurd—claim to "Mexico," at which point his fellow pirates descend upon Hacker in a noisy exchange of cudgels and sword blows. All squabble over their prospective "empires": Mexico, Cuba, and Peru. The racket they make rouses the disguised Polly, who is asleep nearby. Gay's female warrior awakens in this "Brave New World" of warring heroes.

Noticing her, the rogues drop their imperial negotiations. But theirs is only a shift of attention, not of mode. Capstern cries: "Hold, hold, gentlemen, let us decide our pretensions some other time. I see booty. A prisoner. Let us seize him" (II.ii.115–19). Moreover, lest the link between the colonial pretensions of these shiftless pirates and their invocation of Herculean heroism be overlooked, Gay underscores the connection. After seizing their "booty," Hacker demands: "Why, who do you take us for, friend?" Polly replies: "For those brave spirits, those *Alexanders,* that shall soon by conquest be in possession of the *Indies.*" She recognizes correctly, if ironically, that her captors are heroes fully consonant with the mythic variety. Satisfied by their prisoner's reply, her conquerors lead their captive "youth" off to their leader "Morano," the disguised Macheath.[21]

The European presence in the New World, Gay insists, is a chaotic state of war between divergent "Alexanders": rapacious planters and squabbling buccaneers, all of whose "conquests" stem from racism, pillage, cowardice, and greed. Moreover, as Gay goes on to show, this plundering colonialism is no accident. The stuff of "heroism" has for its prototype an ideal of Love and Glory that Gay exposes as an icon of mutual conquest. Representing this gender-based icon are Macheath and Jenny Diver, Gay's Antony and Cleopatra.

Slavery is the key to Gay's anatomizing of the relationship of his parodic Venus and Mars, who form the centerpiece of act 2. Polly's disguise as a hero—spurred by her ennobling and selfless love—has its counterpart in Macheath's disguise as a slave—spurred by his and Jenny's mutual conquest. He says, "I disguis'd my self as a black, to skreen my self from women who laid claim to me where-ever I went" (II.iii.34–35). As a few examples show, Gay's ironic costume-critique of heroic love as a relationship of enslaving ownership comes explicitly out of Dryden's tragedy. In *All for Love,* Cleopatra declares: "I'm to be a Captive: *Antony* / Has taught my mind the fortune of a Slave" (II.i.14–15).[22] Later her sycophant Alexis assures her of her lover's thrall:

> I . . . can see this *Antony,* this dreaded Man,
> A fearful slave, who fain would run away,
> And shuns his Master's eyes: if you pursue him,
> My life on't, he still drags a chain along,
> That needs must clog his flight.
>
> (II.i.88–92)

The journey of Gay's Polly to recover her "enslaved" Antony takes on ironic explicitness when we recall (as Gay's generation unquestionably did) the declaration of Dryden's venturing Octavia:

> He was a *Roman,* till he lost that name
> To be a Slave in *Ægypt;* but I come
> To free him thence.
>
> (III.i.421–23)

This "heroic" bondage, which Dryden imagined as a tragic tension in the paradigm, Gay explodes as indulgence and self-interest. In the typical way that eighteenth-century masquerade functions, Macheath's "skreening" reveals Gay's pirate Antony to be a willing slave.[23] Dryden saw a sympathetic, even tragic Antony entrapped by Cleopatra, vanquished by his own and her all-too-human weakness. With epic candor, Dryden's hero observes: "We have loved each other into our mutual ruin" (II.i.248–49). But while Dryden's Antony is calamitously conquered by passion, Macheath's predicament in love is a matter of costume and expedience, an appropriate slavery of his own determination.

Nor is Jenny's "Love" any nobler. Replaying Cleopatra's intrigue with Dolabella, Jenny upon first sight attempts to seduce the captured Polly, whom she finds "a mighty pretty man" (II.v.40).[24] The language of her seduction reminds us of the political ramifications of love conquests: at issue is power. "If I have put my self in your power," she declares, "you are in mine" (II.vi.60). Thus, Gay pushes to satirical conclusion an ideological connection between gender politics and empire that appears again and again in the plays and poems of his contemporaries. The conflation of the imagery of love on the one hand and of war on the other was a commonplace. In a typical example, Fainall in Congreve's *The Way of the World* (1700) facetiously likens his loss of marital challenges to Alexander's loss of imperial ones: "Nothing remains . . . but to sit down and weep like Alexander, when he wanted other worlds to conquer."[25]

In his literalizing of Dryden's image of enslavement Gay sees not the failure of individuals that Dryden saw but the failure of the ideology itself, particularly as the Augustans imaged it. Thus, Gay's satire links slavery in love to slavery in empire by parodying a discourse of conquest and trade taken directly from *All for Love.* Jenny's "ownership" of Macheath and Gay's exposure of the relationship between empire and the heroic ideal proceed from the crucial speech in *All for Love* in which Antony, believing the misreport that Cleopatra is dead, surrenders his will to fight and even to live. For Dryden, this abdication is high tragedy and a sympathetic emblem of the Herculean dilemma. The tragic Antony cries:

> What shou'd I fight for now? My Queen is dead.
> I was but great for her; my Pow'r, my Empire,
> Were but my merchandise to buy her love;
> And conquer'd Kings, my Factors. Now she's dead,
> Let Caesar take the World—
> . . . for all the bribes of life are gone away.
>
> (V.i.269–76)

But how easily, even in the original, Dryden's imagery tumbles into a problematic burlesque as "Power" and "Empire" in this outburst become "merchandise," "Factors," and finally "bribes" for love. It is but a short step for Gay to take his parodic Antony from Dryden's image of commodities to a willing slavery that exchanges shackling claims of ownership between female Love and male Glory. Macheath's blackface disguise is an ironic emblem of the conquest by which he is enslaved and for which he carries out his debased program of empire. As for Jenny— so committed to slavery is she that at the play's end we find her begging for bondage: "Send me back again with him into slavery, from whence we escap'd" (III.xii.32). Eventually, when her being with Macheath is no longer at issue, slavery still remains her choice: "Slavery, Sir, slavery is all I ask" (III.xiii.64). Jenny's final craving for slavery at the play's end contrasts ignobly with Polly's unwavering resistance to it.

Gay highlights the interlocking relationship between this gender-conquest and empire as he sets up the familiar outlines of the Herculean conflict between *volupta* and *virtu*. "I conquer but to make thee great," sings Macheath to Jenny of his "bribes" for love (II.iii.24). But, "an arrant Cleopatra," Jenny becomes an obstruction to the hero's pursuit of glory. Macheath protests: "Sure, hussy, you have more ambition and more vanity than to be serious in persuading me to quit my conquests . . . one bold step more, may make you queen" (II.iii.1–4). However, such "bribes" notwithstanding, Macheath's Cleopatra urges the conventional retreat: "You have a competence in your power. Rob the crew, and steal off to *England*" (II.iii.50–51). In so doing she sets up as the centerpiece of *Polly* a caricature of the heroic conflict between Love and Glory that is the crux of the conventional Herculean dilemma.

Just as he appropriates the pervasive imagery of enslavement in *All for Love,* Gay literalizes to burlesque the heroic conflict between Love and Glory experienced by Dryden's Antony. The Herculean Antony in *All for Love* stands tragically poised throughout the play between the epic *volupta* of Cleopatra, his "brighter Venus" (III.i.11), on the one hand, and the *virtu* of manly Honor on the other, as represented by his gruff lieutenant, the "old true-stampt *Roman*" Ventidius (I.i.106). In *Polly* Ventidius has his parodic counterpart in Macheath's "plain-spoken" Vanderbluff, who, with farcical inelegance, delivers the familiar chide: "For shame, Captain, what, hamper'd in the arms of a woman, when your honour and glory are all at stake! While a man is grappling with these gil-flirts, pardon the expression, Captain, he runs his reason a-ground" (II.iv.1–4).

Gay's version of the heroic conflict eventually reaches an ironically emblematic climax: a frenzied and parodic tug-of-war between Love and Glory. With Jenny yanking him by one arm and Vanderbluff by the other, the Herculean Macheath is—literally—caught in the middle. Eventually he gives way, as did Antony, to Love. As he does so, Vanderbluff's warning baldly recapitulates Dryden's imagery of "merchandise" and "bribes": "Lose the *Indies* then, with all my heart. Lose the money, and you lose the woman, that I can tell you, captain" (II.ix.31–32).

However, immediately after this farcical reenactment of the Herculean dilemma, Vanderbluff's "Honor," like Jenny's "Love," capitulates to the greed and expedience that ultimately motivate the European "heroes"—whether female or male—in Gay's New World. Jenny admonishes Vanderbluff: "Not so hasty and choleric. I beg you lieutenant. . . . Why should we put what we have already got to the risque? . . . We have money enough. . . . Let us leave the *Indies* to our comrades" (II.ix.34–44). For a moment, Vanderbluff, Glory's spokesman, hesitates: "If it were consistent with our honour, her counsel were worth listening to" (46–47). But Jenny quickly counters: "Consistent with our honour! For shame, lieutenant; you talk downright *Indian*. . . . You may talk of honour, as other great men do: But when interest comes in your way, you should do as other great men do" (II.ix.48–49).

Without more ado, Vanderbluff is persuaded and the three heroic principals—Macheath, Jenny, and Vanderbluff—prepare to sneak away to the ships anchored offshore. Just as they depart, however, word comes that the Indians and the troops from the plantation are blocking their path and forcing a fight. Trapped, Macheath urges glory and empire: "Since I must have an empire, prepare yourself, *Jenny*, for the cares of royalty. Let us on to battle, to victory. Hark the trumpet" (II.x. 10–12). "They must conquer or die who've no retreat," sings this mock-heroic triumvirate in lines that echo Dryden's ironic trumpet call in "A Song for St. Cecilia's Day": "Charge, charge, 'tis too late to retreat."[26]

Jenny's social accusation that, on the subject of "honour," Vanderbluff speaks "downright Indian" represents a moral opposition Gay sets up throughout the play between debased "Europeans"—pirates, slavers, and whores—and noble New World natives imagined along the lines of Aphra Behn's "Oroonoko." By act 3, these nobly pastoral Indians become increasingly important in the play as they speak for "the whole world," against which European piracy has set itself at war. Foils to and victims of the conquest, they further decenter our view of the play's squabbling European Alexanders. Like "Oroonoko," Gay's noble Amerinds dismay most modern readers of *Polly*, who find their stiff courtliness and relentless honor not only too lifeless but indeed, at bottom, too European.[27]

However, our expectations of ethnorealism notwithstanding, the Indians in *Polly* stand in marked contrast to the European "heroes" who are the play's real subjects, and in this contrast is their principal function. Throughout the play Gay's Indians use the term "European" to refer to the pirates and their conquest. In so doing, they remind us of the scope of Gay's satire: the entire European heroic mythology and its consequences for individuals and for whole peoples. Brought before Morano/Macheath, the captured Cawwawkee refuses to talk: "What, betray my friends! I am no coward, *European*" (II.vii.51–52). Of course, by contrast, we have just seen among the pirates betrayal of every kind on every side. Moreover, the "Europeans" before him—Macheath, Vanderbluff, Jenny, Capstern, Laguerre—in lines deeply ironic, further contrast themselves and their civilization with this aboriginal "whole world" against which they war.

VANDERBLUFF: What, neither cheat or be cheated! There is no having either commerce or correspondence with these creatures.
JENNY: We have reason to be thankful for our good education. How ignorant is mankind without it!

CAPSTERN: I wonder to hear the brute speak.
LAGUERRE: They would make a shew of him in *England*. (II.viii.57–63)

That Cawwawkee is anything but a "brute" is precisely the point. Here there is no mistaking Gay's indictment of the colonial enterprise and the arrogance of European ethnocentrism.

Gay's "noble savages" serve the play in three principal ways: (1) They establish, by contrast, the brutishness of the play's European "heroes" and their enslaving will to empire, Gay's real subject. "How different are your notions from ours!" exclaims the baffled Pohetohee (III.1.28). "Heaven guard our country," says Cawwawkee (II.xi.17–18). (2) The nonwhite Indians also underscore the connection that Gay makes between an avaricious and enslaving heroic ideal and European racial arrogance, a connection already made explicit by Macheath's blackface masquerade. Thus, the underling pirates' final mutiny has at its core the same racism voiced by Jenny: "I don't see, Brother Hacker, why we should be commanded by a Neger," complains Culverin (III.v.11–12). And (3) ultimately, the noble Indians supply an ideological free zone beyond the European system that at play's end will afford the masquerading Polly—ironically, the only virtuous and "heroic" European "man" to be found—an avenue of escape from the failed ethos of her race and culture.

Macheath's blackface masquerade, then, is an icon by which Gay metaphorizes his analysis of European heroism as a racially embodied slavery. The issue of slavery, as we have seen, permeates *Polly,* linking the politics of gender and empire. In addition, Gay hinges the plot's last twist upon Macheath's disguise, using it to deal his final dismantling blow to European heroism: the failure even of the virtuous gender-transcending Polly and her female warrior program of rescuing her "hero." In a final climactic battle between the pirate Alexanders on the one hand and Polly and the Indians on the other, the two heroic paradigms upon which Gay constructs the play—Macheath's Herculean tragedy and Polly's female warrior romance—intersect and ultimately undo each other. Failing to recognize in him the disguised Macheath, Polly conquers the slave "Morano" in battle and turns him over to a justice that decrees his death. In this most purposefully anticlimactic of climaxes, Gay completes the unheroic undoing of Macheath and in the process exposes the ultimate failure of our "hero" Polly. Her female warrior heroism can only collapse upon its own success, premised as it is upon loyalty to an ideal of enslaving and being enslaved. As the unmasking at the play's conclusion reveals, Polly's Glory—all we find to admire in the European ethos—depends upon her Love, which remains defined and thus corrupted by the paradigm of Mars and Venus, whose men at base are pirates and whose women are trulls. Gay thus disappoints the last of heroic loyalties: faith in the female warrior motif.

But just how does this final divestiture happen? As we have seen, Gay's play works as it does because he sets before us familiar heroic paradigms whose rules we know and whose conventional outcomes we expect. Indeed, his satire neatly ensnares us into hopes that the familiar ideal of Love and Glory—be it enacted in the female warrior motif or the Herculean dilemma—will work itself out in the expected way: "None but the Brave deserves the Fair," to quote Dryden's famous declaration.[28] Throughout the play, we hope for a satisfaction of our heroic expectations: that Polly's familiar female warrior quest will be rewarded in the necessary way—in the rescue and reclamation of her hero. Juxtaposing these two traditional paradigms, Polly's romantic female warrior and Macheath's tragic Hercules, Gay purposely sets up expectations of the traditional results: the heroic union of the Brave and the Fair that we have been taught to expect, whether in tragic destruction or comedic promise. In overturning these expected results, he anatomizes the failure of Polly's love and in so doing completes his dismantling of the heroic ideal that governs it.

The problem in *Polly* is Macheath: he is not the hero he is supposed to be. As I have noted, Macheath's ignobility may account for the discomfort and dismissal of the play by modern critics, whose satisfaction—like that of any audience—is shaped along the lines of conventional expectations.[29] The problem of the unheroic Macheath can be solved in two conventional ways, both of them working out of the heroic ideal's system of gender reciprocity, the interrelationship of women and men vis-à-vis Love and Glory. Dryden's Ventidius eloquently outlines the two Love alternatives that can intersect with Antony's Glory:

> One would be ruin'd with you; but she first
> Had ruin'd you: the other, you have ruin'd,
> And yet she would preserve you.
>
> (III.i.342–45)

First, there is the resolution posed by the Herculean dilemma: that male Glory can withstand the soft debilitation of female Love—the story of Antony and Cleopatra, Samson and Delilah, Odysseus and Circe, Dido and Aeneas. Tragic "ruin" occurs when it fails. Then, there is a countervailing view of female Love as preserving, redemptive, hero-reforming. In this scenario, fallen male Glory can be restored by the power of female Love. *Polly* deliberately entertains both solutions only to discard them.

Our initial hope arises within the context of the Herculean dilemma: Macheath really *is* a hero, and the problem—simply and tradition-ally—is his "arrant Cleopatra." Of course, Hacker and others have already introduced to us this conventional configuration of manly Glory made impotent and servile in the thrall of womanly Love. Throughout *Polly,* Gay deliberately plays upon the enticing familiarity of this por-trait. Jenny is, after all, an unremittingly unattractive contrast to the sympathetic Polly, whose pluck and fidelity actually bolster hopes in Macheath's character. Indeed, the Herculean dilemma works because of the weighting of the paradigm against the siren Love in favor of Glory. It is a weakness for Antony to deny Ventidius and favor Cleo-patra. But of course Gay's burlesque finally overturns the Herculean solution by collapsing any contrast between the Love of Cleopatra and the Glory of Ventidius: such conquest—be it of a man or a nation—is self-interest. Gay's Vanderbluff affords no redemptive honor for our hero. What expectations the conventional Herculean dilemma raises, Gay quickly dissipates in this shabby world of pirate Alexanders. More complex, however, and ultimately more radical is his dismantling of the heroic hopes that Polly's romance pattern engenders.

Gay deliberately sets up the hope of Macheath's reform not only in the terms of the Herculean dilemma but also as an adjunct to Polly's story in a different but equally familiar configuration of the relationship of women to men. Thus, we are encouraged to hope for the power of Love to reform the rake. Indeed, there is an assumption of Macheath's worth embedded in Polly's female warrior story: he must be something of a hero to command such Love. Moreover, because such Love ennobles and restores to potency such fallen Glory, we can expect of Macheath a final reformation that will prove the hero deserving of this Love, and thus ultimately "Glorious" by implication. "None but the Brave de-serves the Fair." Gay's thwarting of this hope in the power of female Love

to restore male Glory—the ultimate justification for Polly's heroism—
is his last satiric move.

Gay postulates the redemptive function of female Love fast on the
heels of Polly's battlefield success as a male "hero." In this way he brings
into dismantling conjunction the two sides of the paradigm, Glory and
Love. Polly's final plea of love is a "womanly" heroine's plea and brings
about the relinquishing of her "manly" hero's part. After being captured by Polly, the unrecognized "Morano" is led off to be punished for
his crimes. Revealing the true identity of this "runaway slave," Jenny
desperately poses to his captors the one conventional possibility left
to redeem him as a hero—the intercession of love: "He is no black,
Sir, but under that disguise, for my sake, skreen'd himself from the
claims and importunities of other women. May love intercede for him?"
(III.xii.43–45). Momentarily, it does. The astonished Polly—soldier
hero of the day—claims his life as reward for her warrior exploits.

Here we see a final example of Gay's satiric method in this play
as Polly's "claim" literalizes that of Dryden's journeying Octavia.
Throughout Gay exploits and exposes the conquering "claims" that
surface everywhere in Dryden's tragedy. In *All for Love*, for example,
Octavia bids her children approach their father Antony that he may
"own" them—and conversely, that they may "own" him. Indeed, as
we noted, Octavia came to Egypt explicitly to *claim* him. This climactic moment of domestic negotiation over, Antony capitulates—at least
temporarily—amid the imagery of conquest and of legal and financial
ownership:

> I am vanquish'd; take me,
> Octavia; take me, Children; share me all.
> I've been a thriftless Debtor to your loves,
> And run out much, in riot, from your stock;
> But all shall be amended.
>
> (III.i.365–69)

But in Gay's satire, Polly's heroic, virtuous, and fully justified "claims
and importunities" ironically overturn Macheath's slavish "skreening."
Moreover, Polly has yet to learn from this irony. Discovering her conquered foe's true identity, Polly exclaims: "Macheath! Is it possible?
Spare him, save him, I ask no other reward" (III.xiii.46–47). But she is
not in time. Macheath has already been executed. This desperate last-

minute intercession of the hero-heroine Polly comes too late to save him and the ideal that requires, if not his heroism, at least his redemption.

However inconsistent and impossible Polly's hope of reclamation, it is a perfect articulation of one of the conventional functions of female Love in the heroic paradigm: the temporarily lapsed hero is revived to his Glory by the Love of his virtuous heroine. Gay counts on our recognizing and being seduced by this last of his familiar scenarios. Polly's Love, however, is not only too late but also wrongheaded—or, more aptly, wrong-hearted. For all her good intentions, Polly is caught in a web of vice that, though not of her own making, nonetheless falsifies her heroics. Asked by the onlooking Pohetohee to reconcile her commitment to Macheath and her own admission that he is "the most profligate of mankind," Polly declares her hope that her rescuing love will reform, indeed, "reclaim" him. "He ran into the madness of every vice. I detest his principles, tho' I am fond of his person to distraction. Could your commands . . . restore him to me, you reward me at once with all my wishes. For sure my love still might reclaim him" (III.xii.85–89).

But Polly's declaration turns upon itself and exposes her delusion. If Macheath is run into a vicious "madness," Polly's language betrays that she runs along with him, being driven to "distraction" by his "possession" of her. Faced with her own part in his destruction, the distraught Polly cries: "Why could I not know him? All his distress brought upon him by my hand! Cruel love, how could'st thou blind me so?" (III.xiii.49–51). Imagining him as a hero, she could not see him in the slave he chose to be. Moreover, once recognizing him, she still persists in her allegiance to the heroic ideal. "None but the Brave deserves the Fair"; therefore, Macheath must be brave, all evidence to the contrary.

Polly's "sureness" that her love "might reclaim" the hero for whom she has been a hero represents the last unsteady feature of the heroic paradigm that Gay undoes. In short order, he awakens us to the conventionality, real contradiction, and even viciousness of this attempt to preserve the ideal. Immediately after Polly's abortive reclamation attempt, the profligate Jenny voices the identical claim of Love's hero-redeeming power: "I know I have so much power over him, that I can even make him good" (III.xii.7–8). Pohetohee asks the obvious: why didn't she then? Jenny replies lamely that she was "too indulgent," "loth to balk his ambition," and herself possessed of the "frailty of pride"

(III.xiii. 10–14). Pohetohee ponders this acceptance of heroic vice in the remarks of Jenny and, as we now realize, in those of Polly as well: "With how much ease and unconcern these *Europeans* talk of vices, as if they were necessary qualifications" (III.xii. 15–16).

Indeed, in Gay's analysis they are. Polly's conventional hopes tellingly (and futilely) coincide with the ignoble Jenny's. As she so ironically observed earlier in the play, her woman's heroism is ultimately contingent on Macheath and the gender-parsed paradigm of Love and Glory from which she has yet to extricate herself. For these plantation pirates, Gay insists, *are* European heroes. As Macheath declares before his final exit: "*Alexander* the great was more successful. That's all" (III.xi. 59). By the play's end, Gay has thus fully dismantled the gendered ideal of European heroism with its ignobly conquering Macheaths and Jennys, its deluded if virtuous Pollys waging war against "the whole world." Having done so, he sends his gender-confounding female warrior out of the final act in the company of her Indian allies.

It has not been my purpose here to claim dramatic excellence for this barely known and little-appreciated ballad opera. In truth, even recognizing the ambitious and sometimes ingenious sweep of the satire, one can hardly find *Polly* a satisfying play. How can it be when it thwarts, frustrates, and overturns so many of our fundamental and cherished conventions? Moreover, though Gay insists upon the failure of European culture and its conquering enterprise, he does not shed entirely the heroic notions the play so thoroughly dismantles. When he sends Polly off with the Indians, he projects an eventual relationship with "Prince" Cawwawkee, which seems not so much an alternative as a modification of the heroic ideal that he has gone to such lengths to expose.[30] If Gay recognized the need for a point of reference altogether outside the European ethos he so devastatingly dismantled, he nonetheless could not quite imagine a voice for that perspective. It is telling that Gay's *Polly* does not contain even one non-European woman.

But the success or failure of the play is not my concern. Rather, I have attempted to show Gay's satiric dismantling of the European heroic ideal of Love and Glory. As the female warrior motif reveals, heroism itself is a matter of gender. As Gay makes so disruptively plain, this story of female Glory prompted by Love ultimately implies not only the maleness of heroism but also an ethos of conquest. Love and Glory construct each other, and for Gay, the ideologies of both are far from clean. Necessarily intersecting with an ethos of slavery and conquest, even Polly's female warrior heroism must fail. Exiting into a "Third World" of hopeful—if vaguely conceived—Otherness, Gay's boyclad female warrior and her play flee altogether the bounds of a failed and deplorable European civilization.

Notes

1. For a study of the female warrior in Anglo-American literature, see Dianne Dugaw, *Warrior Women and Popular Balladry, 1650–1850* (Cambridge: Cambridge University Press, 1989). See also Dianne Dugaw, " 'Female Sailors Bold': Transvestite Heroines and the Markers of Gender and Class," in *Iron Men, Wooden Women: Gender and Anglo-American Seafaring, 1700–1919,* ed. Margaret Creighton and Lisa Norling (Baltimore: Johns Hopkins University Press, forthcoming).

2. *The Female Warrior* from a 1690s London broadside, reproduced in *The Bagford Ballads,* ed. Joseph W. Ebsworth, 2 vols. (Hertford: Stephen Austin and Sons, 1878), 1:322.

3. For Chaucer's portrait of the Wife of Bath in terms of this astrological conjunction, see "The Wife of Bath's Prologue," in *The Canterbury Tales,* 11:609–20. For discussion of this conjunction, see Walter C. Curry, "More About Chaucer's Wife of Bath," *PMLA* 37 (1922): 30–51.

4. D. K. Wilgus, "A Tension of Essences in Murdered-Sweetheart Ballads," in *The Ballad Image: Essays Presented to Bertrand Harris Bronson,* ed. James Porter (Berkeley and Los Angeles: University of California Press, 1983), 241–42.

5. From an early nineteenth-century Liverpool broadside in Harvard University Collection 54-784, "Miscellaneous Prints," vol. 2, p. 96.

6. This view of the heroic ideal as gender opposition was especially fashionable in the Restoration era, appearing in work after work. Dryden supplied perhaps the most dazzling emblem of the idea in the masque of Cleopatra as Venus and Antony as Mars, which opens the third act of *All for Love.* A broad-

side ballad from about 1665 underscores this opposition, and with an allusion to Antony and Cleopatra. In *The Faithful Lovers Farewell,* "John" counters his "Betty's" proposal that she "put . . . on a Masculine Case" by insisting: "Thou rather wilt hurt, and hinder me, / When we begin the Fray, / When Cleopatra put to Sea? *MARK ANTONY LOST THE DAY.*" See *The Euing Collection of English Broadside Ballads in the Library of the University of Glasgow* (Glasgow: University of Glasgow Press, 1971), 179.

7. Gay was aware of the female warrior of balladry, for he briefly introduced the motif already in *The What D'Ye Call It* (1715). In that "Tragi-Comic-Pastoral Farce," the heroine, Kitty—much-influenced by street ballads—offers to accompany her Tom to war (I.i.73). It is also clear that at the end of the 1720s, Gay had both gender and heroism on his mind, for he followed *Polly* with his third ballad opera, *Achilles,* which took for its subject the episode of the hero's masquerade as a woman at the outset of the Trojan War. Among the last pieces Gay wrote, *Achilles* was staged posthumously in 1733.

8. For a recent discussion of the play, see Calhoun Winton, *John Gay and the London Theatre* (Lexington: University Press of Kentucky, 1993), ch. 9. On the production history, see William E. Schultz, *Gay's Beggar's Opera: Its Content, History, and Influence* (New York: Russell and Russell, 1923; reprint, 1967), 208–20. See also the Introduction of John Gay, *Dramatic Works,* ed. John Fuller, 2 vols. (Oxford: Clarendon Press, 1983), 1:53–55.

9. Quoted in L. W. Conolly, "Anna Margaretta Larpent, the Duchess of Queensbury and Gay's *Polly* in 1777," *Philological Quarterly* 51 (1972): 956.

10. For example, see Schultz, *Gay's Beggar's Opera,* 220, 221, and 223.

11. Bertrand H. Bronson, *Facets of the Enlightenment: Studies in English Literature and Its Contexts* (Berkeley and Los Angeles: University of California Press, 1968), 81.

12. Quoted in Schultz, *Gay's Beggar's Opera,* 209.

13. *Lord Hervey's Memoirs,* ed. Romney Sedgwick (London: B. T. Batsford, 1963; reprint, New York: Penguin, 1984), 20.

14. Patricia Meyer Spacks, *John Gay* (New York: Twayne, 1965), 156.

15. James B. Sutherland, "'Polly' Among the Pirates," *Modern Language Review* 37 (1942): 291–303.

16. For discussion of *Polly* in terms of the Herculean conflict, see Joan H. Owen, "*Polly* and the Choice of Virtue," *Bulletin of the New York Public Library* 77 (1974): 393–406.

17. Thus, Edmund McAdoo Gagey—apparently never imagining that Macheath was not intended as the hero or even the central focus of the play—complains: "Gay was . . . sacrificing the glamour, the charm, and the gallantry of his hero." See *Ballad Opera* (New York: Columbia University, 1937), 49. John Fuller also betrays a hint of bafflement at Macheath's debasement:

"Polly herself cannot carry the play . . . Macheath at least retains his self-confidence . . . In context his presumptuousness lacks charm . . . and his death is ignominious." See Gay, *Dramatic Works*, 1:56. For a reconsideration of Polly's virtue and her importance to *The Beggar's Opera* and its sequel, see Toni-Lynn O'Shaughnessy, "A Single Capacity in *The Beggar's Opera*," *Eighteenth-Century Studies* 21 (1987–88): 212–27.

18. Gay, *Dramatic Works*, 2:83. My references are to this edition. The imagery here also calls to mind the conventional ballad motif of a dead lover—usually an abandoned woman—who pursues her beloved betrayer. See, for example, *The Cruel Ship's Carpenter* (usually titled on broadsides *The Gosport Tragedy*). For versions, see G. Malcolm Laws, *American Balladry from British Broadsides* (Philadelphia, 1957), 268–70 (P-36). On the structure of the female warrior ballads, see chapter 4 of Dugaw, *Warrior Women*.

19. As Fuller observes (Introduction, *Dramatic Works*, 1:56), "a sexual/political metaphor is substituted [in *Polly*] for the criminal/political metaphor of *The Beggar's Opera*." That Gay is developing links between racial slavery and gender slavery is apparent in the first act when the slaver Ducat complains of paying the price of "a dozen Negro princesses" for "a handsome Christian" (I.v.26). Shortly after, Gay weaves into this construction the problem of heroism as Polly, refusing to be Ducat's slave, invokes the unsatisfactory example of Helen of Troy. She declares there "was never yet / So great a wretch as Helen" (I.xi.19–20).

20. Accounts of Hercules' love for Omphale develop this theme of the hero emasculated by love. The exchange of gender-typed clothing and activities is a prominent feature of these stories. See J. Lempriere, *Lempriere's Classical Dictionary* (London: Routledge and Kegan Paul, 1865; reprint, London: Bracken, 1984), 302–4 and 458.

21. The identification of Macheath with Alexander began already with *The Beggar's Opera*. See Bronson, *Facets*, 72–73.

22. John Dryden, *All for Love*, ed. Maximillian Novak, II.i.14–15, vol. 13 in *The Works of John Dryden*, ed. H. T. Swedenberg, Jr., and Alan Roper, 12 vols. (Berkeley and Los Angeles: University of California Press, 1956–). My references are to this edition.

23. Gay's habitual use of disguise as exposure of truth is noted by Spacks, *John Gay*, 139.

24. The intrigue between Cleopatra and Dolabella that provokes Antony's jealous rage occurs in act 4 of Dryden's play.

25. William Congreve, *The Way of the World*, II.i.127–29, in *The Comedies of William Congreve*, ed. Anthony G. Henderson (Cambridge: Cambridge University Press, 1982), 334.

26. John Dryden, "A Song for St. Cecilia's Day" (1687), in *The Poems and*

Fables of John Dryden, ed. James Kinsley (London: Oxford University Press, 1962), 422.

27. For a discussion of Gay's portrait of the Indians in *Polly,* see B. H. Bissell, *The American Indian in English Literature of the Eighteenth Century* (New Haven: Yale University Press, 1925), 127–30.

28. John Dryden, "Alexander's Feast; or The Power of Music" (1697), in *Poems and Fables of John Dryden,* 504. One cannot fail to recognize that Dryden himself, particularly in his later works, took a similarly ironic and subversive stance with regard to this heroic ideal. Unlike Gay, however, he never questioned the rootedness of the ethos in gender.

29. Spacks declares: "[Macheath] has become so conventionally detestable that we find him both boring and distasteful and feel well rid of him" (*John Gay,* 160).

30. In addition, one cannot help but sympathize with Gagey's objections to the Indians and to the play's ending "with its assurance that Polly will eventually marry the sententious Indian Prince, Cawwawkee, and be obliged to listen the rest of her life to his moral apothegms" (*Ballad Opera,* 50).

Lady Mary Wortley Montagu and the Historical Machinery of Female Identity

𝒬𝒜𝒬 *Jill Campbell*

Lady Mary Wortley Montagu is known first to students of the eighteenth century not as the authorial voice heard in her many poems, essays, three volumes of letters, and a play; but as the satiric spectacle conjured in Pope's portraits of her in several of his poems. In his epistle on the characters of women, Pope's Lady Mary, under the name of Sappho, presents the scandalous spectacle of the failed or incoherent construction of a woman's outward beauty:

> Rufa, [he declares,] whose eye quick-glancing o'er the Park,
> Attracts each light gay meteor of a Spark,
> Agrees as ill with Rufa studying Locke,
> As Sappho's diamonds with her dirty smock,
> Or Sappho at her toilet's greasy task,
> With Sappho fragrant at an ev'ning Mask:
> So morning Insects, that in muck begun,
> Shine, buzz, and fly-blow in the setting-sun.[1]

While Belinda's labors at her toilet in *The Rape of the Lock* are the decking of some kind of "Goddess" with the "glitt'ring spoil" of England's world trade, Lady Mary's labors are a "greasy task," a descent into the "muck" supporting the shine of self-presentation, and what she achieves—like all the other women of this epistle—is "at best a Contradiction still": diamonds and a dirty smock. As Louis Landa and Laura Brown have persuasively argued, in the Indian gems, Arabian perfumes, and African ivory with which Belinda adorns herself

64

we see the goods of imperial trade displayed on the body of the "Lady of Fashion," so that that body becomes an ideologically charged figure for the equivocal morality of imperial trade.[2] In the first half of the eighteenth century, during the period of what Brown calls the "first major English expansion" and of what Neil McKendrick calls the beginning of England's "consumer revolution," writers frequently express their responses to this increasing absorption in commercial exchange and world trade—whether responses of enthusiasm, horror, or ambivalence—through their representations of English women, portrayed as the paradigmatic consumers of fashionable goods.[3] Thus, as Brown argues, the contradictions, deceptions, and denials involved in female self-presentation become convenient synecdoches for those of imperial trade and commercial exchange.

For example, Pope repeatedly links what he calls the epic "machinery" of *The Rape of the Lock,* the legion of sylphs who construct and preserve Belinda's beauty, with the economic machinery of the trade in commodities that adorns her; but the agency of both the sylphs and the economic relations that produce Belinda's adornments must remain invisible if the effect of her beauty is to be successfully achieved. In Sappho's "dirty smock" perhaps we see an allusion to the sordid underpinnings of the glittering exterior of a culture based on imperial trade and commercial exchange, again displaced onto the woman—but with the grinding of the machinery of material relations now rendered unflatteringly visible in the evident labors of the woman's material body. Sappho's engagement in the economic and cultural machinery of female beauty only reveals her incoherence as an individual and the extreme ephemerality of her existence, as passing as that of a fly.

The portrait of Sappho in Pope's "Epistle to a Lady" thus takes its lineaments from the established satiric category of the fashionable lady; and it specifically draws into question Sappho's ability to construct herself as a viable individual. The portrait has always been recognized, however, as the depiction of a particular historical woman, Lady Mary Wortley Montagu, as well as of a satiric type. That woman existed not only as a spectacle but also as a voice, writing vociferously against Pope's depiction of herself, against Swift's depiction of women in general, against the reduction of women to mere spectacle, whether charming or grotesque. In the first section of this essay, I will examine the determining historical machinery of female identity as it appears specifically in the restrictive and coded system of female clothing and bodily appearance, which Lady Mary discusses in several issues of her periodical, *The Nonsense of Common-Sense*. However, in her *Nonsense of Common-Sense* essays, Lady Mary also uses the image of a constraining, artificial, or impersonal machinery to describe the production of voice itself: at times she represents herself as entangled in a discursive or specifically literary "machinery" that dictates the terms of gendered identity as deterministically as the required spectacle of female fashion.

When Lady Mary traveled to Turkey as a young woman, she responded enthusiastically to the alternative possibilities for female identity she encountered there in the form of different conventions of dress; but she also applied herself eagerly to learning the Turkish language and studying its literature, as if immersion in another culture might affirm for her ways in which culture itself is not monolithic and therefore cannot thoroughly, or at least straightforwardly, control the content of personal voice. In the second section below, I will consider Lady Mary's letters from Turkey, focusing on her attempts in those letters to use her encounter with cultural difference to figure the historical specificity of eighteenth-century English notions of female identity. In her letters from Turkey, and particularly in the letters that offer a translation of a Turkish love poem and a description of the women's baths, Lady Mary attempts to use her experience of cultural disjunctions to construct a voice that can speak of sexual desire and of aesthetic pleasure—subjects not available to the Belindas or the Sapphos of Pope's poems.

A 1746 engraving, *The Lady's Disaster*,[4] graphically depicts some of the stakes attached to female fashion in this period. The little poem below the engraving's picture informs us that the woman at the center of the satiric scene is named Celia, and it refers to the hoop-petticoat she wears as a "wide Machine." The machine of Celia's fashionable clothing has betrayed her, apparently, catching on what seems to be a window-shutter hook as she snobbishly tossed her skirt in an attempt to avoid the dirty chimney sweep who has fallen at her feet. Celia is thus ironically punished for her snobbery of social class and fashionable appearance by having what underlies that fashionable appearance indecorously revealed to the crowd of common as well as gentle people who have gathered in the street. And the artist of the picture is quite specific about what underlies the machine of her fashionable clothing:

If Fame say true in former Days,
The Fardingale was no disgrace;
But what a Sight is here reveal'd!
Such as oure Mothers ne'er beheld.
A Nymph in an unguarded hour,
(Alas! who can be too secure)
Dire fate has destin'd to be seen,
Entangled in her wide Machine.
While Carmen, Clowns, & Gentle folks
With satisfaction pass their Jokes.
Some view th'enamel'd Scene on high

And some at bottom fix their Eye;
Mark well the Boy with smutty Face,
And wish themselves were in his place:
Whose black distorted features show,
There's something—to be seen below,
And artfull [?] grinning at her Foot
Cries sweep! sweep! Madam for your Soot,
While from his Stall the leering Jew,
Would gladly have a better view.
In moderate bounds had Celia dres't.
She'd ne'er became a publick Jest.

(Drawn from the Fact. Occasion'd by a Lady carelessly tossing her Hoop too high, in going to shun a little Chimney sweeper's Boy who fell down just at her Feet in an artful Surprise, at ye enormous Sight.)

The Lady's Disaster (1746), reproduced courtesy of the Print Collection, The Lewis Walpole Library, Yale University.

both the materiality of her female body and the materiality of the economic relations that have produced her clothing are here revealed as the
repressed content normally hidden under her elegant garments. It is the
very extremity with which Celia's skirt alters and conceals the natural
shape of her body that has led it to unveil that body unexpectedly; as
the picture's poetic caption concludes, "In moderate bounds had Celia
dres't, / She'd ne'er became a publick Jest." When what's under Celia's
skirt is exposed to view, the chimney sweep between her legs holds up a
little phallic-shaped shovel underneath that skirt, as if to emblematize
the crudely sexual nature of the exchange in which her body is destined,
finally, to function; and the shape of his shovel is echoed in the various
phallic images with which Celia finds herself surrounded—the three
bishop's miters on the tavern's sign behind her, the guns held erect by
the men standing nearby, and the post at the edge of the road that seems
almost to have just forced its way out of the ground in response to her
exposure.

More elaborately, the artist has arranged the composition of the picture to suggest that Celia's skirt normally conceals the facts of hard
manual labor and of commercial exchange that support or undergird its
extravagant compass. Crucial to the picture's brief narrative is the figure
of the lowly chimney sweep, who has thrown himself at Celia's feet and
caused her thus to reveal herself. The dirty face and twisted limbs of
the chimney sweep, the marks of his brutal bodily work, make him a
social outcast and a paradigmatic representative of the physical labor
that produces the goods the fashionable lady wears, but that must be
concealed if those goods are to have their proper effect. The man identified by the caption as a "leering Jew," with his display tray of goods to
be hawked, also hovers under the reach of her skirt, a representative of
the relations of exchange that normally remain hidden as well beneath
the carefully constructed image of a fashionable lady. The scandalous
revelation of these hidden features of Celia's self-presentation amuses all
the onlookers on the street; but it is really only the male viewers who can
thoroughly appreciate and enjoy the revelation. The three prostitutes
in the windows of the tavern take an interest in the accident, but they
can savor it only because they have already allowed the purely physical
nature of their claims on men to be exposed. The woman with the fan,
wearing her own enormous petticoat, *thinks* she's a knowing onlooker of
Celia's humiliation, like the grinning men that surround her, but in fact

Celia's disaster is being reproduced, less spectacularly, on her own edge of the picture frame, without her knowing it, as a male dog lifts his leg and urinates on the edge of her brocaded skirt.

The woman at the center of *The Lady's Disaster* is thus made the satiric butt of the artist's disclosure of the material relations concealed by fashionable appearances; and she shares a name, Celia, with the woman at the center of Swift's "The Lady's Dressing Room," whose repellant body, as Laura Brown has shown, is made to figure the hidden corruption of the economic order that adorns that body.[5] The artist of *The Lady's Disaster* and Swift both work to expose the mystified economic realities of commercial exchange, but they do so specifically by locating the unseemly realities they unveil in the body of a woman. When "The Lady's Dressing Room" was first published, Lady Mary herself responded directly to Swift's portrayal of Celia, sharply questioning the male interests that might determine his fixation on the scandalous image of a decaying female body. In her bitter parody, entitled *The Reasons that Induced Dr. Swift to write a Poem call'd the Lady's Dressing Room*, published in 1734, Lady Mary defended Celia from Swift's attack by providing an account of why Swift wrote his poem, imagining that he turned against Celia out of frustration at his own impotence and reluctance to pay her money for sexual acts he could not perform.[6] The analysis of motives, presented in the form of narrative, is telling, if crude; and Lady Mary generalized the analysis several years later in the sixth issue of her anonymously published newspaper, *The Nonsense of Common-Sense*.

There, she complains that it is men who encourage women to devote themselves to the frivolities of fashion; and she scathingly summarizes some of the economic reasons that men would like to believe that women are contemptible, from their resentment of mothers who hold jointures to their desire to be rid of wives who keep them from remarrying some "great Fortune."[7] Both in her parody of Swift and in this essay, Lady Mary thus offers a critique of men's interests in constructing female identity in the specific terms they do. She concludes the *Nonsense of Common-Sense* essay with a warning to women to resist the terms offered by those male authors "who with the sneer of affected *Admiration* would throw you below the Dignity of the Human Species," and with a fantasy of offering her own alternative terms with which to understand and admire women, saying that she hopes to exhibit "a set of Pictures of . . .

meritorious Ladys, where I shall say nothing of the fire of their Eyes or the pureness of their Complexions, but give them such praises as befits a rational sensible Being, Virtues of Choice and not Beautys of Accident" (134). Lady Mary does not, however, ever produce this set of pictures of real female virtue, and she does not even give us a portrait of herself as authoress in these essays—constructing, instead, a masculine persona in which she can appear in print before the public eye.

As the anonymous author of *The Nonsense of Common-Sense,* Lady Mary thus conceals her sex as well as her name, apparently assuming that a woman cannot publicly present her opinions on the political and economic matters she addresses in these essays. In the first two issues of the paper, Lady Mary not only fails to identify herself as a woman writer but also seems to take on a distinctively male point of view, repeating familiar masculine complaints that place what she calls "the Fair Sex" at the center of England's most basic economic and moral problems. Referring to the "present pressure of national debts" and urging her readers to purchase English rather than foreign goods, she focuses her argument in these essays on the image of the fashionable lady, dressed in expensive imported cloth; and she decries that "Fantastic mimicry of our Ladys, who are so accustom'd to shiver in Silks" that they prefer them to good English wool (107–11). In both issues she thus suggests that it is a female habit of mimickry that drives excessive consumption; and her sympathy for women appears only in her exhortation to them to model themselves on something other than mechanically imitative principles. However, although she introduces her first issue of the newspaper with a promise that she will find things to praise in its pages rather than things to satirize or blame, she is unable to body forth the more admirable possibilities for women in anything but negative form. She begins, indeed, by praising the manner in which women are presently dressed, but she explains that they are dressed in sensible fashion only because they have been required by government order to appear in mourning clothes. For the moment, the mechanisms of direct government control have overridden the pervasive mechanisms of imitative female consumption, but the only alternative to the existing norm of the "Fantastic mimicry of our Ladys" conceived in this essay is the negatively defined black dress of mourning, of deprivation and loss. Suggestively, the mourning clothes Lady Mary approves in this essay have been donned to commemorate the death of Queen Caroline: perhaps women can escape the dictates of imitative and conventional identity only under the sign of the cancellation or demise of one representative female figure.

To the extent that Lady Mary provides any depiction of herself as a speaking female subject in these essays, it also appears only negatively, in various forms of indirect references to, or images of, the fragmentary or distorted nature of her voice there. The fifth issue of the paper focuses on the problem of a censorship of views that is the effect not of government restrictions but of commercial interests. Lady Mary tells the story of her difficulty in getting the newspaper published—one printer rejects it because it is not written *against* the ministry, another because it is not directly commissioned *by* the ministry, and one man prints it but tampers with its words, removing some of its sting against male readers and adding gratuitous sexual innuendoes that alter its force. "I am convinc'd," Lady Mary concludes, "that the Liberty of the press is as much block'd up, by the combination of the Booksellers, printers, pamphlet sellers, Authors etc. or perhaps more, than it would be by an Act of Parliament; and that . . . 'tis as impossible for a man to express his thoughts to the public as it would be for one honest Fishmonger to retail Turbots in a plentiful season below the price fix'd on them by the Company" (129). This essay never mentions the author's sex as a source of difficulty in having her thoughts published; it here laments the impossibility, specifically, of a *man* expressing his thoughts to the public, and the references to the author's masculine persona are much more overt and insistent throughout this essay than in any of the others. However, this very insistence, the pointedness of the essay's denial of its writer's sex, seems to speak for an unmentioned means by which the hegemony of commercial powers that Lady Mary refers to in this essay—what she calls "the Company"—either silences her or mediates and revises her words. The system of commercial exchange that she here treats as monolithic not only excludes her from the realm of rational discourse but also shapes what it means to be a woman, or to speak as one.

In this issue of her newspaper, then, the figure of Lady Mary as disguised female author is glimpsed only in the essay's general references to what is systematically excluded from commercial forums of expression. In an earlier issue of the paper, Lady Mary provides a more concretely embodied, though oddly refracted image, for her own compromised voicing of identity in the essay's pages. Lady Mary devotes the third issue of the paper to a letter from an imaginary correspondent about that endless subject of satire in this period, the Italian castrato singers in the London opera. The correspondent, who signs his name Balducci, introduces himself as an expert artisan in statuary and machinery and proposes to replace the highly paid castrati with mechanical substitutes, saying that he has "found out a Method of making a Statue imitate so exactly the Voice of any *Singer* that ever did, or ever can appear upon the Stage, that I'll defy the ravished Hearer to distinguish the one from the other" (115). Balducci describes himself as one whose "chief Principle of Action" is "to serve those by whom [he] can get the most money," and he dwells on the reflex of "mimickry" that creates fashions among audiences and consumers (114–15). The mechanical singers he imagines creating, with their mimickry of life, embody, then, something mechanical both about the profit-seeker and the avid consumer, and Balducci implies that his proposal only literalizes a process already begun by which objects expropriate human relations in a commodity culture: "this Statue," he says, "shall sing any *Opera* Air the Audience pleases to call for, and shall chant it over again and again, as long as they please to cry, *Ancora,* which is an Honour, I presume, they will as often confer upon my artificial Machines, as ever they did upon any of the natural Machines of *Italy*" (115).

At several points in the letter, with broad winks at his reader, Balducci implicitly explains the status of the castrati as "natural Machines" specifically in terms of their sexual incapacity, or their inability to reproduce, but he locates them throughout the essay in a world of new commercial phenomena. The construction of a human idol through animating fetishized commodities might remind us of Belinda, whose adorning objects take on a kind of human agency while her heart becomes a "moving Toyshop," as C. E. Nicholson has shown.[8] The emasculated male singer, here imagined as easily replaced with a purely artificial, well-marketed construction, might then represent also the woman who is only a site for the display of accumulated objects in her culture, deprived of any but mechanical voice and repeatedly accused of operating only on principles of imitation. Indeed, in what she calls an "Autobiographical Romance," when Lady Mary describes her own courtship with Wortley, she imagines him seeing her as the kind of miraculously performing effigy that Balducci designs: at their first meeting, she says (referring to herself as Laetitia), "Tea came in before cards; and a new play being then acted, it was the first thing mention'd on which Laetitia took occasion to criticise in a manner so just and so knowing, he was as much amaz'd as if he had heard a piece of Waxwork talk on that subject."[9] In a culture in which the phallus serves as the guarantor of individual identity, the woman and the castrato share a position below human agency, reduced equally to living waxworks or "natural Machines," although the woman is born into that position, the castrato violently thrust into it.

More subtly, however, the mutilation of the castrato's sexual identity might be said to mirror Lady Mary's own loss of sexual self in these essays—not her original lack of a phallus but her suppression of some defining organ of *female* identity—what she imagines she must give up to aspire to voice on a public stage. The conclusion of the essay detaches its fantasy about mechanical voice from the specific satiric object of the castrati, as Balducci proposes that, were the Pope to outlaw the practice of castration, he might create mechanical simulacra of other famous singers—even Orpheus might be brought upon the stage by his art, he boasts. Unlike the castrati, Orpheus, the mythic singer who could animate the very rocks and trees, seems a figure very far from any specter of the mechanical production of voice. Does Lady Mary's momentary fantasy of a performing Orpheus-machine cast suspicion on the authenticity of privileged male expression itself? Or does it serve, rather, as an image of her own necessarily mechanical, because *female,* imitation in these essays of masculine powers of voice?

Writing to Alexander Pope from Adrianople, Turkey, in 1717, twenty years before the publication of *The Nonsense of Common-Sense,* Lady Mary opened her letter with the speculation, "I dare say You expect at least something very new in this Letter after I have gone a Journey not undertaken by any Christian of some 100 years." "The most remarkable Accident that happen'd to me," she reports, "was my being very near overturn'd into the Hebrus." In itself, this accident seems neither "something very new" nor so newsworthy—it is, after all, only a *near* event. But the particular site of Lady Mary's near-overturning is what makes it the most remarkable accident that has happened to her: "if I had much regard for the Glorys that one's Name enjoys after Death, I should certainly be sorry for having miss'd the romantic conclusion of swimming down the same River in which the Musical Head of Orpheus repeated verses so many ages since." She then provides Pope

with the Latin lines from Virgil's *Georgics,* which describe the passage
of Orpheus's head down the Hebrus, the voice of that severed head still
calling upon his lost love—"Eurydice! Eurydice!"—as it floats. And she
concludes, "Who knows but some of your bright Wits might have found
it a subject affording many poetical Turns, and have told the World in a
Heroic Elegy that As equal were our Souls, so equal were our fates?"[10]

Though Lady Mary might have "near overturn'd" into an English
river, that event could not have provided her with an opportunity to
assert the equality of her soul with Orpheus's. As the accident has occurred in a distant and classical landscape, it provides an occasion to
show off her wit and her learning to Pope—and, more profoundly, as
she construes that accident, it becomes an occasion to lay claims for herself both to *poetry* and to *passion* equal to those of a famous male singer
and lover. Were she to assume either the poetic power of Orpheus, or the
strength of his passion for a lover—and perhaps, even specifically, the
strength of his passion for a female lover—were she to imagine herself
floating down the Hebrus, calling out a woman's name in a passion that
survives death—now, that would be "something very new," something
"remarkable" indeed. Lady Mary's fantasy of a fusion between her own
feminine identity and Orpheus's masculine one evokes the possibility
of an "overturning" of gender categories perhaps more threatening than
the near overturning of the boat itself in this excursion on the Hebrus.
But we should not pass over the element of danger and violence in the
narrative episode with which Lady Mary evokes this possibility: she em-
beds her assertion that "equal were our Souls" within the hypothetical
situation of her own death, suggesting that her death might make her
the subject for someone *else*'s poetic inspiration, and she imagines her
story coinciding with Orpheus's only when the poet has been both killed
and dismembered. Perhaps Lady Mary would need to figure herself as
a severed head, parted from her own female body, were she really to
imagine herself as attaining Orpheus's poetic inspiration or his erotic
passion, both of which are denied to the alternative insubstantiality or
bathetic, commercialized materiality of the female body.

If Lady Mary elsewhere recognizes that the female body exists within
the wide and entangling historical machine of fashionable vestments
and of cultural *in*-vestments, in her writings from Turkey she works to
imagine her temporary release from that machine by interpreting the
culture and landscape around her as outside history, as a place where past

and present, the literary and the natural, coexist. In the letter to Pope, she moves on from the story of Orpheus's and of her own fate to describe the countryside surrounding Adrianople as "a place where Truth for once furnishes all the Ideas of Pastorall"; where the customs, dances, musical instruments, and clothing described by Homer are preserved; and where Theocritus's pastorals prove to be merely "a plain image" of the peasants' actual "Way of Life" (331–32). Here and elsewhere in Lady Mary's letters from Turkey, she not only insists that the distinction between art and nature blurs there but also repeatedly participates in that phenomenon observed by anthropologist Johannes Fabian, by which Western travelers deny the contemporaneity of different cultures, coexisting in the same historical moment, and instead imagine the alien cultures they encounter as inhabiting the distant past of their own culture's history or prehistory.[11] These techniques of describing cultural difference in terms of time do, as Fabian's model would suggest, serve Lady Mary to distance her from the contemporaries she encounters in other countries, and to define those contemporaries in her own terms; but they also serve her particular needs to register, through observations of cultural difference, the essential historicity of gender roles, and to allow her to manipulate the machinery of those roles in some unexpected ways.

The last half of this same letter to Pope offers one good example of this, when Lady Mary provides Pope with an actual sample of Turkish art—a love poem written by the young sultana's suitor, with translations first by Lady Mary's Turkish acquaintance and then by herself. Commenting on the poem's features, she equates ancient and Turkish culture, reminding Pope of Boileau's observation that "we are never to judge of the Elevation of an Expression in an Ancient Author by the Sound it carrys with us, which may be extremely fine with them, at the same time it looks low or uncouth to us," and warning him that "you must have the same Indulgence for all Oriental Poetry" (335). In fact, the feature that pleases her most in the poem is one that she feels may look "low or uncouth" to English people specifically because it defies, in the context of a love poem, their categorical sense of gender terms.

As translated by Lady Mary's Turkish acquaintance, the first two stanzas of the poem end with the lines, "Your Eyes are black and Lovely / But wild and disdainfull as those of a Stag," and its third stanza incorporates the image of this refrain by referring to the sultana as "stag-ey'd." Lady Mary presents Boileau's excuse for ancient or Oriental poetry after commenting on this image: "The Epithet of Stag-Ey'd (tho the Sound is not very agreable in English) pleases me extremely, and is, I think, a very lively image of the Fire and indifference in his mistrisse's Eyes." Disagreeable as she feels it sounds in English, Lady Mary preserves the epithet in her own translation, and explains, "I could not forbear retaining the comparison of her Eyes to those of a Stag, tho perhaps the novelty of it may give it a burlesque sound in our Language" (337). What seems to keep Lady Mary circling around this simple epithet in her commentary—what seems to make her fear that it will seem "disagreable" or "low or uncouth" in English, at the same time that it pleases her extremely and forms an irresistible part of the poem's charm—is that the phrase constructs an image of the poet's mistress in terms of her likeness to an unequivocally male (and famously virile) animal, the stag. If the epithet has an unfortunate "burlesque sound" in English, perhaps it is because it might remind English readers of the comic device of cross-dressing employed on the English burlesque stage.

Acknowledging her uncertainties about the epithet in English, Lady Mary ends her letter with an apology and then a boast, both of which express something about what it would mean for her to think of *herself* as a "stag-eyed" woman. "I cannot determine upon the whole how well I have succeeded in the Translation. Neither do I think our English proper to express such violence of passion, which is very seldom felt among us; and we want those compound words which are very frequent and strong in the Turkish Language.—You see I am pritty far gone in Oriental Learning, and to say truth I study very hard." Seven years earlier, during Lady Mary and Wortley's long, wrangling courtship in letters, some of their first exchanges had to do with her study of the Latin language, a crucial part of the education of eighteenth-century men but rarely of women, and Wortley had praised her intellect, saying, "Had I you, I shoud have at one view before me all the Charms of either sex met together" (26). However, Lady Mary's intellectual gifts also made him question the sincerity of her letters, for, he said, "Shoud you write to me it woud not be a great compliment. Every woman wou'd write instead of dressing for any lover . . . , that coud persuade herselfe she did it halfe so well as you" (52).

To this last suggestion, Lady Mary responded sharply that her accomplishments in writing could never present her in a flattering light. If Wortley's comparison of writing to the female art of dressing were just, she says, she would want to extend it in this way: "perhaps the Spanish dresse would become my face very well, yet the whole Town would condemn me for the highest Extravagance if I went to Court in't, tho' it improv'd me to a Miracle. There are a thousand things not ill in themselves which custom makes unfit to be done" (56). As she had written to Bishop Burnet the month before, "There is hardly a character in the World . . . more liable to universal ridicule than that of a Learned Woman" (45). While Lady Mary's analogy between a woman's learning or accomplishment in writing and an unfashionable foreign dress suggests that it is something that would be condemned as ridiculous by her own society, the analogy does hold open the possibility that there may be some place where her literary accomplishments would seem to suit her and even "improve" her "to a Miracle."

In the same letter, when she responds to Wortley's complaints that she has not expressed sufficient partiality to him in their written exchanges, Lady Mary uses a more extreme comparison to visual appearance to register the unacceptability of passion as well as of verbal ability in women. "You would have me say I am violently in Love," she writes. "That is, finding you think better of me than you desire, you would have me give you a just cause to contemn me. . . . I should not think you more unreasonable if you was in love with my Face and ask'd me to disfigure it to make you easy. . . . amongst all the popish Saints and Martyrs I never read of one whose charity was sublime enough to make themselves deformd or ridiculous to restore their Lovers to peace and quietnesse" (56). No wonder Lady Mary repeatedly insists to Wortley in this correspondence that she is unacquainted with passion. For she suggests here that any expression of passion by a woman is so egregious a violation of decorum in her culture that it would be the equivalent not simply of appearing in outlandish clothing, but of making oneself deformed, or permanently disfiguring one's own face. For Lady Mary to cry out longingly, "Wortley! Wortley!"—much less "Eurydice! Eurydice!"—would be for her to mutilate her own face, if not to sever her own head; and she elsewhere equates expressions of erotic passion by women with death (35).

Thus, when she ends her comments to Pope on the Turkish poem by saying that she does not think "our English proper to express such violence of passion, which is very seldom felt amongst us," her general estimate of English people encompasses a more specific reference to a particularly intractable problem of expression for English women. Though she is uncertain about the success of her translation, the act of rendering the Turkish poem into English, giving voice in her own language to the male suitor's passionate words, gives her temporary access to a passion that, in her own culture, might seem as egregious or paradoxical for a woman as eyes likened to a stag's. Lady Mary feels particularly, she says, the lack within the English language of "those compound words which are very frequent and strong in the Turkish Language"—the Turkish language and culture, apparently, can combine "stag" with "woman" and have it seem "extremely fine" or "elevated," while in English, a compounding of different terms, as of different categories, can only seem awkward, burlesque, even disfiguring. Significantly, one of the few real alterations Lady Mary makes in her own translation is her replacement of a reference in the original to the Persian legend of the nightingale, known for her passionate love for the rose, with a familiar English literary reference to Philomela—a victim of rape and mutilation, rather than a legendary representative of female erotic passion. The latter figure, it seems, does not appear within the realm of English "cultural literacy"; but Lady Mary's voyage into Turkish learning and Turkish life seems to serve her by disrupting her own familiar oppositions of man and woman, past and present, art and nature, even death and life.

Nonetheless, it is her own culture's vocabulary of sexual roles that Lady Mary draws upon as she translates her experience in Turkey into English, and even when she reconstrues her female identity within what she calls "the other world" of Turkish life, she does so primarily by compounding conventional masculine and feminine roles rather than by reimagining either of them. In several episodes, Lady Mary encounters the beauty and the erotic desirability of Turkish women not as the literary subject of a Turkish love poem but as an immediate physical presence. Even then, Lady Mary seems to formulate her erotic and aesthetic response as a kind of translation from male texts—and a translation from traditional English male texts as well as Turkish ones.

In the most famous of her "Turkish Embassy Letters," Lady Mary reports her visit to the women's baths in Adrianople.[12] Even before she describes her entrance into the baths, she prepares us for the highly textualized and allusive nature of the experience to follow: at some length, she describes her passage to the baths in a special Turkish coach that is decorated inside with "poetical mottos" and painted flowers, and from which one can look out and see the world while remaining entirely hidden, like a reader gazing upon a text. After brief and businesslike remarks on the design of the baths and the general civility of the women there, when Lady Mary turns to describing the appearance of the women "in the state of nature," or, as she says, "in plain English, stark naked," she finds herself turning toward the world of European literature and art.

She begins by projecting the Muslim women in the baths back into Judeo-Christian prehistory, as recounted by a seventeenth-century English man: "They Walk'd and mov'd," she attests, "with the same majestic Grace which Milton describes of our General Mother" (314). Quickly, however, she relocates the women within the distant past, placing them within the world of classical mythology, as recreated by Renaissance Italian painters rather than by an English writer, as she likens their "exact proportions" to those of the goddesses and Graces depicted by Guido and Titian.[13] Having represented her experience of the women first by means of this rapid litany of male literary and artistic renderings of women, she pauses to express the pleasure she feels in turning her attention on this occasion from female clothing and female faces, both potentially disfigured by any divergence from custom, to female bodies themselves. "If twas the fashion to go naked," she says, "the face would be hardly observ'd. I perceiv'd that the Ladys with the finest skins and most delicate shapes had the greatest share of my admiration, thô their faces were sometimes less beautifull than those of their companions." Whereas, when she identified with Orpheus in his posthumous passage down the Hebrus, Lady Mary evoked a fantasy about being only a head, released from the sexual fate encoded in her body, she here expresses pleasure in the female body as it appears unmediated by any fashion except the "fashion" of "going naked," and undominated by the status of the face to which it is attached.[14] Once she has acknowledged more directly, in this way, the immediate presence of the female bodies before her, Lady Mary's next allusion to an artistic representation of these bodies brings them up sharply into her own historical moment. "To tell you the truth," she confesses, "I had wickedness enough to wish secretly that Mr. Gervase [that is, the English portrait painter, her own contemporary] could have been there invisible. I fancy it would have very much improv'd his art to see so many fine Women naked."[15]

Lady Mary's wish not only registers the contemporaneity of the Turkish women and herself but also involves a close identification between their bodies and her own—for the portrait-painter she chooses to wish were present to observe these women is one who had, seven years before, painted Lady Mary herself.

When Charles Jervas painted the young Lady Mary's portrait in 1710, he portrayed her in quaint pastoral costume and posture, holding a shepherd's staff and attended by a lamb.[16] This depiction released Lady Mary's body from the social framing of contemporary English fashion, but only into the highly conventionalized space of portraiture's pastoral cliches. Lady Mary repeatedly describes her experience in Turkey as an encounter with a pastoral existence that is alive and present rather than purely literary or artistic. However, her rendering of the world of the baths as, simultaneously, a physical world and a textual or an artistic one ultimately works to de-realize her own body, even as she struggles to realize the immediate presence of the bathers. Finding herself in the position of the observer and interpreter of female bodies rather than that of the observed and represented, Lady Mary can only imagine that position as a male one, and she fantasizes herself as replaced in the baths by an invisible male artist. The problem of the sex of her own body comes back suddenly, though, in the final portion of the letter, as the Turkish women invite Lady Mary to undress as well.

This invitation challenges and so destroys the delicate balance Lady Mary has been maintaining in what precedes, the balance created by a female viewer gazing through the lens of masculine literary and artistic tradition. Could her body in any sense reveal her fantasy identification with male artists in this scene, the results would be fatal, for, as she concludes her letter, " 'Tis no less than Death for a Man to be found in one of these places." But if it were to reveal her physical identity with the Turkish women as merely another woman, she would abruptly be reduced to being an object of vision, just like them, rather than a privileged viewer. Lady Mary excuses herself from the invitation to undress "with some difficulty, they being all so earnest in perswading me. I was at last forc'd to open my skirt and shew them my stays, which satisfy'd 'em very well, for I saw they beleiv'd I was so lock'd up in that machine that it was not in my own power to open it, which contrivance they attributed to my Husband."

Abruptly, Lady Mary's female and English body returns to her, and

returns to her as most rigidly constructed by English fashion and masculine social imperatives. At the same time, she is catapulted from her
fantasy of a place outside history into a sense of urgent present schedules
and time: "I . . . should have been very glad to pass more time with
them, but Mr. W[ortley] resolving to persue his Journey the next morning early, I was in haste to see the ruins of Justinian's church." The sense
Lady Mary expresses here of English female dress as a kind of machine,
and part of the larger historical machinery of patriarchy, helps explain
her great interest in the alternative conventions of female dress that
she encountered in Turkey: she speaks with admiration and envy not
only of women's freedom from dress in the all-female social gathering
of the baths but also of the complete concealment and disguise allowed
by the veils and loose draping clothing that Muslim women wear when
out in the public world of men (328–29).[17] Lady Mary also expresses
great enthusiasm for the Turkish outfit she purchased for herself in
Adrianople, which she describes to her sister by combining English
terms for articles of both female and male dress, saying that it included
"a pair of drawers" and what she refers to as a "wastcoat."[18] Back in
England, however, her Turkish outfit became merely another costume
in which she might be represented by male artists within the frame of
conventional portraiture, neatly substituting an Orientalist look for the
pastoral one in which Jervas had first painted her.[19] This substitution
is particularly visible in a 1719–20 portrait by Sir Godfrey Kneller that
nearly identically reproduces the composition of Jervas's earlier one, but
with Lady Mary in Turkish rather than pastoral guise.

The actual Turkish outfit remained, nonetheless, in Lady Mary's own
possession, as did her sense of the significance of "the other world"
she had encountered while traveling in Turkey. Twenty years later in
her life, when Lady Mary left her passionless marriage with Wortley
to pursue a bisexual Venetian man, Count Algarotti, into Italy, she
would take her Turkish outfit with her into exile, and would formulate
the erotic passion she discovered in middle age in terms of the exotic
experiences of her youth. Abandoning her early claims that she was
incapable of passion, she frequently expressed her love to Algarotti in
images of herself as a fervent male lover. Thus, she still could conceive
that passion only as it was doubly framed by masculine roles and by
the exoticism of foreign lands. Italy (and France), where she was to live
for twenty-three years, served her as a kind of mediating port between

Eastern and Western realms, and when she moved there, her friend
Lord Hervey wrote her that in Italy with Algarotti she might "enjoy
[Mahomet's] Paradise upon earth"[20]—a sensual paradise that, according to eighteenth-century English writers, only the spirits of departed
men were permitted to enjoy.

Notes

1. "Moral Epistle II. To a Lady. Of the Characters of Women" (1735),
lines 21–28. *The Poems of Alexander Pope,* ed. John Butt (New Haven: Yale
University Press, 1963).

2. Louis A. Landa, "Pope's Belinda, The General Emporie of the World,
and the Wondrous Worm," *South Atlantic Quarterly* 70 (1971): 215–35, and
"Of Silkworms and Farthingales and the Will of God," *Studies in the Eighteenth
Century* 2, ed. R. F. Brissenden (1973): 259–77; Laura Brown, *Alexander Pope*
(New York: Basil Blackwell, 1985).

3. Laura Brown, "Reading Race and Gender: Jonathan Swift," *Eighteenth-
Century Studies* 23 (1990): 425–43; Neil McKendrick, John Brewer, and J. H.
Plumb, *The Birth of a Consumer Society: The Commercialization of Eighteenth-
Century England* (Bloomington: Indiana University Press, 1982).

4. I am grateful to Mrs. Frank Sussler, curator of prints at the Lewis Walpole Library, for calling this very interesting print to my attention.

5. Brown, "Reading Race and Gender," 426–34.

6. Robert Halsband made the attribution of this poem to Lady Mary in
" 'The Lady's Dressing-Room' Explicated by a Contemporary," *The Augustan
Milieu: Essays Presented to Louis Landa,* ed. Henry Knight Miller, Eric Rothstein, and G. S. Rousseau (Oxford: Clarendon Press, 1970), 225–31. I have
consulted the copy of it held in Yale University's Beinecke Library.

7. *The Nonsense of Common-Sense,* no. 6, in *Lady Mary Wortley Montagu: Essays
and Poems and Simplicity, A Comedy,* ed. Robert Halsband and Isobel Grundy
(Oxford: Clarendon Press, 1977), 132. Further references to these essays will
be provided parenthetically in the text by page number in this edition.

8. C. E. Nicholson, "A World of Artefacts: *The Rape of the Lock* as Social

History," *Literature and History: A New Journal for the Humanities* 5 (1979): 183–93.

9. "Autobiographical Romance," in *Essays and Poems and Simplicity, A Comedy*, 78.

10. *The Complete Letters of Lady Mary Wortley Montagu*, ed. Robert Halsband, 3 vols. (Oxford: Clarendon Press, 1965), 1:330. Subsequent quotations from letters are cited by page number from this volume of this edition.

11. Johannes Fabian, *Time and the Other: How Anthropology Makes Its Object* (New York: Columbia University Press, 1983).

12. In the last three years, this letter has been frequently discussed in a variety of contexts. Joseph W. Lew provides one extended and very interesting reading of it in "Lady Mary's Portable Seraglio," *Eighteenth-Century Studies* 24 (1991): 432–50. He argues that Lady Mary's letters from Turkey are instructive because they illustrate "not a monolithic, Saidian Orientalism, but a number of discourses competing for hegemony" (435). Other discussions include: Elizabeth A. Bohls, "Aesthetics and Orientalism in Lady Mary Wortley Montagu's Letters," *Studies in Eighteenth-Century Culture* 23 (forthcoming); Marjorie Garber, *Vested Interests: Cross-Dressing and Cultural Anxiety* (New York: Routledge, 1992), 312; Billie Melman, *Women's Orients: English Women and the Middle East, 1718–1918* (London: Macmillan, 1992), 88–92; Marcia Pointon, *Hanging the Head: Portraiture and Social Formation in Eighteenth-Century England* (New Haven: Yale University Press, 1993), 152–54; Ruth Bernard Yeazell, "The Woman's Coffee House, the Painter's Harem: Lady Mary Wortley Montagu and the Origins of Ingres' *Bain Turc*." I am grateful to Professors Bohls and Yeazell for sharing their work on Lady Mary with me in manuscript.

13. Both Pointon and Bohls discuss Lady Mary's use of these literary and artistic allusions, which Bohls calls "the crux of Montagu's rhetorical strategy," to describe the women at the baths. They come to quite different conclusions, however, about the effects of the allusions. Bohls argues that the allusions work to "de-eroticize [Montagu's] readers' imaginary gaze," to associate that gaze with the emerging ideal of disinterested aesthetic contemplation ("Aesthetics and Orientalism"); but Pointon asserts that they serve specifically to sexualize "naked eastern woman," noting that the reference to Milton invokes one "*locus classicus* of female sexuality" and that Guido and Titian are "artists renowned for the sensuousness of their handling" (*Hanging the Head*, 153).

14. Throughout her discussion of visual depictions of Lady Mary, Pointon emphasizes an aspect of Lady Mary's physical experience and appearance that I have neglected here: the severe marking of her face by smallpox in 1715, which was said to have damaged her husband's political career along with her personal pride by making Lady Mary "unsuitable as an object of the . . . royal

gaze" (144). The notion of a society in which "the face would be hardly observed" would have this particular personal meaning for Lady Mary, then, along with more general ones. Pointon argues that Lady Mary employed the refracted image of herself in the "mirror" of "Turkish womanhood" (and specifically, the painted representations of herself in Turkish dress) to "negotiate the relationship between the actual and the idealized female body," allowing the "scarred (misrecognized) and ego-damaged" subject to re-enter "the public domain, and in triumph" (*Hanging the Head*, 144, 151).

15. Note Ingres's fulfillment, of a sort, of Lady Mary's wish, over one hundred years later, in *Le Bain Turc*, based on this passage from her letters. But the position of masculine voyeur constructed by Lady Mary's comments is there greatly heightened, and the women's own erotic and aesthetic responses are reduced to a matter of dazed, sensuous gropings.

In her subtle and illuminating account of the relation between Ingres's painting and its sources in Lady Mary's letters, Yeazell notes two striking ways that Ingres departs from Lady Mary's account: he radically privatizes a scene that Lady Mary makes clear takes place within a specifically public, though all-female, institution, so that the public space of the baths merges in his version with the private space of a harem; and (relatedly) he eliminates the figure of the Western visitor, Lady Mary, in his rendering of the scene ("The Women's Coffee House").

16. The 1710 portrait of Lady Mary in shepherdess's dress is attributed, although not definitively assigned, to Charles Jervas by John Kerslake, the editor of *Early Georgian Portraits* (London: Oxford University Press, 1977). Both the 1710 portrait and the Kneller portrait of 1719–20 mentioned below are reproduced in volume 2 of this work.

17. Lady Mary's interest in the "paradoxically" greater freedom of the Muslim women, in their required veils, has been frequently noted by commentators; see Garber (*Vested Interests*, 313); Melman (*Women's Orients*, 85–89); Pointon (*Hanging the Head*, 151); and Yeazell. Melman and Yeazell disagree, however, about the nature of the freedom claimed by Lady Mary for the Turkish women, and apparently envied and yearned for herself. Melman emphasizes what she sees as the essentially sexual nature of that liberty, whereas Yeazell suggests (more accurately, I think) the importance Lady Mary placed upon mobility and access to public spaces, in themselves and not only as means to pursue sexual aims.

18. Garber has noted this effect, commenting that "this toilette. . . , though entirely feminine, is also virtually identical to the items worn by men, as Lady Mary's 'translations' into an English sartorial lexicon . . . make clear" (*Vested Interests*, 312). Aaron Hill suggests that the English in general may have interpreted Turkish dress as less clearly divided by sex than English

clothing: in *A Full and Just Account of the Present State of the Ottoman Empire* (1709), he comments that "Their Womens Dress *at Home* is just the same, in Britches, Slippers, Shirts, and Wastcoats, with the Mens before describ'd" (95). As Bohls has observed, European travelers (such as Jean Dumont and Paul Rycaut) routinely rendered Turkish men as de-masculinized in a variety of ways, from their dress to their sexual habits and their manner of urination ("Aesthetics and Orientalism").

19. In her chapter-length account of portraits of Lady Mary, Pointon explores the possibility that "Montagu at some level controlled the images of her produced by . . . established society artists who depicted her as a mature adult," including the group of at least seven portraits of her in Turkish-style dress. I am sympathetic to Pointon's effort to question critical assumptions that do "not allow any manner of organizing function for woman in the production and deployment of her own image," although the status of that active, controlling, or "organizing function" finally remains, it seems to me, as equivocal in her analysis of the portraiture and letters of Lady Mary as in mine.

20. Letter of August 17, 1739, quoted in Robert Halsband, *The Life of Lady Mary Wortley Montagu* (New York: Oxford University Press, 1960), 181–82.

Fielding and the Comedy
of Attempted Rape

✒ Susan Staves

In the world of comic romance, female chastity is always safe from violation. The level of violence against women in Henry Fielding's comic fiction is high and the rape of the heroine is frequently enough attempted, but it never succeeds. Indeed, to be the target of a would-be rapist seems to be a necessary sign of female desirability. Consider some of the more memorable examples. In book 2 of *Joseph Andrews,* on a dark evening in the country, Fanny is attacked by an anonymous man who throws her down on the ground and who has almost overpowered her when she is providentially rescued by Parson Adams, who bashes the man with his crabstick. In book 3 Fanny is abducted by the Captain; he intends to deliver her over to be raped by the country gentleman who has earlier roasted Parson Adams. In book 4 Fanny is assaulted first by Beau Didapper, who is not strong enough to subdue her, and then by Beau Didapper's pimp, who might have subdued her but for the opportune arrival of Joseph. In *Tom Jones,* Lord Fellamar determines to rape Sophia, hoping that once raped she will have no alternative but to marry him. His attempted rape is providentially interrupted by Squire Western. Both *Joseph Andrews* and *Tom Jones* establish comic universes in which we can neither doubt the chastity of the heroines nor suppose that—however often their chastity might be attacked—rapists could ever ruin them.

With different tonalities, attempted rape is also a subject of Fielding's parodic, satiric, and more realistic fictions. *Shamela* is almost throughout a story of sexual assault. Mr. Booby begins with lesser assaults but soon enough threatens rape. "You are absolutely in my power," he tells Shamela, "and if you won't let me lie with you by fair Means, I will by Force."[1] In the mordant world of *Jonathan Wild*, attempted rape becomes the subject of a long shaggy-dog story. The narrator tells of Wild's assaults on Mrs. Heartfree, but the longer narrative of subsequent events, featuring repeated attempted rapes, she herself tells after her trials are over and she is reunited with her husband in Newgate. The trials include passionate declarations from a French captain, insolent addresses and "further brutality" from an English captain of a man-of-war, "nauseous kisses" and threats of force from another gentleman on that ship, and an assault by the count who has helped ruin her husband and who catches her in his arms, declaring "that he was determined to enjoy" her "at that moment."[2] Perhaps the oddest variation on the theme of attempted rape is to be found in *Amelia*. There both Colonel James and the noble lord lust after the heroine and scheme against her chastity. Whether or not their schemes will have success generates a sort of suspense in this more realistic novel that we do not feel about the assaults on Fanny or Sophia. There is a threat of violence against Amelia, particularly from the character and past behavior of the noble lord, yet, overtly, such a possibility is denied.

Attempt is simultaneously a natural topos of comedy and a jurisprudentially difficult idea. Unsuccessful attempts are intrinsically comic because villains who huff and puff with all their might and main but only give themselves coughing fits and never actually blow the house down are silly villains who do no real harm. We have to laugh when Jonathan Wild, driven by "violent passion" and with the evilest possible intent, fully intending to rape Mrs. Heartfree, a "poor wretch . . . in the utmost agonies of despair," winds up foiled and tossed into a small boat by a captain who gives him "a half a dozen biscuits to prolong his misery" (102, 104).

In early legal systems that conceptualized criminal sanctions as vengeance or reparation for harm done, attempts at crimes, which produced no damage, were not conceived as criminal. From a modern point of view, however, someone who intends a crime and attempts to commit it may seem as deserving of punishment as the criminal who happens to succeed. The English criminal law of attempt, after intense discussion by legal intellectuals in the 1970s and 1980s has recently been revised to make people convicted of attempted crimes liable to sentences as long as the sentences statutorily set for completed crimes.[3] Why, we may reason, should a criminal who merely happens to be interrupted in the commission of his crime benefit from an accident to escape punishment? Or why should society wait to sanction him until he happens to be caught in a completed crime? On the other hand, it seems not only impractical but wrong for society to punish the mere fleeting thought of committing a crime. How are we to decide when someone has moved from merely contemplating a criminal act to actually beginning to commit it? The question of how to treat attempted crimes is, therefore, a nice jurisprudential problem.

Feminism has now made thinking people wary of venturing to tell rape jokes or of admitting to finding any humor in rape or sexual assault. Susan Brownmiller's *Against Our Will* and similar modern studies have contributed to making us understand rape as a crime of violence and hostility against women, not love or lust gone just a bit too far.[4] But we have also learned that both crime and sexuality have histories, that neither is a transhistorical constant, a simple expression of invariant human nature unaltered from century to century.[5] The project of writing a history of rape is still in an early and contentious stage. Key questions that are being asked include: Are there different rates of rape in different cultures and in different times? What institutions get to control and to administer the definitions of rape and who controls those institutions? How have definitions of rape changed? What levels of "fear of rape" have there been and how has fear of rape been used to limit the behavior of women? And, how have shifts in gender identities been related to rape? Very recently, in many common law jurisdictions, a major change in the definition of rape has been made: at older common law, a wife was understood at the time of her marriage to have consented to all subsequent acts of intercourse with her husband, but now a number of jurisdictions permit criminal indictments of husbands for marital rape, that is, for specific acts of intercourse to which a wife has not consented. Anna Clark, working on the period 1770–1845 in England and focusing on working-class women, has recently argued that significant change also occurred between the late eighteenth century and the early nineteenth century.[6] Perhaps most notably, she believes that in the early nineteenth century the threat of rape was newly used to limit the freedom of working women to move about freely in public space. Both Clark and Antony Simpson, who has independently studied eighteenth-century rape, have been struck by increased reliance on medical testimony to establish the fact of rape at trial, although it is hard to say precisely when in the eighteenth century this occurred.[7] It does seem, though, that at the beginning of the eighteenth century prosecutrixes in rape and attempted rape were more able to have their own accounts heard at trial than prosecutrixes in the early nineteenth century, not only because medical evidence loomed larger in the later period, but also because new constraints of "modesty" made it more difficult for many women to recount—or, if we believe Clark, even quite to comprehend—details of sexual violence. Both Clark and Simpson, in different ways, see connections between the history of rape and economic pressures on men that led men to understand their masculinity differently.[8]

What I would like to do here is to consider Fielding's fictional scenes of attempted rape both as literary variations on a theme and in the context of eighteenth-century criminal law doctrines of rape and of attempt and of narratives from criminal trials. Such a consideration of the legal history, as I shall indicate, has to be made on two quite different levels, the level of practice as recovered from court records and trial transcripts, and the level of doctrine, the more abstract and philosophical ideas of legal intellectuals as they appear in treatises and law reports. This may seem like an unduly heavy-handed feminist killjoy project—perhaps it is—and also one that meanly refuses to enjoy Fielding's comedy. While I agree with Angela Smallwood that Fielding's work shows considerable awareness of contemporary debates about the "woman question" and also that Fielding was eager to attack certain misogynistic ideas, I cannot agree with her more extreme contention that "all of his writing shares the orientation and aspirations evident in contemporary feminist writing in the rationalist tradition." Fielding, I think, was both closer to normative masculine ideas of the period and more complicit in developing new ideals of dependent femininity than Smallwood is prepared to acknowledge.[9] As partial compensation for refusing to find Fielding an advanced feminist, I will offer a small tribute to the prescience of his legal imagination and, eventually, argue that, despite the crude state of criminal law doctrine during the period of Fielding's legal education and practice, his fictional plots productively explore fact situations that were to emerge as doctrinal cruxes.

Why, we may ask, did Fielding find attempted rape such a repeatedly productive source of plot and comedy? One reason, I would speculate, one that has more to do with social history generally than with legal history in particular, was that, along with many of his male contemporaries, Fielding worried that there were no truly chaste women (and that unchaste women were too skilled at pretending to be chaste). He certainly knew that he lived in a world characterized by high levels of male predation. "The Virtue of a young Lady," the narrator tells us in *Tom Jones,* "is, in the World, in the same Situation with a poor Hare, which is certain, whenever it ventures abroad, to meet its Enemies: For it can hardly meet any other." [10] Female beauty, so it appeared to him, evoked male desire, as by some fundamental law of nature. Having described Amelia "all a Blaze of Beauty," the narrator insists, "I am firmly persuaded that to withdraw Admiration from exquisite Beauty, or to feel no Delight in gazing at it, is as impossible as to feel no Warmth from the most scorching Rays of the Sun. To run away is all that is in our power, . . . yet . . . how natural is the Desire of going thither!" (232). Prompted by strong desire, men flirt, cajole, inveigle, deceive, chase, insist, press—solicit female chastity infinitely. With so many strong and resourceful men constantly soliciting desirable women—especially because by contemporary standards desirable women were neither very strong nor very worldly-wise—a man might naturally worry that there might soon be no female chastity left. Roy Porter has argued that Enlightenment England reconceptualized sexuality as an essential part of a good Nature and encouraged naturalistic and hedonistic assumptions. [11] To the extent that this was true, and so long as female chastity continued to be thought erotically desirable, male hedonism had a problem supplying itself with suitable objects. And because a binary opposition between chaste and unchaste women was so fundamental to the eighteenth-century conception of female character, what better way to dramatize that opposition and to ally masculine fears that no pure women remained than to repeat stories of solicitations of chastity proceeding all the way to violence, to show chastity tested not only by persuasion but also by more extreme assaults, and then to ally masculine anxiety by triumphant comic conclusions in which female chastity is preserved?

Fielding's comic plots not only use attempted rape as a sign of female desirability, but they also use vulnerability to rape as a way of distinguishing good women from men and of distinguishing good women from bad women. In *Joseph Andrews,* the narrator proclaims, "How ought Man to rejoice, that his Chastity is always in his own power,

that if he hath sufficient Strength of Mind, he hath always a compe-
tent Strength of Body to defend himself: and cannot, like a poor weak
Woman, be ravished against his Will." [12] (Tell that to the cabin boy on
a man-of-war, we might retort.) Fielding in *Joseph Andrews* is bemused
with the odd asymmetries of gender and makes wonderful comedy out
of his male hero having to defend his own chastity from the assaults of
Lady Booby. Nevertheless, that there should be five attempted rapes of
Fanny is used to indicate how desirable she is; that she requires a male
rescuer on all occasions (except those involving the diminutive bisexual
Didapper) seems to show that she is a true and virtuous woman. Sophia,
similarly, is helpless against Lord Fellamar and requires rescue by her
father.

Less desirable women, in contrast to the perfectly chaste heroines,
are less vulnerable to rape. Shamela, the extreme case, is neither particularly attached to her virtue nor vulnerable to rape. One evening
Mr. Booby comes into her bed, "fell a kissing one of my Breasts as if
he would have devoured it" and is "as rude as possible." But Shamela's
mother has given her secret and apparently foolproof "instructions to
avoid being ravished." Fielding's language is periphrastic, but the trick
apparently entails squeezing or pulling the assailant's penis as hard as
possible. Whatever exactly Shamela does, it inspires Mr. Booby to vow
never again to try to "take her by Force" (341). In keeping with the
relative lowness of *Jonathan Wild,* although Mrs. Heartfree usually is
rescued by men, once she is able to defeat a would-be rapist by a strata-
gem of her own. Mrs. Heartfree, we are given to understand, while a
virtuous married woman, is not so fanatically chaste that she does not
enjoy interpreting the various assaults on her person as tributes to her
attractiveness. On one occasion she gains time by telling the would-be
rapist that she will grant him her favors just as soon as she drinks "a
hearty glass" of punch with him (184). She is then able to get him so
drunk that he falls down the cabin stairs and dislocates his shoulder.
As Shamela has her foolproof rape-avoidance technique, so Mrs. Heartfree, a good woman but not one of the highest delicacy or a particularly
elevated class position, also has at least one self-help option.

The structures of Fielding's plots also contrast, on the one hand,
chaste and beautiful women who are the objects of failed rape attempts,
and, on the other hand, loose and lascivious women who falsely cry
rape to cover up their own delinquencies. Such structuring shows Field-

ing's engagement, at a rather early date, in issues that were to concern Enlightenment jurisprudence. Fielding, of course, studied law at the Middle Temple, was called to the bar in 1740, and served as a magistrate from 1747 to his final illness in 1754. His professionally accurate use of legal terminology has often been noted. Recently, his *Enquiry into the Causes of the Late Increase of Robbers* (1751) and *Proposal for making an Effectual Provision for the Poor* (1753) have attracted renewed attention both from literary scholars and legal historians.[13] These tracts concern crimes committed by the poor and make social policy arguments about how they might be prevented and controlled. Such issues were of great interest to Enlightenment jurisprudence, yet Fielding seems also to have been interested in the more abstract, more purely intellectual questions of legal doctrine, and to have been concerned that legal rules be intrinsically rational. Like a modern law professor who has learned "to love the law," he was fond of intellectual legal puzzles and eager to point out contradictions in the contemporary rule system. For example, in *Amelia* he makes Booth notice that while a necessitous person who stole food or clothes might hang, a person who committed a perjury that led to another person's wrongful execution could only be convicted of a bailable misdemeanor.

The most obvious issue of Enlightenment jurisprudence that concerned Fielding was the issue of evidence. Early modern law rejected the previous model of trials as oath-contests and showed concern with the possibility that testimony given under oath might be false. Remember what happens in book 2 of *Joseph Andrews* after Parson Adams rescues Fanny from the would-be rapist. A group of young men, bird-baiters, come upon them, Adams tells his story, then the would-be rapist promptly concocts an alternative narrative. "Gentlemen," he says to the new arrivals who did not witness his assault on Fanny, "you are luckily come to the Assistance of a poor Traveller, who would otherwise have been robbed and murdered by this vile Man and Woman, who led me hither out of my way from the High-Road, and both falling on me have used me as you see" (141). (Rapists who defended themselves by accusing their victims, especially lower-class victims, of having robbed or attempted to rob them and then concocting a counter-charge of rape in hopes of getting off on the robbery charge were apparently not unusual; the infamous Francis Charteris used this tactic as part of his defense at his rape trial.) [14] The young men are inclined to believe this story rather than Adams's and so is the justice of the peace before whom all three are soon taken.

Criminal law when Fielding was a student at the Middle Temple was—compared to property law especially—doctrinally a very underdeveloped field. A simple reason for this, as John Langbein has argued, was that lawyers were not yet much involved in criminal trials, either for the prosecution or the defense. The law reports of the earlier eighteenth century do not contain many reports of criminal cases. As Langbein points out, "Law reports are largely lawyer's literature; it ought not to surprise us that during an epoch when lawyers were not engaged in criminal litigation, compilers and publishers were not engaged in producing precedent books for a non-existent market." [15] Nevertheless, as the century progressed, lawyers did get increasingly involved in criminal trials and criminal law began to develop doctrinally. There is a small literature of reported rape, attempted rape, assault, and other criminal attempt cases that can help give insight into Fielding's treatment of this subject in his fiction.

In the fiction, the chaste and beautiful women who genuinely attract would-be rapists are structurally set against loose and lascivious women who falsely cry rape to cover up their own delinquencies. The considerable difficulty the world has in reading the evidence as to which is which is emphasized by moments in which the pure heroines are mistaken for loose women: Fanny is believed to be Adams's trull by the bird-baiters and the justice of the peace; Sophia is mistaken for Jenny Cameron, the mistress of Bonnie Prince Charlie; and Amelia mistaken for Booth's mistress when she goes to visit him at the sponging house. Perhaps the most ludicrous example of the lascivious women who falsely cry rape is Mrs. Slipslop in *Joseph Andrews*. The first description of Mrs. Slipslop makes her a grotesque:

> She was a Maiden Gentlewoman of about Forty-five Years of Age, who having made a small Slip in her Youth had continued a good Maid ever since. She was not at this time remarkably handsome; being very short, and rather too corpulent in Body, and somewhat red, with the Addition of Pimples in the Face. Her Nose was likewise rather too large, and her Eyes too little; nor did she resemble a Cow so much in her Breath, as

in two brown Globes which she carried before her; one of her Legs was also a little shorter than the other, which occasioned her to limp as she walked. (32)

In the comic night adventures concluding *Joseph Andrews,* Mrs. Slipslop lies in bed delighted to be mistaken for Fanny by a man who pretends to be an enraptured Joseph declaring himself her lover, but whom she soon—by feel—discovers to be the puny and unsatisfactory Didapper. Disappointed, the narrator tells us, "of those delicious Offerings of which her Fancy had promised her Pleasure," she nevertheless sees an "Opportunity to heal some Wounds which her late Conduct had, she feared, given her Reputation": "At that instant therefore, when he offered to leap from the Bed, she caught fast hold of his Shirt, at the same time roaring out, 'O thou Villain! who hast attacked my Chastity, and I believe ruined me in my Sleep, I will swear a Rape against thee, I will prosecute thee with the utmost Vengeance.' The Beau attempted to get loose, but she held him fast, and when he struggled, she cry'd out, 'Murther!, Murther! Rape! Robbery! Ruin!' " (331). The joke here depends partly on the idea that a woman as old and as ugly as Slipslop would never be the object of a real rape attempt (an idea for which there seems to be no empirical evidence). It also depends on a reversal of gender roles that casts the woman as the big, strong person capable of physically controlling another by holding on despite the other's struggles. Fielding promptly underlines the reversal by having Parson Adams, awakened by Slipslop's outcry, come into the still darkened room and—by touch alone—identify Didapper as the girl and Slipslop as the man: "He made directly to the Bed in the dark, when laying hold of the Beau's Skin (for *Slipslop* had torn his Shirt almost off) and finding his Skin extremely soft, and hearing him in a low Voice begging *Slipslop* to let him go, he no longer doubted but this was the young Woman in danger of ravishing, and immediately falling on the Bed, and laying hold on *Slipslop's* Chin, where he found a rough Beard, his Belief was confirmed" (331–32).

Less broadly, Jenny, as Mrs. Waters in *Tom Jones,* appears to be the object of attempted rape, but is not. Fans of the Tony Richardson movie will remember the scene that follows Tom's rescue of Jenny from Ensign Northerton's assault in the woods: Tom, like Orpheus, leads, while Jenny, a luscious English Eurydice, bare-breasted, follows along behind, Tom all the while heroically and modestly trying not to look back. A first or hasty reading of the Northerton assault on Jenny in book 9, chapter 2 is likely to make it appear an attempted rape. Tom is summoned by "the most violent Skreams of a Woman" in the woods, just as Parson Adams is summoned to Fanny's rescue in *Joseph Andrews* (495). He arrives to see her "stript half naked" and in the hands of a "Villain," whom he bashes with his stick, as Adams has bashed Fanny's attacker with his crabstick. As Jenny falls on her knees to express her gratitude to her deliverer, we descend from the superlatives of romance, yet she does seem an object of erotic temptation: "The redeemed Captive had not altogether so much of the human-angelic Species [as Tom]; she seemed to be, at least, of the middle Age, nor had her Face much Appearance of Beauty; but her Cloaths being torn from all the upper Part of her Body, her Breasts, which were well formed, and extremely white, attracted the Eyes of her Deliverer, and for a few Moments they stood silent, and gazing at each other" (496).

Some chapters later, however, we learn that what appeared to be an attempted rape was not. The narrator slowly unfolds what he titles "*a fuller account of Mrs.* Waters, *and by what Means she came into that distressful Situation from which she was rescued by* Jones" (518). First, we are invited to notice that Jenny seems content that Northerton has escaped and reluctant to have the assault inquired into further. Then we are told that while Jenny lived with Captain Waters as his wife, "there were some Doubts concerning the Reality of their Marriage." Moreover, the narrator continues: "Mrs. *Waters,* I am sorry to say it, had for some Time contracted an Intimacy with the above mentioned Ensign, which did no great Credit to her Reputation. That she had a remarkable Fondness for that young Fellow is most certain; but whether she indulged this to any very criminal Lengths, is not so extremely clear, unless we will suppose that Women never grant every Favour to a Man but one, without granting that one also" (519). At this point in a first reading we are invited to revise our understanding of what appeared to be an attempted rape in book 9, chapter 2.

On the question of whether a woman previously unchaste could be the victim of rape, eighteenth-century doctrine and practice were beginning to disagree. Doctrinally, the early modern writers on rape had begun to insist that, in theory at least, even prostitutes could be raped. Thus Sir Matthew Hale (d. 1676) in *Historia Placitorum Coronae* writes:

> It appears by *Bracton* . . . , that in an appeal of rape it was a good exception, *quod ante diem & annum contentas in appello habuit eam ut concubinam & amicam, & inde ponit se super patriam,* and the reason was, because that unlawful cohabitation carried a presumption in law, that it was not against her will.
>
> But this is no exception at this day, it may be an evidence of an assent, but it is not necessary that it should be so, for the woman may forsake that unlawful course of life.[16]

William Hawkins commented in his *History of the Pleas of the Crown,* "nor is it any Excuse . . . that she was a common Strumpet; for she is still under the protection of the Law, & may be forced. But it was anciently said, to be no Rape to force a Man's own Concubine."[17] Whether this rule is still good, Hawkins does not say. The tendency, instead, was to try to develop doctrine about witness credibility according to which evidence of a woman's previous unchastity could be considered relevant to the issue of consent as well as to the credit of the complaining witness. Yet, in practice, to judge from the reported trials, very likely no woman who, like Mrs. Waters, could be shown to have lived in one illicit relationship and then to have had an affair with another man could have maintained a successful prosecution for rape against the second man in the eighteenth century.

Despite the chivalric unwillingness of the narrator in *Tom Jones* to state explicitly that Jenny has made an assignation with Northerton fully intending to have intercourse with him, we soon enough conclude that she is in love with him and will readily enough consent to whatever he likes to propose. The surprise turns out to be that Northerton had no interest in raping Jenny; he has intended to rob her. Once he learned she had over ninety pounds in notes and cash and a valuable ring, he determined to rob her to secure money, the better to make his escape from the criminal charges already pressed against him. In Fielding's comic world, an unchaste middle-aged woman, one without even a pretty face, cannot be an object of a rape attempt.

But such a woman can readily enough falsely cry rape, as Jenny does soon after at the inn at Upton when Mr. Fitzpatrick bursts in upon Jenny and Tom in bed together. Waking in compromising circumstances and seeking to preserve her reputation, Jenny begins "to scream in the most violent Manner, crying out Murder! Robbery and more frequently

Rape!" (530). The narrator comments, "which last, some, perhaps, may wonder she should mention, who do not consider that these Words of Exclamation are used by Ladies in a Fright, as Fa, la, la, ra, da, & are used in Music, only as the Vehicles of Sound, and without any fixed Ideas" (530). When Jenny persists in complaining that all three men in her bedroom—Tom, Mr. Fitzpatrick, and Mr. Maclachlin, who has rushed in from the next room—were all there with the intention of raping her, the narrator uses the success of her performance to make a paradoxical argument: "And hence, I think, we may fairly draw an Argument, to prove how extremely natural Virtue is to the Fair Sex: For tho' there is not, perhaps, one in ten thousand who is capable of making a good Actress; and even among these we rarely see two who are equally able to personate the same Character; yet this of Virtue they can all admirably well put on; and as well those Individuals who have it not, as those who possess it, can all act it to the utmost Degree of Perfection" (532).

The ideas that women will make accusations of rape as lightly as they can sing fa, la, la, and that women can easily feign virtue are, from a masculine point of view, alarming. From a feminist point of view, it is saddening if not surprising to observe that some of the earliest critical modern thinking about problems of witness credibility developed in rape. Thus, Sir Matthew Hale told of an experience of his own as a judge in a case where a man about to be convicted of rape had proven his innocence by submitting to a physical examination that demonstrated that he was physically incapable of rape. Hale generalized:

> it must be remembered that it [rape] is an accusation easily to be made and hard to be proved, and harder to be defended by the party accused, tho never so innocent . . . [we must be] cautious upon trials of offences of this nature, wherein the court and jury may with so much ease be imposed upon without great care and vigilance; the heinousness of the offense many times transporting the judge and jury with as much indignation, that they are over-hastily carried to the conviction of the person accused thereof by the confident testimony, sometimes of malicious and false witnesses.[18]

Judges' concern that women could falsely allege rape does not seem to have been matched by equivalent concern that male defendants could falsely allege the prosecutrix's prior unchastity and consent—and that

they could and did procure perjured testimony and even forged documents (a letter from a prosecutrix offering to be the defendant's mistress,
for example) in efforts to exculpate themselves. Antony Simpson has
devoted considerable attention to trying to discover whether contemporary masculine complaints that women were likely to use allegations of
rape in blackmail schemes were well-grounded; he has concluded that
they were not.[19]

Fielding contrasts the beautiful, chaste woman who attracts genuine rape attempts and the unpretty, unchaste woman who falsely cries
rape most ambiguously in *Amelia*. The tone of *Amelia* is less comic and
more realistic than the tone of *Joseph Andrews* or *Tom Jones;* we cannot
be so absolutely sure that the plots of Colonel James and the noble lord
against Amelia's virtue will not be successful as we are sure that no
efforts to rape Fanny or Sophia will succeed. The colonel, who ought to
know, says of the noble lord, "If he once fixes his Eye upon a Woman,
he will stick at nothing to get her" (227). Booth and Amelia have a
most peculiar conversation on the nature of the threat the lord poses
when Booth asks Amelia to refuse to accept the masquerade tickets
he proffers. Neither one seems quite able to speak of or perhaps even
to contemplate the possibility that the noble lord is prepared to rape
should seduction attempts fail. Booth expresses his apprehension of the
"Snares" the noble lord might lay for his wife's innocence and adds, "I
feared what a wicked and voluptuous Man, resolved to sacrifice every
thing to the Gratification of sensual Appetite with the most delicious
Repast, might attempt" (250–51). One would think such wickedness
quite likely to result in rape. Amelia, however, responds by resenting
what she takes to be Booth's suspicion of her virtue, and by insisting,
"O Mr. *Booth,* Mr. *Booth,* you must well know that a Woman's Virtue
is always her sufficient Guard" (251). Such a position denies the very
possibility of rape and seems implausible in the sordid and relatively
realistic world of the novel. Amelia's second argument to her husband
also seems silly: she claims that she is too good a judge of character to
be "cheated of her virtue" by being deceived into an affection for an
unworthy man. "No Man breathing," she tells Booth, "could have any
such Designs as you have apprehended, without my immediately seeing
them" (252). The reader, of course, knows that the noble lord in fact
has the designs Booth fears and that Amelia has not suspected them. In
the event, Amelia's virtue is saved not by her discernment or even by

her own virtue acting as a sufficient guard, but by her reliance on her husband's judgment and her obedience to his prohibition.

Amelia is also assisted by the warning of Mrs. Bennett, who confesses what she describes as her own victimization by the noble lord. Mrs. Bennett tells her story of the noble lord's behaving to her as he has behaved to Amelia, winning her confidence by expressions of affection and presents for her child, then finally offering her masquerade tickets. According to Mrs. Bennett, she willingly went home with the noble lord at about 2 a.m. to share "a very handsome Collation." What occurred subsequently has all the murkiness of modern date rape. According to her narrative:

> I was not . . . entirely void of all Suspicion, and I made many Resolutions; one of which was, not to drink a Drop more than my usual Stint. This was, at the utmost, little more than Half a Pint of Small Punch.
>
> I adhered strictly to my Quantity; but in the Quality, I am convinced, I was deceived: For, before I left the Room, I found my Head giddy. What the Villain gave me, I know not; but besides being intoxicated, I perceived Effects from it, which are not to be described.
>
> Here, Madam [she tells Amelia], I must draw a Curtain over the Residue of that fatal Night. Let it suffice, that it involved me in the most dreadful Ruin; a Ruin, to which, I can truly say, I never consented; and of which I was scarce conscious, when the villainous Man avowed it to my Face in the Morning. (295)

Modern literary critics have been almost as quick to doubt Mrs. Bennett's story as eighteenth-century jurymen no doubt would have been.[20] Once she admits that she was willing to be partying and drinking with a man not her husband at 2 a.m. in a private place, her ability to elicit belief in the claim that she did not consent to have intercourse with him is severely impaired.

Let us suppose, though, that Mrs. Bennett's story is true. Would the behavior of the noble lord then be rape? As Fielding no doubt appreciated, this makes a nice legal question. In the eighteenth century, rape was sexual intercourse with a woman against her will. It is probable that the use of force was considered an essential element of the crime. After Fielding's death, as criminal law developed doctrinally, a number of fact situations in which intercourse was had with women without their consent but also without the use of force were much discussed: having

intercourse with a woman rendered insensible by alcohol, having intercourse with a woman who was feeble-minded, and having intercourse
with a woman by fraudulently pretending to be her husband.[21] In all
these fact situations, the woman makes no physical resistance to the
man's act of intercourse. Given an early understanding of rape as a man's
insistence on penetrating the woman against her will and despite her
determined efforts to resist, the judges worried that they might convict
a man who was not fully intending to rape, that is, a man who intended
to stop his assault before penetration should he meet determined resistance. *Reg.* v. *Camplin* (1845) finally established the rule that a man who
gives a woman alcohol intending to render her unconscious, and then,
when she is unconscious, has intercourse with her, commits rape. The
victim in that case was thirteen; the jury found that the defendant gave
her liquor for the purpose of exciting her, and not with the intention
of making her unconscious. But he did, in fact, render her unconscious
and then have intercourse with her. The judges found that under these
circumstances "and also when the prisoner must have known that the act
was against her consent at the last moment when she was capable of exercising her will, because *he had attempted to procure her assent, and failed,*"
he was guilty of rape.[22] Mrs. Bennett, in contrast to this thirteen-year-
old, does not claim to have been rendered totally unconscious by alcohol
or other drugs; she says she was intoxicated, that the drug produced
"Effects . . . which are not to be described" (effects most commentators
have understood without any particular evidence as those of an aphro-
disiac), that she was "scarce conscious" or "semi-conscious," as we might
say, and that she never consented to the intercourse. It is likely that
no court in the 1750s would have found the noble lord guilty of rape
on Mrs. Bennett's facts. We may observe, however, that Fielding here
presciently explored a fact situation that generated important doctrinal
controversy and that finally was recognized as rape in England by the
Sexual Offences Act of 1956 under the rubric of "administering drugs to
obtain or facilitate intercourse."

How difficult it was to get away from the idea that rape was simply
the forcible penetration of a woman against her will and her determined
resistance is evident in the line of nineteenth-century cases involving
men, sometimes burglars, who crawled into the beds of married women
at night when their husbands were temporarily absent and tried to have
intercourse with them. Beau Didapper uses a similar fraud trying to gain

Fanny's consent to intercourse with him by pretending to be Joseph. The narrator tells us he is "an excellent Mimick" and has him say "in *Joseph's* Voice," in darkness: *"Fanny, my Angel, I am come to inform thee that I have discovered the Falsehood of the Story we last Night heard. I am no longer thy Brother, but thy Lover; nor will I be delayed the Enjoyment of thee one Moment longer. You have sufficient Assurances of my Constancy not to doubt my marrying you, and it would be want of Love to deny me possession of thy Charms"* (330–31). This tactic fails because Slipslop rather than Fanny is in the bed. A similar fraud, however, works for Roderick Random, who has intercourse with the apothecary's daughter by pretending to be her lover—and Smollett does not seem to think the worse of Roderick for using it. In an early nineteenth-century case on the facts of a burglar's coming into a wife's bed at night and having intercourse by pretending to be her husband, because he desisted while in the act of copulation but before emission when she realized what was happening and resisted, the majority of the judges considered that there was no intent to commit rape. Chief Justice Dallas "pointed out forcibly the difference between compelling a woman against her will, when the abhorrence which would naturally arise in her mind was called into action, and beguiling her into consent and co-operation." [23] Similarly, in another case in 1822 a father began to have intercourse with his thirteen-year-old daughter when she was asleep; she then awoke but did not resist until observed by another person. This was found not to show "such an absence of consent throughout as to justify a conviction of rape." [24] In yet another of these cases, a fellow lodger insinuated himself into a wife's bed after her husband had gone downstairs in the middle of the night; he had intercourse with her. As soon as she realized the man was not her husband, she pushed him off, rushed downstairs, and hanged herself. The judge found that the facts pleaded did not establish a charge of rape, "as the crime was not committed against the will of the prosecutrix, as she consented, believing it to be her husband." [25] The logic here is partly that the court cannot know for certain whether or not the defendant would have proceeded beyond the woman's resistance, because she offered none, so it is unfair to punish him for rape. The woman's consent is found in her willingness to participate in the intercourse without crying rape or offering physical resistance. This line of cases—the reader may be relieved to know—was first repudiated by the Criminal Law Amendment Act of 1885, which made a man liable for rape if he impersonated a woman's husband in order to have sexual intercourse with her, then further repudiated by the Sexual Offences Act of 1956, which made it a crime to induce a married woman to have sexual intercourse by impersonating her husband and, more broadly, to procure of woman by false pretenses to have unlawful sexual intercourse. Here again, this time in the Didapper mimicry attempt, Fielding describes a fact situation that turned out to be an important doctrinal crux.

So far we have looked at rapes that are attempted but not completed and at rapes that are falsely alleged. Rape itself is not represented in Fielding's fiction. An obvious reason for its absence—and there is nothing wrong with obvious reasons—is that his fiction is fundamentally comic. After all, he was writing comic novels with happy endings, not tragedies like *Titus Andronicus* or *Lucius Junius Brutus.* I would, however, also suggest that Fielding's understanding of rape, and his culture's understanding of rape, made rape quite difficult to represent, not only in fiction but also in court.

We do not know how frequently women were raped in eighteenth-century England, but several students of the history of rape have commented on how low indictment rates seem in the eighteenth century and suggested reasons why rape was probably significantly underreported. Barbara Lindermann, in a study of rape in Massachusetts between 1698 and 1797 counted only 43 indictments for rape and attempted rape over the century. She argued that few assaults that we would now count as rape were perceived as rape: "in a patriarchal and explicitly hierarchical culture, rape committed by men of the upper or middle orders never came to public attention, much less to the courts. Because of their positions of prestige and authority, respectable men of the community could force their attention on servants or single girls, finding a grudging acquiescence." [26] Two recent studies of rape and attempted rape indictments in eighteenth-century England, one by Antony Simpson of Old Bailey and the City of London Quarter Sessions between 1740 and 1830 and another by J. M. Beattie of Surrey and Sussex between 1660 and 1800, show similarly low rates. [27] Indictments for rape and attempted rape at London's Old Bailey and the City of London Quarter Sessions between 1730 and 1759 totaled 103, or 3.43 a year. Combining the Surrey and Sussex figures for both rape and attempted rape from 1700 to 1779 yields 102 indictments, or 1.275 a year. Contrary to Lindermann's argument about Massachusetts and also contrary to what a novel reader might expect, Simpson's London data show that the most frequent prosecutrixes in rape and attempted rape were female servants. Sixty-seven percent of his prosecutrixes for whom information was available were domestic servants. Of 189 female servants complaining of abuse, 35 accused their masters, 8 other workmates, and 35 other members of the households in which they were employed. Beattie suggests that the assaults leading to indictments had a peculiar character: either the victim was so seriously injured "that this not only provided evidence of the attack but also brought it to the attention of others who might have encouraged her to report and prosecute; or the rape had actually been interrupted by witnesses who not only encouraged the prosecution but also provided evidence." [28] My own readings in the law reports support this impression. Absent special circumstances, few women on their own appear to have reported rape to a magistrate. Moreover, Simpson and Clark have independently found in study of some surviving magistrates' minute books that the magistrates further reduced the small number of cases reported to them by declining to indict in many of those cases.

As I noted initially, the category of attempt was not known in the earliest criminal law. In the eighteenth century, however, a doctrine of attempt was slowly developed. In quite a rough and general way, attempts at committing felonies were prosecuted as misdemeanors.[29] Thus, because rape was a felony, attempted rape was a misdemeanor. The *locus clasicus* of early doctrinal thinking on attempt is usually said to be Mansfield's opinion in *Rex* v. *Scofield* (1784), an appeal on an indictment for attempted arson. Mansfield found the defendant guilty of a misdemeanor and said: "So long as an act rests in bare intention, it is not punishable by our laws; but immediately when an act is done, the law judges, not only the act done, but of the intent with which it is done; and, if it is done with an unlawful and malicious intent, tho the act itself would otherwise have been innocent, the intent being criminal, the act becomes criminal and punishable." [30] In theory, therefore, at the first kiss Peter Pounce or Lord Fellamar would be guilty of attempted rape.

In practice, however, and the practice seems reflected in Fielding's treatment of attempted rape, an attempt at rape would have had to have proceeded much farther, would have had to have been much closer to a completed rape, or, in fact, been a completed rape with proof problems in order to have led to prosecutions for attempt. On the basis of his Surrey and Sussex data, Beattie concludes that many women who were, in fact, raped decided to charge their assailants with attempted rape only. By this tactic, the women avoided having to state publicly the details to prove penetration and might well also avoid sustained hostile cross-examination. One pregnant Surrey woman, for example, after having been assaulted and raped by three men in Croyden, "from a great tenderness and Delicacy natural to her, would not swear to a Rape, so that the Prisoners were acquitted of that Charge, and again indicted for an assault only."[31]

It is not only because Fielding's fictions are comic that no one formulates the thought of indicting any of his would-be rapists for attempted rape and that only a few of them receive even minimal punishments, such as blows with a stick or the box on the ears Joseph administers to Beau Didapper. They also are not indicted or seriously punished because, despite the emerging doctrine of attempt, in Fielding's day the law was closer to the older view of no harm, no punishment. None of them do enough physical damage to attract serious legal attention.

The earlier narratives present would-be rapists as motivated by sheer lust and do not weigh their guilt very carefully. But *Tom Jones,* in presenting Lord Fellamar's assault on Sophia, gives a more complex account of motive and a more detailed look at the consequences of attempt. Significantly, Lady Bellaston's plot that Lord Fellamar should rape and forcibly marry Sophia is said to be "a very black Design," but of Lord Fellamar, who is to execute it, the narrator says: "his Reputation was extremely clear, and common Fame did him no more than Justice, in speaking well of him" (784, 788). In a world in which women may be locked up and corporally disciplined by first their fathers and then their husbands, the idea that a young woman might be brought to understand her own best interests by rape and forcible marriage has some plausibility to an ordinarily decent young man like Lord Fellamar. Given the encouragement of the young lady's relative and the belief that she has fixed her affections on a very unsuitable man, all in all the scheme "appeared in no very heinous Light to his Lordship, (as he faithfully promised, and faithfully resolved too, to make the Lady all the subsequent amends in his Power by Marriage)" (792).

What Lord Fellamar attempts, until interrupted by the noisy arrival of Squire Western, would be, if completed, a statutory felony, a capital crime; the mere attempt is a misdemeanor. Yet interestingly and plausibly in the light of the social and legal history of attempted rape, after being discovered assaulting Sophia and after having quite plainly declared his intention to rape her, Lord Fellamar is neither prosecuted nor, apparently, ashamed to show his face. On the contrary, when Squire Western—who never seems to take notice of the fact that his daughter was about to be raped—later rebukes Lord Fellamar for presuming that he has been accepted as a son-in-law and calls him a "Son of a Bitch," Fellamar promptly sends a second to Squire Western to demand an apology or a duel. Sophia, in fact, does not complain to anyone about his attack until Fellamar is again insisted on as a husband for her, this time by Mrs. Western. Like many modern victims of sexual assault or harassment, she is embarrassed to speak of what happened, even to a woman and a relative. Only when her aunt threatens to force her to be alone with Fellamar does Sophia confide: "Indeed, . . . I am almost ashamed to tell you. He caught me in his Arms, pulled me down upon the Settee, and thrust his Hand into my Bosom, and kissed it with such Violence, that I have the mark upon my left Breast at this Moment" (889). Mrs. Western's initial response is to doubt Sophia's truthfulness and to accuse her of inventing the story to persuade her aunt to desist from promoting the match. Subsequently, Mrs. Western forces Sophia to have another private interview with Lord Fellamar, an interview in which Lord Fellamar hopes to have his attempted rape forgiven as a symptom of the "Violence of his Love" (902).

Rape itself was close to being unnarratable in Fielding's world. Even the law reporters sometimes produce sentences like: "the circumstances of this case are too shocking to the feelings of modesty to detail."[32] That rape could occur challenged patriarchal ideology, according to which men were the protectors of women, especially good women. At trial, a woman who had been able to identify her attacker and to have him apprehended had to tell her story, giving details to establish penetration, and produce whatever corroboration she could. A modest woman, especially a genteel woman, one who might really have refused consent to intercourse, was thought to be reluctant to tell such a story. Fielding's chaste heroines, once attacked, shriek and struggle but do not utter the word "rape"; nor do they after rescue initiate proceedings against their attackers. A woman's willingness to tell the story of her rape threatened of itself to constitute evidence of her immodesty and unchastity, to plunge her into the category of loose women such as Slipslop and Jenny, women who cry rape as easily as they sing fa, la, la. Not infrequently, the contest of stories at trial was like the one Clarissa fears would occur should she accuse Lovelace of rape: the woman's tragic narrative against the man's comic one, with the comic story of the ambivalent woman who first consents and then falsely cries rape frequently prevailing. Anna Clark makes the useful point that women who prosecuted for attempted rape rather than rape might seem more credible: while "juries hesitated to hang a man for rape on the testimony of a woman who admitted she was unchaste and unworthy . . . a woman who prosecuted for attempted rape declared publicly that she had risked her life defending her chastity, and that she should be believed because she was still chaste." [33]

Women who alleged rape at trials were usually not believed. Between 1730 and 1830 at the Old Bailey the conviction rate for people indicted for burglary was 0.56, while the conviction rate of men indicted for rape was 0.17. Grand juries in Surrey found true bills in 88.5 percent of the capital property offenses alleged before them, but only in 55.6 percent of the rapes alleged. And when the eighteen men indicted for rape went to trial, fifteen or 83.3 percent were acquitted. [34]

During Fielding's own career as a magistrate he played a small practical role in the legal history of rape and attempted rape. His performance, as recorded in the "Modern History" column of his *Covent Garden Journal,* has drawn mixed reviews. Anna Clark has been most severe, declaring that "as a magistrate Fielding continued to regard rape victims unsympathetically," and objecting to the "sceptical tone" taken in reporting several accusations. [35] Martin Battestin and Ruthe Battestin, Fielding's biographers, have instead stressed Fielding's outrage at an instance of brutal rape and his concern and activism on behalf of young girls who were forced into prostitution. [36] Bertrand Goldgar's new edition of the *Covent Garden Journal* makes the "Modern History" columns more accessible, allowing us to see both the jocularity in some of the narratives of rape and attempted rape allegations and the sympathy at least for those Fielding was convinced were real victims. [37] As a magistrate, of course, Fielding had an obligation to hear both sides of cases before him. While at least one of these cases (Mr. Labrosse's) might provoke feminist suspicion, on the facts before Fielding and reported, a few of the allegations certainly did not appear well-founded. Simpson has discovered that not only did a number of real victims of rape and attempted rape negotiate for monetary damages but also that marriage, even from strangers, was sometimes offered as a recompense, and that "working-class women sometimes accepted marriage as suitable recompense for sexual attack."[38] In one of Fielding's cases, a woman who alleged attempted rape accepted an offer of marriage from the defendant: "and instead of returning before the Justices, they went directly before the Parson" (431). In another, a woman charged a staymaker with rape, whereupon "the Prisoner said to the Woman, 'My Dear, you know very well we were married on Monday Morning at the Fleet.' Upon which she burst out into Tears, and confessed it to be true; alleging as an Excuse for what she had done, that she had been over persuaded to it. The good Man presently forgave the Offence, and they departed very lovingly together" (435). Surely such cases appealed to the comic sensibility of the novelist and to the very human wish to believe that—despite lovers' quarrels—no real harm has been done. Another case, where a young defendant is indicted for the rape of a seventy-year-old woman he claimed to have married, is also treated comically. Yet the willingness to realize detail in these comic mini-scenes, sometimes even adorned with dialog, does contrast with the more generalized, more abstract, language used to represent real injury. From the different point of view of women victims of sexual assault, as Anna Clark's evidence suggests, puzzles over evidence or distinctions between completed rape and attempt, however fascinating to the legal mind, were less important than the humiliation, the fear, and the physical pain and injury they felt it important to describe.

I would like to close with an eighteenth-century rape story from a trial transcript, one in the Harvard Law Library Trial Collection, a story unimaginable in the comic worlds Fielding creates. Sarah Woodcock was a woman in her late twenties, a member of a dissenting church engaged to a fellow dissenter. In partnership with her sister, she had a millinery shop. As was customary in such businesses, she was prepared to call at the houses of potential customers with samples of her wares. On one occasion when she did so, she was forcibly prevented from leaving by a gentleman in a dressing gown. He first held her captive for several days while he tried to seduce her, then had her taken away to his country house at Epsom, where he raped her. This is the testimony of Sarah Woodcock as it was taken down in shorthand at the assizes:

> He turned upon me with all the force he could, and forced himself between me, and said he would get into me: with that he lay upon me with all the weight he could, and strove to push himself into me with all

his might; and I cried and struggled all I could, but he held my mouth together with his fingers, that I might not cry; and strove to lie over me, so much as to smother me. When he had been some time in me, I felt something come from him, and then he turned off from me as he came on, and left me to live or die as I could. . . . After this he asked me if I wanted the pot [the chamber pot]? I said yes. I got out of bed, I don't know how, and there came a great quantity of blood from me.[39]

Sarah Woodcock's story was not believed.

Notes

I should like to thank Hugh Amory, of the Houghton Library, Harvard University, for the invitation that prompted the first version of this essay, delivered as a talk in January 1987 on the occasion of an exhibition, entitled "New Books by Fielding," of the Hyde Collection at Houghton.

1. Henry Fielding, *The History of the Adventures of Joseph Andrews . . . and An Apology for the Life of Mrs. Shamela Andrews,* ed. Douglas Brooks (London: Oxford University Press, 1970), 339. All subsequent references to *Shamela* are from this edition; they will be included in my text.

2. Henry Fielding, *The Life of Jonathan Wild the Great* (New York: New American Library, 1962), bk. 4, ch. 7–8, pp. 180–94. All subsequent references to *Jonathan Wild* are to this edition; they will be included in my text.

3. A basic grasp of the history and theory of the English law of attempt may be derived from: Sir James Fitzjames Stephen, *A History of the Criminal Law of England,* 3 vols. (London: Macmillan and Co., 1883), 2:221–26, 3:108–18; John S. Strahorn, Jr., "The Effect of Impossibility on Criminal Attempt," *University of Pennsylvania Law Review* 78 (1930): 962–98; Paul Kichyun Ryu, "Contemporary Problems of Criminal Attempts," *New York University Law Review* 32 (1957): 1170–1201; Glanville Williams, *Criminal Law: The General Part,* 2d ed. (London: Stevens and Sons, 1961), ch. 14; L[eslie] B[asil] Curzon, *Criminal Law* (London: MacDonald and Evans, 1973), ch. 6.

For an important statement of the recent reform effort, see "Criminal

Law: Attempt, and Impossibility in Relation to Attempt, Conspiracy and Incitement," Law Commission Report No. 102 (London: Her Majesties Stationary Office, 1980). A resulting statute is the Criminal Attempts Act (1981). Debate has continued in: Glanville Williams, "The Problem of Reckless Attempts," *Criminal Law Review* (1983): 365–75; Richard Buxton, "Circumstances, Consequences and Attempted Rape," *Criminal Law Review* (1984): 25–34.

4. Susan Brownmiller, *Against Our Will* (New York: Simon and Schuster, 1975). In England, Jennifer Temkin has played an important role in providing a feminist perspective for law reform. See, for example, Temkin's "Toward a Modern Law of Rape," *Modern Law Review* 45 (1982): 399–419; "The Limits of Reckless Rape," *Criminal Law Review* (1983): 5–16; "Women, Rape, and Law Reform," in *Rape,* ed. Sylvana Tomaselli and Roy Porter (Oxford: Basil Blackwell, 1986), 16–40.

5. Sir James Fitzjames Stephen offers a classic denial that rape might have a significant history in his *History of the Criminal Law of England:* "I pass over many sections punishing particular acts of violence to the person, and in particular the whole series of offences relating to the abduction of women, rape, and other such crimes. Their history possesses no special interest and does not illustrate either our political or our social history" (3:118). For thoughtful comments on some recent writing on the history of rape, see Roy Porter, "Rape—Does it have a Historical Meaning?," in *Rape,* 216–36.

6. Anna Clark, *Women's Silence, Men's Violence: Sexual Assault in England, 1770–1845* (London: Pandora, 1987). For debate on some of her points, see Porter, "Rape."

7. Antony E. Simpson, "The 'Blackmail Myth' and the Prosecution of Rape and Its Attempt in Eighteenth Century London: The Creation of a Legal Tradition," *Journal of Criminal Law and Criminology* 77 (1986): 101–50.

8. Clark thinks that at the beginning of the nineteenth century the "myth of the aristocratic rapist" was used to mask proletarian sexual violence resulting from an upheaval in gender relations faced by working people; women, increasingly dependent on low wages, needed to marry, but working-class men were less and less able to support them because of agricultural depression, low factory wages, and the de-skilling of artisans (*Women's Silence,* 5, 13). Simpson, locating a somewhat similar phenomenon earlier, points to the enclosure movement as creating an ethos of violent masculinity among the lower classes: men, pressured to move from the country where they had property and local reputation, developed a new ethos of violent masculinity as a defense against their consequent loss of earning power and status ("The 'Blackmail Myth,'" 144–45).

9. Angela J. Smallwood, *Fielding and the Woman Question: The Novels of Henry*

Fielding and Feminist Debate, 1700–1750 (Hemel Hempstead, Herts.: Harvester Wheatsheaf, 1989), 173. Smallwood quite consciously attempts to present Fielding as a feminist to reclaim him for liberal humanist criticism. She makes a number of useful points, but a more accurate account of Fielding's final position on the "woman question" seems to me to be offered by April London, "Controlling the Text; Women in *Tom Jones,*" *Studies in the Novel* 19 (1987): 323–33.

10. Henry Fielding, *The History of Tom Jones, a Foundling,* ed. Martin C. Battestin (Middletown, Conn.: Wesleyan University Press, 1975), 616. All subsequent references will be to this edition; they will be included in my text.

11. Roy Porter, "Mixed Feelings: The Enlightenment and Sexuality in Eighteenth-Century Britain," in *Sexuality in Eighteenth-Century Britain,* ed. Paul-Gabriel Boucé (Manchester: Manchester University Press, 1982), 1–25. For further comment on this important essay, see Susan Staves, "Sexuality in Eighteenth-Century Britain," *Etude Anglaises* 38 (1985): 60–62.

12. Henry Fielding, *Joseph Andrews,* ed. Martin C. Battestin (Middletown, Conn.: Wesleyan University Press, 1967), 87. All subsequent references to *Joseph Andrews* will be to this edition; page numbers will be included in my text.

13. For a variety of comment on Fielding's professional legal knowledge and involvement, see Hugh Amory, "Law and the Structure of Fielding's Novels" (Ph.D. diss., Columbia University, 1966); Marvin R. Zirker, Jr., *Fielding's Social Pamphlets: A Study of "An Enquiry into the Causes of the Late Increase of Robbers" and "A Proposal for Making an Effectual Provision for the Poor"* (Berkeley and Los Angeles: University of California Press, 1966); Hugh Amory, "Henry Fielding and the Criminal Legislation of 1751–52," *Philological Quarterly* 50 (1971): 175–92; John H. Langbein, "Shaping the Eighteenth-Century Criminal Trial: A View from the Ryder Sources," *University of Chicago Law Review* 50 (1983): 1–136; J. M. Beattie, *Crime and the Courts in England, 1660–1800* (Oxford: Oxford University Press, 1986).

14. *The Proceedings at the Sessions of the Peace, and Oyer and Terminer, For the City of London, and Country of Middlesex, Held at Justice-Hall in the Old-Bailey, on Friday the 27th of February last . . . upon a Bill of Indictment found against Francis Charteris, Esq.; for committing a Rape on the Body of Anne Bond, of which he was found Guilty* (London, 1730).

15. John Langbein, "The Criminal Trial Before the Lawyers," *University of Chicago Law Review* 45 (1978): 264.

16. Sir Matthew Hale, *Historia Placitorum Coronae* (London, 1736), 628–29.

17. William Hawkins, *A Treatise of the Pleas of the Crown,* 2 vols. (1716; reprint; Abingdon, Oxon.: Professional Books, 1980), bk. 1, ch. 42, p. 108.

18. Hale, *Historia Placitorum Coronae,* 365.

19. Simpson, "The 'Blackmail Myth.' " In fact, he argues, men who alleged sodomy against other men in extortion schemes were a more real threat; false allegations of this kind were consequently made into a felony "regularly productive of convictions" (123).

20. For example, Eric Rothstein, *Systems of Order and Inquiry in Later Eighteenth-Century Fiction* (Berkeley and Los Angeles: University of California Press, 1975), in an important chapter on *Amelia*.

21. For comment on these fact situations, see K. L. Koh, "Consent and Responsibility in Sexual Offences," *Criminal Law Review* (1968): 81–97, 150–62.

22. I Den. C.C.R. 90. See also Sir William Oldnall Russell, *A Treatise on Crime and Misdemeanors,* 3 vols. (London, 1826), 1:677.

23. Rex v. Joseph Jackson (1822), Russ. & Ry. 487.

24. Reg. v. Page, 2 Cox C.C. 133; the girl was also said to have consented to previous intercourse with the father.

25. Regina v. Bernard Saunders (1838), *Cases on the Oxford Circuit,* 265, at 266. The judge also observed to the jury that, although earlier he would have had to direct an acquittal, because of the recent passage of I Vict. c. 85 it would be possible to find the defendant guilty of assault.

26. Barbara S. Lindermann, " 'To Ravish and Carnally Know': Rape in Eighteenth-Century Massachusetts," *Signs* 10 (1984): 80.

27. Antony Simpson, "Vulnerability and the Age of Female Consent: Legal Innovation and Its Effect on Prosecutions for Rape in Eighteenth-Century London," in *Sexual Underworlds of the Enlightenment,* ed. G. S. Rousseau and Roy Porter (Chapel Hill, N.C.: University of North Carolina Press, 1988); Antony E. Simpson, "Masculinity and Control: The Prosecution of Sex Offences in Eighteenth-Century London" (Ph.D. diss., New York University, 1984); Beattie, *Crime and the Courts,* 131–32. Anna Clark's findings, for the slightly later period, and based on some of the same materials Simpson uses as well as on less institutional sources, are similar.

28. Beattie, *Crime and the Courts,* 127.

29. A useful discussion is to be found in Sir William Oldnall Russell, *A Treatise on Crimes and Misdemeanors,* 4th ed., 3 vols. (London, 1865), 1:79–84.

30. Rex v. Scofield (1784), Thomas Caldecott, *Reports of Cases Relative to the Duty and Office of a Justice of the Peace, from Michaelmas 1776 to Trinity 1785* (London, 1786), 379, at 399.

31. Beattie, *Crime and the Courts,* 129.

32. Thomas Leach, *Cases in Crown Law* (London, 1789), 99. This was a case with a child victim. A subsequent sentence does provide some detail: "The prisoner had several times committed a rape upon the body of the deceased, and from his age, violence, and a venereal disorder, had so torn and injured her private parts, that a mortification ensued which was the cause of her death."

33. Clark, *Women's Silence*, 47–48.

34. Statistics are from Simpson and Beattie.

35. Clark, *Women's Silence*, 52. There are also issues of the legitimacy of a magistrate's freeing an accused rapist on bail and of electing to dismiss complaints.

36. Martin C. Battestin and Ruthe R. Battestin, *Henry Fielding: A Life* (New York: Routledge, 1989), 547–57.

37. Henry Fielding, *The Covent Garden Journal and a Plan of the Universal Register-Office,* ed. Bertrand A. Goldgar (Middletown, Conn.: Wesleyan University Press, 1988), appendix 1. See Goldgar's introduction for discussion of the authorship of these columns.

38. Simpson, "The 'Blackmail Myth,' " 123.

39. *The Trial of Frederick Calvert, Esq.; Baron of Baltimore, in the Kingdom of Ireland, For a Rape on the Body of Sarah Woodcock . . . At the Assizes held at Kingston, for the Country of Surrey, On Saturday, the 26th of March, 1768. . . .* (London, 1768), 12.

Mary Delany, Model to the Age

✣ *Janice Farrar Thaddeus*

The definition of woman changed radically in England during the lifetime of Mary Granville Pendarves Delany (1700–1788). In the 1700s and before, women were assumed to resemble men. Even their bodies—though of course considered less perfect—were thought to resemble men's bodies. Hence, women were assumed to be sensual and strong, to be nearly as independent after marriage as before.[1] By 1788 this female being who had been defined chiefly as a lesser man had been redefined as a separate and oppositional being, by "nature" chaste and domestic. Delany successfully maneuvered through the major complexities of this great shift. Edmund Burke said of her in later life that she was "high bred, great in every instance," indicating further that she was a model to the age and even that she would be a model to future ages.[2] Thus twentieth-century historians have often used Delany as a template. The Delany we have assumed to have been Burke's model, however, was not the entire woman. The Delany we have known was actually constructed in the mid-nineteenth century by her great-grandniece Lady Augusta Llanover. By omitting passages from Delany's letters, Lady Llanover made her seem much more sedate than she really was. Born at the beginning of the century, and formed by its looser mores, Delany was in fact much less inhibited than her younger friends. Frances Burney talks of the "benevolence, softness, piety, and gentleness . . . all resident in her face," in a scene that Lady Llanover firmly disbelieved. Lady Llanover characterizes this scene as full of "pert and vulgar dialogue," unworthy of Delany's eighty-two-year-old "dignity and refinement."[3] One of the main purposes of this essay is to revise this Victorian model of Delany, to restore the facets of her character that Lady Llanover found unacceptable, and hence to return her to her proper historical place in the eighteenth century.

I can define most clearly the quality of this model woman's person-

ality and the sources of her power by analyzing her life chiefly through
the perspective of her marriages, recovering omitted passages from
Lady Llanover along the way. Though Delany was less inhibited than
Frances Burney, she too was entrammeled by her powerlessness, and
especially by her position as a woman who needed money and who saw
marriage as her only recourse. Marriage was women's profession in the
eighteenth century. It was difficult to avoid. By midcentury only 5 percent of the population remained single.[4] Although the fictional happy
ending was nearly always a marriage, it is perfectly clear that marriage
in eighteenth-century England was for real women a particularly con-
stricting institution. As Kathryn Kirkpatrick has pointed out in her
essay in this volume, a single woman in the eighteenth century was
in a much stronger position than a married woman. She was equal to
a man before the law; she could own property, and she could write a
will. But when that *"feme sole"* married, unless careful contracts were
executed—and in most cases, even if they were—she became, as Sir
William Blackstone put it, "one person in law," with no more rights
than a lunatic or a child.[5] Samuel Richardson explored some of the
consequences of this view in his sequel to *Pamela,* especially the effects
of the sexual double standard on the faithful wife. Mary Hays, Elizabeth Inchbald, and Mary Wollstonecraft confronted the destructive
ways husbands used their power, and Defoe, Richardson, Fielding, and
Sterne persistently queried the romantic ideal. But marriage in fiction
was constantly romanticized as a goal, the happy ending. Delany wrote
at length about her own marriages, and her ways of reinventing her life
as literature provide an alternative to the narrative shapes of fiction,
supplying by an ever-shifting dialog the distortions and inconsistencies
of experience.

Delany gained control over her life by telling her story—not by publishing it, but by writing it down for her intimate women friends—her
sister Anne and Margaret Cavendish Harley, the duchess of Portland.
She frequently linked her experiences to enabling fictions, struggling
to create out of her often-paradoxical existence an ensemble she could
live by. In spite of all incongruities, Delany attempted to stitch together
her private and public lives, to maintain a continuity between affection
and material needs, to be frank when custom dictated euphemism and
disguise, to question some conventions even as she embodied others.

First, a summary of the facts as we know them. Delany experienced two varieties of eighteenth-century marriage. The first time, being a woman and powerless, when she was forced by her uncle to marry Alexander Pendarves, she was her family's pawn, and she was abundantly unhappy; the second time, she herself chose the Reverend Patrick Delany, a man her family volubly and stubbornly disapproved of, and her rebellion served her well.

In 1717, the year of the first marriage, Delany's family was in desperate need of a pawn. Up to 1714, they had been reasonably prosperous. Her father was an impecunious youngest son of a younger son, but her uncle, who inherited the family fortunes in 1706, had aggressively pursued a political career under Queen Anne. "When," as Samuel Johnson puts it in his *Life*, "the violence of party made twelve peers in a day, Mr. Granville became Lord Lansdown, Baron Biddeford [sic], by a promotion justly remarked to be not invidious, because he was the heir of a family in which two peerages . . . had lately become extinct." [6] In 1712 Lansdowne became Comptroller of the Household and privy councilor to Queen Anne. Predictably, at the accession of George I, the Granville family collapsed in the general debacle. Delany's father was briefly imprisoned, and her uncle spent two years in the Tower. To help recoup the family's depleted fortunes, Delany was at the age of seventeen "not entreated, but commanded" by Lord Lansdowne to marry his friend Alexander Pendarves. Pendarves, in addition to being nearly forty-three years her senior, was physically repulsive ("excessively fat," "negligent in his dress," took so much snuff that he had a "dirty look"—"altogether a person rather disgusting than engaging")—and a drunkard. He controlled his drinking habits for two years after their marriage, "but then he fell in with a set of old acquaintance . . . and to his ruin and my misery was hardly ever sober" (1:26, 34, 35). Delany went to live with this prize catch in his gloomy and ill-kempt castle in Roscrow, Cornwall, with its rotten floors and broken-down ceilings. The detail that depressed her most was that the windows in the parlor were so high that she could not see out of them. Pendarves allowed her to redecorate the castle, which she enjoyed. But she spent most of her time, as she later recalled, governing her temper. Mr. Pendarves, she says, "seemed very happy and well satisfied with my behaviour, and if I showed no delight in being in his company (which my honest heart would not let me do), I took care he should have no reason to accuse me of preferring any other to it. I never made any visits without him, and as he was often confined with the gout, I always worked and read in his chamber. My greatest pleasure was riding, but I never indulged myself in that exercise unless he proposed it" (1:55). Delany behaved in so pleasing a fashion that when they had been married for seven years, Pendarves said one night that he wanted to sign his will at that very moment, that he intended her to have his estate. She demurred, saying that he was tired, that tomorrow was soon enough.[7] The next morning, as she pulled aside the curtains of their bed, she saw that his face was black. Through most of the night she had as usual been kept awake by his labored breathing, but she had slept from four to seven, and during this brief time he had quietly died. His new will was unsigned; his property went to his niece.

After Pendarves's death in 1724, Delany resisted marrying again, though many people asked her.[8] She remained a widow for eighteen years.

Seven years after Pendarves's death, Delany, now thirty-one, made a prolonged visit to Ireland, where she met Jonathan Swift and Dr. Patrick Delany. Dr. Delany was older than she, but only by about sixteen years, not forty-three.[9] Unfortunately, he was just on the brink of marrying a woman whom Delany twice succinctly summarized in letters as "a very rich widow" (1:369–70, 372). Her name was Margaret Tenison and her fortune was indeed considerable; Swift referred to Dr. Delany's wife as "worth fifty thousand pounds," and her income was elsewhere described as fifteen hundred pounds a year.[10] Lady Llanover omits letters that are peppered with Delany's comments about Dr. Delany, even though they are similar to statements she later made in her autobiography: "Dr. Delany is as agreeable a companion as ever I met with, and one who condescends to converse with women, and treat them like reasonable creatures." Or again, "Dr. Delany I promise you will make a more desirable Friend [than Swift, who is evidently at the moment more interested in Miss Kelly] he has all the Qualities requisite for Friendship Zeal, Tenderness, Application I know you would like him because he is worthy."[11] After Delany returned to England, Dr. Delany, in spite of his unavailability, lingered vividly in her mind. She kept in touch with the Delany family. In 1735, they sent her a "trifle" and exchanged letters about it. Dr. Delany writes at length in a friendly and relaxed fashion. He is so confident in their relationship that he dares to tease her: "Be advised madam, abate a little of that ease & politeness that delicate fine turn of thought and phraze & come down Some degrees nearer to the level of common politeness." [12] In this letter also, and in another written four years later, he passes on news about Dean Swift and talks about his own work, or the fact that Delany has helped his niece. Twice she sends greetings to Dr. Delany in postscripts to letters to Swift. One gets the sense that one way or another they were regularly in touch. Both of the extant letters and one of the postscripts are omitted in Lady Llanover's edition, though even by her standards this exchange should have been unexceptional. Dr. Delany always mentions his wife's greetings; the friendship was clearly open and above board. Lady Llanover felt that she needed to be particularly careful, even to omitting one of those postscripts, because Dr. Delany seems to have caught an underlying meaning in this seemingly bland correspondence. When Margaret Tenison Delany died, Dr. Delany wrote as soon as propriety allowed to propose marriage to Mary Granville Pendarves.

The best way to summarize Delany's second marriage, to the man she eventually called "D.D.," is to give her own outline of a typical day in their twenty-five years together. They lived in Ireland, mostly, both in his house Delville, three miles from Dublin, and one hundred miles north in Down, where he was Dean: "We rise about seven, have prayers and breakfast over by nine. In the mornings D.D. makes his visits, I draw; when it is fair and he walks out I go with him; we dine at two; in the afternoon when we can't walk out, reading and talking amuse us till supper, and after supper I make shirts and shifts for the poor naked wretches in the neighbourhood" (2:362, June 11, 1745). Note here that they both have work (he sees parishioners and she pursues her artistic endeavors by drawing); they walk out *together* (and she tells us elsewhere that they made visits in the parish together as well); they read together (they are intellectual equals); and she is steeped enough in Shakespeare to allude to the "poor naked wretches" who are D.D.'s parishioners.

These are the facts in bare outline. What are we to make of them? How can we put this woman into the complexity of history? How can we read the intricacy of history in the texts she has left for us? Lady Llanover's portrait reflected her own assumptions about how women ought to be, and I will struggle to avoid that kind of agenda. Nonetheless, Lady Llanover and I clearly agree that in both of these marriages— different though they were—Delany succeeded against odds and with exceptional energy in maintaining her equilibrium and her propriety. She was certainly, as Burke said, "high bred," and as a consequence, "great in every instance" (5:12). To use the word "great" in this context, as Burke has done, is not misplaced. Maintaining human kindness and dignity in difficult social situations and setting a pattern for others to follow is arguably more important than leading an army to its Waterloo. This was not, however, an argument that Delany would have understood (although she embodied it). Delany died just before the French Revolution, just before Mary Wollstonecraft wrote her manifesto on women's rights. During Delany's lifetime political ideology in England increasingly emphasized the rights of the individual, which for both men and women vied with and to some degree replaced earlier hierarchical assumptions, but the ultimate effect of the developing idea of the social contract in many ways reinforced rather than replaced patriarchalism.[13] Delany's instincts always led her to recognize—if not to defend and possess—fundamental human rights. She said that in her first, forced marriage, she had lost "not life indeed, but I lost all that makes life desirable—joy and peace of mind" (1:29–30). She felt that loss so deeply that she compares herself to Iphigenia, who was also sacrificed for higher political motives; Delany actually envies Iphigenia her death, which seemed like a better fate than the life to which she was condemned. Joy and peace of mind, the sources of life, came from attachment, consideration for others—responsibilities based on human connection. Forced connection, for the sake of money alone, destroyed "all that makes life desirable." In the eighteenth century, the definition of woman's body and her separate sphere changed, but throughout the period, the ideal of human connection was perceived—with an emphasis that we still retain—as a distinctly feminine value, and it was one of the values that Delany maintained throughout her life, in spite of the political and social changes she witnessed. These values were the essential source of her high breeding.[14]

Delany tried, in this period when separate spheres were gradually being defined, to join as fully as she could her public to her private self, and to judge her public self by her private morality. Her uncle Lord Lansdowne seems to have made little attempt to join his discrete personalities, occasionally transferring the language of the marketplace into the home. Though called by Alexander Pope "*Granville* the polite," [15] Lansdowne departed from his accustomed decorum by threatening to drag his niece's presumed lover (the invented reason for her reluctance to marry Pendarves) "through the horse-pond." Delany comments, "Such an expression from a man of my uncle's politeness, made me tremble, for it plainly showed me how resolute and determined he was, and how vain it would be for me to urge any reasons against his resolution" (1:27–28). Further, it showed that his private values had peremptorily vanished in this public situation. In other situations, Lansdowne used yet another discourse. In one of his poems, for instance, which Susan Staves summarizes as "a cautionary poem against women marrying for rank and wealth," [16] he describes in relentless detail some of the possible eventualities when "Cleöra has her Wish, and weds a Peer"; in public, she lives a "gaudy" life, happily making all the other women envious, but her private life is different, and agonizing:

> View her at home in her Domestick Light,
> For thither she must come, at least at Night.
> What has she there? A surly, ill-bred Lord,
> That chides, and snaps her up at ev'ry Word;
> A brutal Sot, who while she holds his Head,
> With drunken Filth bedawbs the Nuptial Bed.

A closer summary of Delany's life with Pendarves would be difficult to find. But Lansdowne does not stop there; he imagines what sexual intercourse must be like with such a man:

> But most she fears, lest waking she should find,
> To make amends, the Monster wou'd be kind:
> Those matchless Beauties, worthy of a God,
> Must bear, tho' much averse, the loathsome Load. [17]

The inevitable result is venereal disease, described in reeking detail. To save face, the husband accuses poor, hapless Cleöra of adultery; she loses her public reputation as well as her private joy. She has no way to defend herself against this perfidy. Her friends abandon her. All she has left is the consciousness of her own innocence. Luckily, Delany escaped Cleöra's public fate and the worst of her private fate. She had learned the lesson this poem tenders. But Lansdowne had not; he wrote this poem long before he forced his niece to marry his sottish, aged, unattractive (but wealthy) friend. In his mind, the message evidently did not travel from one type of discourse to another. It was such habits of mind that were to underlay the establishment of the separation of the sexes into their separate spheres.

Within the parameters set by consideration for others, Delany attempted to the greatest degree possible to deal honestly with other people, a further effort to maintain continuity between her private and public selves. She describes herself as having a "sincere" (1:34) nature, but her social situation frequently forced her to practice deception. Although she indicated clearly to Pendarves that she disliked him, she hid this dislike from her parents. Toward Pendarves she did behave as openly as she could. She tells the duchess of Portland how she attempted to fend off the marriage proposal: "In order to prevent it, I did not in the least disguise my great dislike to him; I behaved myself not only with indifference but rudeness; when I dressed, I considered what would become me least; if he came into the room when I was alone, I instantly left it, and took care to let him see I quitted it because he came there" (1:24). Delany was deliberately flouting some of the most widely accepted eighteenth-century restrictions for women of her class. These women were assumed and also enjoined to be agreeable, polite, and pretty. In *The Ladies Calling,* first published in the 1670s and reprinted throughout the century, one of the chief virtues listed is affability, along with modesty, meekness, compassion, and piety.[18] As for being pretty, the influential Joseph Addison, while making in *Spectator* No. 10 praising references to women "that move in an exalted Sphere of Knowledge and Virtue," commended them nonetheless chiefly in a dehumanizing phrase as "the most beautiful pieces in human nature."[19]

Raised in this stifling milieu, Delany against her inclinations rebelliously endeavored to be rude and ugly. Only a seventeen-year-old could have hoped to reverse the situation in which Delany found herself by intentionally choosing her most ungainly dress. More adroitly, Delany appealed to her aunts, but her aunt Laura "called me childish, ignorant, and silly," placing her not merely in the hierarchy of male-female but of adult-child, adding "that if I did not know what was for my own interest, my friends must judge for me" (1:24). Although Delany openly declared her dislike to Pendarves himself and informed her relations that she objected to their choice of a husband, she deluded her parents, aware of their poverty and hers, paradoxically *fearing* that they would object to this marriage she abhorred. She knew that if through their interference she demurred, Lord Lansdowne would wreak his resentment on his brother as well as on her: "These considerations gave me courage, and kept up my resolution" (1:29). This part of Delany's strategy was successful; her parents delightedly approved the match. Lady Llanover, writing slightly more than a century later, comments that this parental blindness was typical of the times, "a very striking illustration of the complete disregard shown in marriage at that period to everything but the worldly settlement in life" (1861, 1:32). At least one twentieth-century historian emphatically agrees. Lawrence Stone calls Delany's marriage "a classic case of an arranged marriage purely for money and influence." [20] Alan Macfarlane has shown that in theory the romantic marriage was by the traditions of the canon law, at least from the twelfth century on in England, a possibility, that legally a woman had the right during the marriage ceremony simply to say "I do not" instead of "I do." By Roman law, parental consent was necessary, and in many countries Roman traditions edged out canonical traditions. Macfarlane notes that "as late as 1907 under the French Civil Code, a son under 25 and a daughter under 21 could not marry without parental consent." [21] In England from 1753 to 1823, during the period of the Hardwick Marriage Act, parental consent was required for those under twenty-one; otherwise there was no legal way to force children into wedlock. Yet in 1717, Delany saw no way to escape, save the forlorn hope that her husband-to-be would be daunted by her aversion. In this case, as in many others, in spite of the legal situation, one woman's emotional needs counted for nothing when weighed against power and money.

Some women—especially those who had lost their reputations—resisted their oppression by proclaiming their many-sided personalities, as opposed to the more acceptable, unified character attributed to women. Their memoirs, as Felicity Nussbaum puts it, "disrupt conventional paradigms of that female character." [22] This was Laetitia Pilkington's strategy when she defined herself as a "heteroclite." Unlike Pilkington, Delany always retained her reputation, but like Pilkington, she availed herself of the strongest prop she could find by writing her own story. The most important factor in Delany's general success, even in adverse circumstances, was her ability to contain her experience, and to objectify it, through language. She defined in speech, in letters, and in her ongoing autobiography, as clearly and sharply as she could, the society in which she found herself and her place in it. To her chosen, private, feminine audience she named her options and reinterpreted conventions. Here is one example. During her first widowhood, when she was about to turn twenty-eight, she wrote to her sister Anne Granville this opinion of the married state: "Matrimony! I marry! yes, there's a Blessed Scene before my Eyes of the Comforts of that State. a Sick Husband and Squawlng Bratts, a cross Mother in Law, and a thousand unavoidable impertinences" (MS. f. 1; March 19, 1728). What most distressed Delany about marriage—and Moll Flanders makes the same point—was losing control of her life. The central word in the statement quoted above is "unavoidable." Delany knew the facts I mentioned at the start of this essay: a single woman in the eighteenth century, besides being equal to a man before the law, was mistress of her own body and of her finances. When she married, as Mary Astell and subsequent commentators make clear, she lost her separate legal existence, not to speak of control over her body (besides the "loathsome load," year-in, year-out pregnancies were a usual if not inevitable result),[23] and impertinences were then unavoidable. Marriage, as Delany describes it here and elsewhere, is a kind of jail.

The metaphors Delany uses to evoke her first marriage are similar to those that Susan Gubar and Sandra Gilbert have noted in *The Madwoman in the Attic.* In our effort to reestablish women's changing position over time, we should not altogether deny the continuities—continuities both of language and of experience. Delany's husband is her tyrant and her jailer, and she is incarcerated; in fact, she comes to prefer incarceration to display, to prefer the prison to the zoo. When he introduces her to all of his friends, she "would much rather have hid myself in a cave, than have been exposed to the observation of any body" (1:34). In this case, she wanted to put *herself* away, to stay in her cell, return to the womb undisturbed, not to be exhibited by her jailer. Worse, in this cage she discovered that Pendarves was excessively jealous, and she had very little room to pursue her own interests (such as riding), or to escape the sometimes extremely aggressive seducers who chased the pretty girl married to an ugly old man. She said she "would rather have had a lion walk into the house, than any one whose person and address could alarm" Pendarves (1:50–51). Caged as she was, she felt guilty: "I must do him the justice to say he was very obliging in his behaviour to me, and I have often reproached myself bitterly for my ingratitude (if it can be strictly called so), in not loving a man, who had so true an affection for me. That is a most painful reflection, and has frequently added to my anxieties" (1:55). I have not been able to locate the original text of this autobiography and I do not altogether trust Lady Llanover's version. If this *is* what Delany said, her eighteenth-century doublethink was very well honed. What does she mean by "obliging"? The man who so insensitively insisted that she marry him, in spite of her clear aversion; who after the marriage allowed her at the age of seventeen to deny herself simple outdoor activities in order to watch over his gouty frame; who allowed his sister to bully her; who had her every move monitored for fear she might betray him—was this man so affectionate that Delany needed to berate herself for "ingratitude"?

Such moments of self-reproach enter rarely into this account, however. Delany's handling of language on the whole is extremely confident. She furthered her command of her text—and hence of her life—by taking over the male prerogative of naming. Her uncle may have initiated her into this habit of using pet names. Lansdowne invariably refers to her husband as "Pen," which makes him seem somewhat more attractive than he appears in Delany's narrative. Like Swift, Delany made use of "Stella" for one of her friends.[24] Eventually, she also had a model in Samuel Johnson, whose intimate acquaintances sometimes objected to sobriquets like "Goldy" and "Sherry Derry," if not to "Bozzy." Naming is a powerful tool, and Delany was aware of this. Besides simply shortened versions of her friends and acquaintances' names, Delany made use of a more general lexicon. She adopted pet names for her friends and fictional names for her autobiography. Some of her names are particularly apt. The fact that the Honorable Henry Hervey became both "Ha Ha" and "Apollo's Imp" indicates how well she understood his character. Like the sunken ditch that created an invisible fence, Hervey had a double character. "Described by his father as fit to live nowhere but a jail,"[25] Hervey nonetheless inspired Johnson to his famous dictum: "If you call a dog HERVEY, I shall love him."[26] He was an imp, but Apollo's imp. Many of the other names are equally well chosen. Lansdowne becomes "Alcander," a little-known character in Plutarch's life of Lycurgus. To find him, Delany need not have gone to the original source, though quite possibly she had read Plutarch. Alcander appears as one of the examples of compassion in *The Ladies Calling:* "Lycurgus not only forgave *Alcander,* who had struck out his eye, but entertain'd him in his house."[27] It seems as if Delany called Lansdowne Alcander because she had—against odds—forgiven him. An added twist is that Alcander had been a member of a mob that had attacked Lycurgus because he insisted that everyone should live on an equality, without ostentatiously spending money. More sharply, Delany impales her niece-in-law, Pendarves's heiress, as "Fulvia." Pendarves himself becomes "Gromio," who was Bianca's aged but rich suitor in *The Taming of the Shrew;* the ludicrousness of the name makes him seem somewhat less of an ogre. On the other hand, his castle is more fiercely called Averno, that hell which—as we know from Virgil—is easy to enter but laborious to escape. Delany herself is Penny, which may have little significance beyond the fact that it is a feminine version of Pen. On the other hand she also took Aspasia to herself—Pericles' mistress, center of Athenian literary and philosophical life. Lady Llanover was careful to imply in a footnote that some of the overtones of "Aspasia" were not appropriate; it was "a favorite appelation of the period, where beauty and accomplishments were united, without reference to its being inapplicable from other circumstances" (1:40, n. 2). To combine the characters of Aspasia and Penny, on the page if not always in life, was in this period a particularly difficult feat. Joy was what Penny-Aspasia feared to lose in her marriage to Pendarves, and she may have lost for a while what she called joy, but she never lost her spirit of fun. At times she signs herself Penelope Darves.

This naming and renaming is a fictional technique, and it is remarkable how vividly Delany's life both as a first wife and as a young widow resembles fictional representations. In the eighteenth century, as Lennard Davis has made clear to us, the separation between news and novel, fact and fiction, was a permeable partition.[28] "What Novel's this?" says Wisemore in Fielding's *Love in Several Masques,* upon hearing the details of a complicated maneuver in letter-switching.[29] Richardson turned to *Pamela* in the midst of writing letters less literary women could use on appropriate occasions. He included documents in *Clarissa,* such as Clarissa's will in its entirety. He also distributed portions of his manuscript to friends so that they could comment on it, and he included some of their suggestions. Samuel Johnson reported as parliamentary debates speeches written by himself. Lady Vane's memoirs appeared in the middle of Tobias Smollett's *Peregrine Pickle.* In novel after novel, authors claimed simply to be editors of found autobiographical manuscripts. This fluidity of discourse throughout the century is reflected in eighteenth-century discourse on marriage.

Susan Staves has discussed these permeations and complexities as they relate to marriage. She points out, for instance, that a letter produced in a court case as authentic can use rhetoric as high-flown as any romance. The facts about particular marriages undergo permutations depending on whether one is reading *Town and Country* magazine or court records. Part of the difference has to do with spheres of discourse. Marriage manuals enjoin obedience in all cases but fail to mention specific abuses. Court cases, of course, mention little else. In one of the instances Staves gives, a husband asks two of his friends to hold his wife down while he reasserts his conjugal rights; in addition, he threatens to incarcerate her in isolation somewhere abroad unless she signs over to him her rights to her own separate property. Staves laments that "perhaps the most serious problem that confronts us in writing a history of eighteenth-century marriage is that so much female feeling, so much female bitterness, was not only unexpressed but almost inexpressible." [30] We need to read with our senses preternaturally awake, to distinguish carefully among different spheres of discourse, to hear the message in such statements as the postscript that Lady Llanover omitted, "I beg my particular compliments to Dr. Delany." [31]

Delany borrowed many of the appurtenances of fictional discourse even in her letters, but she especially heightened her autobiography, not only by using fictional names but also by including scenes and stories told with the sort of dramatic detail, including dialog, that we are accustomed to find in the novel. In content as well as form, Delany's account of the Pendarves courtship uncannily resembles Clarissa Harlowe's experience with the disgusting Solmes, and a comparison helps to characterize the situation and the relationship and to emphasize Delany's ability to dramatize—and hence to survive—her experiences. Like Clarissa, Delany made her aversion very clear—but to no avail, as we know. Pendarves was as obtuse as Solmes, though he was more agreeable. Clarissa was more physically afraid; she looks at Solmes "with disgust little short of affrightment," but as in Delany's case, "his courtship indeed is to *them*," her family. [32] Who influenced whom? The evidence is somewhat unclear. Delany met Pendarves in 1717, but according to Lady Llanover, she dated her longest autobiographical fragment 1740, although she added to it later; if she wrote or revised her autobiography after 1747, she might have deliberately enhanced the resemblance to *Clarissa*. If Delany wrote before Richardson, as she probably did, this is one more instance of the harrowing accuracy of his tale. [33] Indeed, Delany's story is in some ways more distressing than Richardson's, because its denizens are so well-intentioned, so likable—too nice to be indulging in a flesh-trade like this.

Self-dramatization came so naturally to Delany, though, that some of the seemingly fictional intensities may simply arise from that Boswellian habit. For instance, with frequent professions of her own innocence and surprise, Delany nonetheless depicts herself as quite a femme fatale. One admirer succumbed to a palsy brought on by her marriage to Pendarves, and though unable to speak, he poured out in writing (as was revealed to her years later) his love for Mrs. Pendarves, and died with one of her cut-paper mosaics under his pillow. Another man, a married friend of her husband, loved her to distraction, even threatening suicide, though when rejected he rushed off like Betty the chambermaid in Fielding and seduced someone else. During her first widowhood the aspiring lovers seem multitudinous. Toying with love and resisting marriage seems to have been her primary activity. This was of course the prescribed activity at this period for women in her position. But what is exceptional about Delany is that she seemed always to control her enforced passivity, to remain powerful even in a position of weakness, theatrically assuming other names and other periods of history, enlarging her cage through the diversity of her personality. Energy—seizing life as it passed by, fixing it and redirecting it both in language and in what might be called the feminine arts—this energy seems to have been Delany's chief and saving characteristic.

During the interregnum of this first widowhood, in spite of sharply negative statements about marriage like the one quoted above, Delany did consider remarrying. She knew that—to use her own phallic and yet despairing simile—she might founder on the "Rock" she was so explicitly naming. The very force of the rejection gained its power from the pull toward acquiescence. Her favorite was Lord Baltimore, but like Lovelace, Baltimore staged a quarrel, and she had to break off the relationship. Delany's first description to her sister of the final break was rather vague; she explained later to the duchess of Portland a more nearly Richardsonian situation. In this case the personal letter is less revealing than the autobiography, another instance of the way twentieth-century assumptions can be denied by eighteenth-century discourse. Perhaps Delany's pride prevented her from telling the full story at the time, or she was inhibited by her desire to protect her as-yet-unmarried sister from such disillusioning conduct on a man's part. She frequently attributes to the duchess of Portland a reiterated, even unrelenting pressure to continue, to explain, to reveal. The fact, then, as she tears it out of herself for the autobiography, is that Baltimore had insisted that she prove her love to him before their marriage; given such an insult to her virtue, she had no recourse but to drop his acquaintance. Baltimore soon married a woman with more money, whom Delany with some residual jealousy later described as dressing her hair so unflatteringly as to look like "a *frighten'd owl,* her locks strutted out most furiously greas'd or rather gumm'd and powder'd" (MS. f. 2; 2:72, January 22, 1740). The vividness of the description served to neutralize the rival. In 1751, however, she blandly delivered the coup de grace in a letter to her sister: "I saw in the newspapers that Lord Baltimore was ill: is he dead? *He had some good qualities.* . . . I fear his poor children at Epsom have been sadly neglected: I suppose he suspects they are not his own, but that *cannot justify his neglect*" (3:5, January 12, 1751). Lady Llanover rushed to defend the comment about the frightened owl, but the insinuation of cuckoldry she passes over in complete silence. Perhaps she thought it was simply true.

On the evidence of Delany's refusal to prove her love to Lord Baltimore, Stone argues that she was "basically frigid."[34] He suggests that she might have driven Pendarves to drink, that "this may have been one solution to the torment of sleeping in the same bed as an attractive young woman for whom he had great affection, but who found him physically revolting."[35] He further argues that Baltimore might have been worried about this possible "frigidity," that this fear might have sparked his rakish request that she prove her love. The text, however, refutes this interpretation. Delany distinctly says that Pendarves drank to excess before his marriage. Further, Delany makes her affection for Baltimore so abundantly clear in her narrative that he must have been aware of it in the flesh. She simply respected herself too much to risk in such a judgmental society the kind of commitment he asked of her. As for the possibility that Delany had refused to cohabit with Pendarves, this conjecture seems equally unlikely. Even Lansdowne's Cleöra had to bear the "loathsome load" of her husband's caresses. Delany was not enough of a renegade to refuse her husband his conjugal rights. Stone has been misled by Lady Llanover's editorially selective version of Delany. Lady Llanover carefully excised the fact that whenever Delany mentioned a marriage in her letters, she dwelt on the bedding of the wife, saying of Lady Sunderland, for instance: "I was at the supper and helped to put her to bed . . . we plagued her a little as there is no forbearing on such occasions."[36] Delany may not, however, have successfully pretended that she enjoyed her husband, a failing that she mentions in a general way, one that embarrassed her somewhat. She often apologized to the duchess on this account. Nonetheless, her descriptions in the autobiography and elsewhere contain a great deal of physical detail, an awareness of the corporeal that belies the complex state of mind and body that used to be called frigidity. She never became pregnant, but this does not prove that she avoided sex. At the end of her first letter, remembering her marriage, she trembles so violently that she has to retire to compose herself.

Delany's story resembles Richardson's in some of its details and its emotional intensities. An even more similar tale appeared in Sarah Scott's novel *Millenium Hall,* published in 1762, and in this case Delany's marriage was clearly the source for the fictional version. Scott was Elizabeth Montagu's sister, and Delany certainly knew her, though not well. In 1752, when Delany commented in a letter to her sister that "Mrs. Scot [*sic*]" had made a "foolish choice" of a marriage partner, her information was secondhand. "Mrs. Montagu wrote Mrs. Donnellan word that she and the rest of her friends had rescued her out of the hands of a very bad man, but for reasons of interest they should conceal his misbehaviour as much as possible" (3:115). Scott's husband kept half of her fortune when they separated after a brief marriage. Of her many books, which she wrote both before and after her marital disaster, *Millenium Hall* was the most popular. The book presents a utopian alternative to marriage while concurrently emphasizing that men should respect women more, and that they should voluntarily abjure the double standard. Millenium Hall is a female residence, where women who are unmarried or widowed gather to study and work together. The women aid other subordinated groups—taking in people who are physical freaks and educating young girls who need their help. Their benevolence stretches far into the community around them. Although the subtext in this book occasionally betrays assumptions about women that the text denies (that they are more destructively curious than men, for instance), the point Scott is making was radical for her time and remains radical today. She is asking that men model themselves on the virtues persistently defined as feminine—connection and personal responsibility.

The women who live in the cooperative house that they call Millenium Hall tell their own and other women's stories to the novel's male interlocutor.[37] Miss Melvyn's experiences are based on Delany's. Miss

Melvyn was forced by her father and stepmother to marry Mr. Morgan, a "gentleman, in whom age had not gained a victory over passion."[38] Mr. Morgan disgusts her, and Miss Melvyn tells him so, but he assumes that her disgust will vanish when it becomes her duty to love him. Mr. Morgan is also a drunkard, lives in a gloomy house, allows his termagant sister to bully his wife, and overwhelms her with "nauseous fondness" (85). Miss Melvyn argues: "I am insensible to all joy but what arises from the social affections. The grave, I confess, appears to me far more eligible than this marriage, for I might there hope to be at peace. Mr. Morgan's fortune is large, but his mind is narrow and ungenerous, and his temper plainly not good. If he really loved me, he would not suffer me to be forced into a marriage which he well knows I detest" (78). This passage, with its mention of joy and peace, linking their loss with a desire for death, resembles Delany's account too closely to reflect pure coincidence. The female narrator of this story says that she had to obtain it secondhand, because Mrs. Morgan was always loyal to the memory of her husband; she never openly complained about him. Some elements are different, as if Scott wanted to make her characters generic, not so much as to write a roman à clef as to supply the patterns of bad marriages in order to define by contrast a good marriage. Scott's version is more stereotypical than the true story. In Scott, a scheming stepmother turns Miss Melvyn's father against her by implying that she is about to elope with a farmer, whereas Lord Lansdowne really seems to have deluded himself into the belief that he was settling his niece in a comfortable way of life. Lady Llanover convincingly argues that his letters to her after her marriage indicate his discomfort.[39] Mr. Morgan's grounds are as gloomy as his house, whereas Pendarves's surrounding countryside was quite beautiful; Mr. Morgan insists that Miss Melvyn abandon her best friend and concentrate on him alone, whereas Delany was allowed to bring her brother Bunny with her for companionship; Mr. Morgan does sign over his estate before dying, and he dies more conventionally and slowly. It is with his money that the women have founded Millenium Hall.

In spite of the radical tendencies in *Millenium Hall*, it lacks the energetic grasp of language one so often finds in Delany.[40] Of course this verbal rebellion, naming things as they actually were, was even for Delany not always sufficient. Sometimes it was necessary not only to define her environment but also to change it. When she wanted to marry again, her family disapproved. Delany set to work to change their minds. She was successful in convincing her mother and her sister that Dr. Delany was a worthy choice, but she was unable to win over her brother. In choosing to marry Dr. Delany, Delany was by her family's standards falling below their expectations. Dr. Delany was the son of a servant and therefore represented the kind of liaison a Granville should not really consider. Although Delany promised to abide by her brother's decision, she eventually convinced herself—and allowed Dr. Delany to convince her—that his objections were unreasonable and unfair. She was willing to follow the rules; she strained and struggled to gain her mother's consent, but at the age of forty-three, she simply rebelled against her brother, the one remaining objector. Frances Burney did the same when her father opposed her marrying General d'Arblay.

Delany defined clearly in her autobiography what appealed to her about the man she came to call D.D. A twentieth-century reader notices immediately that she liked D.D. because of his feminine characteristics. "His wit and learning were to me his meanest praise; the excellence of his heart, his humanity, benevolence, charity, and generosity, his tenderness, affection, and friendly zeal gave me a higher opinion of him than any other man I had ever conversed with" (1:296). These are the attributes to praise in a woman, not the honor or courage that was always cited as the chief masculine virtue. Further, when D.D.—turned widower—wrote asking her to marry him, he approached her as an equal, styling himself as "a man whose turn of mind is not forreign from yr own, (& for yt only reason not wholy unworthy of you) a man who knows yr worth, and honours you as much as he is capable of honouring anything yt is mortal" (MS. f. 9; 2:211). Qualities of mind come first, and then respect—respect that comes through knowing her "worth"—and all is placed in the context of religion and their mortality. Dr. Delany does not take the male prerogative of power. This is spare language and in its very lack of adornment it rings true.

There was also the question of money. Money had been the primary consideration in Delany's first marriage, but she had learned from this experience how to husband her own assets, and she retained in marriage a sense of her own economic independence. She herself was never a spendthrift, and she was eminently able to live on her income even if it was small, so long as it was sufficient. Lansdowne had argued when he first suggested that Delany marry Pendarves that she could not refuse "his offer of settling his whole estate on me" (1:27). Later, this plan foundered. Pendarves apparently made important financial mistakes, or at any rate redistributions. "Bad tenants and a cheating steward" was his excuse to Delany when he explained that he could not provide enough money to deck her out when they moved to London. But "his old friends" hinted "that he had some *very near relations* to maintain" (1:62–63). At Pendarves's death, she retained only her jointure, and even that had to be wrested from "Fulvia" by a good lawyer recommended by Lord Lansdowne. Lady Llanover describes this income as a few hundreds a year. Delany was perfectly content with this: "As to my fortune, it was very mediocre, but it was *at my own command*" (1:109). Evidently her own fortunes became somehow entwined with those of her youngest brother, Bevil, who died in 1736. "Had it not been for the misfortunes and misconduct of my youngest brother," she complains, "I should have been very happy, but I suffered infinite vexation on his account for some years" (1:109–10). She was cautious about money; D.D. was more extravagant, though upon his marriage to Margaret Tenison, Swift remarked that D.D. was "very modest in his new prosperity."[41] Much of his money was swallowed up in a lawsuit to prove that his first wife had intended him to inherit—at least during the remainder of his life—her fortune. At his death, Delany was certainly not rich. D.D. had said in his letter proposing marriage that though he had "twelve hundred pds. a year, clear income, for my life," he had only "a trifle to settle"; he was unable to leave her much beyond their houses (MS. f. 9; 2:211). Even so, though the duchess of Portland provided friendship and frequent refuge, Delany never accepted any of her money. At her death in 1785 the king provided a pension of three hundred pounds a year and a house at Windsor. Delany also maintained throughout a home at St. James Place in London. A few hundreds a year seems to have been her usual condition, but she did not live beyond her means. She learned early that there were things more important than affluence.

The fact that Delany had some money of her own provided a source of strength that helped to sustain her marriage to D.D. She had lived alone and been self-sufficient for eighteen years. She was managing well enough, although she was attempting to find herself a position at Court. Many good marriages in the eighteenth century contained similar elements by which the husband's power was somewhat depleted. Note, for instance, in the Thrale-Piozzi marriage, Piozzi's Catholicism and lower status as music teacher; or in Burney's case, d'Arblay's position as emigré, which meant that except when they lived in France, Burney had to support him. Delany wanted D.D. not for material support but for companionship. Similarly, he wanted not power, not money, but someone whose turn of mind resembled his own.

Delany was, like many thoughtful women of her era, suspicious of men. During the period when Lord Baltimore was fluttering about her, she remarked that Lord and Lady Fitzwilliam were about to be divorced after twenty-five years of marriage, adding this observation: "Fine encouragement this to wedlock. Shall I devote my life, my heart, to a man that after all my painful services will be glad of an opportunity to quarrel with me?" She asks herself what "security" she has against such a fate, and answers that she has to choose the right man, "a man of sense and judgment" (1:204–5). She also—in passages omitted by Lady Llanover—openly deplored the fact that virtuous wives could contract venereal diseases from their husbands. She mentions to her sister that "Lady Frances Williams is dying with ye foul disease, & that monster her husband never told her what ail'd her. they are parted. such husbands and such wretched wives abound."[42] Like her uncle, who had stressed the irony that the wife was blamed for the husband's disease, Delany points out that poor Frances Williams is ignorant as well as innocent. Yet Delany retained a relish for the sexuality of marriage, and as mentioned before, she continually refers both to the fun of teasing a bride and to other traditions connected with bedding a couple on their wedding night. Given Delany's concern about venereal disease, one might think that she would have asked her second husband about his sexual past before accepting him. We have no record that she did so, but we do have Dr. Delany's letter of proposal, and he says in a passage omitted from Lady Llanover's published text: "I thank god I am still in health & strength, wth a constitution never impaired or endangered by vices, or diseases of any kind" (MS. f. 9). Surely she was meant to read that as, among other things, saying: "I am still sexually active, and I have no venereal diseases." Dr. Delany realized that his bride would want information about his body as well as his mind.

Delany's instincts also led her in another important direction. She liked women. In spite of the fact that eighteenth-century mores tended to separate women from one another, to founder them in petty jealousies and reputation-saving rejection, Delany sought out friends. J. S. C.

Muriel goes so far as to say that "she had no interest in men. All her life, her friends—her real friends—were women." [43] This may overstate the case, but Delany's respect for women is everywhere apparent, much more generally diffused through her papers than in the work of Sarah Scott, whose demeaning assumptions—as noted above—frequently burst through as subtext. Even in ticklish situations, Delany was unusually generous to women. When Lansdowne's wife tried to inveigle Delany into an affair with one of her cast-off lovers, Delany was resistant but on the whole forgiving. When a certain Miss Hawley, whom she had helped to introduce into London society, managed to become pregnant and lose her position at Court, Delany was less judgmental than Burney would have been, perhaps because of her aristocratic upbringing. Her final word on the subject has to do with male perfidy—both incest and sexual opportunism: "To complete this horrid tale, the suspicion fell heavily amongst many others upon her uncle Wm. Balenden.—Col. Win, a man of as little delicacy as morals, had planned, for some time to secure her for himself, and carried her off into Wales, as his mistress since which time I have never heard of either of them" (MS. f. 9; 1:69). This story, which is marked by Lady Llanover in the manuscript as "not fit for publication," actually does appear in a bowdlerized version in her edition, at the proper chronological moment. Lady Llanover changes the name from Miss Hawley to Miss H———, omits the hint of incest, and by cutting out the phrase "as his mistress," leaves slightly ambiguous Colonel Win's motives (1:69).

Why did Lady Llanover go out of her way to include this story of Miss Hawley, which even in its truncated form described a woman who had borne an illegitimate child? Lady Llanover was an extremely meticulous editor, rendering most of the text with scrupulous exactitude. When she excised a portion of a letter, she was careful not to destroy the context. In a reputation-saving effort, she carefully cut out the ambiguous footnote reference to Dr. Delany, but she went further, saving not only reputation but also character. And her definition of character apparently was narrower than Burke's. She even excised such tame comments as one about breast cancer, and another about a painter who liked "fine fat white backs" and had painted Hagar with such a back. The body was evidently for Lady Llanover a particularly undesirable subject. She also omitted a description of a new man the young widow Delany noticed in the neighborhood who was lucky enough to possess such assets as "cherry cheeks, dimpled chin," and "rolling Eyes" (MS. f. 1). She carefully removed Delany's description of a boat ride where she had laughed so hard that her fellow passengers "swore I bewater'd my self" and refused to exonerate her until it became inarguably clear that the boat was leaking (MS. f. 1; June 8, 1731, 1:275ff). For reasons that are not altogether clear, she cut out Delany's more fulsomely affectionate greetings to her sister, and some of her silliest expressions,[44] of which the following addendum to her sister is typical: "whilst Life doth last thou hast me fast" (MS. f. 1, March 19, 1728). Yet Miss H—— remains. I would hazard two explanations here. Lady Llanover removed expressions for which Delany herself was responsible. *She* was not supposed to be thinking about wetting her pants or noticing men's cherry cheeks, but if other people misbehaved, their sins and idiosyncrasies might be included. In the case of Miss Hawley, there is one additional motive. When asked to give the name of the father of her child, Miss Hawley said that the "Devil should pick her bones, before she confessed," and though "pick" is changed to "eat," this statement remains in Lady Llanover's version. It seems to me just possible that Lady Llanover included this story because of this riveting expression. It may be on similar grounds that she failed to omit Delany's summary of the widowed duchess of Leinster's marriage to the children's tutor, Mr. Ogleby: "perhaps she thought it incumbent (as Lady Brown says of her Grace) to marry and make an honest man of him" (MS. f. 5; 5:89). Both instances were satisfyingly attributed to other people, and both were verbally inventive. Lady Llanover wrote myriad footnotes to her edition, and she is clearly one of those rare people who can hone a clear sentence and appreciates a vivid phrase.

Lady Llanover's ancestor Mary Delany was not a true heteroclite. She never lost her reputation, never needed publicly to redefine her character in order to claim its contradictions. Nonetheless, one of her chief preoccupations was repairing the disjunctions between the required public self and the irrepressible private self. She clearly condemned, though she did not rebel against, many of the social constructions that hemmed women in. She retained throughout her life a rambunctiousness she never even tried to suppress. When her young friend the pox-scarred Letitia Bushe visited at Delville, her Irish home, she played Puss in the Corner, a game where one person stands in the middle of the room and four others hold the corners. When those in the corners switch places, the player in the middle tries to capture one of the empty spots. Her mention of this game is so matter-of-fact that Lady Llanover doesn't bother to delete it (2:334). Burney, on the other hand, was embarrassed when the king caught her at the same sport. Delany's rambunctiousness was not, of course, a sufficient outlet for her abilities. Pursuing her other halted desires was more difficult. She could not easily practice her artistic crafts. During her marriage, at the age of forty-five, she called her work "amusements" and stressed that D.D.'s encouragement was necessary to keep her at her task. "*Eager* as I am," she wrote to her sister, "in all my pursuits I am *easily checked,* and the least disapprobation or snap, from the person I wish to oblige, in thought, word, or deed, would soon give me a distaste to what was delightful to me before!" (2:395). Later, as a widow, without obliging anyone in particular, she perfected her technique of cutting colored paper into the shapes of flowers, and these flowers are now recognized as extraordinary. Only at the end of her life, unmarried, was she able to create art for a more nearly public purpose.

Yet even when married to Pendarves, Delany successfully mediated between the claims of obliging others and pleasing herself, between duty and desire. She escaped from the forced passivity marriage required partly by self-dramatization. She always moved easily in and out of fiction, and though this was not unusual for the early eighteenth century, it was more pronounced in Delany than most. This habit disturbed Lady Llanover. The scene in Burney's diary Lady Llanover disapproved of, the one full of "pert and vulgar dialogue," depicts Delany, Hester Chapone, and the duchess of Portland playfully referring to Burney's characters as if they were real. Delany, aged eighty-two, her eyesight failing, "archly" eggs on the duchess, who launches into praise of *Cecilia,* and the two of them very nearly reenact their disagreement over the character of Mrs. Delvile, whose firmness Delany admires, and whose fierceness the duchess hates (255). Delany could dramatize her life, and laugh at it, chiefly because she valued herself. George Ballard, who—with her reluctant permission—dedicated to her the second half of his *Memoirs of Several Ladies of Great Britain,* described her in terms similar to Burke's, but with a more clearly gendered application, as befitted the context: "To Mrs. Delany the truest judge and brightest pattern of all the accomplishments which adorn her sex."[45] Delany was the pattern, but she was also the judge, the passive recipient and the active discriminator, the woman who carefully defined the elements she most disliked about the married state and then avoided them as best she could. The strength, the humor, the energy, the self-dramatization, and the articulate defining of life's possibilities that had enabled Delany to choose D.D. and to live as his equal, empowered her to seize life as fully as a woman could in the incarcerating institution of marriage—both times. Born with the century, she is definitively not the Victorian woman we have met in Lady Llanover's delicately bowdlerized version of her autobiography and correspondence. We have always known that Delany was clear-eyed and blunt. Now we know that this model eighteenth-century woman was much less inhibited than we had thought. She did not want to be praised, and she did not want to be published, but she spoke frankly about the body, writing myriad phrases that in 1862 were considered not fit for publication.

Notes

1. See Thomas Laqueur, *Making Sex: Body and Gender from the Greeks to Freud* (Cambridge, Mass.: Harvard University Press, 1990). Laqueur shows clearly that early pictures of women's sexual organs, drawings by Vesalius and others, depict the uterus as an inverted penis (78ff.), and that "sometime in the eighteenth century, sex as we know it was invented. The reproductive organs went from being paradigmatic sites for displaying hierarchy, resonant throughout the cosmos, to being the foundation of incommensurable difference: 'women owe their manner of being to their organs of generation, and especially to the uterus,' as one eighteenth-century physician put it" (149).

2. This quotation appears in Lady Augusta Llanover, *The Autobiography and Correspondence of Mary Granville, Mrs. Delany*, 6 vols. (London: Richard Bentley, 1861–62), 5:12. Edmund Burke's statement comes to us on slightly tenuous evidence. Samuel Johnson conveyed it to someone at the home of Delany's niece, who wrote it down. Three copies survive, jotted down on separate scraps of paper in a notebook. It seems doubtful that anyone would have made it up (three times) out of whole cloth; the full statement is several sentences, and it certainly rings true. Historians who have taken Delany as a

model include Randolph Trumbach, for instance, who uses Burke's summation of Delany as his frontispiece and touchstone in *The Rise of the Egalitarian Family* (New York: Academic Press, 1978). Besides Lady Llanover, a number of people have written biographies of Delany, relying heavily on her edition of the autobiography and letters. These include: George Paston [E. M. Symonds], *Mrs. Delany* (London: Grant Richards, 1900), a useful, unromantic, and fairly accurate summary that includes some material Lady Llanover omitted; R. Brimley Johnson, *Mrs. Delany at Court and Among the Wits* (London: Stanley Paul, 1926), chiefly "arranged" from Lady Llanover, with an introduction (this book is full of inaccuracies, but interesting; Johnson also claims to have introduced if not new material at least new spelling, the lady's own); Simon Dewes [J. S. C. Muriel], *Mrs. Delany* (London: Rich and Cowan, 1940), a popularized account; "The Artist," in Alice Anderson Hufstader, *Sisters of the Quill* (New York: Dodd, Mead, 1978), 142–95, a brief, unfootnoted, but well-researched account; Ruth Hayden, *Mrs Delany: Her Life and Her Flowers* (London: British Museum Publications, 1980), marvelously illustrated with pictures of the cut flowers. Lady Llanover's edition is the source for all unattributed parenthetical quotations in the text. Some of the manuscripts that Lady Llanover used are now in the Newport (Gwent) Central Library; they are scattered throughout her career, so that listing them here is impracticable. Unfortunately, the autobiography is not among them. The Newport collection is the source for all unattributed manuscript references in the text and in the notes. I wish to thank Mrs. B. Strong and her assistants for their help while I was examining the manuscripts, and the National Endowment for the Humanities for the grant that enabled me to travel to Wales.

3. *Diary and Letters of Madame D'Arblay*, ed. Charlotte Barrett (London: Henry Coburn, 1842), 2:249–58; Llanover, *Autobiography*, 6:127–28.

4. John R. Gillis, *For Better, for Worse: British Marriages, 1600 to the Present* (Oxford: Oxford University Press, 1985), 110.

5. Janelle Greenberg, "The Legal Status of the English Woman in Early Eighteenth-Century Common Law and Equity," *Studies in Eighteenth-Century Culture* 4, ed. Harold E. Pagliaro (Madison: University of Wisconsin Press, 1975), 172–73.

6. Samuel Johnson, *Lives of the English Poets*, 3 vols., ed. George Birkbeck Hill (Oxford: Clarendon Press, 1945), 2:291.

7. This detail does not appear in the narrative; it may be a later embroidering. According to a footnote, Delany told this story to Lady Llanover's mother (1:107, n. 2).

8. Lady Llanover includes material indicating that Lord Tyrconnel was among these; but she omits material that shows that he almost certainly was not.

9. The *Dictionary of National Biography* dates Dr. Delany's birth at 1685 or 1686.

10. Jonathan Swift, *Correspondence,* ed. Harold Williams, 5 vols. (Oxford: Oxford University Press, 1963–65), 4:77 and n. 2.

11. Paston (alias Symonds), 73, February 6, 1732.

12. MS. f. 9, February 8, 1735.

13. For a complex treatment of this subject, see Susan Staves, "Separate Maintenance Contracts," *Eighteenth-Century Life* 11, no. 2 (May 1987): 78–102, and her book *Married Women's Separate Property in England, 1660–1833* (Cambridge: Harvard University Press, 1990).

14. Delany, as socially constructed in her period, continually reflects the psychology of women described by Carol Gilligan: "The psychology of women that has consistently been described as distinctive in its greater orientation toward relationships and interdependence implies a more contextual mode of judgment and a different moral understanding." *In a Different Voice* (Cambridge, Mass.: Harvard University Press, 1982), 22.

15. "An Epistle to Dr. *Arbuthnot,*" line 135, in *The Twickenham Edition of the Poems of Alexander Pope,* ed. John Butt, 6 vols. (New Haven: Yale University Press, 1939) 4:105.

16. Susan Staves, "Where Is History but in Texts? Reading the History of Marriage," in *The Golden and the Brazen World,* ed. John M. Wallace (Berkeley and Los Angeles: University of California Press, 1985), 130. Staves shows in detail in a number of instances that: "Not only were there different attitudes toward marriage in different classes or social circles—among the Methodists or the rakes—but the same people were perfectly capable of taking one attitude or tone in one social circumstance and another in another social circumstance" (132).

17. Lord Lansdowne, *Poems Upon Several Occasions* (London: J. Tonson, 1712), 112–14.

18. *The Ladies Calling in two parts. By the author of the Whole Duty of Man, &c, the Tenth Impression,* attributed to Richard Allestree (Oxford: Printed at the Theater, 1717).

19. *Spectator,* ed. Donald F. Bond, 5 vols. (Oxford: Clarendon Press, 1965), 1:46–47.

20. Lawrence Stone, *The Family, Sex, and Marriage* (New York: Harper and Row, 1977), 313.

21. Alan Macfarlane, *Marriage and Love in England: Modes of Reproduction, 1300–1840* (Oxford: Blackwell, 1986), 126.

22. Felicity Nussbaum, *The Autobiographical Subject: Gender and Ideology in Eighteenth-Century England* (Baltimore: Johns Hopkins University Press, 1989), 179.

23. Regarding the dangers and ultimate bodily effects of childbirth in

the eighteenth century, see Ruth Perry, "The Veil of Chastity: Mary Astell's Feminism," in *Sexuality in Eighteenth-Century Britain,* ed. Paul-Gabriel Boucé (Manchester: Manchester University Press, 1982), 145–52. Perry shows that a woman who had six children "had at least a ten per cent chance of dying" (148).

24. Stella was Delany's name for Melusina de Schulemberg, countess of Walsingham, an illegitimate daughter of George I who in 1733 married the earl of Chesterfield.

25. Walter Jackson Bate, *Samuel Johnson* (New York: Harcourt, 1977), 166.

26. James Boswell, *The Life of Johnson,* ed. George Birkbeck Hill, rev. and enlarged by L. F. Powell, 6 vols. (Oxford: Clarendon Press, 1934–50), 1:106.

27. *The Ladies Calling,* 63.

28. See Lennard Davis, *Factual Fictions* (New York: Columbia University Press, 1983).

29. Henry Fielding, *Love in Several Masques* (London: John Watts, 1728), 4.4, 54.

30. Staves, "Texts," 141.

31. Mary Pendarves to Jonathan Swift, September 2, 1736, British Library Additional MS. 4806:166.

32. Samuel Richardson, *Clarissa* (1747–48; reprint, London: Everyman, 1932) 1:32, 33.

33. Richardson's biographers mention the similarities between the Pendarves story and Clarissa's, and also note that Lord Baltimore's insulting proposal to Delany is comparable to Lovelace's to Clarissa. They do not assume influence either way. T. Duncan Eaves and Ben D. Kimpel, *Samuel Richardson* (Oxford: Clarendon Press, 1971), 174.

34. Stone, *The Family, Sex, and Marriage,* 313.

35. Stone, *The Family, Sex, and Marriage,* 312.

36. MS. f1; this letter of December 12, 1724, concerning the wedding of Lady Sunderland and Sir Robert Sutton, was wholly omitted by Lady Llanover.

37. The frame of the story is, as Melinda Rabb has pointed out, "the voice of a male narrator, and in other ways seems to subscribe to male authority over language." "Making and Rethinking the Canon: General Introduction and the Case of *Millenium Hall,*" *Modern Language Studies,* 18, no. 1 (Winter 1988): 12.

38. Sarah Scott, *A Description of Millenium Hall* (1762; reprint, New York: Penguin, 1986), 55. I would like to thank Betty Rizzo for pointing out this parallel.

39. "This letter . . . clearly indicates that Lord Lansdowne was not altogether easy or happy at the match he had insisted upon, and at the same time he is careful to remind Mr. Pendarves that the family interest of his wife is of no small importance to him" (Llanover, *Autobiography,* 1:42).

40. The names of the characters in *Millenium Hall* are perhaps the most

striking instance of Scott's tendency toward blandness. A plethora of names begins with "M." Besides Mrs. Morgan, and Miss Melvyn, there is Mrs. Maynard, and Miss Mancel. To confuse matters further there is also a Miss Selvyn. This seems like such a clear reflection of Melvyn that one longs to assume that this look-alike and mirror naming serves a purpose. Perhaps Scott intended to emphasize that women share qualities and experiences, that these individual women taken together represent Woman. Many of the names contain the letters M-A-N. But the effect, even if one can find an argument to support this practice, is at best confusing and at worst deadening. Delany's wider reference extends her experience into history and myth. One longs for the likes of Gromio and Fulvia.

41. Swift, *Correspondence,* ed. Williams, 4:91.

42. MS. f2, November 12, 1742; Lady Llanover's version of the letter is on 2:198.

43. J. S. C. Muriel (alias Dewes), *Mrs. Delany,* 62.

44. Nearly every letter commenced with a full page of loving salutation; Lady Llanover may have cut this material simply to save room, since her project was already running to six hefty volumes. This affectionate language reached a crescendo during the first trip to Ireland, when Delany had lost Lord Baltimore and was feeling particularly bereft. She claimed that no one could love her sister better than she: "I fancy my heart was form'd to Love yo better than all the world beside" (MS. f1, June 21, 1732).

45. George Ballard, *Memoirs of Several Ladies of Great Britain Who Have Been Celebrated for Their Writings or Skill in the Learned Languages, Arts and Sciences,* ed. Ruth Perry (1752; reprint, Detroit: Wayne State University Press, 1985), 235. Sarah Chapone, Delany's old friend "Sappho," objected to the phrasing of "adorn her sex," saying that it made an intellectual woman sound like a bride. Delany herself was somewhat unnerved at having to undergo this public adulation, but D.D. convinced her to do it.

A Night at the Opera: The Body, Class, and Art in *Evelina* and Frances Burney's *Early Diaries*

𝕊𝕃𝕊 *Beth Kowaleski-Wallace*

In volume 1 of Frances Burney's *Evelina*,[1] among the many social "tortures" to which the heroine is subjected is a trip to the opera in the company of her underdressed and overbearing relations, the Branghtons. From the beginning, the outing is a nightmare, for—unlike Evelina—the Branghtons know nothing of the proper behavior associated with a night at the opera. Evelina's mortification begins with her relations' ignorance of the proper door through which to enter; wandering about in a dress "so different from that of the company" that attends her, she finds herself attracting "general notice and observation." Discovery of the proper door only elicits an embarrassing outburst from Mr. Branghton, who quarrels loudly about the exorbitant price of admission. After much discussion of the expense, the party enters and climbs to the gallery, where the relations express their disappointment with their surroundings and persist in comparing English and Italian theaters. Although Evelina is soon ready to let herself be swept away by the signing of Signor Millico—in real life, a famous castrato, whom Burney herself admired—her concentration is constantly interrupted by the inane and persistent chatter of her relations. When at last, despite the distracting behavior of her cousins, Evelina succumbs to the pleasures of the music, she is ridiculed for what is perceived as a pretension on her part. Her own pleasure in the music is nearly ruined by the comments of Mr. Branghton, who declares "they've caught me once, but if ever they do again, I'll give 'em leave to sing me to Bedlam for my pains: for such a heap of stuff never did I hear; there isn't one ounce of sense in the whole Opera, nothing but one continued squeaking and squalling from beginning to end" (*Evelina*, 89–93).

I will argue that this scene warrants our attention for an important reason: here Evelina's utter horror—indeed her total mortification in response to her cousins' behavior—translates as a nearly phobic representation of what it means to be threatened by the very social forces against which one has struggled to define oneself. That Evelina's behavior *is* phobic is not immediately apparent, because the scene is constructed in such a way as to obliterate any alternative viewpoint: because of the epistolary form, we *must* read the scene exclusively through the eyes of the beleaguered heroine. Evelina's extreme embarrassment, her pain, becomes the reader's pain. Implicitly as well, her struggle to differentiate herself from her cousins, and to protect herself against their obtrusive behavior, becomes the reader's struggle. In this scene, Evelina takes her self-definition in relationship to what she is not, and the reader is positioned to participate in that act of self-definition. Yet this missing alterity, this militant defense against any other perspective on the Branghtons, or on the proper behavior associated with the opera, is one of the clearest signs of an ideology at work.[2]

In *Evelina,* the image of the beleaguered protagonist, leaning forward enrapt by a song both "slow and pathetic," temporarily oblivious to the ridicule of her companions, suggests a portrait of the artist herself; one need not search far in Burney's biography to find evidence of her own deep and passionate attachment to the opera and of her own occasional defensiveness about the art in the presence of skeptics. For Burney as for her heroine, the opera was a symbolic space in which anxieties about the public display of the body were foregrounded and potentially resolved. Burney's novel presents the opera as the "natural" location for an elevated consciousness, which leaves behind the body, to express itself. But Burney's early diaries lay the groundwork for this presentation. That is, they establish how, in the moment of operatic performance, the physical becomes sublimated in favor of a transcendent "voice."

As my summary from *Evelina* is meant to suggest, however, class is also a factor in the construction of this symbolic space. For the insistence on a refined and elite public sphere, which is the proper setting of opera as performance and art, means simultaneously the sublimation of the body and the identification of those (like the Branghtons) who, through ignorance or will, insist on "living the body" differently. As Peter Stallybrass and Allon White have shown us, to the extent that those who "live the body" differently are almost always of another class, the construction of the symbolic space necessarily entails class opposition.[3]

Thus, to examine the opera scene in *Evelina* is to consider how Burney's novel, offered as "The History of a Young Lady's Entrance into the World," gives rise to unstated ideological tensions. In pursuing the meaning of this scene, I am extending work done by feminist critics such as Mary Poovey or Nancy Armstrong.[4] These critics suggest how we might consider "the rise of the domestic woman," who is embodied in Evelina, in relation to late eighteenth-century class politics. They argue that the eighteenth-century novel offers us not just a mimetic representation of a historical, eighteenth-century female "experience" but a vibrant, multivalent textuality, which can be understood against a backdrop of social and political forces. What matters about a novel like *Evelina* is not just the "reality" it reflects, but the social process it encodes.

More recently, in an essay entitled "Evelina and the Problem of the Female Grotesque," Heidi Hutner examines how Burney "utilizes a discourse of bodily repression to promote Evelina's fairy-tale ascent."[5] Refuting the idea that Evelina is both "separate from and invested in the patriarchal discourse of the novel," Hutner remarks that "Evelina's supposed simultaneous disdain for and interest in the trivial pursuits of the public world and 'conventional modes of female employment' are precisely what make her a proper domestic woman" (192). Central to Hutner's analysis is the figure of Evelina's grandmother, Madame Duval, who serves as a warning of what Evelina must avoid becoming— "the lower class, self-assertive, loud-mouthed woman" (202).

Like Hutner, I also see Evelina as engaged in a politics of self-definition by negation, and I suggest that the social dynamic which Hutner describes is especially pronounced in the opera scene. During the eighteenth century, the opera was a highly disputed form of entertainment with a contentious history for writers from Addison to Pope, Smollett to Dr. Johnson.[6] In Burney's own work, the opera is a recurring image, one to which she returns often and one which is central to the problem of self-definition for both Burney and her heroines. Elsewhere I have written about the likely grounds for projection and identification between Burney and the castrato, whose presence was central to the eighteenth-century opera.[7] In this essay, I am interested in reading the opera scene from *Evelina* against a series of passages taken from Burney's *Early Diary*.[8] In these passages, certainly among the most colorful of the opera anecdotes, Burney describes the visits of the "celebrated Signora Agujari," "detta la *Bastardini* from some misfortune that preceded her birth, but of which none is so innocent as herself" (*Early Diary*, 2:1–2).

First, the Agujari anecdotes show us how Burney was able to deal with the display of one particularly flagrant body through a series of transformations. Second, the opera scene from *Evelina* demonstrates how, despite the successful sublimation of the body in operatic performance, another representation of the body continues to assert itself in the opera audience. For important reasons, that audience is also configured as Evelina's *family*, and the family become the backdrop against which Evelina will assert her class-bound identity.

In 1775 Agujari paid a much-anticipated call on the Burney household. Burney records her first impression: "She is of the middle stature, and has the misfortune to be lame; owing perhaps if there is any truth in the story to her being mauled when an infant by a pig, in consequence of which she is reported to have a silver side" (*Early Diary*, 2:2). Introduced first through a story about her body, Agujari is presented as something of a freak, a woman whose physical appearance already signals a sordid and bizarre (if fascinating) history, one that certainly places her life story outside the parameters of a "lady's" life. That her lameness is reputed to have been caused by a pig is highly suggestive, for this offhanded reference to the pig introduces an image of what Peter Stallybrass and Allon White call the "low grotesque" into Burney's narrative. The effect of such a remark is to call attention to the singer's perilous proximity, on a physical level, to a world of dirt, disorder, chaos, and clamor. The reference to the pig, in other words, foregrounds the class difference that distinguishes the opera singer from Dr. Burney's daughter.[9]

Yet Agujari flaunts her weird physicality, bringing it to the fore in a series of self-aggrandizing gestures designed to bring attention back to her body—and implicitly as well, back to her class. She is, according to Burney, "immensely proud," and although civil, "her excessive *vanity* [is] perpetually self betrayed," and Burney substantiates this judgment with several examples. Asked about her rival, la Gabriella, Agujari confesses never to have heard her, for she solemnly believes that the two singers "could never be in the same place together" or, as a guest explains, "Two suns are never seen at once" (*Early Diary, 2:3*). Moreover, she tells Dr. Burney that she always leaves the room when she finishes her own song. Burney comments, "How conceitedly incurious! But she chuses to make it known, that no singing can please her but *own*" (*Early Diary, 2:4*). This narcissistic refusal to demonstrate humility is consistent with Agujari's implicit insistence that all regard *her* and her alone. Furthermore, Burney is amused by the prima donna's theatrical mannerisms, mannerisms that once again bring the singer's body into view. A question about whether the Burneys had ever attended the Pantheon is accompanied by a series of melodramatic gestures. When she discovers they have not, Agujari lifts up her hands and eyes, "doubtless concluding [the Burneys] to the highest degree barbarous and Gothic, not to have flown on the wings of—*half Guineas*—to see and hear this Wonder of the World" (*Early Diary, 2:3*).

Theatrical in her self-presentation, Agujari also fails to be discreet about her private affairs. Burney's sister Susan is temporarily thrown off guard when she discovers that Agujari's "companion," one Signor Colla, "to whom she is reported to be married," is not her husband at all.[10] Thus a touch of raciness attaches itself to this celebrated singer. The illegitimacy that attends the circumstances of her birth extends into her personal life, and the description of Agujari's visit introduces the theme of the illicitly lived body. In other words, everything about Agujari's self-presentation signals an excessive physicality, a life-style dictated by the appetites of the body. Her first appearance makes her resemble Madame Duval more than Evelina: somewhat vulgar, even crude, loud, and narcissistic, Agujari is not socially equal to the Burneys.

Indeed, Frances Burney's tolerance of Agujari's moral "eccentricities" is all the more remarkable when we remember, in contrast, her extreme reluctance to sit in an opera box with the author Mrs. Brooke because Mrs. Yates—a celebrated actress—was already seated there (*Early Diary, 1:329*).[11] Yet Burney makes allowances for Agujari because of the tremendously affective power of her singing. If the circumstances of the prima donna's life-style are beyond the pale of the "acceptable," all can be forgotten in the pleasure of her song. As we shall see, Agujari's body becomes sublimated in the space of operatic performance. Because of this sublimation, class differences between the performer and her audience are temporarily negated as well.

On June 10 Burney writes to Samuel Crisp about a private performance given by Agujari for the benefit of the Burney household.
Insisting that this singer could be compared to nothing, Burney writes
of Agujari's astonishing "compass": "reaching from C in the middle of
the Harpsicord, to two notes *above* the Harpsicord! Every tone so clear,
so full, so charming!" (*Early Journals,* 1:154). Thus her voice is literally
transcendent, as the singer is capable of making sounds beyond the reach
of Dr. Burney's instrument. Moreover, Agujari's voice demonstrates
incredible flexibility and variety, qualities that also suggest Agujari's
transcendence of her physical limitations: "Besides it's [sic] great power,
her voice is all sweetness, & when she pleases, all softness and delicacy.
She sings in the highest style of Taste, & with an *Expression* so pathetic,
it is impossible to hear it unmoved" (*Early Journals,* 2:154). Feminine
traits that seemed lacking in Agujari's public presentation—softness,
delicacy, taste, the ability subtly to affect her audience—surface in her
singing, and the same theatricality that earlier seemed overblown in the
Burneys' drawing room greatly enhances her singing as "she sung in
twenty different styles":

> The greatest was son Regina & sono amante from Didone. Good God!
> what a song! & how sung! Then she gave us two or three *Cantibles,* sung
> divinely, then she chanted some *Church Music,* in a style so nobly simple
> & unadorned, that it stole into one's very soul! Then she gave us a Bra-
> vura, with difficulties which seemed only possible for an Instrument in
> the hands of a great master—Then she spoke some Recitative, so nobly!
> In short, whether she most astonished, or most delighted us, I cannot
> say, but she is really a *sublime* singer! (*Early Journals,* 2:155)

What is "sublime" is literally lofty or elevated; in its origins the word
carries with it the sense of something having been "refined," rendered
finer as in purity or essence. Thus Agujari's singing simultaneously elevates her, placing her above the body, and "purifies" her of the body
that seemed so intrusive in her initial introduction. Burney's description
of a subsequent visit reinforces the idea of the singer's transcendence.
Singing an "Arria parlante," Agujari "began with a fullness and power of
voice, that astonished us beyond all our possible expectations. She then
lowered it to the most expressive softness; in short she was *sublime:* I
can use no other word, without degrading her" (*Early Diary,* 2:81–82).
Burney's insistence on the word "sublime" testifies to the perception of a

transformation that has rendered Agujari's body innocuous. To Burney's mind, the sublimity of Agujari's singing allows for the transcendence of her body, as art elevates the singer above any trace of physicality; her body is thus *sublimated* in the moment of her operatic performance.

Burney goes on to compare Agujari to "her darling Millico," the very performer whom Evelina admires in the opera scene in the novel: "His *sensibility* in singing seemed more unaffectedly genuine and *touchant* than any other human being's I have heard." In contrast, Agujari has vocal *talents:* "She began *Son Regina,* with a dignity I scarce had an idea of, and then proceeded to *e son amante,* in a tone of voice so sweetly pathetic, so softly clear, that it almost melted us to tears to hear it; then when she grew more animated,—never was expression more impassioned" (*Early Diary,* 2:82). Thus, though presumably less "genuine" and more "affected" than Millico's, Agujari's power is of a different order, for her singing gives testimony to the transformative power of art. The effect is captivating, as the Burneys find themselves transfixed, transported to new regions of emotion. If, as a female visitor, Agujari engages in certain forms of behavior Burney finds vaguely distasteful—for example, the brazen disregard of social convention or the flagrant display of a theatrical bent—these same behaviors cease to matter at the moment of performance. Agujari's eccentricities are no longer the sign of manipulativeness but of a superior sensibility, of Agujari's rare and refined ability to move her audience to another realm of experience.

Not surprisingly, according to Burney, Agujari is a *"slave* to her voice": "she fears the least Breath of air—she is equally apprehensive of Any heat—she seems to have a perpetual anxiety lest she should take Cold; & I do believe that she niether [sic] Eats, Drinks, sleeps, or Talks, without considering in what manner she may perform those vulgar duties of Life, so as to be most beneficial to her Voice." Yet Burney hastens to defend this sort of obsessive behavior: "However, there are so few who are gifted with eminent Talents, that it is better to cultivate them, even labouriously, than to let them suffer Injury from Carelessness or Neglect" (*Early Journals,* 2:78). This kind of explanation foregrounds the synecdochical connection between the singer and her voice: after all, Agujari *is* her voice. To be a "voice"—as opposed to a "mouth," for instance—is to surpass the body, for the voice is no longer a bodily part but an instrument, the medium of the singer's art. In contrast, the "mouth" is an orifice traditionally located in relation to the grotesque body. But Burney's observations insist precisely upon the "voice" as the appropriate trope for the singer.

Thus, while the physical portrait of Agujari introduces a touch of the illicit, sordid, and low grotesque, the description of Agujari's singing erases all hints of illegitimacy and transforms "la Bastardini"—literally the illegitimate child—into something far more spiritual. But it is also important to recognize that the physical portrait carried with it the marks of class: initially Agujari did not belong to the same social circle as the Burneys because she "lived her body" in a radically different fashion from that followed by the Burneys. Her association with "Signor Colla," for instance, or the crude display of her weird physicality were the indicators that she belonged to a different social order. In the eye of the audience, however, operatic performance sublimates Agujari's body. Moreover, to the extent that the body is what designates her as a member of a particular class, operatic performance also negates important class differences (differences that were once imaged in her affiliation with the pig) and makes possible her acceptance in "respectable" households such as the Burneys'.

When we pair Burney's journal entries with the opera scene from *Evelina,* an immediate contrast arises: whereas, in Burney's journals, the moment of operatic performance sublimates the body, making obvious class differences between the performer and the audience disappear, the scene in the novel brings another "body" back into view, exacerbating class tensions in the process. Here, of course, that "body" no longer displays itself on the stage but in *the audience,* in perilous proximity to the protagonist who finds herself sitting next to it: that "body" is represented by the foregrounded physicality of the Branghtons.

For it could be argued that part of what mortifies Evelina about her relations is the fact that their bodies are simply too much in evidence. Loud, improperly dressed, and "ill-behaved," the Branghtons display ignorance about what to do with their bodies in a refined public place like the opera house. Making too much noise, from Evelina's vantage point, they are also too visible, too present. The clamor that issues from their bodies is the opposite of the transcendent song that issues from the opera singer's sublime voice. Thus they seem to image a displaced physicality, a metaphorical "body" associated with a class lower than Evelina herself. The spectacle they make of themselves eclipses the spectacle on the stage, while their mannerisms, their chatter, their obtrusive behavior, all betray them as members of a class not educated in the ways of the elite connoisseur. In contrast, Evelina knows how to behave and she also physically deports herself appropriately to her elegant surroundings. In the absence of her cousins' outlandish behavior, she would blend anonymously into the refined crowd and she would let the music overtake her. Indeed, she would be allowed temporarily to forget that she has a body at all. She would be swept along, through the medium of the castrato song, to a world where bodies cease to matter. She would, in short, arrive at the very place where Burney found herself while listening to Agujari's private performance.

What then are we to make of this contrast? What do these two representations of the body—one sublimated at the moment of operatic performance, the other painfully present as an inappropriately public display in the audience—have to do with each other? To answer this question, we might begin by thinking about what in particular so mortifies Evelina about the Branghtons. Their very existence comes as something of a surprise to her: Madame Duval, Evelina's crass and overbearing maternal grandmother, forces these relations upon her at a time when Evelina would prefer to be in the company of her dear friend Mrs. Mirvan.

Evelina registers her initial impression of Mr. Branghton, who "keeps a silversmith shop." To her guardian she confides that her new relation is not wanting in "a common understanding, though he is very contracted and prejudiced" (68). Evelina's obvious feelings of superiority do not prepare her for what follows: the new relations condescend to *her* as a pitiful social outcast. Riveted by the tragic tale of Evelina's mother (whose husband refused to recognize their marriage), the Branghtons openly stare at Madame Duval's unfortunate granddaughter, while Madame Duval entertains them "with all the most secret and cruel particulars of [her] situation!" (69). Mr. Branghton's daughters are especially fascinated by the fact that Evelina *has never seen her father.*

Anyone who has ever read the novel knows that this point—the refusal of Evelina's father to recognize her existence—is the single most important fact of Evelina's life. It is a source of great anguish to her, anguish that is only barely resolved by the dramatic confrontation scene that occurs in volume 3. Critics often write that, without her father's acknowledgment, Evelina symbolically lacks both her patrimony and her proper identity. Without the benefit of her patrilineage, Evelina is, as Margaret Doody succinctly writes, "unfathered and unauthorized." [12] So, when the cousins confront Evelina with the curious fact that she has no father, they manage to touch upon Evelina's most sensitive point, the point that proves unbearable. Evelina runs from the room, later reflecting upon how extraordinary it is that Madame Duval "can put [her] in situations so shocking, and then wonder to find [her] so sensible of any concern" (70). Far from being a suitable mother-figure, Madame Duval is Evelina's tormentor: she finds the very spots where her granddaughter is most vulnerable and exposes her every time.

The opera scene follows out of this first, mortifying encounter. Though her relations begin planning the trip to the opera immediately, Evelina has no plans to accompany them. The Branghton girls simply appear as she is in the process of dressing in order to attend Mrs. Mirvan. When they cannot convince Evelina to go with them, Madame Duval blows in an explosive rage and insists that Evelina come with her. Under a volley of abusive language, and in the presence of Sir Clement Willoughby, Evelina is dragged off. So Evelina's appearance at the opera is framed by a series of painful encounters with a group of people who are, in every way, determined to claim her for themselves.

In forcibly dragging Evelina to the opera with the Branghtons, Madame Duval insists that Evelina belongs to *her.* The subtext of her coercive behavior is that Evelina has no real control over who she is: she is powerless to assert herself or to make the claim that she belongs elsewhere. Indeed, her chief fear at the opera is that Sir Clement Willoughby will recognize some connection between her and the Branghtons; she dreads that he might hear Miss Branghton call her "cousin." To her guardian she explains, "I fear you will think this London journey has made me grow very proud, but indeed this family is so low-bred and vulgar, that I should be equally ashamed of such a connexion in the country, or any where" (94).

If Evelina's condition is to be "fatherless and unauthorized," then the nature of the menace that the Branghtons represent is clear: as her relations, they are "relative to" her. While she wants publicly to claim they have "nothing to do with her," in reality they are (at this point in the novel) the only true family "connexions" she has. Paradoxically, they have everything to do with her, as they tie her back to her matrilineage.

Thus their presence is so disturbing because they threaten to undo her fragile fiction of herself, namely the fiction that she is *her father's* daughter. They disturb her delicate attempt to "authorize" herself in a world that does not recognize her as such. Moreover, they shadow her with a particularly physical image, with an insistent reminder that only a series of behaviors, manners, and attitudes distinguishes the Branghtons from the daughter of Sir John Belmont. In sum, the opera scene resonates with tensions that prove the crux of Evelina's painful dilemma: how can she establish herself socially in the absence of an "authorizing" figure? Who *is* "Evelina—"? How can she make the world receive her as she would like to be received?

The opera setting is especially appropriate because so much of Evelina's struggle depends upon her presentation of her body as a cypher to be encoded and interpreted in a particular fashion: where better to dramatize the problem of self-presentation than at the opera? By the latter part of the eighteenth century, the opera house had become one of those places that consolidated class interests by allowing for the public display of a series of recognizable class behaviors. Referring to those behaviors, Burney's novel implicates itself in an ideological struggle that is central to the construction of the heroine's class-bound identity. During the eighteenth century the opera house was one of the "new cities of assembly," which, as Stallybrass and White explain, were being regulated "according to manners and norms more significantly different from those places they were displacing," [13] namely, large public assemblies such as the fair. The opera is thus a symbolic space, and what Stallybrass and White write of the theater applies equally well here: "[W]hat is new, and contrasts strongly with the Shakespearean stage, is the urgent attempt to expel the lower sort altogether from the scene of reception, to homogenize the audience by refining and domesticating its energy, sublimating its diverse physical pleasures into a purely contemplative force, replacing a dispersed, heterodox, noisy participation in the *event* of the theater by silent specular intensity." [14]

The point is that *Evelina* obscures the history of how proper behavior at the opera evolved, as it must in order to assure the heroine's ascendancy. Burney's novel works to convey the idea that Evelina's behavior is "naturally" called for by the elegant setting, and Burney shows that Evelina's refined sensibility "naturally" finds itself at ease in the opera house. Her "natural" behavior becomes the inevitable sign of her superior class. But there was little that was "natural" in the scene framing Burney's heroine. First, Evelina's intense response to the highly artificial music of a real-life castrato signals not a "natural" sensibility but a historically specific and culturally attuned taste, one that many of Burney's own contemporaries did not share. Second, Evelina's behavior is also culturally and historically specific to its moment. Even a brief consideration of the history of the opera suggests that eighteenth-century audiences responded to the operatic spectacle in a number of different ways. In recapitulating these details, I do not mean to represent exhaustively a social history of the opera, but rather to suggest that, over the course of the eighteenth century, as the opera spectacle moved from Italy to England, "proper" behavior in the audience had to develop and be codified as such.

In the earlier part of the century, we find Addison, for example, complaining about the wrong sets to be found at "the Opera, the Play, the Waterworks, and other publick Meetings, where their whole Business is to draw off the Attention of the Spectators from the Entertainment and to fix it upon themselves." That he classes the opera together with the play and the waterworks surely indicates his belief that all three could be classed equally as "public spectacles." But his subsequent remark is especially revealing about the activity level of the audience to be found at such amusements: "I am at a Loss to know from whom People of Fortune should learn this Behaviour, unless it be from the Footmen who keep their places at new Play, and are often seen passing away their Time in Sets at *All-fours* [a card game] in the Face of a full house, and with a perfect Disregard to People of Quality sitting on each Side of them." [15]

Writing specifically of the "opera seria" (and not the "opera comique," where one might expect a certain amount of high spirits in the audience), one historian of the opera in Italy states "Contemporary audiences, far from regarding the opera as a serious dramatic spectacle, looked upon it merely as an amusement":

> De Brosses reports that performances in Rome began at eight or nine in the evening and lasted to midnight. Everyone of any consequence had a box, which was a social gathering place for friends. "The pleasure these people take in music and the theatre is more evidenced by presence than by the attentions they bestow on the performance." After the first few times, no one listened at all, except to a few favorite songs. The boxes

were comfortably furnished and lighted so that their occupants could indulge in cards and other games. "Chess is marvelously well adapted to the monotony of the recitatives, and the arias are especially good for interrupting a too assiduous concentration on chess."

The historian also cites Dr. Burney, who "mentions faro tables at the Milan opera; at Venice, where the pit was usually filled with gondoliers and workmen, 'there is a constant noise of people laughing, drinking, and joking, while sellers of baked goods and fruit cry their wares aloud from box to box'; at Florence it was the custom to serve hot suppers in the boxes during the performance." [16] Of course, these accounts refer to a different time and place, and they do not reflect upon English custom. Still, it is interesting to try to imagine the steps leading from the scene described by De Brosses or Dr. Burney to the setting described by Frances Burney: what changes in attitude toward the opera must have occurred in the interim, in the time during which Italian opera made itself an integral part of English culture, and how did the public consensus come to settle on the "decorous" and "refined" behavior we still associate with opera attendance today? [17] Anyone who enjoys opera may want to defend established social practices as most conducive for the reception of the music: and indeed a well-behaved audience does facilitate certain kinds of listening pleasures. What is at stake here is not that pleasure but the way in which Burney's novel invites us to be attentive to the ideological underpinnings of the history of the audience behavior at the opera.

Looking at the opera scene in isolation, then, allows us to see more clearly the nature of the tension between Evelina and her relatives. In refusing to succumb to the charms of the opera, the Branghtons jeopardize Evelina's efforts at self-creation. They do so by offering an image of resistance to the self-disciplined, bodily practices and behaviors that are crucial to Evelina's project of defining herself as a new domestic woman. Their bad behavior threatens her with an image of *what she must not be,* but also with an image of *what she could easily be.* In other words, this scene functions in a similar way to the scene in book 2, where Evelina views her trussed-up grandmother in a ditch. Dirtied, disgraced, the object of a cruel practical joke, Madame Duval is, as Hutner points out, an image of the female grotesque. [18] In both the opera scene and the scene from book 2, the reader compares the heroine's decorous and self-contained body with a grotesque body or bodies on display. In both instances, the plot advances at the expense of a class-bound image that must be repressed. The full ideological weight of the opera scene cannot be recognized, however, until Evelina's behavior is recognized for what it is: the result of a historical process involving the sublimation of physicality in order to privilege a particular kind of social and aesthetic experience.

In conclusion, the opera scene in *Evelina* also invites us to consider another historical process—the rise of the professional author. Stallybrass and White tell us that the regulation of the body and crowd behavior was one of two "concomitant" processes during the eighteenth century: the regulation of the crowd resulted in the establishment of the refined public sphere that, at the same time, gave credence to the "distinct notion of a professional authorship." [19] The implication is that the two processes had to occur together: that is, the notion of "professional authorship" means little without the corresponding changes in the notion of the "public sphere." The application of their work to Burney and to *Evelina* is, I think, obvious: for it becomes clear that Burney's own status as professional author depended upon the availability of a public sphere receptive to her art. During the eighteenth century, according to Stallybrass and White, that public sphere was being configured in relation to newer kinds of performance, which elicited a more "refined" response from their audiences. Clearly opera was one notable kind of such performance. On stage, it "detached" the voice from the body, allowing it (apparently) to transcend the body, even while, paradoxically, the very plots of opera could perpetuate the themes of the body. From its audience, opera increasingly demanded—and received—the "silent specular intensity" denying the body its more audible expressions and ensuring a "refined" atmosphere.

Thus, following Stallybrass and White, we can see a series of connections between Burney's *Early Diaries,* which are invested in the notion of operatic performance as transcendent art, and the representation of the opera in *Evelina.* In the *Diaries,* the assertion of a transcendent art facilitated Burney's own belief in a refined artistic sphere where class differences—and the body that denotes those differences—would cease to matter to the artist and audience alike. However, when Burney represents the opera in her novel, she returns to the reality of the situation—that an audience cannot be counted upon to participate in the conventions that sustain the illusion of a transcendent art.

In refusing to participate in the spectacle of the opera, the Branghtons jeopardize Evelina's efforts at self-creation. However, they also represent a potential threat to Burney's construction of her identity as "professional author." If the audience can refuse to participate in the conventions of the opera, if they can remind one of how arbitrary, after all, those conventions are, can they not also refuse to recognize the conventions that designate the author as standing in a particular relation to the public sphere? Can they not also refuse to acknowledge the author's own need to "authorize" her own text? My reading suggests that the opera scene in *Evelina* is phobic precisely because so much is at stake for both the character *and* the author. For the author, the opera represents a powerful symbolical space where art ought to achieve its ultimate transcendent status. The Branghtons, however, function metaphorically as an image of what can disrupt that symbolical space.

In conclusion, in *Evelina* the opera is important simultaneously to the heroine whose very identity is at stake and to the author whose ability to claim for herself any kind of authority results from the implementation of a refined public sphere. In other words, in *Evelina,* both the validation of the heroine and the establishment of narrative authority depend upon a series of behaviors and attitudes that come into full view during a night at the opera.

Notes

1. Frances Burney, *Evelina* (New York: Oxford University Press, 1982). Further references are cited parenthetically.

2. I am thinking here of Terry Eagleton's expansion of Althusser's definition of ideology. As Eagleton explains, the absences or "not-saids" of a work are precisely what "bind it to its ideological problematic: ideology is present in

the text in the form of eloquent silences. . . . What the text says is not just this or that meaning, but precisely their meaning and separation. . . . An ideology exists because there are certain things which cannot be spoken of" (Eagleton, *Criticism and Ideology: A Study in Marxist Literary Theory* [London: Verso Editions], 1978), 89–90.

3. See *The Politics and Poetics of Transgression* by Peter Stallybrass and Allon White, especially chapter 2 (Ithaca: Cornell University Press, 1986). See also Frederic Jameson, who writes about how one class distinguishes itself from another in its way of "living the body" (*Marxism and Form* [Princeton: Princeton University Press, 1971], 380). For a more elaborate account of how the body is deployed in the class politics of two late eighteenth-century women writers, see my study *Their Fathers' Daughters: Hannah More, Maria Edgeworth, and Patriarchal Complicity* (New York: Oxford University Press, 1991).

4. Mary Poovey, *The Proper Lady and the Woman Writer* (Chicago: University of Chicago Press, 1984), and Nancy Armstrong, *Desire and Domestic Fiction* (New York: Oxford University Press, 1987).

5. Heidi Hutner, "*Evelina* and the Problem of the Female Grotesque," *Genre* 22 (1990): 191.

6. Opera had long been identified as an "effeminate"—and effeminizing—art form. Addison complained about the "vast sums which have been laid out upon Opera's [*sic*] without Skill or Conduct, & to no other Purpose than to suspend or vitiate our Understanding" (*Spectator,* ed. Donald Bond, 5 vols. [New York: Oxford University Press, 1965], 4:480). In *The Dunciad,* Pope characterized the opera as "A Harlot form, soft sliding by, / With mincing step, small voice and languid eye; / Foreign her air, her robe's discordant pride / In patch-work flutt'ring, and her head aside" (book 4, lines 45–48). For a description of Pope's relation to opera, see Pat Rogers, "Noise and Nonsense: The Critique of Opera in *The Dunciad,*" in *Literature and Popular Culture in Eighteenth-Century England* (New York: Barnes and Noble, 1985), 102–19. On Smollett's response to the castrato in the opera, see James Carson, "Commodification and the Figure of the Castrato in Smollett's *Humphrey Clinker,*" *Eighteenth-Century: Theory and Interpretation* 33 (1992): 24–46. In the *Rambler* for March 2, 1751, Dr. Johnson classed the opera with "fashions, frolicks, routs, drums, hurricanes, balls, assemblies, ridottos, masquerades, auctions, plays, puppet shows, and bear gardens." See also " 'Warring Eunuchs': Opera, Gender, and Sexuality on the London Stage, 1705–1742," by Thomas McGeary, in *Restoration and Eighteenth-Century Theatre Research* 2d ser., 7 (1992): 1–17.

7. Another important opera scene occurs in *Cecilia,* where the heroine attends a rehearsal by Pacchierotti, a real-life castrato with whom the Burneys were acquainted (chapter 8 of book 1). See my essay "Shunning the Bearded

Kiss: Castrati and the Definition of Female Sexuality," in *Prose Studies: History, Theory, Criticism* 15 (1992): 153–70, where I discuss the relationship between Burney and Paccheriotti.

8. The definitive edition of Burney's early journal is *The Early Journals and Letters of Fanny Burney,* ed. Lars Troide, 2 vols. (Oxford: Clarendon Press, 1990). However, Troide omits selections from the 1775 journal, including the six-page account of Agujari's visit. In what follows, a parenthetical reference to *Early Diary* refers the reader to Annie Raine Ellis, *The Early Diary of Fanny Burney,* 2 vols. (London: George Bell and Sons, 1907). A parenthetical reference to *Early Journals* refers the reader to the Troide edition.

9. This issue of class difference is complicated: although Burney's paternal grandfather had been a dancer, musician, and portrait painter, she was encouraged to think of herself as upwardly mobile, as evidenced by her father's later pressure on her to accept a position in the court of Queen Charlotte. It could be argued that, in creating the profession of "musicologist," Burney's father assured his own enhanced social status: a profession that has no precedent can be conveniently perceived as upwardly mobile. Thus, though the Burneys' social status would seem to have been scarcely higher than that of the performers they often entertained, they appear to have been concerned with distinguishing themselves from their company.

10. Cf. Burney, *Early Journals,* 2:75–76.

11. Eventually coerced by Mrs. Brooke to sit in the presence of Mrs. Yates, Burney wrote of the incident, "All I can comfort myself with is, that it was only at the Opera-House that we met, and that of *late years* Mrs. Yates has had no harm said of her" (*Early Diary,* 1:329).

12. Margaret Anne Doody, *Frances Burney: The Life in the Works* (New Brunswick: Rutgers University Press, 1988), 40. On the consequences of being "unauthorized," see Julia Epstein, *The Iron Pen* (Madison: University of Wisconsin Press, 1989), chapter 3. For two readings of the confrontation scene, see Irene Fizer, "The Name of the Daughter: Identity and Incest in *Evelina,*" in *Refiguring the Father: New Feminist Readings of Patriarchy,* ed. Patricia Yaeger and Beth Kowaleski-Wallace (Carbondale: Southern Illinois University Press, 1989), 78–107, and Mary Poovey, "Fathers and Daughters: The Trauma of Growing Up Female," *Women and Literature* 2 (1982): 39–58.

13. Stallybrass and White, *Transgression,* 84.

14. Stallybrass and White, *Transgression,* 87.

15. Joseph Addison, *Spectator,* ed. Donald Bond, 5 vols. (New York: Oxford University Press, 1965), 2:163.

16. Donald Jay Grout, *A Short History of the Opera* (1947; reprint, Columbia University Press, 1965), 200.

17. Among other factors, the situation had something to do with the eco-

nomics of the opera—with the rise in cost of production and the corresponding rise in ticket prices. See E. D. Mackerness, *A Social History of English Music* (London: Routledge and Kegan Paul, 1964), chapter 3.

18. Hutner, "Female Grotesque," 191.

19. Stallybrass and White, *Transgression,* 83.

Bluestockings in Utopia

৩৯২ *Ruth Perry*

The utopian impulse is at once an urge to represent the most perfect social relationships and institutions that one can imagine and a temptation to satirize one's own society; this makes utopian fiction a splendid medium for examining the values of any culture. A comparison of four utopian novels published between 1762 and 1781, two by men and two by women, offers an opportunity to examine the imaginative projections of four eighteenth-century English writers about ideal social and economic arrangements. Each was published without the author's real name on the title page; two earned their authors about thirty pounds.[1] All four novels are suffused with the instrumental rationality that characterized the period; all are filled with schemes for maximizing happiness and productivity, often confusing the two.

The utopian societies imagined in these books take root in the British Isles. The two written by women, *Millenium Hall* (1762) by Sarah Scott and *Munster Village* (1778) by Lady Mary Hamilton, are set in the English countryside and convey in their very names the feudal manorial ideal on which each is based. Although very differently imagined in terms of social organization and purpose, each looks back to the precedent power of aristocratic women on their medieval estates. The class-inflected meaning of these two titles reminds us that as with men's power, women's power in England had been based in class privilege throughout the Middle Ages and the Renaissance. The particular devaluation of women as women, the notion that (as Mary Astell put it) "the greatest Queen ought not to command but to obey her Footman" because he was a man and she was a woman, while an advance for democratic class leveling, diminished women's power in English society from the end of the seventeenth century into the eighteenth century.[2] These women's utopian novels retain a whiff of the class privilege that had guaranteed women's social agency in early periods although, as we shall see, many details of social organization of these imagined communities were intended to undo class privilege.

The two utopias written by men, on the other hand, are situated in the wilderness of Wales and are named after features of the natural landscape domesticated by human will and labor. *Shenstone-Green; or, The New Paradise Lost* (1779) by Samuel Jackson Pratt (under the name of Courtney Melmoth) and *Mt. Henneth* (1781) by Robert Bage carry in their titles the suggestion of outdoor public spaces, areas recalled from nature and tamed to the uses of men. These meanings are also embodied in the material and social arrangements of their imagined utopias, in the exercise of personal power on the part of their founding fathers for private satisfactions rather than for the public good or in the interest of general social reform.

Munster Village and *Millenium Hall* do have the feel of matriarchies: experiments conceived of and financed by high-minded women concerned to better the conditions of humankind and to bring out the best in human nature. Their purpose is nothing less than to resocialize society, even at the expense of some personal comfort or private satisfactions. *Shenstone-Green,* on the other hand, represents a failed and foolish attempt to improve the conditions of a hopelessly fallible human race, and *Mt. Henneth* envisions a collection of intelligent, educated gentlemen and their wives coming together to form a more or less "democratic" community based on equal membership, equal labor, and equal conjugal power.[3]

In none of these cases is the imaginative conception behind these utopian visions the least bit anthropological: none describe complete societies with their own systems of customs, manners, and institutions such as those encountered by travelers in *Gulliver's Travels* or *Candide*. None is imagined as developing organically over generations. Each is constructed, built overnight from the ground up, so to speak, by the agency of—in most cases—a single person. All organize class and gender somewhat differently in their best of all possible worlds; all position themselves differently in relation to colonialism. Let me first introduce these texts and then make some preliminary observations about them.

Sarah Scott's *Millenium Hall* is the earliest and most serious blueprint for a better society among these fictional utopias, and the only one really interested in exploring alternative social structures. Based to some extent on the life the author led with Lady Barbara Montagu in Bath and Batheaston, it describes what can be done by five women of intelligence and enterprise when they pool their resources in a country establishment. Like *Munster Village,* the other woman's novel in this set of four, the heart of *Millenium Hall* is its defense of women's capacity for art and learning and for the production of culture. This contested ground is clearly held by women in this novel, although a ridiculous "learned lady" named Lady Brumpton appears briefly to draw fire from women who aspire too high—much as pedantic Mary Bennet in *Pride and Prejudice* draws fire from her sister Elizabeth and from the author herself. In both utopian novels by men, on the other hand, learned women are represented as pretentious and comical. As I will argue later, this difference is accompanied by a willingness to perpetuate other forms of exploitation and is symptomatic of a difference in attitude about profit, class, and colonialism.

Millenium Hall opens with two gentlemen travelers—an English colonist just back from Jamaica and a libertine ready for a change of pace—taking shelter from the rain in a country mansion. The speaker, who describes his mind with Lockian optimism as "a sheet of white paper," is shown into what at first appears to him to be an "Attick school." In a large room furnished with tables and bookcases, an orrery, a globe, and a harpsicord, he sees a number of women reading and taking notes, translating from French, drawing, painting, sewing, writing, carving, engraving, and cutting linen. An ensemble gathers around the harpsicord, joined by the steward, a shepherd, a lame youth and a blind fellow. The players take up their instruments, including a lute, bass, flute, violincello, and a French horn, and begin to play.

This opening scene figures the operations of the community in a number of ways. It is our first introduction to the five founding members of the community: Mrs. Mancel painting, Mrs. Trentham carving, Lady Mary Jones engraving, and so on, disposed around the room as in an artists' colony, engaged in activities to entertain, educate, and exercise the mind, to produce durable goods for use and for charity, and to produce art for ornament and sale.[4] Their personal stories—what brought each of them to Millenium Hall—create what narrative interest there is, alternating with descriptions of the educational and philanthropic projects they have undertaken, the regulations they have decided upon, the funds they have allocated to these projects, and the profits they have realized. The chamber music group, whose harmonies result from co-operation of rich and poor, young and old, handicapped and whole, men and women, is a foretaste of the planned interdependence of the geron-tological commune of old women, the farm maintained by sideshow freaks, the staff of crippled servants, and the boys' and girls' schools. The visitors' meal, "more elegant than expensive," supplied by the pro-duce of the estate and dictated by common sense rather than by a taste for the uncommon and exotic, is one example among many of an econ-omy set up explicitly to undo market values. Wages, for example, are determined by laborers' needs rather than the calculus of production. The projectors of Millenium Hall encourage economic self-sufficiency within each of their experimental units and the sharing of resources, rather than economies geared for growth and expansion.

Everywhere the best in human nature is turned to account. Old, failing women are housed in cottages on the estate and they, in turn, undertake to support all children after the fifth born to poor women in the neighborhood—and to train up these charity children to knit and spin, read and write. A large house is turned over to a group of indigent gentlewomen—toadeaters—governesses and ladies' compan-ions—"the most unhappy part of creation"—who are set to work to educate the young and work for the poor.[5] Creatures from circuses and sideshows, deformed objects of curiosity and ridicule in the outside world, also find a home on the estate. They live on their own corner of land, surrounded by a high fence to keep out prying eyes, where they raise chickens and maintain an elaborate kitchen garden. When they first came to Millenium Hall, we are told, they used to argue like kept women about whose keeper made the most money exhibiting them. Now they keep to themselves with only their beautiful gardens visible to the public: emblems of their well-ordered spirits.

Millenium Hall was fairly popular in its own day. Published in 1762, it went through four editions by 1778. It influenced the other three novels under consideration here, although none of the others manifested the same serious interest in practical realities—such as the amount of capital necessary to keep, educate, and apprentice so many children; or how soon a carpet and rug manufactory might be expected to pay off. Neither Lady Mary Hamilton, Samuel Jackson Pratt, nor Robert Bage was so interested in imagining the human dynamic that made commu-nity possible, the mix of self-sustaining labor and expressive pleasure, the balance between personal freedom and responsibility for others, the proper ratio between production for subsistence and production for art, or what early twentieth-century Americans called "bread and roses."

Especially concerned with the problems of eighteenth-century women, *Millenium Hall* can be read as a set of interventions in both the labor market and the marriage market. Imagined as a plausible retreat for women from an oppressive society, its author shows how much could be done on a pooled income of several thousand pounds a year: the ladies of Millenium Hall provide dowries for working-class women who want to marry but need a stake; retreats for "superfluous" women of all ages and conditions; and support and education for unwanted children. It is imagined as a place that redeems otherness, whether figured as monstrosity, physical handicap, or merely femaleness—all are restored here to their full human dignity. Even animal rights are defended at Millenium Hall in an impassioned diatribe against menageries and zoos. In a sense, the virtues of this community are the virtues of women writ large: care for the old and feeble; education of the young; frugality and a labor-intensive, self-sufficient household economy; cleanliness and orderliness—indeed the text is obsessed with cleanliness and orderliness. The author has imagined a comfortable and worthwhile retreat from a heartless world, although she has not tried to imagine how to change that larger world.

Munster Village, while sharing with *Millenium Hall* the urge to represent women's intellectual and artistic capacity for cultural production, has none of its interest in self-sustaining economies or experiments in human collectivity. A semi-epistolary text like *Millenium Hall,* this novel has a larger cast of characters and more variety of correspondents. It tells of the creation of a seat of culture by Lady Frances, heiress to Lord Munster's large fortune and guardian and educator of her niece and nephew. Finding herself in possession of a long-neglected property with an income more than adequate to rebuild it, Lady Frances sends for the famous Mr. Brown, who, as the author writes in a rare moment of wit, "found great *capabilities* in the situation: under his direction it is now one of the finest places in England" (22).

Describing the construction of *Munster Village,* intended as a center of learning, permits Lady Mary Hamilton to prove her encyclopedic knowledge of Western culture. One hundred new houses are laid out with classical symmetry around a tribuna whose walls are adorned with representations of the world's nine greatest libraries (Babylonian, Athenian, Alexandrian, Palatine, etc.),[6] the inventors of ancient letters (such as Adam, Abraham, Mercius, Aegyptus, Pythagorus, etc.), and in whose central hall is a white marble statue of Lady Frances herself, "inviting the lovers of literature to make use of the helps which she has provided for them" (22). Two hundred male scholars are to be admitted, and twenty women, with preference among the women given to "those who labour under any imperfection of the body—endeavouring, by increasing their resources *within themselves,* to compensate for their *outward defects*" (25). In addition, Munster Village contains an astronomical observatory furnished with the best instruments, galleries of sculptures and paintings, an anatomy amphitheater, and a library, about which the author is more particular than anything else.

> This library is open at stated times, (like that of the Vatican, and the French king's). . . . This was greatly wanted in this kingdom. London, after so many ages, remains without any considerable public library. The best is the Royal Society's: but even that is inconsiderable; neither is it open to the public; nor are the necessary conveniences afforded strangers for reading or transcribing. The British Library is rich in manuscripts . . . but it is wretchedly poor in printed books: and it is not sufficiently accessible to the public; their revenue not being sufficient to enable them to pay a proper number of attendants. (23)

Lady Mary Hamilton appears to know a great deal about libraries. Indeed, the library is a perfect emblem of this novel, much as the large busy room in the opening scene of *Millenium Hall* is emblematic of the human relations envisioned in that book—of its communal domesticity and its mixtures of work and play. The thoroughness of this passage on libraries is characteristic of *Munster Village,* whose dominating impulse is collecting, creating a repository of knowledge, gathering up the treasures of art and science in one place. The utopia Lady Mary Hamilton imagines is like a living museum; Lady Frances has skimmed off the best the world has to offer, the best of Western culture and the best of colonial agricultural resources. Thus her farmers pull their plows with water buffalo because they are stronger than oxen and eat less; and they cultivate India corn for the reeds it produces as a by-product. She produces silk, too, both raising the worms and using hydraulic weaving machines to manufacture the cloth. The description of what Lady

Frances brought to her estate from the four corners of the earth provides an opportunity for the author to record her remarkable range of opinions and information on every conceivable subject.

This listing of the accouterments of Western civilization at the opening of the novel is matched by another cultural pageant at the end, a textual celebration of the learned woman who is the creator and benefactress of Munster Village—and by extension, the learned woman who has created this highly learned novel. The occasion is Lady Frances's wedding anniversary, celebrated with a masquerade for three hundred people. Guests at this fete, ferried to a temple of Minerva by a boatman called, for the evening, "Charon," dress up as Romans (Cicero, Lucretius, Livy, Virgil, Horace, Ovid), as Italians (Michaelangelo, Raphael, Titian), as Englishmen (the duke of Buckingham, Dryden, Locke, Waller). A man dressed as Lord Chesterfield is told that he should burn his book "wherein he depreciates women, and considers them only as the toys of dalliance" (136). The procession ends with Homer and Ossian, with lavish poetic tributes by the figure representing Ossian to Lady Frances as a daughter of Albion.

Threaded through the often tedious recitations of learning are the melodramatic stories of parental tyranny and criminal abduction that comprise the rest of the novel. Thus, the narrative impulse in *Munster Village* is divided between displaying the knowledge and sensibility of a highly experienced connoisseur, and relating staple romantic episodes about the trials of beautiful young high-born women (Miss Burt, Countess de Sons, Miss Harris) and the heroic, faithful men who follow them (Sir Harry Bingley, Marquis de Villeroy). The productive arrangements of Munster Village hardly interest Lady Mary Hamilton at all. The charities—the schools and hospitals—are disposed of in a few sentences. But it is made clear that within a few years of Lady Frances's taking over her estate, building her community of scholars, improving her land, and caring for the people who live on it, her investment pays off. "The sums Lady Frances expended in bringing these plans to perfection, diffused riches and plenty among the people, and has already doubled the estate" (29).

The economic base of her community, hardly discussed at all, is Lady Frances's fortune, inherited from her father, Lord Munster, to whom we are introduced briefly at the beginning of the novel. Judging from his title and the references to his political machinations at Court, his ambition and cabals, one assumes that his wealth is "old money," based in land and accruing from rent rolls. So Lady Frances's capital derives ultimately from English feudal privilege rather than from any of the newer market-based forms of exploitation such as trade, manufacturing, or colonial holdings.

Shenstone-Green; or, The New Paradise Lost (1779) by Samuel Jackson Pratt, although literarily located in this group of novels by several intertextual references, is the only one of these fictions skeptical about the perfectibility of human life. *Millenium Hall* offers the possibility of human perfectibility through benevolence and mutual aid; *Munster Village* collects in one place whatever is most glorious in human achievement; and as we shall see, *Mt. Henneth* proposes the rational association of forward-looking, entrepreneurial young industrialists and their educated wives. But the bumbling old-fashioned sentimental fool who is the narrator of *Shenstone-Green* and the benefactor of the community, a cross between Sir Roger de Coverley and Henry Mackenzie's "man of feeling," has in mind neither the maternal model of community outlined in *Millenium Hall* nor the educated tastes of the connoisseur who constructed *Munster Village.* This Quixotic old gentleman is led into folly by trying to put into action the sentimentalized values he has learned, in part, from novels. Without a serious vision of an alternative way of life, *Shenstone-Green* must be read as a reaction to the high period of sentimentalism in English fiction—the 1770s—and as a parody that reinscribes the formulas of the sentimental novel even as it mocks them.

The book opens with Benjamin Beauchamp's explanation that he is writing this book for the use of "all those projectors who build towns upon poetical principles." He then describes the fatal sequence that led to his decision to build Shenstone Green. After saving eight kittens from being drowned, avoiding stepping on an ant (whose burden he imagines as food being taken to a sick friend), convincing his gardener to spare a "pregnant" linnet, and letting insects sting him Uncle Toby–like rather than lift a hand against them, he takes too much to heart a passage that his beloved daughter, Mathilda, reads to him of William Shenstone's:

> Had I a fortune of eight or ten thousand pounds a year, I would, methinks, make myself a neighborhood. I would first build a village with a church, and people it with inhabitants of some branch of trade that was suitable to the country round. I would then, at proper distances, erect a

number of genteel boxes, of about a thousand pounds apiece, and amuse myself with giving them all the advantages they could receive from taste. These would I people with a select number of well-chosen friends, assigning to each annually the sum of two hundred pounds for life. The salary should be irrevocable in order to give them independency. The house, of a more precarious tenure, that, in cases of ingratitute, I might introduce another inhabitant.[7]

In a paroxysm of sensibility, Mathilda kisses the page and urges her susceptible papa to invest most of the ten thousand pounds a year that she is to inherit in this utopian scheme. One thousand pounds a year is enough for her, she urges; the remaining nine thousand pounds a year might finance this benevolent plan (1:22). They decide to go to Wales to make this fairy tale come true, taking with them Samuel Sarcasm, Beauchamp's steward of twenty-eight years, whose hardheaded sense of reality—repeatedly confirmed by the narrative—is proof against the foolish enthusiasms of his employers.

En route to Wales, the steward Samuel Sarcasm buys a copy of *Millenium Hall,* and in a chapter called "A Panegyrick on Women and Books" mocks its vision of harmonious cooperation: "Do you think that Miss Mansell, and Miss Morgan, Lady M. Jones, Mrs. Selvyn, Mrs. Trentham, and all other Lady Bountifuls, could live together in the same house without *lovers, husbands,* or *quarrels*?" he asks (1:53). Confidently he affirms that "times and seasons would come about, if you were *with* them, when Mrs. Maynard would throw her orrery at Mrs. Selvyn, who, like a true woman, would throw her book at Mrs. Maynard etc." (1:54). Explicitly, then, *Shenstone-Green* is imagined as a refutation of the utopian maternalism of *Millenium Hall.*

The rest of this comic novel plays out the absurdity of providing ideal conditions for fallible humans. Workers gather quickly on the building site in Wales, attracted by Beauchamp's money. Not surprisingly, everyone wants to live in the houses constructed for the gentry, with two-hundred-pound annuities, and they importune Benjamin Beauchamp with hard luck stories and flattery. Our narrator reflects that London is a sort of Shenstone-Green and the king of England a Benjamin Beauchamp, "providing his fine folks with a house and an annuity for—*doing nothing*" (1:158). Mathilda dreams of a poetical and picturesque spot, with verdant walks and waterfalls, winding valleys and dark woods. She plants "roses, jessamines, pinks, honeysuckles, and lillies" everywhere at great expense (1:116) and invites her friend Eliza Eliot to join them, a woman whose excessive delicacy burlesques the sentimental heroine.

Into this feminized universe, masculine corruptions are introduced: horse racing, cockfighting, gambling, prostitutes, mountebanks, dueling, and debtors from the Fleet. The women clamor for theatricals and masquerades. Fights break out; venereal disease is discovered; the inhabitants mortgage their annuities to one another to pay gambling debts; the statue of Shenstone is plastered with advertising bills; the grounds are trampled. In an attempt to encourage learning that calls to mind *Munster Village,* Benjamin Beauchamp establishes an Academy of Dispute where philosophers can argue about the nature of God and of matter. But the place is soon overrun with lawyers, usurers, peace officers, and zealots of all sorts; there is no religion, no decorums, no order. Sectarians and fringe religionists hold forth with "weak heads and strong lungs"; pandemonium reigns.

An anecdote about a bricklayer named Henry Hewitt furnishes an example of the class relations imagined in this novel, which, like the other ills of society, Sir Benjamin Beauchamp tries to rectify. Kind to a fault, he wipes his worker's brow and believes every story of misfortune he hears.[8] He gives a house and a two-hundred-pound annuity to Henry Hewitt, who has had his share of trouble. But before long, the bricklayer appeals to his softhearted benefactor to restore him to his former state. He is miserable in his idleness. He cannot read or write. He no longer sleeps soundly at night. He misses his work and weeps over his trowel as over an old friend. He asks to be given work and to be paid for it—to repair the brickwork in Shenstone Green. The narrator's coy aside about the disparity between Henry Hewitt's prosaic request and the readers' romantic expectations about life continues his parody of sentimental novels: "To make any comment on this behavior on the part of our bricklayer, would be to suspect the readers' sense and sensibility. I leave it therefore, with his feelings" (2:109).

A gentleman who has watched this fiasco from the sidelines in disguise, in reality the wealthy Sir Matthew Davies, whose fortune comes from East India trade, advises Benjamin Beauchamp to give up his experiment—to convert the Academy of Dispute into a hall for breeding cattle and to turn the mansion house into a combination orphanage, boys' free school, and old-age almshouse. Rents from the outlying houses can then be used to maintain this charitable enterprise. He suggests that the hardheaded Samuel Sarcasm stay on to oversee the operation and get the best possible rents for the premises. Human nature, it seems, makes utopia impracticable. As Benjamin Beauchamp writes, "this little paradise, which I have raised, like a second Eden, around me, may, like the first, which was regulated by more powerful patronage, be equally lost" (2:94). Only a very few people can be governed by their own virtue, explains practical Sir Matthew Davies; the rest need laws, "the check of governments."

Sir Benjamin Beauchamp reminds one of other loveable incredulous idealists of eighteenth-century fiction, men such as Henry Fielding's Parson Adams, Sarah Fielding's David Simple, Oliver Goldsmith's Dr. Primrose, or Henry Mackenzie's Harley, men whose trust and unsuspecting generosity often landed them in painful and ridiculous situations. Represented as nostalgic vestiges of a bygone era, they only survive because they are protected by shrewder men of the world. But *Shenstone-Green* can also be read as the failure of feminine values of nurture in a masculine world of profit and calculation. This feminized view of the world, epitomized by the copy of *Millenium Hall* Sir Benjamin and his entourage carry with them, and by the way Sir Benjamin is governed by his daughter Mathilda, gives way to better business practices, to the masculine instrumentality of market capitalism embodied in Sir Matthew Davies, successful East India merchant. The idea of community is abandoned; the houses will be rented. Henry Hewitt begs for his trowel and the proper relations between capital and labor are reestablished.

Shenstone-Green is not a gloomy book; there is not a trace of bitterness or frustrated idealism. The tale is told with a wry shrug: life is not a novel; human nature must be kept in check. Certain economic facts of life are reaffirmed on its pages: the need to work hard, to stay within one's station in life and not to expect to live as fine ladies and gentlemen do.

Of the four utopian fictions I am examining here, Robert Bage's *Mt. Henneth* reads most like an eighteenth-century novel—full of character and incident and lively dialog. Fully staged as an epistolary novel, Bage's characters speak in different voices. The plot entwines the fates of three sets of friends: a young gentleman and his sister who must earn their own livings in the world; a pair of financially independent brothers, the elder with a fortune and the younger with a competency; and the wealthy patriarch who bankrolls the community in the end, with his Clarissa-perfect daughter and her spirited Anna Howe–like friend. The result is a social web in which both class difference and gender difference have distinct resonances.

I have noted that *Shenstone-Green* was written in reply to *Millenium Hall* and *Munster Village,* to show how benevolent principles opened one to sharpers and opportunism, and how the attempt to gather together the best that culture has produced gets you nowhere. The most practical use of the Academy of Dispute was to turn it into a barn for breeding animals. *Mt. Henneth,* in turn, was written with *Shenstone-Green* in mind. At the end of the novel, after the characters' many adventures in love and in commerce, when all are ready to retire to *Mt. Henneth,* the projector of this utopia observes that the principles by which he intends to operate are very different from those of Sir Benjamin Beauchamp.

> On the east side of the said mountain he hath determined, after the example of Sir Benjamin Beauchamp, to build himself a green, to be called the Green of Association.
>
> But he hath not, like Sir Benjamin, determined to people the said green with vice and folly, to the utter exclusion of common sense and common gratitude. (224)

Unlike Benjamin Beauchamp's ill-fated community, this one will be based on rational principles. Not a simple agricultural community, or even a country village, Mt. Henneth is imagined as a commercial pastoral, located on four thousand acres. The plan is summed up by Dr. Gordon, an idealized representative of the Enlightenment, a canny Scottish medical man: learned, industrious, impatient with superstition, free and independent in his thinking. "We must have manufacture, that other folks may be as happy as ourselves. . . . We must have commerce, or the manufacture will be useless" (238). The most advanced knowledge in science and technology is to be harnessed to economic production in Mt. Henneth: "every man among us should be a man of business, of science, of pleasure," writes Dr. Gordon. They will fell timber and build ships, grow and gather medicinal herbs and make medicines, manufacture linen, glass bottles, and spectacles. As for the women, all neatly paired off with the forward-looking, enterprising young men, Mrs. Gordon writes the following to a friend: "We breakfast early, because our gentlemen are all men of business, and generally devote the hours till three, the hour of dinner, to it. In fine weather, we ladies have a world of work in our plantations, groves, and grots. . . . When the air is sharp or rainy, we have our harpsicords, our tambours, and our pallets. At such times, the gentlemen have their philosophical experiments" (239). Thus the perfect life that Robert Bage has imagined for the members of his community is that of an experimentally minded country squire, intent on improving his land, making the most rational use of his resources, and maximizing his profit. The men he imagines for this life are practical, energetic, prosperous, scientific. The women are educated and tractable. This is the end to which he has directed his plot, for which he has married off four young couples: to form an ideal neighborhood, combining the best of country living with civilization and the virtues of family life with community. The quadruple marriage at the end of the novel is thus the threshold of the utopian community, which is imagined for the most part to accommodate these couples and to ensure some social formation larger than a family.

There are continuities between this vision and the stock character of the successful gentleman farmer, the *beatus vir,* of eighteenth-century fiction. Often presented in interpolated tales, this enlightened agrarian acts as his own steward, keeps his own accounts, introduces the latest improvements in crops and irrigation, and takes good care of his laborers. A capable wife and two rosy children crown his prosperity. Usually offered in contrast to a wasteful, debauched, fashionable way of life, this productive retirement is the alternative to a worldly concern with politics and power. It is the story of Mr. Wilson in *Joseph Andrews* (1742), Mr. Franklin in Clara Reeve's *The Two Mentors* (1783), and the Percy family in Maria Edgeworth's *Patronage* (1814).

In building his society, Mr. Foston exhibits considerable managerial skill in assembling about him grateful men and women as laborers in a diversified economy. Wherever misery is protected—debts paid and repossession forestalled—there grateful labor is gathered for the new community. A widow with three small children, whom Mr. Foston found weeping because the bed in which her husband died was being repossessed for debt, is offered a position as a dairymaid to eight cows, to produce milk and butter for the inhabitants of Mt. Henneth. A worthy brother and sister saved from debtor's prison for something under twenty pounds are enlisted respectively as a construction worker and a manager of a cheese and bacon coffee shop. The interpolated tale of a cobbler named Hugh Griffith makes it clear that workers are expected to stay within their allotted sphere and not imitate their betters. He explains to Mr. Foston how he had built up his business until he employed six other workers and was exporting his wares when he married an impoverished but genteel daughter of a clergyman. After a few contented years, his wife, egged on by her sister, began to tease our virtuous cobbler for the refinements enjoyed by the wives of other genteel tradesmen in the neighborhood. She had their brick floor boarded, their whitewashed walls wainscotted, grew shrubs in the kitchen garden rather than cabbages and peas, and spent far too much money on tea and other imported luxuries. As a result of this mismanagement, Hugh Griffith's business fell off and his fortunes spiraled downward. In return for paying off his debts, he asks James Foston to reinstate him in his old way of life, to return him to his brick floor, his simple furnishings, and his life of labor. Like Henry Hewitt begging Sir Benjamin Beauchamp to hire him back as a bricklayer rather than treating him like a man of leisure, Hugh Griffith asks James Foston to redeem him from his upwardly mobile spending habits and return him to his proper station and class.

Robert Bage was one of the more progressive thinkers of his day, and so the reaffirmation of class hierarchy in this sequence is particularly striking. On the issue of women's rights, for example, he quoted Mary Wollstonecraft with approbation in *Hermsprong* (1796). In an otherwise laudatory essay on his fiction, Sir Walter Scott criticized him for being too lax on the issue of female chastity.[9] A member of the progressive community around Birmingham that included such luminaries as Joseph Priestley, James Watt, and Erasmus Darwin, Bage was apparently present at the famous incendiary dinner celebrating "the ideas of 1789" that set off the Birmingham riots of 1791. But his representation of class relations in this utopian novel is hardly revolutionary. He imagines bringing in workers to provide the labor necessary to operate Mt. Henneth—labor bought and paid for with the capital earned in a colonial system of exchange.

If class arrangements are not disturbed in *Mt. Henneth,* neither are gender arrangements. Most of this novel concerns itself with the stories of the four couples who marry at the end—stories of true love interrupted, thwarted, misunderstood, postponed—in which women play utterly conventional roles. There is one scene in particular that demonstrates how Bage leaves gender hierarchy undisturbed and illustrates how the handling of gender—and women's learning—is symptomatic of the representation of other social relations in the novel.

Julia Foston, the projector's perfect daughter, and her lively friend are out walking with the son and daughter of Sir Owen Caradoc, a pair of young sophisticates. We are told by one of our trusted narrators that "the son is an eminent member of the Antiquarian Society; the lovely daughter is monstrously enamoured of virtue; she minces snails to multiply the breed, kills cats in an air-pump, and generates eels in vinegar" (183), thus distinguishing between science when practiced as a hobby of the idle rich—especially by women—and science practiced by industrious men in "philosophical experiments" on rainy days, for practical results that might be useful to manufacture or medicine. This group of young people then see an ass and a mare rutting in a nearby field. Miss Caradoc calls attention to the scene and begins to discuss it. "Brother," she says, "you have constantly asserted that copulation betwixt animals of different species is unnatural, and always committed by a rape of the female—see the contrary" (183). Julia Foston and the other young ladies in the company turn away, embarrassed. "Sister," her brother replies, "the naturalists have not considered an ass and a mare so much of different species, as differing in specie." Shamelessly Miss Caradoc continues to discuss animal reproduction and the narrator tells us that "a learned dispute followed betwixt these two originals, in which the whole science of generation was discussed. The brother maintained the egg system; the sister, Lewenhoeck's. They ended at last with an inquiry into the political cause of circumcision" (183).

Taken out of context, one might have concluded both from Bage's reputation for egalitarian attitudes and from the way he privileges scientific knowledge in this novel that Miss Caradoc would be admired for her learning. But the narrator makes it clear that the most likeable and trusted characters in this scene find the thoroughly modern Miss Caradoc unpleasantly arrogant and unpredictable. Her question about rape and her brother's reply about specie, although suggestive of continuities about sexual and economic domination, serve merely as pedantic jokes and are quickly forgotten. The old prejudice that learning is antithetical to femininity, that women with knowledge give themselves airs and are insufficiently modest about sexual matters, is reinforced by this incident. There is no place for bluestockings in this utopia. The role of women in Mt. Henneth is to feed people or to play entertainingly on the harpsicord, not to participate in discussions of science.

Another author might have made something of the pun on specie and species, with their common Latin root in spectacle or seeing, as the group stood and watched the ass, who "had broke through three several barriers" to reach the mare, "eager to reap the fruits of his bold enterprise." There are also connections to be made between invest-ment capital—specie—and the breeding of animals of different species, which was indeed a new enterprise in this period.[10] Curiously, Bage's associations in this brief scene—among the terms of capital and rape and difference—turn out to be the central terms of Mr. Foston's story of how he met his wife and made his fortune. Sent to India as an agent of the East India Company, his first adventures demonstrated to him the relativity of religious belief, the equal viability of Christianity and Buddhism. Another sequence of events led him to rescue his wife-to-be, an Indian woman, and her maid, from two villains who were in the act of violating them. He subsequently marries this woman and acquires her father's immense fortune. This, then, is the source of the capital he invests in Mt. Henneth: an Indian fortune earned by interrupting a rape and multiplied by colonial trade. It is a story whose terms are parodied in the conversation between the Caradoc brother and sister: rape, specie, and species. Nor is the rest of their conversation insignifi-cant either, although Bage obviously meant to ridicule their choice of topics: the science of generation, the relative importance of the egg or the sperm, and the political meaning of circumcision.

I offer these details to suggest that attitudes toward learned women in these four novels are patterned predictably with respect to hierarchi-cal social relations—whether gender, class, or colonial power. Where women's intellectual capacity is mocked and their subordination to men taken for granted, the economic exploitation of other classes—whether at home or in the colonies—is assumed. Where women's capacity for the production of culture is emphasized on the other hand, that intellectual and artistic activity is embedded in an economic system whose guiding principles are communalism and self-sufficiency. Nor do these economic systems necessarily harken back to earlier "golden age" agricultural models. In *Munster Village* the imaginative benefactress introduces the latest technological innovations in the form of hydraulic weaving machines; in *Millenium Hall* the "manufacture of carpets and ruggs" employing several hundred men, women, and children is booming at the end of the novel and likely to expand. These enterprises provide a secure economic base for their workers and extend the reclamation of society; their object is not to accumulate capital or enrich their owners. Indeed, in *Millenium Hall,* the profits from the rug factory are explicitly distributed to workers according to need rather than productivity. The effect is to "enrich all the country around" (201).

Moreover, as I have already noted, the initial capital invested in these women's utopias is older wealth deflected into philanthropic purposes; it did not come from the exploitation of colonized labor. The mansion house given over to destitute gentlewomen at the end of *Millenium Hall* was once owned by a dissolute and intemperate nobleman; the present use of his property redeems his sins both in terms of class and gender. Similarly, Lady Frances's generosity in *Munster Village* sets to rights her father's selfish tyranny and makes use of her estate to benefit a broader class of people. Although Lady Frances trains her nephew to enter the world of international trade, the author, Mary Hamilton, deliberately complicates his relation to race, ethnicity, and class in the stories of his adventures. She inverts all the usual colonial relations, for example, in a scene in which he meets, rescues, and befriends a black slave merchant who, it turns out, has delivered his closest friend, another European aristocrat, from slavery on a prison galley. "Nothing can be more unjust than to confine the instance of humanity within the narrow circle of a few European nations," reflects the rescued Marquis de Villeroy. "We have savages in Italy; and there are worthy men amongst those we call savages" (121).

The community on Mt. Henneth on the other hand—whose purpose is to create a neighborhood and to provide companionship for the young, educated, newly wed entrepreneurs who are going to settle there—is made possible by the fortune James Foston made in the East India Company. His money and his wife were his plunder, so to speak, from his colonial adventures in India. Like Sir Matthew Davies, the millionaire in *Shenstone-Green* who pulls the solution to the disastrous utopia out of his hat, Foston's money was generated by English imperialism—portrayed unproblematically by Bage despite my associative reading of his narrative. Thus, in both novels written by men, rational experiments in living are made possible by surpluses generated by colonialism.

In Sarah Scott's *Millenium Hall,* by contrast, the colonial merchant is a sick and weary traveler who needs to recover from his debilitating sojourn in the West Indies. In *Mt. Henneth* he is alert and enterprising and ready to create his own protected society after travel has taught him that all cultural practices are relative. That is, European and Christian moral superiority is illusory, but English manufacture, science, and trade *are* superior, Bage suggests, and can provide the material basis for gentility. The West Indian plantation owner visiting Millenium Hall seeks a remedy for his spirit as well as his bodily health in the salubrious environs and harmonious visions of cooperation at Millenium Hall, where activity is motivated not by profit but by charity, regulated not by the demands of luxury but by the needs of subsistence. The English trader returned from India in *Mt. Henneth,* on the other hand, has been energized in mind and spirit by his colonial experiences and wants to consolidate his happiness in a protected space, maximizing the partnership of rational instrumentality, trade, and manufacture that has served him so well already.

Constructed expressly to rectify the injustices of earlier generations, both *Millenium Hall* and *Munster Village* are grounded in critiques of existing forms of social domination. *Shenstone-Green* and *Mt. Henneth,* on the other hand, while poking fun at many fashionable pieties of sentimentalism and religion, essentially reinscribe the existing social relations of class, gender, and colonialism both in their characters' attitudes and in their narrative structures. Although there are obvious ways to complicate this formulation, gender is key in determining how radical the utopian vision actually is. Attitudes toward women's capacity for cultural production—whether civic planning or the creation of intellectual or artistic works—appear to be a good index of other attitudes involving status and power. Where the education of women is either deemed irrelevant or a matter of debate, where intellectual women are ridiculed in what was, after all, the "age of reason," the social relations of power are re-inscribed rather than re-imagined. And where women's claims to the life of the mind are honored and encouraged in these eighteenth-century texts, it signals a belief in human potential—across gender and across the social dimensions of race, class, and nation as well.

Notes

1. Sarah Scott told her sister Elizabeth Montagu that it had taken her a month to write *Millenium Hall* and at that rate she had earned a guinea a day. Sylvia Harcstark Myers, *The Bluestocking Circle* (Oxford: Clarendon Press, 1990), 188. Robert Bage sold *Mount Henneth,* his first novel, to Thomas Lowndes for thirty pounds. Peter Faulkner, *Robert Bage* (Boston: Twayne Publishers, 1979), 22.

2. Mary Astell, preface to *Some Reflections upon Marriage,* 3d ed. (London, 1706), 1–2. For a discussion of the tensions between the claims of class and gender in the political philosophy of this period, see my "Mary Astell and the Feminist Critique of Possessive Individualism," in *Eighteenth-Century Studies* 23 (1990): 444–58.

3. Pages from these works cited in this article are from the following editions: Sarah Scott, *Millenium Hall,* intro. Jane Spencer (London: Virago Press and Penguin Books, 1986); Mary Hamilton, *Munster Village* (New York: Pandora Press, 1987); Courtney Melmoth, *Shenstone-Green; or, The New Paradise Lost. Being a history of human nature . . . Written by the proprietor of the Green,* 3 vols. (London: 1780); Robert Bage, *Mt. Henneth,* vol. 9 of Ballantyne's *Novelists Library,* ed. Sir Walter Scott, 10 vols. (London: Hurst, Robinson and Co., 1821–24).

4. The market for painting as well as for writing opened up new earning possibilities for women. Emblematically, each of the two novels by women in this set represents a female painter who earns money for the art she produces. Louisa Mancel in *Millenium Hall* earns part of her living from selling her paintings, and impoverished Lady Finlay in *Munster Village* is represented as earning enough from the sale of one of her paintings to support her family for two years. Sarah Scott, who herself depended upon what she earned from her writing, makes no comment upon this way of earning money. But aristocratic Lady Mary Hamilton felt called upon to justify her character's entry into the market as follows: "Good blood cannot be kept up without the shambles of the market, so it is no scandal to procure *that* by ingenuity or industry, when the appendages of gentility are so far reduced as not to afford it otherwise" (16).

5. In Charlotte Lennox's *Henrietta* (1758), written four years later, Miss Courtney, the heroine, prefers earning her own living as a governess to being a parasitical ladies' companion—a subservient toadeater.

6. As in Clara Reeve's later *Progress of Romance* (1785), there is an aware-

ness in *Munster Village* that Greek classical civilization was itself derivative, although its influences were often overlooked by learned men who liked to trace their tradition to the Greeks. The narrator of *Munster Village* notes: "An ingenious Persian lately in England, gave an account of many thousand Arabian manuscripts, totally unknown to the gentlemen of the university of Oxford. It is to be wished these were procured. The Orientals and Hebrews were the parents of knowledge, and the Greeks no more than their scholars: how gross were their notions of prudence and *virtue,* till Orpheus, and the travelled philosophers taught them better" (23).

7. This remark comes from Shenstone's essay "Egotisms," reprinted in his *Essays on Men and Manners* (London: Bradbury, Evans, & Co., 1868), 165.

8. In the person of Benjamin Beauchamp, Pratt satirizes the feminized, feeling heroes of the novels of the 1760s and 1770s. See, for example, the Miss Minifies's *The Histories of Lady Frances S——, and Lady Caroline S——* (1763) or Mrs. Woodfin's *The Auction* (1770). Harley, in Henry Mackenzie's *The Man of Feeling* (1771), with his highly developed sensibility, comes dangerously close to parodying the ideal he embodies. An examination of the nature of masculinity and macho attitudes and behaviors was very much on the agenda of fiction by both men and women in these decades.

9. Sir Walter Scott, "Prefatory Memoir to Robert Bage," in Ballantyne's *Novelists Library,* 9:xxvii.

10. On the breeding of animals for maximum productivity in the new scientific agricultural practice, see Harriet Ritvo, "Possessing Mother Nature: Genetic Capital in Eighteenth-Century Britain," forthcoming in *Early Modern Conceptions of Property,* ed. John Brewer and Susan Staves (New York: Routledge).

Arthur Young, Agriculture, and the Construction of the New Economic Man

Beth Fowkes Tobin

In *Desire and Domestic Fiction* Nancy Armstrong argues that in the mid-eighteenth century, the emerging ideology of feminine domesticity authorized "a whole new set of economic practices that directly countered what were supposed to be seen as the excesses of a decadent aristocracy." It was, Armstrong contends, the new domestic woman with her capacity to supervise herself and her home, and not "her counterpart, the new economic man, who first encroached upon aristocratic culture and seized authority from it." I will argue in this essay that while the new economic man may have not been the first to challenge aristocratic hegemony, he, like the domestic woman, is a historically constituted subject who arose out of specific, historical circumstances having to do with the middle-class challenge to aristocratic authority. I think it important to stress the constructedness of the image of the new economic man so that we may recognize that the "competitive desires and worldly ambitions" that have been ascribed to men are a cultural rather than a natural difference.[1]

The new economic man's attributes were depicted in a body of literature that I will call the discourse on agriculture.[2] This new discourse differs markedly from the old farmer almanacs with their chatty tone and jumble of miscellaneous information that included cures for headaches and deafness, recipes for pickles, wines, beer, and rat poison, advice on the care and maintenance of fishing tackle, and "a great number of choice receipts for the Cure of Cattle."[3] The new "scientific" discourse on agriculture, which began with the publication of Arthur

Young's *The Farmer's Letters to the People of England* (1767) and flour-ished well into the second decade of the nineteenth century, consisted of manuals on estate management, dissertations on the new agricultural practices, treatises on plants and animals, travel literature describing "tours" through England's agricultural districts, the collected papers delivered at the regional meetings of various agricultural societies, and *The Annals of Agriculture*, a serial published by the Board of Agriculture. Topics discussed in these various forms of agricultural writing include how to raise hybrid flowers, how to use marl, a chalky clay, to fertilize the soil, how to get rid of a bad tenant, how to keep an account book, how to build a boat to transport sheep to market, and how to write out a bill of exchange.

The most prominent and prolific writer of this new discourse was Arthur Young, secretary of the Board of Agriculture and author of dozens of volumes describing his tours throughout England. Young and other influential agriculturalists such as John Mordant, Nathaniel Kent, and William Marshall held ambiguous positions in society: all with the exception of Mordant had owned and had managed a mod-estly sized estate, and all at one time or another had been stewards on great estates. Neither of the lesser gentry nor of the servant class, they positioned themselves as experts and professionals, as highly trained, well-educated, informed managers of property. With their treatises on crop rotation, turnips, and fertilizers, they used the new scientific dis-course on agriculture to establish themselves as professional experts on land and productivity. By displaying their wealth of information and skills as quantifiers and organizers of land and labor, they planted in the minds of their readers the need for professional estate managers, and by constructing the new "apparatus of efficient estate management," they inserted themselves into the rural economy between landowners and their tenant farmers.[4] Conferring upon themselves a position of power and authority, they created a space for a class of professional men who, like themselves, possessed accounting and valuation skills, technical knowledge, and a talent for management and organization.

The Professional Estate Manager

Young and his colleagues constructed this new economic man, the professional estate manager and agricultural expert, in opposition to notions of aristocratic masculinity. While aristocratic males displayed their power and authority by indulging their appetites for blood (hunting, dueling, and cockfighting) and sex, males of the newly emergent middle class sought to demonstrate with their power through the "cerebral control of the world" that "the pen and the ruler" were mightier than the "sword and the gun."[5] As historians Leonore Davidoff and Catherine Hall argue, "the valuation of actions and materials in monetary terms . . . was an essential part of the middle-class challenge to the aristocratic male whose skills lay with gambling, duelling, sporting and sexual prowess" (205).

As participants in this middle-class critique of upper-class masculinity, agricultural writers sought to discredit the management abilities of the landed upper classes, portraying them as pleasure-seeking, self-indulgent, and incapable of exercising the self-control necessary to run a commercial venture. Young argues that gentlemen do not make good farmers because they are incapable of paying attention to detail and of giving a "farmer's attention to the business."[6] "No profit," he contends, "can arise to any gentleman that does not give the business constant attention, and descend to *minutiae;* which may be too disagreeable for him to submit to" (293). It cannot be expected, Young argues, that a gentleman will "forgo his diversions, his excursions of pleasure, the company of his friends, the joys of society" to supervise the daily running of a farm; nor will his wife "renounce opera or a ball for the pleasure of dancing attendance on her butter and cheese in the dairy" (296). Without careful and constant supervision, a farm will not profit: "Cattle of no kind will thrive but in the master's eye: every variation of the season to be remarked; the lucky moment for ploughing, harrowing, sowing, reaping, etc. to be caught, and used with diligence and foresight; fences for ever to be attended to; and, in short, a million of other things, which require constant thought and endless application" (297). None of these tasks, Young argues, could a gentleman be expected to perform with consistency and regularity and still remain a gentleman pursuing gentlemanly pleasures.

When agriculturalists describe the few farming gentlemen they meet on their tours of agricultural districts, they represent these gentleman farmers as rough, crude, and boorish, as if they have been debased and brutalized by their involvement in the daily business of agriculture and by their entry into the market economy. William Marshall describes how a gentleman "coming into a good paternal estate, discharged his tenants and commenced farmer." Without a steward or even a bailiff, he handles every aspect of farming. "He attends fairs and markets—sells his own corn and his own bullocks." As a result of his direct involvement in farming, "his person is gross and his appearance bacchanalian—his dress that of a slovenly gentleman . . . his conversation bespeaks a sensible, intelligent mind; borne away, however, by a wildness and ferocity which is obvious in his countenance."[7] This gentleman farmer has lost his gentility, at least in the eyes of Marshall, and has debased himself, no longer entitled to the appellation "gentleman."

Agricultural writers as a group sought to discredit not only the abilities of the gentry but also of tenant farmers whom they represented as uneducated boors, deficient in the skills required to run an efficient business. In *The Complete Steward* John Mordant despairs over the sloppy and idiosyncratic bookkeeping of farmers, who, he says, are "the most ignorant and illiterate of all others that are in any creditable employ."[8] Farmers are "dilatory in keeping accounts, there being but few of these sort of people that keep any accounts at all, either of their income, or their out-goings, which should be carefully done by every person in business" (2:382). Describing the kind of bookkeeping that drove agriculturalists like Mordant to frustration and anger, historians Davidoff and Hall recount how one Essex farmer used an account book but did not distinguish between domestic and business transactions. He had entered "purchases of food, school fees, rates, wages, horse medicine and nails jumbled with incomings from sales of corn, rents from small property as well as of payments in kind" (202). Mordant as well as Young preached accounting to these "illiterate" farmers, Young exhorting them to "keep a ledger" and to "account for every article in the farm." Young writes that "the farmer should in this book directly without the intervention of a waste-book or a journal, enter all his expenses; . . . and before he balances his books at the end of the year, it is necessary for him first to cast up the sundry accounts, such as tythe-poor levy—various expenses—and divide them in the same matter as rent."[9] Young, Mordant, Marshall, Kent, and other agriculturalists argued that the business of agriculture, with its focus on profit and loss, was not something a gentleman could engage in without endangering the manners and lifestyle that marked him as a gentleman, and they also insisted that the business of agriculture required organizational skills and a scientific education that a farmer did not have access to. These writers championed the emergence of a new class of professionals, who, as Newby observes, ensured the "rational administration of estate practice" and instituted "a complex structure of managerial authority . . . whereby the estate itself was managed by professional administrators" (25–26). Mordant, a steward himself, argues that every large estate needs a resident agent who will manage land and labor effectively, and who will compensate for the farmers' and the landlords' lack of business sense. Marshall writes that "there are men who are losing hundreds (perhaps thousands) annually, by neglect, or mistaken frugality, in the management of their estates, yet who will consider this executive establishment, and these forms and regulations of business, as unnecessary and extravagant." [10]

According to agricultural writers, Mordant and Marshall in particular, property can only be effectively managed by professional land agents whose qualifications are varied but require an ability to manage land, labor, and the law. They must possess knowledge of land evaluation, cost-accounting bookkeeping, agriculture, architecture, and engineering, as well as the ability to perform scrivener's duties such as drawing up leases, receipts, bills of exchange, letters of credit, bills of debt, bonds, bills of sale, and letters of attorney (Mordant, 266–68). A steward, unlike a farmer or a gentleman, will, according to Mordant, possess "tolerable skill in mathematicks, surveying, mechanicks, architecture, hydraulicks, etc., and particularly that he understands book-keeping" (2: 207). Marshall lists among the "requisite acquirements of an acting manager" a knowledge of "agriculture," "land-surveying," "mechanics (the business of an engineer)," "rural architecture," "planting," "natural history," and "accounts" (338–39). [11]

Young and Marshall stress the importance of organizing the estate's records, documents, maps, and legal transactions in a central office from which the estate or estates of a landowner can be rationally and efficiently managed. Young praises the orderly arrangement of the estate office of Sir Joseph Banks; it contains "156 drawers of the size of an ordinary conveyance . . . all numbered. There is a catalogue of names and subjects, and a list of every paper in every drawer; so that whether the inquiry concerned a man, or a drainage, or an inclosure, of a farm, or a wood, the request was scarcely named before a mass of information was in a moment before me." [12] Marshall argues that the "Office, or Place of

Business" should be in the "proprietor's principle residence" and should contain:

> 1. Maps . . . 2. Rentals and books of accounts . . . 3. Books of valuation: . . . registers of the number, name, and measurement, and estimated value of each field, and every parcel of land, as well as of each cottage, or other building, not being part of a farmstead, on the several distinct parts of the estate . . . 4. A register of timber trees . . . 5. A receptacle of ordinary papers,—such as contracts, agreements, accounts, letters of business . . . 6. A safe repository of documents . . . 7. . . . pocket registers of the farms . . . 8. . . . mechanic instruments . . . earth borers, . . . a theodolite, . . . leveling instruments . . . also models and drawings. (346–49)

In stressing the importance of the routinization of time, space, and money in the responsible management of an estate, the agricultural writers were representing their middle-class skills of quantification and commodification as crucial factors in the economic viability of the landed estate.

Commercialization of Land and Labor

In their role as professional experts on the management of land and labor, agricultural writers introduced accounting techniques and agricultural practices that promoted cost-effective management of land, productive materials, and labor. Arthur Young, the most prolific and enthusiastic supporter of the new regime of high-yield agriculture, encouraged the enclosure of wastelands and open fields, the engrossment of small farms, and the consolidation of scattered holdings. Young's enthusiasm for enclosure permeates his description of what he perceives as agricultural improvements: "All the country from Holkam to Houghton was a wild sheep-walk before the spirit of improvement seized the inhabitants; and this glorious spirit has wrought amazing effects; for instead of boundless wilds, and uncultivated wastes, inhabited by scarce any thing but sheep; the country is all cut into inclosures, cultivated in a most husband-like manner, richly manured, well peopled, and yielding an hundred times the produce that it did in its former state." [13] One farm, consisting of 2,500 acres "all gained from sheep-walks" and "now is regularly inclosed," captures his attention because it "yields immense crops of corn" and is now a very profitable enterprise. The practice of replacing many small farms with a few large ones received Young's repeated praise and recommendation. "Great farms have been the soul of the Norfolk [agri]culture: split them into tenures of an hundred pounds a year, you will find nothing but beggars and weeds in the whole country. A rich man keeps his land rich and clean." [14]

Though an enthusiastic supporter of enclosure and engrossment, Young admits that engrossment can ruin many farmers who lack the capital to employ a greater number of laborers and to buy the seed and stock necessary to cultivate the land. "The bad success of great numbers" of farmers, Young observes, "is owing to their not having a sufficient sum of money to begin with, which inevitably involves them in difficulties, and reduces their profit in every article of their produce." Without sufficient capital, farmers "grow poor, in spite of all possible industry, judgment, and application" (*Farmer's Letters,* 286–87). Nathaniel Kent also expresses his concern that small farmers would go bankrupt trying to compete with large farmers who could invest capital in improvements. Kent argues that when agriculture is "monopolized and grasped into a few hands," "it must dishearten the bulk of mankind, who are reduced to labour for others instead of themselves; must lessen the produce, and greatly tend to general poverty." [15] Small farms, he believes, would make England a strong agricultural producer and safe from the disaffection and discontent of displaced and pauperized farmers. Small farms "reward merit, encourage industry, fill the markets with plenty, increase population, and furnish the best class of men in all subordinate stations of life," [16] and those "who persist in the ruinous practice of throwing too much land into one man's hands, are blind to their own interest, and deaf to the cries of humanity." [17]

But Nathaniel Kent, with his distrust of the efficacy of engrossment, stands out as a lone dissenting voice in the late eighteenth-century discourse on agriculture, which was dominated by Arthur Young and his insistence that enclosure and engrossment represented a desirable rationalization in land management. The essential feature of the new scientific and cost-effective agriculture that Young and his colleagues promoted was their reconstitution of land and labor as commodities to be "bought and sold under conditions of market competition and according to a calculation of profitable return." [18] His books describing his tours through the agricultural districts of England exemplify the new discourse on the commodification of property and labor. When Young examines an estate, he counts the number of acres capable of producing crops and stock that can be sold for cash and he takes into account the expenditures such as maintaining horses, oxen, and laborers that inevitably reduce the size of the profit reaped from the land. He does not sentimentalize land, nor endow it with human meaning, the way William Wordsworth does in his poem "Michael" or Henry Mackenzie does in *The Man of Feeling,* when he describes how Edwards feels about his patrimonial farm: "there was not a tree about it that I did not look on as my father, my brother, or my child." [19] Young's reconceptualization of land erases all signs of the web of social and economic relations that permeated the land and enmeshed it in moral obligation and social customs.

Young expertly calculates the profitability of land and labor by quantifying and commodifying all aspects of the productive process. Young shows his readers how to think in terms not only of enumerating and recording every step in the productive process but also of assigning a monetary figure to each step. Sprinkled throughout his books are tables and charts demonstrating the profit-cost principle. For instance, in his *Six Weeks Tour, Through the Southern Counties of England and Wales,* Young sketches the "general economy and management" (54) of a middle-sized farm of 250 acres with a list:

80 of them [acres] grass.	5 labourers.
10 horses.	25 cows.
2 men.	60 sheep.
2 boys.	

By indiscriminately including land, people, and animals on his list, Young reduces land, labor, and cattle to the same interchangeable category of expense. To Young's way of thinking, they are all commodities to buy or sell.

Young's ability to commodify agricultural processes is perhaps most noticeable when he describes labor. In enumerating the cost of growing potatoes, he takes into his calculations the cost of ploughing, planting, harrowing, manuring, hoeing, weeding, and digging up the potato crop; he assigns a numerical value to each act performed by a laborer, and thereby reduces social relations to numbers to be computed in a

profit-loss ledger.[20] Young insists that farming is like any other business in that it requires constant and careful attention to detail and the
keeping of "regular accounts" (*Farmer's Letters,* 294), both middle-class
masculine skills.

The Commodification of Land

Young's efforts to reduce complex sets of social and economic
relations to simple cost accounting was a part of a larger movement
by middle-class men to redefine land and labor as commodities in an
attempt to displace the old society's paternal economic and social arrangements. By emphasizing the legal and exclusive rights to the land,
middle-class agricultural writers sought to erase traditional definitions
of land based on customary practice, common usage, and verbal agree-
ment, and worked to transform land from a historical and social relation
into a "thing, a discreet physical commodity . . . freed of any social
obligations that had hitherto rested upon its ownership" (Newby, 14).

To appreciate the significance of the agriculturalists' redefinition of
land and labor, we must examine the economic and social relations
of the old society, relations that historian Harold Perkin has called
paternal. According to Perkin, the old society was hierarchical, bound
together by "vertical links" of patronage and friendship. Perkin argues
that the "social nexus peculiar to the old society" was "vertical friendship," which was "a durable two-way relationship between patrons
and clients." It was "less formal and inescapable than feudal homage,
more personal and comprehensive than the contractual, employment
relationships of capitalist 'Cash Payment.'" These "personal bonds of
the old society" formed a chain of reciprocal relations that ran up and
down the ranks of society and formed a "mesh of continuing loyalties."[21]
A patron was obliged to aid and to protect those dependent on him, and
his dependents were obliged to repay their debts with gratitude, deference, and loyalty. In almost every interaction in the old society, a person
would assume at various times, depending on the situation, either role
of patron or dependent, and participate in what J. G. A. Pocock has
called the dynamic of "ruling-and-being-ruled."[22]

The hierarchical yet reciprocal relations of paternalism bound society
together in a chain of connection, to use William Cobbett's description
for paternal ties.[23] Nathaniel Kent in his *Hints to Gentlemen of Landed*

Property explains how the paternal relation works: "The landlord, tenant, and labourer are intimately connected together, and have their reciprocal interests, though in different proportions; and when the just equilibrium between them is interrupted, the one or the other must receive injury" (259). He argues that it is the landlords' duty and interest as "guardians of the poor" to "attend their accommodation, and happiness" and to "act as their friend and protector," for the landlord has "a lasting interest in the prosperity of the parish" (240). The rich's generosity to the poor, and the landlord's generosity to his tenants and laborers, were key in the functioning of the paternal system, for as Robert Southey argues, without the "generous bounty" of the landlord, there is no "grateful and honest dependence," and the "bond of attachment is broken." [24]

Land under the old paternal system, as Howard Newby remarks, could not be "separated from a network of social and economic relationship that surrounded it: land was, indeed, these relationships as much as the physical commodity itself" (15). The strictly legal definition of land as an object of private ownership, one that Locke helped to forge and the agriculturalists promoted, freed land from social and economic obligations, and dislodged it from its communal function. Landowners gained "exclusive rights to the access of the land," and those who did not own but lived and worked on the land were forbidden access to it to perform traditional activities such as "gleaning, grazing, the gathering of fuel or the killing of game" (Newby, 15). This transformation of land from a complex web of customary practice "embedded in the social fabric of the local community" to a "form of economic capital" represents, as Newby observes, "a fundamental, qualitative and decisive break" with the past, with the old manorial system, and its protection of "traditionally defined customs, rights, and obligations" (8–16), a system that the middle-class agriculturalists subtly subverted.

In his book *On the Management of Landed Estates,* William Marshall discusses the moral authority and social significance of customary practice as opposed to purely legal rights. In a section titled "The Proper Treatment of Existing Tenantry," Marshall cautions estate superintendents that "established customs and usages," though not formed by "legal contracts . . . ought to be strictly observed until better can be placed in their stead." [25] Tracing the dissolution of customary practice and the institution of legal definitions and contracts to regulate landlord-tenant relations in his book *The Rural Economy of Yorkshire,* Marshall describes how in the past Yorkshire "tenants were in full possession of the farms they occupy; which, until of late years, they have been led, by indulgent treatment, to consider as hereditary possessions, descending father to son, through successive generations; the insertion of their names in the rent-roll having been considered as a tenure, almost as permanent and safe as that given by a more formal admission in a copyhold court."[26] This "species of tenantry," Marshall says, is called being a "tenant at will," meaning the "only tie between the owner and the occupier being the custom of the estate,—or of the country in which it lies;—and the common law of the land" (*Management,* 378). Most tenants relied on this custom and did not have formal leases, as they felt they had an understanding that had worked for generations. They were to maintain the property—fixing gates and repairing hedges, harvesting timber to make repairs and to fashion farm implements, and gathering brushwood for fuel. Marshall notes that "while the necessary confidence on the part of the tenants remained, these principles of management were abundantly sufficient" and the tenants "took care of the estate as their own" (*Yorkshire,* 1:36).

But when the landlords, realizing they need not be bound by the custom and obligation, raised the rents, their tenants grew dissatisfied and felt "rack-rented" and refused or were unable to maintain the good condition of the property. "New regulations respecting timber and the management of lands," Marshall says, had to be introduced. When Marshall states that the "woodlands have been enclosed, and woodwards appointed," he is indicating a complete breakdown in the landlord-tenant relations (*Yorkshire,* 1:36). The implication is that the tenants previously had free access to timber to use as they saw fit to improve the property, but with the institution of high rents, and the consequent loss of the tenants' loyalty and identification with the landlord's interest, the tenants had, in turn, cut timber to pay the high rent. Because the tenants cut timber for sale and abused their privileged access to the woodlands, they were forbidden access to them, woodwards having been hired to protect the forests from the tenants' "illegal" use of the timber.

Marshall concludes that the only way to remedy this messy situation is to institute "legal agreements specifying covenants, and binding a responsible tenant" (*Yorkshire,* 1:37). "Legal contracts or written agreements" are, he believes, the only "rational method of tenanting an estate" (*Management,* 377–79). The tenant at will, the "species of tenantry" Marshall describes as having once been the norm in Yorkshire, is "now fast going into disuse" (378). The reason Marshall gives for the disappearance of tenants at will and copyhold leases is that long-term leases are not advantageous for the proprietors. "The depreciation of the circulatory value of money, and the consequent nominal rise, in the rental value of the land," has rendered such leases impractical because they are unprofitable (378).

In his discussion of the change in tenancy practices in Yorkshire, Marshall chronicles the transformation of land from an entity that is constituted by a complex system of social and economic relations based on obligation and trust into a commodity that has a strictly legal definition as an object of private ownership. While Marshall insists that "legal contracts" are the only "rational method of tenanting an estate" (377), he registers a note of sadness for the passing of the old manorial system that was based on trust and personal negotiation between landlord and tenant. Despite the tone of regret that occasionally surfaces in Marshall's description of the disappearance of the tenant at will and the institution of signed contracts granting ten-year leases, his narrative naturalizes this shift from a customary to a legal definition of land; he assumes that this change is a natural process involving the decay of old, obsolete forms and the growth of new and improved methods of conducting relations between classes.

Middle-Class Masculinity and the Rise of Capitalist Relations

In their efforts to establish themselves as expert managers of land and labor, agricultural writers like Young and Marshall engaged in a redefinition of masculinity that valorized the capacity to quantify, commodify, and organize. Marshall's faith in the law and its ability to establish rational relations between landlords and tenants, and Young's zealous promotion of cost accounting were part of the middle-class redefinition of social and economic relations. But when the agriculturalists generated a discourse that promoted their middle-class skills, they also participated in the construction of what Max Weber describes as the "preconditions" necessary for the existence of "rational capital accounting"—the cornerstone of capitalism. The agriculturalists' accounts of new breeds of cattle, new ideas on crop rotation, new ways to draw up leases, new plans for building canals to transport sheep to market,[27] and new methods for draining wetlands and reclaiming common wastelands contribute to what Weber sees as the six preconditions necessary for the existence of "rational capital accounting." Weber's six preconditions are the use of "rational technology," "the appropriation of all physical means of production," the presence of "free labor," "the absence of irrational limitations on trading in the market," the establishment of "calculable adjudication and administration," and "the commercialization of economic life."[28]

With his tables and charts quantifying and correlating the cost of labor, seed, cattle, tools, and rental of land, Young promoted the commodification of the agricultural processes through the use of rational capital accounting. Marshall, Mordant, and, to a lesser degree, Kent also participated in this new discourse that commodified land and labor, rationalized agricultural production, and maintained control over resources with rational capital accounting. Not only did these writers generate a discourse that established themselves and men like them—who possessed middle-class skills of quantification, valuation, and organization—in positions of authority and power, but more important, they contributed to the capitalistic redefinition of land and labor, transforming them into exchangeable commodities.

While some historians credit this new "professional stratum" of estate managers with being the catalysts for change (Newby, 25–26)—with G. E. Mingay observing that "the land stewards were a vital factor in this progress" and were "an essential ingredient of that complex process known as the agricultural revolution"[29]—most historians tend to look to merchants, financial entrepreneurs, and industrialists when locating the origins of capitalism, overlooking what happened on the land and what happened to the language that described that land. Immanuel Wallerstein gets the closest to recognizing the significance of the "agricultural revolution" when he suggests that "might not the changes in the social relations of production on the land have been an essential element in the process of industrialization." But when he explains why these new social relations were transformative, he argues that either they "made available manpower for industrial work" or they "were a prerequisite to the technical innovation," locating the origin of capitalism in cheap labor and new machines, in short, in the means of production, ignoring the power of language to transform social and economic relations.[30]

Clearly, I am claiming for discourse the power to transform economic relations, an argument that owes much to Nancy Armstrong, Michel Foucault, Louis Althusser, and Raymond Williams, and I am arguing that it is very important to realize that discourse, whether it promotes domestic femininity or the commodification of land, is both class- and gender-inflected. Middle-class men generated the discourse on agriculture not only to procure a space for themselves in the rural economy but also to establish the value and virtue of their middle-class brand of masculinity and to offer it as a viable and potent alternative to the violence and display of aristocratic masculinity. The ability to commodify a social relation is, as every Marxist will attest, a historical phenomenon, but what is less obvious is that it is also a gendered one.

Appendix

This potato crop table is representative of the many tables and charts that fill Young's agricultural narratives.

Expenses	L.	s.	d.
Four ploughings, at 5s.	1	0	0
Three harrowings, at 6s.		1	6
Twelve loads of dung, half price 1s. 6d.	0	18	0
Carriage of ditto		6	0
Planting, men and women	0	2	0
Seed, 30 bushels, cut, &c.	2	0	0
Rolling	0	0	6
Skim-hoe twice	0	2	0
Hand-hoe	0	3	6
Earth up twice	0	2	0
Weeding	0	1	6
Gathering Tops	0	2	0
Taking up and pying	2	0	0
Rent	1	7	0
Taxes	0	6	0
	9	8	8
Produce			
480 bushels worth, in feeding bullocks, young cattle, horses, &c. 8d. a bushel	16	0	0
Expenses	9	8	8
	6	11	4

Source: Arthur Young, *General View of the Agriculture of the County of Lincoln* (1799), pp. 143–44.

Notes

1. Nancy Armstrong, *Desire and Domestic Fiction: A Political History of the Novel* (New York: Oxford University Press, 1987), 73, 59, 59.

2. See G. E. Mingay's essay "The Eighteenth-Century Steward," in *Land, Labour and Population in the Industrial Revolution,* ed. E. L. Jones and G. E. Mingay (London: Edward Arnold, 1967), 3–27, and Howard Newby's chapter on the agricultural revolution, in *Country Life* (London: Weidenfeld and Nicholson, 1987), 6–28. Agricultural and economic historians have relied on Young's writings for their data about the agricultural revolution, the price of foodstuffs, and the living conditions of laborers. For a brilliant discussion of the political and ideological underpinnings of Young's tours, see John Barrell's *The Idea of Landscape and the Sense of Place, 1730–1840* (Cambridge: Cambridge University Press, 1972), chapter 2. With the exception of Leonore Davidoff and Catherine Hall, historians have not thought to analyze Young's writings for its gendered ideological content.

3. *The Complete Family Piece; and, Country Gentleman and Farmer's Best Guide* (1741), 415. For a discussion of the ideological significance of this shift from compendium to treatise, see Keith Tribe, *Land, Labour and Economic Discourse* (London: Routledge, 1978), chapter 4, "The Agricultural Treatise, 1600–1800." A few recipes from *The Complete Family Piece* will illustrate its folksy tone, unscientific approach, and its non-gender-specific subject matter. "An approved Remedy for present Deafness. Take of the Breast-Milk of a Woman that has had her first Male-Child sometime before, and drop three or four Drops of it warm, as it comes from the Nipple, into the Part affected" (72). A remedy for headaches is equally quaint: "Take green Hemlock that is tender, and put it in your Socks, so that it may lie thinly between them and the soles of your Feet; shift the Herbs once a day" (72).

4. Howard Newby, *Country Life: A Social History of Rural England* (London: Weidenfeld and Nicholson, 1987), 25. Subsequent references to this work will be placed in parentheses following the quotation.

5. Leonore Davidoff and Catherine Hall, *Family Fortunes: Men and Women of the English Middle Class, 1780–1850* (Chicago: University of Chicago Press, 1987), 205. Subsequent references to this work will be placed in parentheses following the quotation.

6. Arthur Young, *The Farmer's Letters to the People of England* (London, 1767),

294. Subsequent references to this work will be placed in parentheses following the quotation.

7. William Marshall, *The Rural Economy of Norfolk: Comprising the Management of Landed Estates and the Present Practice of Husbandry,* 2 vols. (1787), 2:200–201.

8. John Mordant, *The Complete Steward; or, The Duty of a Steward to his Lord. Containing several new methods for the improvement of his Lord's estate,* 2 vols. (London, 1761), 2:382. Subsequent references will be placed in parentheses following the quotation.

9. Arthur Young, *Rural Oeconomy and Farmer's Kalendar* (1770), quoted in Newby, *Country Life,* 27.

10. William Marshall, *On the Landed Property of England, an elementary and practical Treatise; containing the Purchase, the Improvement, and the Management of Landed Estates* (London, 1804), 349.

11. In the table of contents to his book *On the Landed Property of England,* Marshall has outlined his section "The Business of Valuation," a systematic analysis of assigning a monetary value to property:

12. Arthur Young, *A General View of the Agriculture of the County of Lincoln* (London, 1799), 20.

13. Arthur Young, *A Six Weeks Tour, Through the Southern Counties of England and Wales* (London, 1768), 21–22.

14. Arthur Young, *The Farmer's Tour through the East of England,* 4 vols. (London, 1771), 2: 161.

15. Nathaniel Kent, *Hints to Gentlemen of Landed Property* (London, 1775), 205.

16. Nathaniel Kent, "On the Size of Farms," *Georgical Essays* 15 (1803): 281.

17. Kent, *Hints to Gentlemen,* 227.

18. Newby, *Country Life,* 11. Susan Staves describes this change in ideas about property as "a shift from qualitative distinctions (for example, forest versus meadow, freehold versus copyhold, life tenant versus terms of years) to quantitative valuation (equivalency in numerical cash terms)." See her *Married Women's Separate Property in England, 1660–1833* (Cambridge: Harvard University Press, 1990), 211.

19. Henry Mackenzie, *The Man of Feeling* (1771; reprint, New York: Oxford University Press, 1987), 88.

20. See Appendix for an example of Young's use of charts to quantify labor.

21. Harold Perkin, *The Origins of Modern British Society* (1969; reprint, London: Routledge and Kegan Paul, 1985), 49.

22. J. G. A. Pocock, *Virtue, Commerce and History* (New York: Cambridge University Press, 1985), 48.

23. William Cobbett was very concerned about the dissolution of paternal ties between farmers and their laborers. Attacking the shift from moral to political economies and the creation of what he called the "farming aristocracy, who now mix with attorneys, bankers, jews, jobbers, and all sorts of devils," he fears that "the link in the connection, the community of feeling, between the farmer and the labourer is broken" (14). See Cobbett, *Cobbett's Weekly Political Register* 39 (April 7, 1821): 2–22.

24. Robert Southey, *Sir Thomas More; or, Colloquies on the Progress and Prospects of Society,* 2 vols. (London, 1829), 2:224–25.

25. William Marshall, *On the Management of Landed Estates* (London, 1806), 373. Subsequent references to this work will be placed in parentheses following the quotation.

26. William Marshall, *The Rural Economy of Yorkshire,* 2 vols. (London, 1787), 1: 23.

27. See Arthur Young's *Six Months Tour through the North of England,* 4 vols. (1770) for an elaborate description of the construction of Duke of Bridgewater's canal, which, according to Young, "will be the easiest, cheapest, and best way of sending goods of all kinds from and to Liverpool and Manchester" (1:287).

28. Max Weber, *On Charisma and Institution Building,* ed. S. N. Eisenstadt (Chicago: University of Chicago Press, 1968), 140–42.

29. G. E. Mingay, "The Eighteenth-Century Land Steward," in *Land, Labour and Population in the Industrial Revolution,* ed. E. L. Jones and G. E. Mingay (London: Edward Arnold, 1967), 27.

30. Immanuel Wallerstein, *The Modern World System III: The Second Era of Great Expansion of the Capitalist World-Economy, 1740s–1840s* (New York: Academic Press, 1989), 14–16.

Sermons and Strictures: Conduct-Book Propriety and Property Relations in Late Eighteenth-Century England

✎ *Kathryn Kirkpatrick*

> Conduct material is instructive, not only because it probably
> served a prescriptive function for mothers and daughters,
> but also because as products of the everyday discourse of
> eighteenth-century propriety, the essays are themselves
> expressions of the implicit values of their culture. Indeed, in
> many respects this conduct material provides the best access
> both to the way in which this culture defined female nature
> and to the ways in which a woman of this period would have
> experienced the social and psychological dimensions of
> ideology. For in reproducing the ideological configurations
> that protected bourgeois society, both the hierarchy of values
> and the rhetorical strategies contained in these works provided
> real women with the terms by which they conceptualized
> and interpreted their own behavior and desires.
>
> —Mary Poovey, *The Proper Lady and the Woman Writer*

Judging from sales, James Fordyce's *Sermons to Young Women* (1766) and Hannah More's *Strictures on the Modern System of Female Education* (1799) were two of the most popular conduct books in late eighteenth- and early nineteenth-century England. The former ran to fourteen editions by 1813 and the latter to thirteen editions by 1836.

As Mary Poovey suggests, these works give us access to the ways in which gender was constructed during this period—their very existence was founded on the assumption that gender characteristics *could* be prescribed, and they demonstrated the fact by outlining the particular qualities that constituted the social naming and differentiation of the sexes.

Although Fordyce addressed his *Sermons* to "young persons in genteel life," and More subtitled her book with "a View of the Principles and Conduct prevalent among Women of Rank and Fortune," Maurice Quinlan gives a clearer idea about the audience that provided a market for these works. In *Victorian Prelude: A History of English Manners, 1700–1830,* Quinlan links the rise of conduct books with the emergence of the middle classes in England and the increasing access to property and status through capital: "It was not surprising that books of etiquette were popular at a time when many people found themselves in a class superior to that in which they had been born. To the new middle classes, who were not quite sure of the proprieties to be observed in the upper walks of society, any information upon manners was naturally welcome." [1] Information on *women's* manners in particular appears to have been welcome because conduct books for women far outnumbered those published for men during this period. [2] Part of Fordyce's response to his perception of increasing social mobility was to attempt to convince his female readers that, though the boundaries between class might be becoming less rigid, the boundaries between codes of gender behavior were not. More, on the other hand, attempted to contain class mobility by making strict distinctions between the behavior of middle-class and upper-class women. If middle-class women were to fulfill their God-given duties, she argued, they were necessarily prohibited from aspiring to the *upper* classes. [3] Both works, I would argue, not only give us access to the prevailing gender codes of behavior, but they also helped to formulate these codes.

In my reading of Fordyce's and More's texts, I am particularly interested in exploring how material and economic relations helped to define what was considered "proper" in the behavior of middle-class women. I want, therefore, to focus on the connections between property and propriety in these texts: first, by examining the rhetorical strategies both authors employ (specifically, their frequent use of property metaphors to outline rules of propriety); and second, by describing the ways that Fordyce's and More's prescriptions set up a proprietary relationship between women and their reputations, and then seek to appropriate women's propriety for bourgeois ideology.

If we grant language the capacity to register changes in social relations, then there is certainly linguistic support for examining property's relation to propriety during this period. The *OED* tells us that both *property* and *propriety* derive from the same Old French word—*propriété*—and that until around the middle of the eighteenth century the two words were used interchangeably in England. Hence, we find *property* defined as "the condition of being owned by or belonging to some person or persons; the holding of something as one's own," and *propriety,* similarly, as "the fact of being owned by someone, or of being one's own; the right of possession or use." The first definition remains with us, while the second has become obsolete. Moreover, while we still use *property* in the sense of "a piece of land owned; a landed estate," the equivalent definition of *propriety*—"a piece of land owned by someone, a private possession or estate"—makes its last recorded appearance in British English in *Athenaeum* in 1889. In the meantime, *propriety* began to take on a life of its own; as early as 1782 we find it paired with a different concept: "conformity with good manners or polite usage; correctness of behavior or morals."

A similar material base exists in the etymology of another common conduct-book word—*improvement.* The *OED* gives its early definitions as "the turning of land to better account; the cultivation or occupation of land" and "a piece of land 'improved' by enclosure or building." By around 1700, the meaning of *improvement,* like *propriety,* began to become more generalized to "the action or process of making or becoming better; betterment or amelioration."

The shift from a specific to a more generalized meaning in the etymologies of both of these words has at least one significant result—it occults the continued relation of both concepts to property. The issue becomes more complex when we discover that the meaning of *property* had itself changed: it did not include the ownership of land until the early eighteenth century. In the Middle Ages, *property* meant "an attribute or quality belonging to a thing or person." This was a definition it shared with *propriety.* What we have, then, in both property and propriety, is an initial move away from the description of human attributes toward a description of relations with things outside the self, particularly land. When *propriety* comes again to be associated with human attributes, it is in a new relation to them, for now the attributes are themselves external—they take the form of "manners," "polite usage," and "behavior."

As we shall see, the redefining of *property* finds its counterpart in this period in economic and social relations—by readjusting legal definitions of ownership away from communal land-use toward exclusive private use, capitalists were able to exclude large groups of farm laborers from access to land and a livelihood. Similarly, married middle-class women found their already tenuous access to property in land severed by a new emphasis on personal or moveable property. What both groups gained, however, was a new sense of ownership of the self. That is, laboring men and women possessed their labor to exchange on the market for wages, while a middle-class woman possessed her reputation, her propriety; this she might also exchange on the market for one of the few forms of financial support prescribed for her class—a marriage settlement with a reasonably wealthy man. That conduct-book authors of the period recognized propriety as a commodity is implied by their assumption that a woman might be given a pattern by which to "make" herself. But we shall see that "making" the self by prescription became inseparable from the appropriation and use of that self by the prescribers.

Before I turn to a discussion of Fordyce's and More's texts, I want to describe an economic and social change in relations to property in eighteenth-century England that parallels the linguistic unhinging of property and propriety.

From about 1760, wealthy landowners in England began to use their considerable influence in Parliament to speed up the process by which large areas of common land were being enclosed as private property. The enclosing of common land began as early as the thirteenth century and was carried out extensively in the fifteenth and sixteenth centuries. In the latter half of the eighteenth century, enclosing again increased: thus, while there were just over two hundred enclosure acts in the sixty years before 1760, the period 1761 to 1801 saw the number rise to two thousand.[4] In all, under the enclosure acts of the late eighteenth and early nineteenth centuries, six million acres of common land in England were divided into approximately five thousand enclosures.[5] It was the climax of a process by which farmland was consolidated in the hands of a relative few and countless others were left without access to this land.

In *The Making of the English Working Class*, E. P. Thompson describes the enclosure acts as a "plain enough case of class robbery, played according to fair rules of property and law laid down by a Parliament of property-owners and lawyers."[6] In fact, enclosure acts registered their own opposition, for they were only necessary when a landowner met with protest from the villagers and cottagers who used the common land in accordance with long-standing rights of custom and tenancy. Enclosure commissioners tended to disregard these rights. So too did judges who "sought to reduce use-rights to an equivalent in things or in money, and hence to bring them within the universal currency of capitalistic definitions of ownership."[7]

These were the maneuvers that agrarian capitalists masked with the term "improvement." While landowners with capital were able to employ new farming techniques to increase crop production and profits on their enclosed property, small farming families and cottagers lost the right to graze their cattle and cut wood or turf on common land, activities that, combined with wage labor and a small holding, had allowed them a small measure of independence. Among cottagers, who often relied upon the combined resources of the husband's wage and the wife's productive work in the home (sometimes including her revenue from domestic industries such as spinning), the decline of domestic industries and the loss of access to land for gardens, and for the raising of poultry as well as other common rights such as gleaning and collecting firewood, meant that married women were reduced for the first time to complete economic dependence on their husbands.[8] If they became wage laborers, as many of them did, they were paid far less for their work than men. Moreover, widows and single women, who had been able to support themselves through the sale of eggs and dairy products (from poultry and cattle raised on village common land), now often found themselves dependent on the parish.[9]

The village poor were not the only victims of the process of enclosure. Tenant farmers, who had the financial resources to hold out for a time, were eventually pushed off their land by higher rents and their "inability to adopt the new methods of their richer neighbors."[10] This group, together with the local landless, comprised a new class of laborers who owned nothing except their labor, which they were obliged to hire out for wages if they were to survive. These dispossessed laborers thus either became entirely dependent upon those who now exercised exclusive control of the land or moved to urban areas where the terms of employment—in workshops or small factories— were essentially the same.

The change in relations to the land created a change in social relations. The old order had been (at least in some senses) feudalistic. That is, in addition to the right of access to common land, farm laborers had also relied on the guardianship of their landlord. According to John Harrison in *The Birth and Growth of Industrial England:* "In a deferential society, squirearchical leadership, while it preserved the interests of a privileged minority, also provided a form of public service. The squire and his family recognized obligations towards 'their' people in the village and dispensed justice and charity in a patriarchal manner."[11] As Harrison suggests, this social order was firmly hierarchical and ensured the status of a privileged few—the wealth and independence of roughly 130,000 aristocrats and gentlemen and their families was supported by over five million farmers, tradesmen, and laborers.[12] Yet the compensations for the less privileged included the economic security and social certainty of a contractual relationship with landlords and the right of access to common land.

With rural society increasingly geared to cash production for the market and landownership increasingly determined not only by birth but also by cash purchase, the paternalistic order of reciprocal duties and responsibilities gave way to the enlightened self-interest and profiteering of the capitalist classes. In the process, generations of laborers experienced displacement and extreme poverty. The triumph of bourgeois relations in the countryside was marked by the failure of the Speenhamland system, enacted in 1795 to assure laborers a subsistence level wage. That these measures were necessary at all reflects the deterioration of the reciprocal bond between landlords and laborers. That landowners took advantage of them to cut wages still further marks the beginnings of an antagonistic class society.

In the transformation of economic and social relationships toward capitalistic definitions of ownership, middle-class women found their relation to productive labor radically changed. Ivy Pinchbeck, in *Women Workers and the Industrial Revolution,* outlines the effects of agrarian capitalism on the lives of these women: "The mistress of a large farm who at the beginning of our period [1750–1850] was actively concerned in the management and productive work of a large household, had at the end of it as a result of the increase in wealth, joined the ranks of the leisured classes."[13] Women joining the middle class enjoyed an advance in social status but lost the exercise of practical and business capacities. They no longer supervised dairies and cheesemaking enterprises or kept financial accounts or oversaw gardens and orchards. Their lives, in this sense, appeared empty of productive content.

In a parallel move, women lost what little legal control they had had over the landed property they brought to marriage. Common law protection of married women's real property (freehold land) had always been heavily qualified—husbands controlled its income during marriage and a woman was unable to will it. But a husband's rights were limited to the use of his wife's land; he could not sell it without her court-recorded consent, and at his death this property came into her exclusive possession and control (until she married again). In the Middle Ages, when land constituted the chief form of wealth, married women thus had some limited control of real property and widows could own it. But this marginal control of property was eroded during the transition from feudalism to capitalism. In the late eighteenth century, daughters of merchants and tradesmen were more likely to bring personal property to a marriage than land: "money from earnings and investments, household furnishings and stock in trade."[14] Over such personal property a husband had absolute control: he could spend it or will it, and if he died, his wife received no more than half of their combined personal property.

For rich women there was a form of protection. Separate estates in equity allowed for trustees to manage a married woman's separate property free from the control or possession of her husband. But even this remedy had less to do with a woman's actual access to property than her family's desire to protect it from a spendthrift husband.[15] Here, too, a woman's relation to wealth was mediated by a trustee, often appointed by her family. Not infrequently, the family appointed her husband himself. Although in theory obliged to follow the instructions of his wife, the husband's actual uses of settlements suggested that the wishes of the wife usually conveniently coincided with those of the husband and his family. As Susan Staves has observed, the wife who did attempt to control her own property was further hindered by the complexity of property law itself: "The more abstract and remote the newer forms of property, the more difficult women, in the absence of appropriate education and socialization, were likely to find understanding their entitlements or controlling their assets." [16]

Thus, a married middle-class woman's relation to property, as it had been redefined in capitalistic terms of ownership, was both materially and legally alienated. In this sense, she had, like the farm laborers, been dispossessed. That the new terms of ownership—enclosure, private property, and improvement—were used to articulate conduct-book prescriptions for middle-class women during this period is telling: the new domestic woman was to be constructed precisely for her usefulness to the propertied male. [17]

One of the most striking conduct-book uses of property metaphors appears in *Sermons to Young Women* (1766). In this book, Fordyce uses the tropes of private property and common land to counsel his readers on how best to avoid the dangers of seduction:

> Even the worst men are struck by the sovereignty of female worth, unambitious of appearing. But, if a young person (supposing her dispositions, in other respects, ever so good) will be always breaking loose through each domestic enclosure, and ranging, at large the wide common world, those destroyers will see her in a very different point of light. They will consider her as lawful game, to be hunted down without hesitation. And, if her virtue, or (which, to a woman, is in effect nearly the same) her reputation, should be lost, what will it avail the poor wanderer, to plead that she meant only a little harmless amusement, and never thought of straying into the abhorred paths of vice? [18]

Though Fordyce begins this passage by affirming the self-evident nature of "female worth," we quickly see that this worth does not travel very well—it is more self-evident in some contexts than in others. For here the metaphor of enclosing common land is used to circumscribe the private sphere, "the domestic enclosure," where women of propriety most properly reside. In "breaking loose," "ranging" and "straying" into the "wide common world," a woman threatens her status as *private* property; she becomes freely accessible to other men.

Moreover, by likening women to "game" in danger of being "hunted down," Fordyce puts class conflict at the service of gender prescription. Among the luxuries of enclosing landlords was "the new practice of preserving game for competitive massacre and the increasingly savage laws against poaching."[19] The sentences for poaching included transportation and even death; they effectively enforced the landowner's exclusive use of property. By identifying women as "game" in this passage, Fordyce thus locates them at a nexus of particular violence, for in addition to hunting for necessary food on enclosed land, laborers during this period also engaged in the destruction of property—the burning of buildings and wounding of cattle—as a form of protest against their rescinded user-rights to the land. Fordyce deflects this class violence onto women and uses it as a powerful threat.

But the threat is a complicated one, for it obscures the real terms of the class conflict it evokes. Poaching, by definition, could only take place on *enclosed* land. But because Fordyce wishes to equate enclosed land with the domestic enclosure as the proper sphere for middle-class women, he cannot represent the enclosure as the place where class violence actually occurred. Instead, he inverts the terms. Common land becomes the site of danger for middle-class women. Here a woman becomes "lawful" game because she loses the status of private property. The fact that defining land and game as private property for exclusive use had created the real terms of the danger to which she is exposed is denied. In this way, the middle-class woman who strays from the domestic enclosure can be represented as the agent of her own destruction. Thus, Fordyce has evoked class conflict in this passage only to distort its actual terms so that he can make use of it as a threat.

By naming the site of "female worth" as the domestic enclosure, Fordyce positions himself firmly on the side of capital and allies himself with the wealthy enclosures of land. That common land fills in as the negative value of public space, the location of "destroyers" and "abhorred paths of vice," makes doubly clear that Fordyce has little sympathy for those without the power of private property. Indeed, his treatment of "female worth" parallels the capitalist formula of value created by the circuit of capital, for outside the circuit of private property, a woman's value, be "her dispositions . . . ever so good," collapses. Thus, prescribing women's propriety becomes inseparable from appropriating it because only men, and men with private property, can give it value.

The rhetorical strategy that we find in the passage above—a prescription for behavior backed up with a threat—occurs frequently in Fordyce's *Sermons*. His arguments tend to go something like this: he begins by reminding women of their dependence (and for dependence read *economic* dependence) on men. Then he moves on to suggest that women are often uninformed about men's true opinion of them, for Fordyce has often observed that when women are not present, for example, after dinner in the library over brandy and tobacco, men are in fact often "unkind" and "unjust" to them. At this point in his argument, Fordyce has placed himself in a position of considerable power with his readers, for it is *he* who can inform them of what men really think of them. The first forecasts are not good. Fordyce muses, what would happen if *all* men thought women were "foolish" and "vicious," "what would become of humankind?" (13). Fordyce is quick to tell us, and in a manner that ensures his indispensability as a prescriber of conduct. If the view of women as "vicious" and "foolish" were to become widespread, men would cease to ally themselves with women and thus exclude them from the economic support of marriage. Indeed, he maintains, an unwillingness to heed these warnings involves considerable danger. For women who are not concerned about the opinion of men must, by definition, be unconcerned with their own characters, for it is the opinion of men that gives these characters value. For Fordyce, this sort of heedlessness prevails in women who have already "lost their native honours" and "sense of shame," "an infamy to which they would have hardly descended had they not first sunk in their own estimation" (14).

Thus, in order to make use of propriety for profit, Fordyce counsels young women to tend their reputations by observing the rules of conduct that he lays down for them—their reward, he assures his readers, will be a profitable settlement. Certain behaviors are sure to alienate those who possess property—men. And if men turn against women and refuse to marry, they effectively deny women's access to what they must have to live—property. Hence, the wise woman tailors her conduct to the demands of the market.

In her essay "The Rise of the Domestic Woman," Nancy Armstrong observes: "After reading several dozen or more conduct books, one is struck with a sense of their emptiness—a lack of what today we consider 'real' information about the female subject and the object world that she is supposed to occupy."[20] As we have seen, the lives of these women *had* been emptied of a great deal of productive labor. Conduct books reflect that change: "In contrast with earlier domestic economies, the eighteenth-century conduct books ceased to provide advice for the care of livestock or the concoction of medicinal cures." [21] Such productive activities gave way, in Fordyce's opinion, to two activities: reading and prayer.

In his prescriptions for reading, Fordyce is most fond of books like his own, for such books "tell you most convincingly what you are, and what you ought to be"; they "address themselves with the greatest power to the spirit of ingenuity, humility, contrition, self-denial, solid virtue and affectionate devotion" (274). Besides reading conduct books, a woman might also read religion and history. Of the latter, the two most desirable works included biographies and memoirs that offered sheltered women mediated experience of the "wide common world." Such books, however, were not without perils and Fordyce was quick to prescribe the requisite effects of this reading. There were two desirable aspects. First, biographical works should "inspire gratitude for the peculiar blessings of our country," and second, they should "excite pity for those in ignorance and barbarity and admiration for their virtue in dealing with such heavy disadvantages" (163). Works that met such criteria would thus assure the middle-class reader that she lived in the best of all possible situations.

For Fordyce, his prescriptions for reading were eventually to become so internalized by the reader that they became her "own" taste: "you will be disposed to choose and adhere to those waters, of whatever communion, that are calculated to make you most in love with your Saviour, and your duty" (273). One of the duties that the middle-class woman was to learn from her reading was how to contain and control her own feelings as well as those of her husband. To be "in love with" her Savior required the pious woman to engage in frequent and fervent prayer. Although Fordyce claimed to be no advocate of a Methodistical "wild enthusiasm," his recommendation that a woman converse with God throughout the day and lock herself in her room after sermons in order to meditate on her faith, are clearly means of directing and appropriating strong feeling. She was to "silence" her passions in this way and in turn tame the passions of her husband so that "the calm, yet interesting joys, he tastes in her society, occupy all his leisure" (242). Hence, to internalize Fordyce's standards for reading was also to internalize the code of behavior that these prescribed texts contained. In this way, the middle-class woman was to become the agent of her own surveillance and control.

This linking of reading, religion, and duty is not arbitrary in Fordyce's work; they come together to form the middle-class wife's primary domestic function: "Your business chiefly is to read Men, in order to make yourselves agreeable and useful" (162). In her "reading" of men, a woman's religious lessons in humility, self-denial and affectionate devotion were all to be exercised, for if husbands were wayward or restless, it was chiefly because wives had failed them in the exercise of their duties:

> had you behaved to them with a more respectful observance, and a more
> equal tenderness; studying their humours, and overlooking their mis-
> takes, submitting to their opinions in matters indifferent, passing by
> little instances of unevenness, caprice or passion, giving soft answers
> to hasty words; complaining as seldom as possible, and making it your
> daily care to relieve their anxieties, to enliven the hour of dullness, and
> call up the ideas of felicity; had you pursued this conduct, I doubt not
> but you would have maintained, and even increased their esteem. (332)

Here the "improvement" of a middle-class wife is along capitalistic lines of ownership—her value is determined exclusively in terms of her usefulness to her husband. This is the end toward which all Fordyce's prescriptions tend. Even his chastisement of vanity, fashionable dress, and going frequently into society is based on the fear of disrupting a man's domestic sanctuary. This sanctuary was threatened when women adopted the behavior of bourgeois individualism. For what was so disturbing about women going in public was that they risked picking up the behaviors common to the world, including the competitive habits of the laissez-faire marketplace. In Fordyce's words, this would produce "rivalship in figure" and "quarrels for conquest." The danger is that "the folly and presumption before diffused and practiced on all, are now, perhaps, concentrated and turned upon the husband" (330).

The reason that, like Armstrong, we cannot find a recognizable female subject in Fordyce's conduct book is because it was an escape from the world of competitive subjects that the middle-class man wished to find in his home. Not surprisingly, then, the most reputable woman in *Sermons to Young Women* is a dead one. In fact, she is the only woman in the book who receives a name. And Fordyce's ideal woman,

Isabella, is actually a child: "Her mind was very early accomplished; it was that of a woman, when she was but a child" (347). The mind of a woman in the body of a child. Such creatures exist (happily) only in heaven: "Heaven beheld so gentle a spirit with complacence, and took her way from the evil to come; took her to itself, in all the purity of untainted virtue" (357). Finally, the evil that *Sermons to Young Women* seeks to combat is the desire of women to *be* subjects.

Fordyce begins his denigration of women as active subjects in his description of the abuses of study and learning: "That men are frighted at Female pedantry, is very certain. A woman that affects to dispute, to decide, to dictate on every subject; that watches or makes opportunities of throwing out scraps of literature, or shreds of philosophy, in every company; that engrosses the conversation as if she alone were qualified to entertain; that betrays, in short, a boundless intemperance of tongue, together with an inextinguishable passion for shining by the splendor of her supposed talents; such a woman is truly insufferable" (176). If we compare this to the earlier passage on women's duties toward their husbands, we find that what must be tolerated in a man is "insufferable" in a wife. For here a woman's energies are enlisted on her own behalf—she disputes, she decides, she dictates, she makes opportunities. For Fordyce, she is clearly unenclosed and uncontrolled—"boundless" and "inextinguishable." This woman has no time to "read" men; she is too engaged in asserting herself, a self that Fordyce reads in order to dismantle her—for her talents are "supposed"; she is only a fraud. And of course, in this case, men need not be "frighted."

But Fordyce saved his most damning indictments for women who presumed to take their propriety into their own hands. Such women used prescribed codes of behavior to secure their own ends: "Those more accomplished ensnarers are sufficiently aware, that there is no allurement equal to that of maiden virtue; and therefore, having lost the reality, they study to retain the appearance" (64). This is one way of violating male authority over female propriety—to *seem* to possess "maiden virtue," to use prescribed standards of proper conduct to "ensnare." The violation, of course, is of male control of female desire (and it is interesting here that it is men who become the game and women the poachers). A lovely example of just such a woman appears in Jane Austen's early novel *Lady Susan*. Here the heroine uses the conventions of propriety as shrewdly as any businessman—she arranges appearances to attract the attention of lovers, acquires docility and grace to gain residence at her in-laws', and exploits the affections for a time of an "unexceptionable" Sir James to relieve herself of the burden of her daughter. The danger of such women for Fordyce is clear—they deny appropriation of their propriety by men.

For Fordyce, to behave in this way is to behave precisely like a man. It is a short step to the overt display of male gender behavior: "Next to this, is the dislike we feel to her who has contracted a certain briskness of air, a levity of deportment, which, though by good nature, or courtesy or custom, distinguished from the brazen front and the bold attack of the prostitute, does yet, I cannot help saying, approach too near them, and can never, I am sure, be pleasing to men of sentiment" (65). By invoking the image of the prostitute, a woman whose ownership of herself manifests itself in the literal selling of her body on the market to men, Fordyce unwittingly reveals the essential terms of his own prescriptions. It would be left to Mary Wollstonecraft and Mary Ann Radcliffe to make the obvious connections.

But of course in the real social life of Fordyce's time, some women were unconvinced by persuasive argument. For these he reserved a subtext of male violence—the final remedy for the wife who refused to surrender her status as a subject. And not only did men have the right to employ violence to subdue such women, but they were also invited to do so by the women themselves. Fordyce insisted that male resistance was a necessary evil that women brought upon themselves when they refused "soft compliance and meek submission": "a disputatious, perverse, and stubborn female, will always offend; and, where there is any manhood left, will often provoke to a dangerous degree" (324). Indeed, the threat of male violence was for Fordyce retroactive; a controlling and insolent fiancée reaped in marriage as she had sown in courtship: "She forgets how soon an immoderate fondness is cured by connubial familiarity, and what severe revenge may be taken after marriage by him whom she treated ill before it, were he disposed to retaliate" (322). Against an abusive husband during this period, a wife had few legal remedies. Even for a serious injury, such as causing the loss of an eye, a husband was usually subjected only to a light fine.[22] Moreover, it was illegal to give shelter to a fleeing wife without the consent of her husband, and should she choose divorce, she could succeed only rarely. Before 1857, only four

Englishwomen in a 150-year period petitioned Parliament for divorce, and in these cases "adultery had to be aggravated by bigamy, incest or rape."[23] Thus, Fordyce's threat was not empty. What is instructive is that he admits violence as an option and one for which *women* rather than men are ultimately responsible.

Fordyce's work did not go unnoticed by the objects of his prescriptions. In Jane Austen's *Pride and Prejudice,* we find Fordyce's *Sermons to Young Women* in the hands of the pompous and insinuating curate Mr. Collins. After asserting that he never reads novels, Mr. Collins picks up *Sermons* and begins to read aloud. Here is the response of a young woman present: "Lydia gaped as he opened the volume, and before he had, with very monotonous solemnity, read three pages, she interrupted him."[24] She interrupts him with an account of her day and thereby counters the attempt to prescribe her behavior with her own lived experiences. That Lydia is seduced by and eventually elopes with the notorious Wickham shows us how well and truly she has ignored Fordyce's advice. But for this violation of prescribed rules of conduct, she suffers neither prostitution nor abandonment nor death. Although the wayward couple live an unsettled life, "always moving from place to place in quest of a cheap situation, and always spending more than they ought," Lydia's punishment amounts only to economic disappointment; her rash marriage has meant that she finds herself maintained not quite in the manner that she would have liked.

Indeed, even for prostitutes themselves prospects were not always inevitably bleak in late eighteenth-century England. By 1786, the charitable Magdalene Asylum had admitted 2,414 repentant prostitutes and returned 1,571 to "decent places in society."[25] Yet even these exceptions suggest that Fordyce's representations err only in degree; the penalties for becoming a female subject were, by anyone's standards, high—if not death, then economic disappointment; if not prostitution, then displacement. As with laborers in the face of game laws and enclosure acts, small victories might be won, but the campaign was always, for the time being, lost.

In turning to the work of the moralist Hannah More, we cannot help but be struck by an enormous contradiction. How does a woman, fettered by the prescriptions of docility, modesty, and chastity, confined to the "domestic enclosure" of the home, enter the public realm of discourse on propriety without violating the very codes she is engaged in putting forward? Indeed, "writing for publication . . . cultivates and calls attention to the woman as subject, as initiator of direct action, as a person deserving of notice for her own sake." [26] More introduces two remedies for the apparent contradiction. First, she positions herself among women of "rank and fortune" for whom teaching middle-class women their proper place is an acceptable (if self-serving) duty. Second, she becomes an evangelist. By redefining women's role according to the religious doctrine of good works in the world, Hannah More creates a sanctioned realm of action for herself as a woman writer. [27]

These remedies were themselves not without contradictions. For one thing, it was neither rank nor an inherited fortune that made possible More's very active and public life. Her father had been the master of a charity school and her mother was the daughter of a farmer. Moreover, the independent income that allowed for her freedom of movement was money she earned herself—from a successful girl's school in Bristol as well as from her religious works, conduct books, and tracts—added to a two-hundred-pound annuity she had accepted in 1773 "as recompense for a broken engagement." Thus, although More located herself in her works as upper class, her origins and sources of income have led Mary Waldron and Donna Landry to describe her as middle class. As Waldron observes, "She moved in an upper-class circle in London as a privilege rather than by right of birth. That she was aware of this is evident from the almost unbearably obsequious tone she chooses to adopt in letters addressed to those above her station." [28]

As if to deny her own ambiguous class status, More spent her life formulating prohibitions against exactly the sort of social mobility from which she herself had benefited. An obsession with outlining and enforcing the distinctions between ranks runs through her work. Even her monumental efforts in the founding of schools for the poor were marked by an insistence on controlling and directing their energies toward service of the upper classes. What she taught them, she wrote to her friend Wilberforce, was the Bible, the catechism, and "such coarse works as may fit them for servants. I allow for no writing for the poor." [29]

In *Strictures on the Modern System of Female Education,* More displays a similar preoccupation with rank by dissuading her middle-class readers from aspiring to the accomplishments of the "great." For middle-class women, drawing, music, and languages are not appropriate pursuits: "Their new course of education, and the habits of life, and elegance of dress connected with it, peculiarly unfits them for the active duties of their own very important condition; while, with frivolous eagerness and secondhand opportunities, they run to snatch a few of those showy requirements which decorate the great." [30] For More, only upper-class women have the leisure to perform these "showy requirements" well. The knowledge of a foreign language in a middle-class woman, for instance, is simply ridiculous. Because most of her time is required for "domestic offices," she is unlikely ever to run into a foreigner to whom she might speak this language; and as for foreign literature, middle-class women "have seldom time to possess themselves of all that valuable knowledge which the books of their own country so abundantly furnish" (1:65).

Like Fordyce, More sometimes resorted to ridicule in the face of female assertiveness. Such a strategy appears in her discussion of women who turn to writing for either personal solace or making money: "Is a lady, however destitute of talents, education, or knowledge of the world, whose studies have been completed in a circulating library, in any distress of mind? The writing of a novel suggests itself as the best soother of sorrows! Does she labour under any depression of circumstances? Writing a novel occurs as the readiest receipt for mending them" (1:171). In a footnote to this passage, More makes an exception for "females of real genius"; as a former playwright, she no doubt numbered herself among them. Moreover, membership in an exclusive Bluestocking group presumably gave More access to a higher standard of taste than those women whose resources limited them to the holdings of a circulating library. Having thus exempted herself, what remains is a rather vicious class attack no less insidious than Fordyce's gender-related posturing. For here More assures her readers that middle-class women cannot write and that therefore any bid for independence by them on this front is futile.

It was perhaps her new commitment to religious writing that More felt exempted her from the attacks she made on women novelists. In 1794, she wrote in her diary, "I now read little of which religion is not the subject." [31] Yet even the province of the spirit presents More with some problems. In harnessing the energy of women for the evangelical crusade, she must allow them to act, albeit in a limited realm. Here is how she counsels them:

the character of a consistent Christian is as carefully to be maintained, as that of a fiery disputant is to be avoided; and she who is afraid to avow her principles, or ashamed to defend them, has little claim to that honourable title. A profligate, who laughs at the most sacred institutions, and keeps out of the way of everything which comes under the appearance of formal instruction, may be disconcerted by the modest yet spirited rebuke of a delicate woman, whose life adorns the doctrines which her conversation defends. (1:8)

Here is a woman who avows her principles and adorns doctrines, who is modest yet spirited, who rebukes with delicacy. The formula is confusing enough, but when coupled with More's description of why women in particular make good Christians, her prescriptions for action become truly bewildering:[32]

as women are naturally more affectionate than fastidious, they are likely both to read and to hear with a less critical spirit than men: they will not be on the watch to detect errors, so much as to gather improvement; they have seldom that hardness which is acquired by dealing deeply with books of controversy, but are more inclined to works which quicken the devotional feelings, than to such as awaken a spirit of doubt and scepticism. They are less disposed to consider the compositions they peruse, as material on which to ground objections and answers, than as helps to faith and rules of life. (2:34)

Unlike Fordyce, for whom the separation of a woman and her reputation serves the function of convincing her that she can pattern herself along the lines he suggests, More is concerned with describing an essential nature for women. This enables her to chart out a small province for women without seriously violating conduct-book codes. For it is woman as naturally tender, impressionable, and feeling that makes her such a suitable candidate for Christianity. And it is the rewards of Christianity in turn that are to console her for the lack of privilege she experiences in the present life:

Let the weaker sex take comfort, that in their very exemptions from privileges, which they are sometimes disposed to envy, consist their security and happiness. The christian hope more than reconciles Christian women to these petty privations, by substituting a noble prize for their ambition, "the prize of the high calling of God in Christ Jesus." By substituting, for that popular and fluctuating voice, which may

cry "Hosanna" and "crucify" in a breath, that "favour of God which is
eternal life." (2:36, 38)

Here the Christian claim that the meek shall inherit the earth makes
a good fit with conduct-book prescriptions of subordination to men.
More goes on to argue that the gender-code behavior of men exposes
them to worldly temptations from which proper women are safe. The
commerce of men with the world exposes them to the impieties of philosophy, the paganisms of literature, and the pride of knowledge. The
implication is that if women suffer from a patriarchal earthly life, they
will get their own back in a matriarchal heaven.

What then are middle-class women allowed to do? First, they are to
stay at home and remain chaste so that they do not distract men from
their proper work in the world. For More, a wanton woman simply
takes up men's time, time that must be preserved for other matters.
Prosecuting such crimes as adultery served to block the channels of government "til senates seem, / For purposes of empire less conve'd / Than
to release the adultress from her bonds" (2:46). Hold for a moment the
word "empire" while we look at what the chaste middle-class wife does
do. Quite simply she trains up her children in the way that Hannah More
prescribes. And note the terms of the charge: "in this sacred *garrison,*
impregnable but by neglect, you too have an awful post, that of *arming*
the minds of the rising generation, 'with the *shield* of faith, whereby
they shall be able to quench the fiery darts of the wicked'; that of *girding*
them with 'that *sword* of the spirit, which is the work of God' " (2:53,
emphasis mine). We might explain the military metaphors by pointing
to their prevalence in Saint Paul's epistle and in the Christian discourse
of several epochs or by acknowledging that Hannah More was writing
during the period of the Napoleonic Wars. Doubtless both offer partial
explanations, but I think there is strong evidence for something more
at work here. John Harrison gives us the key: "By the early nineteenth
century, strengthened by evangelical morality and utilitarian reforming
zeal, the ideology of imperialism was well established." [33] I would argue
that what Hannah More was advocating as the work of middle-class
women amounted to the domestic support of men so they could make
an empire, and the raising of young Christian soldiers to keep it. In fact,
she makes the point overtly when she quotes Virgil, "the most polished
poet of antiquity to the most victorious nation": "Let us leave to the

inhabitants of conquered countries the praise of carrying to the highest degree of perfection, sculpture and the sister arts; but let *this* country direct her own exertions to the art of governing mankind in equity and peace, of shewing mercy to the submissive, and of abasing the proud among surrendering nations" (2:78–79). If we substitute Hannah More for "the most polished poet of antiquity" and exchange England for "the most victorious nation," if we look forward to the Congress of Vienna and the acquisition by England of Malta, Mauritius, Ceylon, Heligoland, and the Cape, and finally, if we posit a generation brought up on the "evangelical morality and utilitarian reforming zeal" that Harrison describes, then we have set the stage for British overseas expansion. That Hannah More had in mind a vision of what the British Empire ultimately became when she wrote *Strictures* is hardly likely. But she and other Evangelicals helped to put into place an ideology that made such an empire possible. Yet before exporting the system to the colonies, it was necessary to perfect it at home. As we shall see, More's work in educating the laboring poor contributed to the effective colonization of an entire class.

In addition to laying the groundwork for the development of what became the British Empire, More's work contributed to establishing middle-class control over the new class that emerged during the Industrial Revolution—the working class. E. P. Thompson suggests the reasons for such a task and More's place in it: "The sensibility of the Victorian middle class was nurtured in the 1790s by frightened gentry who had seen miners, potters, and cutlers reading *Rights of Man*, and its foster parents . . . were William Wilberforce and Hannah More." [34] In the spring of 1792, a cheap edition of the second part of Thomas Paine's *Rights of Man* was published. In a month it sold over thirty-two thousand copies. [35] The first part had called for full political reform— universal male suffrage, an annual Parliament, and secret ballots; the second called for world revolution. Thomas Paine was indicted for sedition and radical booksellers were jailed. Although some blamed Evangelical reformers such as More for the founding of the Sunday schools that had made literacy possible for the poor, others called on her "to produce some little popular tracts which might serve as counteraction to the poisonous writings of Tom Paine." [36] Her response was "Village Politics."

Addressed to "All the Mechanics, Journeymen, and Labourers, in Great Britain," "Village Politics" counsels passivity and obedience. It posits two alternatives for the arrangement of society—the existing order in England at the time or a state of nature. In More's representation of the existing order, she obscures the inequities of the class system by substituting a necessary division of labor: "suppose in the general division, our new rulers were to give us half an acre of ground a-piece; we could to be sure raise potatoes on it for the use of our families; but as every other man would be equally busy in raising potatoes for *his* family, why then you see if thou wast to break thy spade, I, whose trade it is, should no longer be able to mend it. Neighbor Ship would have no time to make us a suit of clothes, nor the clothier to weave the cloth for all the world would be gone a digging." [37] Like a bad joke, this passage rests on literal readings to create its absurdity. The challenge to the power of amassed property becomes equivalent to the preposterous half acre for raising potatoes—in this way its political content is misrepresented and trivialized. By submerging such reforms as male suffrage and extended Parliamentary representation in a half acre of land, changing the existing order is represented as impracticable. It is important here that those portrayed in the division of land are not those landowners who actually possess it; in this way its distribution can be represented as a disrupting and displacing activity. In fact, as we have seen, it was the consolidation of land in the hands of a relative few that created the greatest destruction of a whole way of life for the laboring poor during this period. And, of course, ownership for the enclosers of land did not require them to cultivate each half acre themselves. That was done by the laborers for the lowest possible wage.

It is a short step from the half-acre plan to the state of nature. For equitable distribution here implies the absence of rulers, and without rulers the rule of Might prevails: "I'm stronger than thou; and Standish, the exciseman, is a better scholar; so that we should not remain equal a minute. I should out-*fight* thee, and he'd out-*wit* thee. And if such a sturdy fellow as I am, was to come and break down thy hedge for a little firing, or take away the crop from thy ground, I'm not sure these newfangled laws would see thee righted. I tell thee, Tom, we have a fine constitution already, and our forefathers thought so" (*Works,* 59). Here again the real actors in the conflict are displaced; it is the existing order that protects laboring men from *each other.* In fact, a fine constitution had not protected farm laborers who had lost access to land for crops and a little firing. But by locating the site of conflict among laborers themselves and representing the existing order as protecting laborers from each other, More mystifies actual relations of power and property. Thus, the final message in this "Burke for Beginners" is faith in authority and resignation to the status quo. "Study to be quiet, work with your hands, and mind your own business," Hannah More advises (*Works*, 63). As we have seen, she gave similar advice in her conduct books to middle-class women.

Convinced now that educating the poor without providing them with "safe" reading materials was a mistake, Hannah More turned to the writing of tracts that were cheap and unspeculative.[38] The *Cheap Repository Tracts* were financed by subscriptions from the propertied classes and they were powerful propaganda indeed. Priced to undercut the more usual ballad sheets of hawkers, these tracks imitated the language and appearance of the material they were designed to outsell. Hannah More wrote over fifty of them herself and they were distributed throughout England, Scotland, and Ireland. Between March 3 and April 18, three hundred thousand copies had been sold. By March 1796, the number had risen to over two million.[39]

In "The Shepherd of Salisbury Plain," we find an example of the sort of advice Hannah More gave to the poor. Just as she urged middle-class women to rejoice in their lack of public power, so she counseled the poor to be thankful for privations: " 'You are exposed to great cold and heat,' said the gentleman: 'True sir,' said the shepherd; 'but then I am not exposed to great temptations; and so throwing one thing against another, God is pleased to contrive to make things more equal than we poor, ignorant, short-sighted creatures are apt to think. . . .' 'You think then,' said the gentleman, 'that a laborious life is a happy one.' 'I do, sir; and more so especially, as it exposes a man to fewer sins' " (*Works*, 191). Here laborers, like middle-class women, find themselves better equipped for Christian piety than those who suffer the "temptations" of power and wealth. In fact, such a blessing makes earthly lots "equal." So bountiful are the blessings of religion for the poor in this tract, that like the multiplying of fishes and loaves, it feeds them when they have nothing to eat: "I have had but a lonely life, and have often but little to eat, but my Bible, has been meat, drink, and company to me" (*Works*, 192).

Here More repeats the rhetorical strategy that she had used in "Village Politics" by literalizing abstractions. Religious faith is represented as actual food for the hungry. For the shepherd of Salisbury Plain, just the thought of angels appearing to shepherds at Bethlehem "warmed my poor heart in the coldest night, and filled me with more joy and thankfulness than the best supper could have done" (*Works,* 192).

If the shepherd's lot is to brave the elements and his hunger cheerfully, it is the duty of his wife to make sure that poverty does not become desperation and want does not lead to despair. The shepherd's clothes prove "the exceeding neatness, industry and good management of his wife": "His stockings no less proved her good housewifery, for they were entirely covered with darns of different colored worsted, but had not a hole in them; and his shirt, though nearly as coarse as the sails of a ship, was as white as the drifted snow, and was neatly mended where time had either made a rent, or worn it thin" (*Works,* 191). Besides making clear that a poor man with a good wife will never go naked, this passage encourages attention, concern, and hard work from women in the face of almost overwhelmng need. We are assured by the number of darns and the quantity of mending that this woman has not given up even in the face of circumstances calculated to make her do so. Her industry, moreover, ensures her worth, for a "poor woman, who will be lying a-bed, or gossiping with her neighbors when she ought to be fitting out her husband in cleanly manner, will seldom be found to be very good in other respects" (*Works,* 191).

After undergoing several more tests of faith, including the refusal of beer on a Sunday and the payment of a debt with money that might have bought necessary food, the shepherd and his family are rewarded for their good behavior by a local cleric. They are moved into a house where the roof does not leak and given charge of a Sunday school in order to teach others the honor of poverty. The salaries are kept low, for as the cleric observes, "I am not going to make you rich, but useful" (*Works,* 200). Hannah More thus rewards subservience and piety with the meaans of subsistence.[40]

As I have suggested, Hannah More's prescriptions for the poor bear some similarity to her advice to middle-class wives. Both groups are enjoined to accept their limited sphere and to equate earthly privation with heavenly privilege. An incident in More's own life brings the issues of gender and class together in a yet more striking way, for in her career as a Bluestocking, More experimented with the power of patronage in a way that allowed her to use a traditional male vehicle for the control of property with a woman of lower-class status.

In 1784 More was shown some poems by a poor Bristol milkwoman and decided to collect subscriptions from her aristocratic friends in order to publish them. When the volume appeared and Ann Yearsley asked for the proceeds as well as the money that had been collected on her behalf, More and her friends refused. They decided instead to invest the money and to set up a trust to ration out funds; in this enterprise, Ann Yearsley was forbidden even the status of joint trustee. When Yearsley retaliated in public with speeches and written protests in newspapers, Hannah More withdrew from the affair completely. She remained, in private, angered and baffled by Yearsley's response. "Gratitude and sub-mission were the due returns of the lower orders for the beneficence of their superiors. Hannah More's conscience was clear. Her intentions were generous and philanthropic."[41]

In the Yearsley affair we see that it was not only men who could control women's access to property. Although she had made her own fortune in terms not dissimilar, Hannah More used wealth and acquired rank to exclude another woman from the financial independence she herself enjoyed. In More's hands class became as powerful a tool of domi-nation as gender was for the propertied male. Finally, it is worth noting that in this incident it was Yearsley who made her claims in public and Hannah More who sulked in private. The poet exercised the terms of her entry into public discourse precisely by acknowledging them; the moralist worked by subterfuge, leaving in place a social hierarchy from which she had found a way to benefit.[42]

"If a man select a picture for himself from among all its ex-hibited competitors, and bring it to his own house, the picture being passive, he is able to *fix* it there: while the wife, picked up at a pub-lic place, and accustomed to incessant display, will not, it is probable, when brought home stick so quietly to the spot where he fixes her; but will escape the exhibition room again, and continue to be displayed at every subsequent exhibition, just as if she were not become pri-vate property, and had never been definitively disposed of" (*Strictures,*

1:163). In advising prospective brides against going too often into public, Hannah More lays bare the essential terms of the marriage contract, or rather, the terms that the *good* wife abides by. The good wife behaves like private property; she stays where her husband "sticks" her.

There was, however, one place that the middle-class woman could go outside the domestic enclosure. She could take her lessons in obedience to the poor. The suggestion had already been made in a minor way by Fordyce, who, in *Sermons to Young Women,* counseled "habitual mildness to those of inferior rank." He did not yet make the prescription one of seeking the poor out as Hannah More was to do, but he urged women to conduct themselves toward such "inferiors" as servants in a manner that would ensure the latter group's good behavior: "An unaffected propension to use them well, without partiality, and without caprice, argues confirmed benevolence. Those who use them otherwise, will urge indeed their mercenary spirit, their want of gratitude, their want of worth" (*Strictures,* 2:335). It was the duty of a middle-class woman, then, to convince the poor that the upper classes meant them well. As Hannah More put the case, such benevolent behavior: "would serve to combine in the minds of the poor two ideas, which ought never to be separated, but which they are not very forward to unite,—that the great wish to make them happy as well as good. Occasional approximations of the rich and poor, for the purposes of relief and instruction, and annual meetings for the purpose of innocent pleasure, would do much towards wearing away discontent, and contribute to reconcile the lower class to the state in which it has pleased God to place them" (*Strictures,* 1:145). It has been often suggested that the increasing involvement of women in charity work in the late eighteenth and early nineteenth centuries served the function of "maintaining the conservative political order."[43] As we have seen, it was precisely this sort of containment that Hannah More and others like her consciously sought to impose through "good works." Moreover, as E. P. Thompson has observed, Methodist revivalist recruitment rose in England among the poor during periods of particular despair; it was when the poor felt the least hope of political remedy that they turned to religion as consolation.[44] As Hannah More's tracts reveal, political quiescence and subservience were among the requirements for salvation. That conduct-book writers enlisted middle-class women, whose status they had already defined as private property, to enclose and improve the poor as part of their own improvement, marks a particularly triumphant moment in bourgeois ideology. It had become a system of belief in which dominated middle-class women might, with all good intentions, ensure the oppression of the laboring poor.

Notes

Portions of this essay were presented at two conferences: the British Studies Section of the Southern Humanities Historical Society, Lexington, Kentucky, in 1989, and the Modern Language Association, Chicago, in 1990.

For their helpful suggestions on drafts of this essay, I thank Patricia Hilden, Lore Metzger, and Timothy Reiss.

1. Maurice Quinlan, *Victorian Prelude: A History of English Manners, 1700–1830* (New York: Harper and Row, 1941), 139.

2. Nancy Armstrong, "The Rise of the Domestic Woman," in *The Ideology of Conduct: Essays on Literature and the History of Sexuality,* ed. Nancy Armstrong and Leonard Tennenhouse (New York: Methuen, 1987), 99.

3. See P. J. Miller, "Women's Education, 'Self-Improvement' and Social Mobility—A Late Eighteenth Century Debate," *British Journal of Educational Studies* 20 (1972): 302–14, for a discussion of how eighteenth-century conduct books for women addressed the issue of class mobility.

4. John Harrison, *The Common People of Great Britain* (Bloomington: Indiana University Press, 1985), 229.

5. E. J. Hobsbawm, *Age of Revolution: Europe, 1789–1848* (London: Weidenfeld and Nicolson, 1962), 153.

6. E. P. Thompson, *The Making of the English Working Class* (New York: Vintage Books, 1966), 218.

7. E. P. Thompson, "The Grid of Inheritance," in *Family and Inheritance: Rural Society in Western Europe, 1200–1800,* ed. Jack Goody, Joan Thirst, and E. P. Thompson (Cambridge: Cambridge University Press, 1976), 341.

8. Ivy Pinchbeck, *Women Workers and the Industrial Revolution, 1750–1850* (1930; reprint, London: Frank Cass, 1977), 28.

9. Ibid., 45.

10. A. L. Morton, *A People's History of England* (1923; reprint, New York: International Publishers, 1974), 327.

11. John Harrison, *The Birth and Growth of Industrial England* (New York: Harcourt Brace Jovanovich, 1973), 12.

12. Ibid., 3.

13. Pinchbeck, *Women Workers*, 7.

14. Lee Holcombe, "Victorian Wives and Property: Reform of the Married Women's Property Law, 1857–1882," in *A Widening Sphere: Changing Roles of Victorian Women,* ed. Martha Vicinus (Bloomington: Indiana University Press, 1977), 6.

15. Susan Moller Okin, "Patriarchy and Married Women's Property in England," *Eighteenth Century Studies* 17 (1983–84): 125.

16. Susan Staves, *Married Women's Separate Property in England, 1660–1833* (Cambridge, Mass.: Harvard University Press, 1990), 222.

17. For more on the rise of separate spheres ideology, see Judith Lowder Newton's *Women, Power and Subversion: Social Strategies in British Fiction, 1778–1860* (Athens: University of Georgia Press, 1981).

18. James Fordyce, *Sermons to Young Women* (1766; reprint, Philadelphia: Thomas Dobson, 1787), 68. Subsequent references to this source are given in parentheses in the text.

19. E. J. Hobsbawm, *Industry and Empire* (New York: Viking Penguin, 1969), 19.

20. Armstrong, "The Rise of the Domestic Woman," 97.

21. Ibid., 105.

22. Pricilla Robertson, *An Experience of Women: Pattern and Change in Nineteenth Century Europe* (Philadelphia: Temple University Press, 1982), 455.

23. Ibid., 246.

24. Jane Austen, *Pride and Prejudice* (New York: Penguin, 1974), 113.

25. Susan Staves, "British Seduced Maidens," *Eighteenth Century Studies* 14 (1980–81): 134.

26. Mary Poovey, *The Proper Lady and the Woman Writer* (Chicago: University of Chicago Press, 1984), 36.

27. For details on how Hannah More became an evangelist, see M. G. Jones's biographical study, *Hannah More* (Cambridge: Cambridge University Press, 1952).

28. Mary Waldron, "Ann Yearsley and the Clifton Records," in *The Age of Johnson* (New York: AMS Press, 1987), 311.

29. *Dictionary of National Biography,* 864.

30. Hannah More, *Strictures on the Modern System of Female Education,* ed. Gina Luria, 2 vols. (1799; reprint, New York: Garland Publishing, 1974), 1:63. Subsequent references to this source are given in parentheses in the text.

31. Jones, *Hannah More,* 129.

32. In *Their Fathers' Daughters: Hannah More, Maria Edgeworth, and Patri-*

archal Complicity (New York: Oxford University Press, 1991), Elizabeth Kowaleski-Wallace makes a similar point about the portrayal of Lucilla in More's novel *Coelebs in Search of a Wife:* "Paradoxically, she strikes him 'at first sight' because of the fact that she does not particularly stand out" (50).

33. Harrison, *Birth and Growth*, 65.

34. Thompson, *Working Class*, 57.

35. Richard Altick, *The English Common Reader: A Social History of the Mass Reading Public, 1800–1900* (Chicago: University of Chicago Press, 1957), 70.

36. Jones, *More*, 132.

37. Hannah More, *The Works of Hannah More* (New York: Harper, 1855), 59. Subsequent references to this source are noted as *Works* and appear in parentheses in the text.

38. Jones, *More*, 138.

39. Ibid., 141.

40. While Kowaleski-Wallace makes some similar points about "The Shepherd of Salisbury Plain" in *Their Fathers' Daughters,* her analysis is grounded in psychoanalytic theory; she argues that More's political activities arise in part from an aversion to the "maternal," a universal and unchanging aspect of the unconscious. Thus, More's efforts to control the poor become a way of containing her own anxiety about the maternal body. My own reading is feminist materialist and makes socio-historical and economic elements central.

41. Jones, *More*, 76; Mary Waldron argues that More's ambiguous class status "may have lain at the root of her insensitive treatment of Yearsley. In her anxiety not to offend her own benefactors, she forgot that her protégée's position might also have its subtleties" (311); similarly, Donna Landry, in *The Muses of Resistance* (Cambridge: Cambridge University Press, 1990), observes that More's behavior toward Yearsley exhibited "a middle-class fear of social mobility generally, especially if it can be obtained through a literary livelihood" (21).

42. In this assessment of More and her work, I differ from Mitzi Myers, who in "Hannah More's Tracts for the Times: Social Fiction and Female Ideology," *Fetter'd or Free? British Women Novelists, 1670–1815* (Athens: Ohio University Press, 1986), argues that reading the Cheap Repository Tracts as women-centered texts shifts their emphasis from the public and political to "more complex configurations fashioned around private amelioration and women's religio-moral concerns" (269). By reproducing the separate spheres doctrine in her critique of More's work, Myers ignores the ways in which the construction of domestic ideology during this period involved rewriting laboring class unrest as moral degeneracy requiring religious instruction. More recently, Christine L. Krueger has argued that the significance of the Cheap Repository Tracts lies in "More's discovery of the lower-class voice as a vehicle

for converting her peers" to her religious principles as well as for introducing them to the lives of the poor" (*The Reader's Repentance: Women Preachers, Women Writers and Nineteenth-Century Social Discourse* [Chicago: University of Chicago Press, 1992], pp. 111–12). Again, by focusing on More's efforts to find a public voice, Krueger downplays the class conflict that made that voice possible. For more on the relation of gender and class in the reading of texts, see Mary Poovey, *Uneven Developments: The Ideological Work of Gender in Mid-Victorian England* (Chicago: University Chicago Press, 1988).

43. Quinlan, *Victorian Prelude*, 159.
44. Thompson, *Working Class*, 388.

"A Peculiar Protection": Hannah More and the Cultural Politics of the Blagdon Controversy

Mitzi Myers

> The sound of a woman's authoritative voice can have only two
> effects on male desire: a deadly or sexually electrifying one. . . .
> Man's response in both private and public to a woman who
> *knows* (anything) has most consistently been one of paranoia.
>
> —Alice Jardine

> Power can lodge in dangerous nooks and crannies. . . . It can
> be informal, unpredictable, unaccountable, frittered away, or
> saved for important occasions. It needs to be examined in its
> full complexity.
>
> —Natalie Zemon Davis

> The practice of piety was also a play of power relationships, a
> theater for social drama, and a cultural mechanism for change
> and continuity. Historians have only begun to read the clues of
> human interaction behind the face of piety.
>
> —Barbara Ritter Dailey

Mary Russell Mitford provocatively describes Hannah More:
"masculine not in a good sense, but a bad one; she writes like a man in
petticoats, or a woman in breeches. All her books have a loud voice, and
a stern frown, and a long stride." By way of orienting the reader to the
representational strategies and power politics of an unfamiliar historical site, I begin with this epigrammatic assessment and two revelatory

dialogs.[1] Together they code the cultural meaning of gender difference and the positioning of woman in culture as trespasses of social space, elisions of boundaries that thus transgress accepted classifications. Emblematic maps to the late eighteenth-century controversy that is my subject, each of the paired dialogs deflates a presumptuous woman's imposture as cultural agent by reallocating social space or reaffirming female objectification, by putting woman back in her place as representational object rather than desiring subject. First, a comic version of deflation: that inveterate gossiper Mrs. Papendiek, reader and wardrober to Queen Charlotte, describes a purported encounter between Hannah More and Samuel Johnson when More was a newcomer to the literary world. Eager to obtain an interview, she was at last promised a meeting. Shown into his library, she cast herself into a big leather chair to await his entrance, exclaiming, "This is doubtless the great man's chair! I will try to gain from it a few sparks of his genius." Johnson drily responded to her confession of encroachment with, "Unfortunately, I never sit in that chair. I should be afraid of its gloomy inspirations."[2] The fond friendship that developed between the two doesn't pluck the rejoinder's dismissive sting.

The March 1804 *Christian Observer* carried an epistle titled "Hints towards forming a bill for the abolition of the White Female Slave Trade" from "An Enemy to All Slavery." Written at the height of More's career (and shortly after the Blagdon Controversy), the pseudonymous letter converts a private literary space to a site of spiritual authority and public reformist goal. The letter's generic strategies miniaturize negotiation between female "genius" and hegemonic culture, a seeming marginality nevertheless invested with ideological and discursive force; for More as author—at once woman and sage—repeatedly confounds interpretive models of anxious female writing.[3] But the piece is even more interesting for its overt gender content than for its generic implications. Witty and wily, the essay exploits the homology between black slaves abroad and white Englishwomen, many of whom are the "wives, daughters, aunts, nieces, cousins, and grandmothers, even of those very zealous African abolitionists themselves." Critics of the abolitionists liked to jibe that they wept over blacks abroad while ignoring the plight of white (male) wage slaves at home. Hannah More, herself an abolitionist, extends the charge to her culture's totalizing disciplinary representation of women, "the system of domestic slavery": "here, there is one, arbitrary, universal tyrant, and . . . he never dies. FASHION is his name." With "aston-ishing fortitude" women hug their socially mandated chains; if a very few "have manfully resisted the tyrant," their transgression of cultural boundaries erases their identity as women, reducing them to psychic and spatial limbo: "*they are people whom nobody knows.*" More's emancipa-tory parable was quickly countered by "A White Slave Trader": "these white negroes occupy that place in the scale of society to which nature destined them. They are an *inferior order of beings.*" Women's bodies, the satiric excursus continues, are sites of pollution and duplicity; because "their inferiority is proved, like that of the Africans, by their *complexions* and their *hair,*" similar enclosure within an approved social space is their proper destiny.[4]

Assessing the problematics of late eighteenth-century gender con-structions implicit in such vignettes as these also entails assessing Hannah More (1745–1833). Among the authors busily examining and redefining woman's situation at the century's close, More figures con-spicuously; strange as it appears in our secular age, she was a top contender for the most widely read, most influential female writer of her day. From America to India, all her works were extraordinary best-sellers, her varied audiences eagerly consuming recipes for their reform. Her Cheap Repository Tracts addressed the poor and middling classes; works such as *Thoughts on the Importance of the Manners of the Great to General Society* (1788) and *Estimate of the Religion of the Fashionable World* (1790) sought to shape up their social superiors. *Strictures on the Mod-ern System of Female Education* (1799) urged a new model of Evangelical womanhood on female readers, and *Coelebs in Search of a Wife* (1808), her didactic novel codifying woman's sphere, responsibilities, and powers, celebrated the Evangelical new woman and the reformed Evangelical male who would prove himself worthy of her.[5] Contemporary testi-monies abound, commemorating More's accomplishment and certifying her authority as moral spokeswoman: "an example and an instructor to the world"; "the warning voice which yet would save us"; "one of the most illustrious females that ever was in the world . . . one of the most truly evangelical divines of this whole age"; "No age ever owed more to a female pen than to your's" [sic]; "From you . . . I date the regeneration of the people of this country."[6] Because his Unitarian creed was an Evangelical bête noire, Henry Crabb Robinson's assessment after reading More's letters in 1836 is even more telling. He rightly thinks the compiler "a poor creature, but it has left a very high opinion of Saint Hannah. . . . Her retreat from genteel society had something heroic in it—nor was she illiberal, though her sect is."[7] Heady flattery such testimonials might seem now—but they are not without foundation. Modern historians, too, find it "difficult to overestimate More's influence throughout much of the nineteenth century." After all, her life and her works, her "non-political feminism," were "so eminently good and respectable and useful, so eminently Victorian."[8]

Yet despite her outstanding public achievements, More has won nothing like the attentive respect now accorded her liberal antitype, Mary Wollstonecraft. (Indeed, More's usual fate is enlistment as pietistic foil to Wollstonecraft's radical romanticism.) Modern critics touching on More either define an Evangelical (sometimes sympathetically, sometimes harshly, as authorial taste or class politics dictate) or else they examine her as a case history of the period's conflicted female writer. For example, some feminist critics typically restate the More enigma, seizing on the apparent disjunction between her individual position as a witty and charismatic bluestocking—Dr. Johnson's flirtatious pet, the Garricks' perennial houseguest, the pioneer social worker, the revered adviser of Wilberforce and a whole train of bishops, one of the influential Clapham Sect's great men despite her sex—and her directives to her sister readers valorizing a distinctive feminine sphere, a gendered space furnished with characteristically female values and concerns. Modesty, humility, piety, altruism—domestic retirement punctuated by charitable endeavor: how does More's own formidably energetic public career conform to these seemingly repressive contours? Some would argue that she hypocritically says one thing and does another, seeing herself as atypical, special; she was, one recurrent claim goes, "an anti-feminist who enjoyed a freedom condemned by her as unsuitable for other women"—and other classes, the most recent critique adds.[9] But another interpretation might read More's career as paradigm rather than paradox, noting (as do recent historians of philanthropy) that her religious pursuits and moral reforms typify fresh channels for women's achievement, channels eventually feeding into other kinds of organizations and other modes of militance. Clearly, More's experience illustrates her sex's cultural predicament and strategies at the eighteenth century's close, a period of ideological crisis, spiritual revival, and social change. Just as clearly, More resists any unitary reading as either feminist heroine or compliant patriarchal victim. Her lengthy career is thus ripe for revaluation from any number of recent critical and theoretical perspectives, from the linguist's to the psychoanalyst's to the cultural historian's.[10]

But I want here to analyze just one symptomatic episode—the so-called Blagdon Controversy that erupted over More's Sunday school work—and to read what happened in that topographical locale, and how what happened has been reported, in terms of ideological space, specifically of a gendered cultural space. Deconstructing received readings of the controversy and drawing on the work of social anthropologists Shirley Ardener and Mary Douglas, I will argue that a revisionist look at the terrain in terms of ground rules and social maps, of the taboo that attends the crossing of gendered boundaries, illuminates not only More's experience but also the rhetoric of sexual spheres pervading Georgian and Victorian thought. Viewing Sunday schools as emergent cultural spaces subject to alternative gender codings and to ambiguous definition as public or private, clerical or lay, sacred or polluted, explicates the explosion of print and passion Blagdon occasioned. In periods of stressed social structure, as were the French Revolutionary years, physical crossing of socially defined demarcations signifies wicked pollution. "Dirt," Douglas notes, is a cultural category for "all events which blur, smudge, contradict, or otherwise confuse accepted classifications," a violation of habitual arrangements and values; the polluter is doubly reprobated, for transgressing lines and endangering others as well.[11] Spatial boundaries signify social constructions: the female sage may turn sorceress.

The Blagdon dispute thus precipitates key queries about the dynamic interplay of women's culture, feminism, religion, society—larger questions rooted in cultural politics and branching toward communal power. Few careers evince so instructively as More's the strains and ambiguities native to female ideology in transition; no episode highlights those tensions more sharply than Blagdon. These are major claims for minor intrigues, but moderns must concur with contemporary participants that the altercation "involves questions of more importance" than superficially apparent.[12] Investigating eighteenth-century women's political involvement, one historian has recently lamented those gaps inevitable in records of covert activity, because "influence" is conducted at one remove, measurable only by male actions, and hard to assess.[13] Blagdon presents a lavish exception to this dearth, for it is richly documented in public report and private memoir (including many letters conspicuously absent from More's official biography).[14] Blagdon problematizes the binary opposition of separate public and private spheres that's conditioned thinking about woman's cultural place for so many years; despite the accumulating mass of hard data calling into question this abstract paradigm, it still pervades thinking about eighteenth- and nineteenth-century women.

Moreover, winnowing Blagdon polemic, sorting out charge and countercharge, propaganda and actuality, yields additional rewards, illuminating not only the workings of Evangelic womanhood, front-stage and backstage, but also Evangelicalism's general challenge to the establishment, its critique of things as they are. For when More's usurpation of clerical prerogative escalated from a parish spat to a national issue, Blagdon came to symbolize in the public mind the whole conflict between Evangelical innovation and the status quo. Blagdon thus miniaturizes a larger cultural clash between traditional patriarchal mentalities and newer structures of feeling; it is a trope for the transition from the decaying paternalism documented by E. P. Thompson and others to an emergent pattern of social attitudes that might well be termed "maternalism" (though it was not held by women alone), a proto-Victorian ethic of responsibility and nurturance. Blagdon, then, functions as a restricted area within which we can hear clearly the dialog between gender ideology and social action and from which we can watch that dialog being (mis)recorded in desexualized twentieth-century historical representations.

Understanding what Evangelical ideology meant to women—what it offered, why it appealed, where it constrained—requires catching it in motion. More's participation in the Blagdon Controversy furnishes just such an opportunity to sample Evangelical intricacies, to see how its canonical doctrines of female influence and religious service tested out in a particular locale and how goodness and usefulness took the form of spatial relationships. A late and initially most satisfying addition to the Sunday school network More's labors had spread over the impoverished Mendip Hills in the 1790s, Blagdon became a turn-of-the-century *cause célèbre* that generated some thirty pamphlets pro or con and exercised journalists for several years. Although issues multiplied confusingly and the cast expanded as discord metastasized, the protagonists and their actions are captured to the life in personal correspondence, as well as pamphlet and review.

Early in 1801, Thomas Bere, Blagdon's now-suspended but still officiating curate (and also its magistrate, which was handy because the justice could thus take affidavits to support the curate), published letters of those involved to buttress his complaints: that his superiors declined to reveal the grounds of his ouster and that More refused to discharge her schoolmaster Henry Young (or Younge) for supposedly Calvinistic enthusiasm and Methodistical practices. More's champion Sir Abraham Elton printed additional documents in his rebuttal, as did other controversialists, many of whom knew More and her project firsthand. Meanwhile, roused to protect her schools, by now defined as her vocation and lifework, More herself was detailing her anxieties and frenetic series of defensive maneuvers in her journal and letters, most revealingly in those to her second major public defender, Thomas Sedgwick Whalley, her replacement for Elton when he proved too wishy-washy an attacker for her purpose. For the background of the conflict, Patty More's journal *Mendip Annals,* a vividly detailed account of late eighteenth-century philanthropy by the sister who labored alongside Hannah, is invaluable. And warring periodicals such as the *Anti-Jacobin Review and Magazine* (anti-More), *British Critic,* and *Christian Observer* (pro) complicate matters with extensive editorial comment and reader response.[15]

The main facts go like this. Blagdon was, in More's account contemporaneous with the schools' founding, "a very large, ignorant, poor, and wicked parish," notorious for crime and litigation. "Perhaps England hardly contains so lawless a parish," she exclaimed some months later. In any case, a 1795 crime wave prompted Bere and district officials, having heard of neighboring villages meliorated by More's social therapy, to beseech her aid toward "instruction and reformation."[16] One of the deputation, "full six feet high, implored us with particular eagerness to come, because, he said, there were places where they were personally afraid to go. . . . here it was," drily notes Patty, Hannah's indefatigable lieutenant in every campaign (to appropriate the terminology of the women themselves), "that these tender-hearted churchwardens wished to send two nervous women." But if God mysteriously calls "delicate instruments" to "athletic service," he safeguards too. Congratulating More on her thriving charities, John Newton (Cowper's father-confessor was also hers) pertinently observes that no prudent minister dared attempt "such an extensive inroad into the kingdom of darkness . . . but your sex and your character afford you a peculiar protection." [17] Begun in 1789, the Mendip schools and societies were scattered over ten or so Somerset parishes by the time Blagdon erupted; enrolling between two and three thousand children and adults, employing a staff of thirty-odd, they were a well-publicized, much-visited showcase, an "annually puffed and paragraphed" model for imitators. [18]

More launched operations at Blagdon under the direction of Young (transferred from Nailsea where, significantly, he had already stirred trouble); he established schools for young people as well as children and instituted evening meetings for adults, following More's customary routine. She knew adult schools were regarded as dangerous irregularities, but thought clerical neglect justified " 'proclaiming open Methodism,' as I suppose it will be called." [19] The organizations flourished, the village improved, and Bere repeatedly wrote grateful letters to More. In fact, despite his being what she called from the first "a hard man," he actually burst into tears at the villagers' eager amendment; these were the halcyon days of what the Mores regarded as a hallowed mission transforming a "Botany Bay" to "one of our finest and most prosperous schemes." [20] Yet by 1798 trouble surfaced. Jealous at the sisters' success where he had failed (their version) or suspicious of mischievous innovations, a "new religion" (his version), Bere was rumored to be preaching insinuations against the Evangelical schools and even veering toward unorthodoxly rationalistic Socinianism. Hannah shamed "this son of Belial" into temporary good behavior. [21] But before long, Bere was openly criminating the adult meetings. Bere thought Young's supposed sermon-reading was really an illegal religious assembly and the putative educator in actuality a schismatic preacher self-consciously rivaling the incumbent. Early in January 1799, Mrs. Bere had complained to More of Young's private Monday evening schools for adults. More did not reply directly, but had Patty speak to the teacher. By April 1800, the war was on, Young by now having insulted Bere personally. "I love Sunday Schools," asserted Bere, when he went public with his grievance over breached clerical boundaries, "but it does not necessarily follow, that therefore *I must support unlicensed conventicles.*" [22]

Bere amassed further charges, but rather than removing Young as he

demanded, More went over his head. Dr. Moss, the bishop of Bath and
Wells, had always "behaved handsomely" in earlier troubles with clerics
who grew restive at More's intrusions; however, that aged diocesan had
become so feeble that his son Chancellor Moss transacted most episcopal
business, and his admiration for More's labors was more politic than his
father's unbounded enthusiasm.[23] Thick missives circulated from the
grievants to Dr. Crossman, Blagdon's timid, absentee rector, anxious to
placate all parties, to the Mosses and back again—hot potatoes nobody
wanted to handle. If Bere found the teacher unorthodox, More soon
countered by clandestine reports of Bere's religious heterodoxy, accusations she refused to back publicly and later disavowed, though her
denial is more narrowly worded than supporters accepting her total non-
involvement in the fray have noticed.[24] The ecclesiastical powers eventually hinted that Young should go. More's allies then exacted a public
hearing because Bere had obtained evidence irregularly and did not
allow Young to confront witnesses against him. Bere's packed "court"
of local gentry and anti-More clergy vindicated his proceedings, but
More denied their jurisdiction; she responded by dissolving the Blagdon
schools entirely in November 1800. Shortly thereafter, though, the old
bishop, finally personally involved, deputed Crossman to cashier Bere
and urged More to reopen the schools, which she did, Young still pre-
siding, in January 1801. Not only had More and her local cadre secretly
impeached Bere, his supporters claimed, but her friend Beilby Porteus,
bishop of London, was her instrument in influencing Moss to hand down
the curate's dismissal.[25] But Bere simply refused to vacate his curacy,
though one of More's entourage was appointed, and, playing in turn the
victim of injustice, he sought outside help, from bishops and politicians
(unsuccessful) and from London journalists (decidedly the reverse).[26] He
published his grievances and the strife intensified; from then on, all was
attack, riposte, move, countermove, faction, coterie. Finally, because
Bere's critics declined to substantiate their censures, he was reinstated
in September 1801, and More withdrew the Blagdon schools for good,
conforming to her avowed "principle of not acting against the resident
clergyman." [27] Throughout, no matter how her adversaries goaded, no
matter how her reputation and all her schools were jeopardized, she
answered no arraignment personally, took no public action, though assured by Lord Chancellor Loughborough that slanders against her were

actionable.[28] More's energetic invasion of clerical space and her behind-the-scenes activities to maintain her inroads contrast strikingly with this decorously feminine official posture, shrinking from public exposure.

And to perplex matters still further, the controversy wrangled on long after Young was out and Bere back in, each new indictment more venomous, more indicative of threatened patriarchal boundaries than the last. More's opponents insinuated that there was not just one zealot at issue but mushrooming colonies, and they wondered who really controlled these renegade seminaries of fanaticism. Not the officiating clergyman, they concluded, despite More's claims, unless he happened to be one of her henchmen. In any case, mere clerical inspection and actual direction of the schools differed, they pointed out. Sunday schools, they feared, menaced church and state, period, breaking down cultural partitions between classes as well as laity and clergy and sapping religious order by undisciplined appeals to the gospel and the heart. Perhaps their patroness was a Methodist herself, specially dangerous because of her reputation and influence. More's enemies discovered with glee that she had taken communion at William Jay's dissenting chapel, thus, they reasoned, proving herself no churchwoman; certainly she knowingly employed Methodist teachers and consorted with dissenters and antislavery quixotes, social malcontents all.[29] Evangelicalism itself, they concluded, was merely Methodism in disguise; because its adherents valued the private space of the individual conscience over formal public observance, it spelled schism and its practitioners were "nondescripts," half in, half out of the established church. Denying the moral malaise and spiritual destitution that More and her sect diagnosed, they dismissed Evangelicals as puritanic gadflies forever nagging the clergy and gentry for dereliction of duty. More and her schools, they declared, were not healing, but spreading immorality and irreligion. For her part, More grieved that her High Church opponents readily leagued with Jacobins and infidels to crush "Methodism, (or what they call so)": "nothing is thought a crime but what they are pleased to call enthusiasm."[30]

This tangled skein of charges deserves unraveling and translation because it encodes key cultural issues, alternative and mutually opposing social visions, fought out in religious idiom. No wonder modern researchers vary wildly when each tugs one thread of interpretation. Just as did contemporary opponents and partisans, historians register

More's spiritual activism and—in Patty's apt phrase—the "violent explosion" it precipitated, while nuanced and comprehensive assessment eludes them. Indeed, most recent studies compound the difficulty by face-lifting old stereotypes and echoing the original disputants. *Mendip Annals* precisely capture these opposing viewpoints: More insisting that "it is a kind of struggle whether Christian instruction shall be continued or abolished in this country"—Bere complaining that the More sisters "were undermining both Church and State by our sly practices, under the specious mask of doing good, and instructing the poor," both sides claiming the right to define Christianity and to determine its social and spatial manifestations. From the Evangelical William Roberts, More's pioneer biographer, down to M. G. Jones, her most recent, More biographies embrace their subject's appraisal. Here is Jones: "The real issue . . . was whether the lower orders should be educated at all, and, if so, by whom."[31]

False, asserts F. K. Brown, whose *Fathers of the Victorians: The Age of Wilberforce* includes a detailed, entertaining, and very biased study of the furor. As his title indicates, Brown (like Jones, whose initials conceal her sex) fails to factor gender into his account. Admirers of More who present her adversaries as "obscurantists opposed to education have wholly missed the point," he declares, for the Mores cared nothing about lower-class education or well-being. Rather, the Sunday schools, together with their attendant institutions—the evening readings, the schools of industry, the female benefit clubs, the charities, even the holiday outings—were pure pretext, toeholds for takeover, established solely because "Hannah More could only in that way introduce Evangelical religion and morals into parishes where . . . the regularly licensed priests of the church, were greatly opposed to them."[32] For Brown, then, who judges his subjects from a modernist, secularist perspective, Blagdon signally instances Evangelical infiltration, exemplifying that superbly organized, puritanically moral Evangelical Reformation whose sinuous plots to seduce the great and quell the poor constitute his thesis. The "victim of his materials" (as one reviewer of his book remarks), Brown merely updates such contemporary jibes as "A Squint at St. Hannah," touching up half that angel-devil stereotype forever shadowing More, who figures in his pages as a spiritual wolf in the Lamb's clothing, her condescending Tory paternalism mocking the pure robes she arrogates.[33] Only those who have tasted primary sources can relish how Brown's massive study, hailed as "refreshingly controversial," savors of Bere and his contentious supporters.[34] With one significant exception: accurately documenting opposition charges of More's covert influence and retaliatory intrigues—the "secret whispers, confidential letters, and private communications" so often complained of—Brown nevertheless dismisses as quite wrongheaded their obsessive linkage of puritanism and revolution, their fear that Evangelicalism implied "subversion of our establishments in church or state."[35] The Mores were politically orthodox, he says, their reforms merely moral, hence conservative; impeccable loyalists, they were heterodox only in the thoroughness of their conservatism. No subversive thrust inheres in moral reform for Brown, as it did for More's opponents, only bleak and insensitive repression, good deeds done with ulterior motive and high hand, crusts in exchange for souls, spiritual press-gangs scavenging among the defenseless poor.

More briefly and suggestively, Thomas Laqueur, arguing that Sunday schools nourished working-class culture, rapidly becoming *by* the people as well as for them, situates Blagdon in the context of lay intervention.[36] Because revivalism engendered folk-directed networks independent of clerical control, the question of how much laymen—and women—might participate in revitalizing their churches fueled dissension. This laicization and decentralization many read very differently from Brown, noting that changing religion gave ordinary people confidence to propagate their own faith actively, remodeling religious institutions to fit their individual notions, freely assessing ministers and challenging clerical hegemony. Never the schismatic her opponents branded her, More yet pronounces the church "more in danger from internal rottenness" than from what barren formalists mislabel enthusiasm.[37] Picturing themselves as crusaders for their country's regeneration, Evangelicals rebelled not only against high and dry religion but also current manners and morals, against all forms devoid of Christ's spirit. What really mattered was within, hence their relative disregard for orthodox spaces, ceremonies, and boundaries between sects. Ecumenically oriented, armed with moral fervor and political savvy, Evangelicals projected a more inclusive and interdependent cultural vision, garnering the good of every class and winnowing the wicked.[38] Greedy monopolizers and tyrannical magistrates, the dissipated and the absentee must mend their ways and shoulder their responsibilities, More argues tirelessly: "Those petty despots, the rich farmers . . . insolent aristocrats" must learn they and the poor share the "same common nature." More's schools and her moral suasion—her letters, visits, and what she herself terms her "clamour"—self-consciously challenged customary oppression with a vision of charity as reform: "instructing the poor, as the grand means of saving the nation." Poorhouses, she writes with indignant maternal compassion, are "mansions of misery," their overseers murderous: Parliament must be mobilized.[39] And new organizational techniques—voluntarism, pressure groups, propaganda— evolved to satisfy Evangelical social conscience (legacies for future uses that laywomen especially would master to negotiate boundaries between private activity and public responsibility). From this perspective, More's enemies correctly perceived Evangelical imperialism as not only a threat to orthodox religion but also to their comfortable status quo. Socially hierarchical, spiritually egalitarian Tories who foster radical causes like antislavery and lower-class education fit uneasily into conventional political schemes. Hence More and her congeners are sometimes stigmatized as repressive social controllers, cold-blooded and artful reactionaries, sometimes alternatively located as avant-garde humanitarian reformers, contributors to an emergent middle-class consensus that transformed and liberalized nineteenth-century society.[40]

But if these oil and water views of Evangelicalism still obtain, the interaction of gender ideology and reformist religion is yet more problematic. To clarify this interplay, I want now to look more closely at the jarring representations of More that Blagdon generated. Because her reputation, influence, actions, and motives still remain key issues in current reinterpretations of this period, my analysis juxtaposes the controversy's alternative readings in order to situate More within the cultural space available to the late eighteenth-century female moral imperialist. Canonized by the bishops in her pocket and Evangelical confreres identifying her cause with religion itself, More was savagely attacked—"battered, hacked, scalped, tom-a-hawked," as she describes it—by Cobbett, Gifford of the *Anti-Jacobin,* and scurrilous pamphleteers such as the pseudo-biographer "Sir Archibald Mac Sarcasm." [41] By Blagdon, More had secured a formidable reputation for useful exertions in behalf of religion, morality, and social order. Displaying a remarkable talent as publicist and propagandist, she had reproved the rich, improved the poor, and rectified her own sex. Antidotes to revolution and specifics against Paine, her Cheap Repository Tracts had sold two million copies in one year; many, such as Bishop Porteus, claimed she saved the country from anarchy. She had valuable connections from her socially triumphant bluestocking days, with godly ones superadded, and entrée to the highest echelons, even royalty itself; circles polite and prelatic alike were struck by her lively gifts and especially her piety. If she worried constantly about falling short of her image, she deftly wielded her feminine goodness and graces to achieve social impact; her virtue served as virtù—psychic power. As one adversary sneers, "She has had the art to dazzle the optics of those who fill the highest civil and religious stations, and even to draw from their pockets the means of carrying her views into effect."[42] Personifying the good woman, she had abundant resources within and without when opposition flared. John Newton warned her that those whose territory she invaded might "shew their teeth"; in fact, her adversaries had proved good biters from the very beginning, as *Mendip Annals* splendidly document: Patty's journal bristles with superstitious laborers, lazy clergy, cantankerous farmers, and reactionary gentry certain that religious lower orders would spell property's demise, all of them having to be stroked into acquiescence "as though . . . soliciting a vote." But More quickly "improved in the art of canvassing," patronage, and placement; recognizing leadership's susceptibility to feminine alchemy, she wove informal networks of influence and established enclaves of activism in the only ways available to women.[43] Lord Loughborough and others bestowed livings for More's young pet preachers; the old bishop of Bath and Wells granted her diocesan carte blanche: "They come and tell me things sometimes, but I only answer them, '. . . I ask no questions when I know it is Mrs. More: I know she is doing right, and that it is all as it should be.' "[44]

In sharp contrast, the anti-Evangelicals' More is a self-aggrandizing, apostate she-saint to be purged from the church calendar for transgressing clerical boundaries and biting the sacerdotal hands that flattered her. "Unexampled success" is dangerous; the activist woman risks vilification for assuming masculine prerogatives, however exemplary for "female excellence and Christian charity." The High Church's More epitomizes duplicitous power, a devilish "Amazon" clothed as an angel of light, "able to 'Ride in the whirlwind, and direct the storm.' " Her premier traits being address and craft, cunning and finesse, she exerts her "secret, sly, hidden powers" in "Machiavelian machinations." This

"Imperial Juno of Literature and Methodism," this *"Pope Joan,"* this *"She-Bishop"* is the "founder of a Sect . . . drawing within the vortex of her petticoat" clerical dupes she "can wrap, twine or use" as she pleases, "like a piece of waste paper."[45] Cobbett's imperious "Old Bishop in petticoats . . . famous for *sophistry*" is replicated in Brown's domineering and single-minded "field commander of her forces, planning, scheming and directing," expertly deploying her "go-betweens, intriguers, arbitrators and referees," manipulating her puppet authors Elton and Whalley and the Reverends Boak and Drewitt, all of them mouthing "bland and unconscionable falsehoods."[46] Both find it maddening that a woman's subterranean influence dismisses "worldly" ministers and installs "serious" ones (these are loaded words in Evangelical discourse) and then, most goading of all, retreats behind impregnable bunkers of feminine rectitude, "contumaciously mute." But then propriety carried More's own ideological imprimatur as "the first, the second, the third [female] requisite." Stung from its normally dependable chauvinism, the *Anti-Jacobin* wished she had "manfully fought her own battle."[47]

Thus, if the opposition's wildest slurs—prostitution, murder, treason, reactionary warmongering as Pitt's hireling—cancel out, they yet leave a residue of charges that demand further investigation, charges quite at variance with the classic biographic, or rather hagiographic, portrayal of More the saintly victim of unmerited persecution, a Christian martyr who steadfastly maintained what Roberts calls the "dignity of silence." More biographies image pious magnanimity, heroic virtue elevated above the fray: she makes no secret charges, never sullies her hands with rebuttal or retaliation, but leaves "her cause quietly to make its own way."[48] Repeatedly, More calls attention to that inviolable public reticence. "I resolve not to defend myself, let them bring what charges they will," she writes Wilberforce. God's restraining grace, she tells another friend, "has preserved me, not only from attacking others, but from defending myself." The letters and journals Roberts prints reveal intense anxiety and repressed rage, certify physical and mental suffering. A lifelong prey to nervous complaints, More sickened for months together as censures multipled. Nonplused at such condemnation while in God's service, she prays to know the "reason of this late visitation." Too much worldly vanity, that "delicious poison" of reputation, she fears: "I set too much store by human opinion," am "wounded just where I am most vulnerable."[49] The anguished bafflement, the prayers for submission ring movingly true. But Roberts includes none of More's many letters to her public champion T. S. Whalley.[50] Other early biographers such as Henry Thompson had access to this correspondence but ignored it; so does Jones, whose sole reference misidentifies the editor, who attributes the *Animadversions on the Curate of Blagdon's Three Publications* that More so carefully fostered to the wrong Whalley.

Just where *Mendip Annals* terminates abruptly (the silence motif again), the Whalley letters pick up, in November 1800 with Bere now in the ascendant. More's almost daily bulletins richly exhibit her clandestine involvement in Blagdon's cultural politics. Like the enclaves of her educational and charitable endeavors and her networks of private influence, her letters constitute a feminized domestic locale whereby she can safely exert pressure on public space, crossing gender boundaries without publicly appearing to do so. Wonderfully fertile in plots and plans, she supplies the minutest instructions for Whalley and other defenders who, helped along by intelligent flattery, chivalrously carried them out. "Burn this," her letters often conclude—with good reason. A typical example: "I do not want myself to be praised, but Bere exposed. Suppose you were to say that, as Bere has coupled my name with . . . sedition, I am advised to bring an action against him, but that both my temper and declining health prevent me. Should not his democratic speeches . . . be glanced at?" Despite her carefully worded later denials, she was clearly delegating people to come forward on the "heresy business." Her letters show her rendering the wavering Crossman "a complete convert," passing on to him rumors about Bere's heretical preaching, carefully securing his "promise not to name me as the repeater. . . . I can't bear the thought of being again brought forward, or anything from me quoted, not even to advance the cause." More privately germinated a clerical *Statement of Facts* correcting Bere's misrepresentations; invaluable testimony to her schools' worth endorsed by nine ministers, it became her advocates' vade mecum. Her protégés took it in hand; her friends among the ladies urged their local priests to sign. More also masterminded the prolonged campaign that transformed four of the five ministers on Bere's "court" into her auxiliaries. She rallied allies, consulting all "friends, Members of Parliament and Bishops," even seeking help from less well-disposed politicians such as William Windham. She prompted endless letters and visits to pressure Crossman and the chancellor, circulated supportive material among London politicians and the episcopacy, gathered and transmitted information about Bere and his perjured witnesses, and kindled various anti-Bere sermons and pamphlets, priming her partisans with factual evidence and shrewd suggestions. Tireless and businesslike, often chafed by obtuse proxies, she grasped the situation better than her front men, whose "sacred awe" of her reputation and descriptions of her as a "Scipio in petticoats" only further inflamed the sensitive issues of her national services and influence.[51] She was "a fine fighter." She was also a combatant in conflict, wondering whether she should be fighting at all, as the letters' dizzying shifts from very real illness to adroit management indicate. Christian meekness and feminine decorum pulled toward submission and seclusion; Christian militance and human aspiration demanded that she save her schools and her reputation—"that vital vulnerable part, on which one's usefulness depends." Resignation did not come easily to one who would always "rather *work* for God than *meditate* on him."[52] More early recognized that the controversy threatened her entire missionary effort; at the calumny's height, even her great supporter Bishop Porteus suggested she give her schools up entirely, but she refused even to consider such a step.[53]

Clearly, neither pro- nor anti-Moreites fully engage her equivocal conduct, the ambiguities and complexities of her situation. Neither spotless martyr nor monster of dissimulation, not just an Evangelical, but a female Evangelical, More was a woman enmeshed in cultural politics; a forceful personality compelled to indirection, she tries to balance orthodoxy with innovation on dual fronts, tensions involving her sex as well as her religion. In her definitive statement on "this ever-painful Blagdon business" (it remained a long-term obsession), she herself pinpoints gender's salience. Detailing her case to win over Dr. Beadon, her new diocesan (Bishop Moss died in April 1802), More complains of "a wantonness of cruelty, which . . . few persons, especially of my sex, have been called to suffer. To that defenceless sex, and to my declared resolution to return no answers, I attribute this long and unmitigated persecution"—and she stresses her disinterestedness, her being "not of a sex to expect preferment."[54] Astutely linking womanhood and controversy, More yet oversimplifies. Persecuted she was, but hardly defenseless. Intent on self-justification, she displays her feminine vulnerability, that hysterical dread of public exposure which haunts the Whalley letters. Patty writes, for example, that the proposed libel suit must be "set aside by Hannah's inability, even to have it named to her; only talking of it once brought on the ague." Like that dignified "delicacy" much commended by her party, such salutary illnesses spurred friends, shamed foes, gave her space to maneuver behind what she terms the "good blind" of vindicators like Whalley, whose every word she superintends lest he seem not wholly a volunteer, "uneasy," says Patty, with amusing understatement, "lest there should possibly be any part of your book which could betray her knowledge of it, or assisting in it." [55] Pace Brown, More's feints and evasions evince less Evangelic or personal duplicity than that inherent in feminine convention. Literal facts, her compulsive silence and sickness also achieve metaphoric status, suggesting women's mutedness and impotence, the constraints within which female agency operates in this milieu. Yet, Janus-faced, peculiar protections work two ways, sheltering and inhibiting but also enabling. They permit resistance, active as well as passive aggression. The elastic formularies of goodness grant, to the creative woman, entitlement, sanctioned license to advance female priorities and preoccupations, to set woman-defined goals.

Certainly, Blagdon, like More's whole career, handsomely illustrates her characteristic pragmatism, her genius for strategically adapting feminine prescription while decorously observing all rules. If she submits to propriety's curbs, she also plies them to advantage, testimony to the strength and complexity of the Evangelical inheritance. More was indeed, as Roberts puts it, "a woman of business in all the concerns of humanity," endowed with "righteous cunning." Enjoying the peculiar protections of sex, she expands female prerogatives, backed by religion's legitimating premise. With the liveliest autobiographic glee, *Mendip Annals* enacts the dialectical interplay of piety and achievement. Peopled by exemplary moral reformers such as the self-portrait Mrs. Jones, the Cheap Repository tales mandate feminine social action, cultural changes addressing female needs, reforms justified in terms of women's specialization in nurturing, caring, teaching: "The best clergyman cannot do every thing. This is ladies [sic] business." Defining the dimensions of femininity, *Strictures* and *Coelebs* quite consciously extend women's behavioral repertoire: if domesticity is the female "profession," that vocation entails a measure of activism. Women are not to remain cloistered at home, but must export their sanative function as moral arbiters, God's instruments: the "superintendance of the poor" is "their immediate office"; *"charity is the calling of a lady; the care of the poor is her profession."* [56] Moreover, aggressive female piety assails male bastions of power and privilege, attacks the double standard, demands that men forsake license for domesticity—public houses, blood sports, gentlemanly codes of honor must go: Christian virtues are feminine virtues. [57]

Scrutinizing More as both ideologue and actor within this limited frame of Evangelical activism highlights typical complexities and conflicts, demonstrating why she could be recently described as at once a "feminist educational reformer" and the stellar propagandist for Evangelical inhibition, for a brand "new ideal of womanhood" based on "total abnegation." That religious ideal, some allege, was painfully confining—obsessed with domesticity, deference, and good works—rendering women slaves to convention, propriety, and patriarchal domination. [58] Certainly, changing religion meant changes for women. Yet it can also be argued that if the religious nexus constricted female life in some ways, it challenged, even liberated, in others; the wearer's ideational corset braced no less than it bound. Because Christian virtues were preeminently feminine virtues, Evangelical ideology mobilized women's culture for service in domestic and social reform movements. If it lauded domesticity, motherhood, familial responsibilities, and home values, it also invested female duties with national importance and legitimated the expansion of those duties beyond the home into organized charities and societies networking the land. [59] Nurturing, fostering, and improving became the feminine specialty abroad as well as within doors. And whatever Evangelicalism's penchant for propriety, it nonetheless defined women as minds and spirits rather than bodies, upgraded their education, and provided a rationale for agency, autonomy, and some measure of activism. "Non-political" in reference to Wollstonecraftian feminism's unthinkably "radical" objectives, the ideology of Evangelical womanhood yet bore significant political implications. Female influence, so the conduct books urged, could remodel the public order and sacralize society, for being "good" meant being useful, God's instruments vigorously correcting this world while ripening for the next—not, it is important to note, God's vessels as female religious endeavor had been typically described in the past.

More's emphasis on the reformist responsibilities inherent in Evangelical female ideology helps explain her enemies' virulence. Factoring

gender into Blagdon complicates but also clarifies. For, along with pre-
dictable antifeminine jibes, Bere's faction betrays a new nervousness
evoked by female moral imperialism. The Evangelical phalanx, they discover, manifests more than danger to clerical hegemony, for Bere, both
minister and magistrate, emblematizes in their diatribes a threatened
male establishment. Critical of women's public activities and impact,
they specially resent that female effrontery that anatomized the extant
order's flaws, seized the power of social definition, called men to answer
for their conduct. More, in a double bind, is castigated for both cunning femininity and masculine feminism. Beaten at their own game,
the *Anti-Jacobin* reviewers rage like baffled bulls when confronted by so
successful an example of that feminine influence they loved to extol.
But the gravamen of the charge is power. Though all More's irregu-
lar ecclesiastical adjuncts were dangerous, her adult evening meetings
initiated controversy because they most strikingly embodied encroachment, Evangelical lay intrusion, female intrusion. Religious and moral
instruction belonged to the clerical domain, not woman's province.
"Put not the Women into Pulpits," thunders one antagonist, for the
church is lowered by association with an "enthusiastic Female." And the
indictment extends beyond More personally to *Strictures,* her didactic
blueprint for the new Evangelical woman, the conservative counterpart to Wollstonecraft's feminist. For just as Evangelicalism generally
critiques establishment deficiencies, so More's revisionist female ideology replaces the existent accommodatingly feminine ideal with an
activist model. She is "a corrupter of the morals of the sex"; her *Strictures* "ought to be publicly burnt." She wants, say her detractors, to
exchange traditional womanly delicacy, simplicity, sensibility, and orna-
mental accomplishments for an "IT, HE, SHE creature," compounded
of study, religion, and ambition, who, empowered by faith, speaks on
social issues, voices her own concerns, defines her own values—a "non-
descript" in both gender and churchmanship.[60] Perhaps the orthodox
were right to fear holy women bearing texts.

Notes

Epigraphs are from Alice Jardine, *Gynesis: Configurations of Woman and Modernity* (Ithaca: Cornell University Press, 1985), 97–98; Natalie Zemon Davis, " 'Women's History' in Transition: The European Case," *Feminist Studies* 3, nos. 3–4 (Spring–Summer 1976): 90; Barbara Ritter Dailey, "The Visitation of Sarah Wight: Holy Carnival and the Revolution of the Saints in Civil War London," *Church History* 55 (1986): 455.

1. The geographical site may also be unfamiliar: Blagdon is one of the several villages in the Mendip Hills of Somerset that made up Hannah More's provincial missionary network. The quotation comes from Mary Russell Mitford, *Letters of Mary Russell Mitford: Second Series,* ed. Henry Chorley, 2 vols. (London: Richard Bentley, 1872), 1:95–96. Because she herself had been ripped by reviewers as a vulgar virago and because she defended Mary Wollstonecraft's womanliness against Victorian prudery, Mitford's assessment is especially interesting.

2. Mrs. Vernon Delves Broughton, ed., *Court and Private Life in the Time of Queen Charlotte: Being the Journals of Mrs. Papendiek, Assistant Keeper of the Wardrobe and Reader to Her Majesty,* 2 vols. (London: Richard Bentley, 1887), 1:113.

3. Sandra M. Gilbert and Susan Gubar's influential scenario of how women writers author-ize themselves—*The Madwoman in the Attic: The Woman Writer and the Nineteenth-Century Literary Imagination* (New Haven: Yale University Press, 1979)—has recently been challenged by Nancy Armstrong's *Desire and Domestic Fiction: A Political History of the Novel* (New York: Oxford University Press, 1987), which argues that the "domestic" female writer's cultural positioning is public, political, and central, though Armstrong deals specifically with very few actual women writers. She in effect revises the canonical inscription of Jane Austen, but it's writers such as More, famous in their day but since occluded, who most urgently demand consideration in female literary history. Useful paradigms of the Victorian woman writer as cultural sage with implications for earlier authors like More include Deirdre David, *Intellectual Women and Victorian Patriarchy: Harriet Martineau, Elizabeth Barrett Browning, George Eliot* (Ithaca: Cornell University Press, 1987); Mary Jean Corbett, "Feminine Authorship and Spiritual Authority in Victorian Women Writers' Autobiographies," *Women's Studies* 18, no. 1 (1990): 13–29; and Thaïs Morgan,

ed., *Victorian Sages and Cultural Discourse: Renegotiating Gender and Power* (New Brunswick: Rutgers University Press, 1990).

4. *Christian Observer* 3, no. 3 (March 1804): 156–57; "Remonstrance of a White Slave Trader," *Christian Observer* 3, no. 5 (May 1804): 285. More's essay is reprinted as "The White Slave Trade," in *The Works of Hannah More,* rev. ed., 11 vols. (London: T. Cadell, 1830), 3:385–96. For an encyclopedic survey of the intersections between female activism and antislavery, see Moira Ferguson, *Subject to Others: British Women Writers and Colonial Slavery, 1670–1834* (New York: Routledge, 1992).

5. More was taken seriously for her literary skills as well as for her religious and educational authority. Jane Austen notes the novel's fame, and Mrs. John Farrar (Eliza Ware Rotch) recalled in 1866, "When I was a young girl, I was constantly hearing the praises of Miss Hannah More. Everybody had read, or was reading, her religious novel" (*Recollections of Seventy Years* [1866; reprint, New York: Arno Press, 1980], 219). See *Jane Austen's Letters to Her Sister Cassandra and Others,* ed. R. W. Chapman, 2d ed. (London: Oxford University Press, 1959), 256, 259. The novel came out at the end of 1808; I own a tenth edition of 1809 (2 vols. [London: T. Cadell and W. Davies]), and that wasn't the last. The anti-Evangelical wit Sydney Smith made merry with More's didacticism in his essay on *Coelebs* for the *Edinburgh Review* (14, no. 27 [April 1809]: 145–51), but he nevertheless set up Sunday schools and used her Cheap Repository Tracts; see K[enneth] Charlton, "Sydney Smith and the Education of His Day," *Researches and Studies* (University of Leeds Institute of Education) 24 (1962): 28–39.

6. *Memoirs of the Life and Correspondence of Mrs. Hannah More,* ed. William Roberts, 4 vols. (London: R. B. Seeley and W. Burnside, 1834), 3:67 (Elizabeth Carter); *Journals and Correspondence of Thomas Sedgewick Whalley, D.D.,* ed. Hill Wickham (London: Richard Bentley, 1863), 2:168 (Mrs. Piozzi); Roberts, 3:161 (Alexander Knox), 3:94 (Tomline, bishop of Lincoln), 3:431 (Jane Porter). Subsequent references to Roberts are to this edition unless otherwise noted.

7. *Henry Crabb Robinson on Books and Their Writers,* ed. Edith J. Morley (London: J. M. Dent, 1938), 480.

8. Barbara B. Schnorrenberg, with Jean E. Hunter, "The Eighteenth-Century Englishwoman," in *The Women of England from Anglo-Saxon Times to the Present: Interpretive Bibliographical Essays,* ed. Barbara Kanner (Hamden, Conn.: Archon Books, 1979), 201, 204. Historians of Evangelicalism rate More similarly; for a typical assessment, see L. E. Elliott-Binns, *The Early Evangelicals: A Religious and Social Study* (London: Lutterworth Press, 1953), 337–38.

9. My concern here is not with the intersection of class and gender but with

competing rhetorics of benevolence, as they help us re-vision the notion of separate public and private spheres that still informs women's history. M. G. Jones, *Hannah More* (1952; reprint, New York: Greenwood Press, 1968), 229. For sources that exemplify the simple paradox approach referred to in the text, see Miriam Leranbaum, " 'Mistresses of Orthodoxy': Education in the Lives and Writing of Late Eighteenth-Century Women Writers," *Proceedings of the American Philosophical Society* 121, no. 4 (August 12, 1977): 281–301; Lynne Agress, *The Feminine Irony: Women on Women in Early-Nineteenth-Century English Literature* (Rutherford, N.J.: Fairleigh Dickinson University Press, 1978); and Marilyn Williamson, "Who's Afraid of Mrs. Barbauld? The Blue Stockings and Feminism," *International Journal of Women's Studies* 3, no. 1 (January–February 1980): 89–102. When I wrote the first draft of this essay in 1980 (I styled it as a mystery story), Hannah More was terra incognita for theorized feminist inquiry. In 1983, R. L. Brett, unaware of American work, remarked, "It is strange that the women's movement has never taken more interest in Hannah More" ("The Bishop in Petticoats," *Times Higher Education Supplement* no. 578 [December 2, 1983]: 13). That's begun to change only recently, with feminist studies currently most interested in class. See, for example, Beth Kowaleski-Wallace's arguments for More's patriarchal complicity, problematic class affiliation, and self-division in "Milton's Daughters: The Education of Eighteenth-Century Women Writers," *Feminist Studies* 12, no. 2 (Summer 1986): 275–93; "Hannah and Her Sister: Women and Evangelism in Early Nineteenth-Century England," *Nineteenth-Century Contexts* 12, no. 2 (1988): 29–51; and *Their Fathers' Daughters: Hannah More, Maria Edgeworth, and Patriarchal Complicity* (New York: Oxford University Press, 1991). For critiques of More's relationship with her protégée Ann Yearsley in terms of class, see Moira Ferguson, "Resistance and Power in the Life and Writings of Ann Yearsley," *Eighteenth Century: Theory and Interpretation* 27, no. 3 (Fall 1986): 247–68; and Donna Landry, *The Muses of Resistance: Laboring-Class Women's Poetry in Britain, 1739–1796* (Cambridge: Cambridge University Press, 1990). For an interesting commentary on the middle-class academic's inevitable and ironic alignment with the historical commodification of the Other that she critiques, see Donna Landry, "Commodity Feminism," in *The Profession of Eighteenth-Century Literature: Reflections on an Institution,* ed. Leo Damrosch (Madison: University of Wisconsin Press, 1992), 154–74. For atypical alignments of More and Mary Wollstonecraft, see my "Reform or Ruin: 'A Revolution in Female Manners,' " *Studies in Eighteenth-Century Culture,* vol. 11, ed. Harry C. Payne (Madison: University of Wisconsin Press, 1982), 119–216; and Lucinda Cole, "(Anti)Feminist Sympathies: The Politics of Relationship in Smith, Wollstonecraft, and More," *ELH* 58, no. 1 (Spring 1991): 107–40; Kathryn Sutherland, "Hannah More's Counter-Revolutionary Feminism," in *Revo-*

lution in Writing: British Literary Responses to the French Revolution, ed. Kelvin
Everest (Philadelphia: Milton Keynes/Open University Press, 1991), 27–63.
Sutherland's essay (which wasn't available to me when I revised this essay)
interestingly expands the reformist argument of my two earlier More essays.

10. "Pastoral power," as Michel Foucault notes, is a very real power, im-
plicated in the formation of both the modern subject and the modern state,
("The Subject and Power," *Critical Inquiry* 8, no. 4 [Summer 1982]: 783).
Yet women's philanthropy and educational endeavors are just beginning to
receive the nuanced feminist investigation they deserve; if it's simplistic to
equate Lady Bountiful with activist saint or feminist model, it's equally re-
ductive "to identify the turn to Evangelicalism as a female strategy for allaying
bodily anxiety" (Kowaleski-Wallace, "Hannah," 46). A huge mass of material remains unnoticed in eighteenth- and nineteenth-century periodical
and popular literature. For useful listings, see Barbara Kanner's entries on
education and on philanthropy, social service, and reform in *Women in English
Social History, 1800–1914: A Guide to Research,* 3 vols. (New York: Garland
Publishing Company, 1990), 1:660–809 and 2:178–376, respectively. F. K.
Prochaska's *Women and Philanthropy in Nineteenth-Century England* (Oxford:
Clarendon Press, 1980), stimulating in its stress on positive achievement,
barely addresses More's early period. See also Jane Rendall's chapter on "Evan-
gelicalism and the Power of Women," in *The Origins of Modern Feminism: Women
in Britain, France, and the United States* (London: Macmillan, 1985), 73–107;
and two essays in *Fit Work for Women,* ed. Sandra Burman (London: Croom
Helm, 1979): Catherine Hall's "The Early Formation of Victorian Domestic
Ideology," 15–32, and Anne Summers's "A Home from Home—Women's
Philanthropic Work in the Nineteenth Century," 33–63.

11. See Shirley Ardener, "Ground Rules and Social Maps for Women: An
Introduction," in *Women and Space: Ground Rules and Social Maps,* ed. Shirley
Ardener (London: Croom Helm, 1981), 11–34, for the argument that spatial
partitions "speak." For the crossing of barriers and "dirt," see Mary Douglas,
Purity and Danger: An Analysis of Concepts of Pollution and Taboo (1966; rev. ed.,
London: Routledge and Kegan Paul, 1979), 39–40, 139; and *Implicit Meanings:
Essays in Anthropology* (1975; reprint, London: Routledge, 1991), 51. The latter
work's chapter "Pollution" (47–59) develops arguments set up in Douglas's
earlier book.

12. *Anti-Jacobin Review and Magazine (AJRM)* 9 (July 1801): 294.

13. Karl Von Den Steinen, "The Discovery of Women in Eighteenth-
Century English Political Life," in *The Women of England,* 229. More's confession to Mrs. Garrick, "under the seal of the strictest secrecy," on the origin
of *Village Politics,* one of the great polemic successes of the 1790s, exemplifies
Von Den Steinen's point: the bishop of London "importuned me in the most

earnest manner" (January 8, 1793, Folger Shakespeare Library MS). Typically, the fiction of secrecy enabled the writing, dissipating as soon as the work was published. Another example is provided by More's 1793 political pamphlet, *Remarks on the Speech of M. Dupont . . . on the Subjects of Religion and Public Education,* a frank assault on French revolutionary atheism recently reprinted under the 1794 American title, *Considerations on Religion and Public Education,* intro. Claudia L. Johnson, Augustan Reprint Society no. 262 (Los Angeles: William Andrews Clark Memorial Library, 1990). More writes that "my full intention was to remain unknown as the author, for fear people wou'd think I was meddling with which the Bishops and the Clergy ought to have done— But I publish it with a view to give the profits to the French Emigrant Clergy," and it appeared under her name (HM to Mrs. Garrick, May 20, 1793, Folger Shakespeare Library MS). More's "private" interventions in public affairs presage her maneuvers during Blagdon.

14. I have room to mention only a very few letters here; More wrote an enormous number, a large proportion of which remain unexamined in private collections. They richly demonstrate her involvement with public issues; for example, she writes to Mrs. Garrick, "I hope you read the papers if only to qualify yourself to talk politics with me and that I shant find you so much behind hand as usual" (January 9, 1799, Folger Shakespeare Library MS). Thorough examination of eighteenth-century women's letters problematizes the prevalent mythology of woman's private domestic sphere versus man's public arena. I am grateful to Janice Thaddeus for bringing the Folger letters to my attention. Other useful holdings are at the Huntington Library and the Wigan Public Record Office. The printed correspondence is not only limited but also censored and Victorianized.

15. Jones prints an incomplete list of pamphlets (*More,* 260–61). Her citation of periodicals covering the controversy (reprinted from Hopkins's earlier biography) errs; the fullest London coverage is in the following: *Anti-Jacobin Review and Magazine* 9 (June 1801): 201–3; (July 1801): 277–96; (August 1801): 391–97, 415–19; 11 (February 1802): 193–94; (April 1802): 417–31; 12 (May 1802): 97–112; (July 1802): 301–8; (August 1802): 428–44; 13 (September 1802): 97–98; (October 1802): 195–211; (November 1802): 326–28. *British Critic* 17 (April 1801): 444–45; (May 1801): 526–30; 18 (August 1801): 216–17; (October 1801): 437–39; 19 (January 1802): 90–94; (April 1802): 439; 19 (June 1802): 654–55, 663–64. *Christian Observer* 1, no. 1 (January 1802): 14–15; 1, no. 3 (March 1802): 176–85. *Cobbett's Annual Register* 1 (May 29–June 5, 1802): cols. 651–57; 2 (July 24–31, 1802): cols. 119–22. See also *Letters from William Cobbett to Edward Thornton Written in the Years 1797– 1800,* ed. G. D. H. Cole (London: Oxford University Press, 1937), 10–12. Provincial papers also carried much material, often reprinted in London.

More's editors frequently misdate and print letters out of order, confusing the sequence of events.

16. *Memorials, Personal and Historical of Admiral Lord Gambier,* ed. Georgiana, Lady Chatterton, 2 vols. (London: Hurst and Blackett, 1861), 1:289; *Mendip Annals; or, A Narrative of the Charitable Labours of Hannah and Martha More in their Neighbourhood. Being the Journal of Martha More,* ed. Arthur Roberts (London: James Nisbet, 1859), 198; Chatterton, *Memorials of Admiral Lord Gambier,* 1:304, 289.

17. *Mendip Annals,* 167, 27, 46.

18. Thomas Bere, *An Appeal to the Public, on the Controversy between Hannah More, the Curate of Blagdon, and the Rev. Sir A. Elton* (London: G. G. and J. Robinson, 1801), 34. Cheddar was the earliest and most famed of the schools; More took visitors on what she called the "Cheddar round." Bere (and other adversaries) were sharply critical of the Mores' appearance in the charitable limelight. My figures are conservative estimates based on the Mores' scattered accounts.

19. Chatterton, *Memorials of Admiral Lord Gambier,* 1:180.

20. Ibid., 1:290; *Mendip Annals,* 197; Chatterton, *Memorials of Admiral Lord Gambier,* 1:382.

21. Thomas Bere, *The Controversy between Mrs. Hannah More, and the Curate of Blagdon; Relative to the Conduct of her Teacher of the Sunday School in that Parish; with the Original Letters* (London: J. S. Jordan, 1801), 21; Chatterton, *Memorials of Admiral Lord Gambier,* 1:382; see also *Mendip Annals,* 215–16. That J. S. Jordan had been the only publisher sufficiently radical to chance prosecution with Paine's *Rights of Man* throws an interesting light on Bere's charges; see Holcroft's letter in *The Life of Thomas Holcroft,* ed. Elbridge Colby, 2 vols. (1925; reprint, New York: Benjamin Blom, 1968), 1:xli: "Not a single castration (Laud be unto God and J. S. Jordan)."

22. Bere, *The Controversy,* 25. "Pride, and a consciousness of really tolerable abilities seem to be the besetting sins of Mr. Younge," diagnosed Patty (*Mendip Annals,* 128).

23. Chatterton, *Memorials of Admiral Lord Gambier,* 1:262.

24. See Henry Thompson, *The Life of Hannah More: With Notices of Her Sisters* (London: T. Cadell, 1838), 203 (also in Roberts, *Memoirs of More,* 3:125).

25. See, for example, *AJRM* 9 (August 1801): 393–94.

26. For Drewitt's appointment to Blagdon, see *AJRM* 11 (April 1802): 425.

27. Wickham, *Journals and Correspondence of Whalley,* 2:201.

28. For Loughborough, see Roberts, *Memoirs of More,* 3:122; Wickham, *Journals and Correspondence of Whalley,* 2:209; *The Correspondence of William Wilberforce,* ed. Robert Isaac Wilberforce and Samuel Wilberforce, 2 vols. (1840; reprint, Miami, Florida: Mnemosyne, 1969), 1:234. More's collected

Works (modestly prefaced) were in a sense a reply; an occasion for the *British Critic*'s defense, they provoked *The Life of Hannah More: With a Critical Review of Her Writings,* by "Sir Archibald Mac Sarcasm" (London: T. Hurst, 1802).

29. More sometimes employed talented Methodist "schismatics" because she valued evangelical efficacy over mere orthodoxy; see Robert Isaac Wilberforce and Samuel Wilberforce, *The Life of William Wilberforce,* 5 vols. (London: J. Murray, 1838), 1:247; *Mendip Annals,* 18 (also in Roberts, *Memoirs of More,* 2:208); Chatterton, *Memorials of Admiral Lord Gambier,* 1:370–72.

30. Roberts, *Memoirs of More,* 3:208 (Misdated 1804, this letter refers to the August 1802 *AJRM*'s about-face review of Mac Sarcasm's *Life,* a work it found rife with dreaded revolutionary "French principles"); 3:147; see also 3:102.

31. *Mendip Annals,* 227, 230–31; Jones, *More,* 172.

32. Ford K. Brown, *Fathers of the Victorians: The Age of Wilberforce* (Cambridge: Cambridge University Press, 1961), 193, 191.

33. David Newsome, "Father and Son" (review essay), *Historical Journal* 6, no. 2 (1963): 295; for similar criticisms of Brown, see Elisabeth Jay, *The Religion of the Heart: Anglican Evangelicalism and the Nineteenth-Century Novel* (Oxford: Clarendon Press, 1979), 9 n. 26, 17 n. 4, 286. For the squib, see Wickham, *Journals and Correspondence of Whalley,* 2:215.

34. Geoffrey Best, "Evangelicalism and the Victorians," *The Victorian Crisis of Faith: Six Lectures,* ed. Anthony Symondson (London: SPCK, 1970), 44. For a particularly clear anticipation of Brown's plot thesis, see Edward Spencer, *Truths Respecting Mrs. Hannah More's Meeting-Houses, and the Conduct of her Followers* (London: G. and J. Robinson, 1802), 68–69.

35. *AJRM* 12 (May 1802): 106; 11 (April 1802): 428.

36. Thomas Walter Laqueur, *Religion and Respectability: Sunday Schools and Working Class Culture, 1780–1850* (New Haven: Yale University Press, 1976), 74–76. For a useful overview of lay control in elementary education, see Robert J. Hind, "Working People and Sunday Schools: England, 1780–1850," *Journal of Religious History* 15, no. 2 (1988): 199–218; and Phil Gardiner, *The Lost Elementary Schools of Victorian England: The People's Education* (London: Croom Helm, 1984). For the centrality of the lay intervention issue to Blagdon, see Bere, *The Controversy,* 83n; *AJRM* 13 (October 1802): 199–201.

37. Chatterton, *Memorials of Admiral Lord Gambier,* 1:211. More is here criticizing Anglican clergymen and praising the dissenter William Jay, her friend and Wilberforce's, an association that preoccupied controversialists. Exemplary clerics people More's Cheap Repository Tracts, but her letters feature the faulty. Having just described one of the latter, she jokes, "Do we not stand in need of a little visit from the French?" (Roberts, *Memoirs of More,* 2:396).

38. For the Evangelical credo, see the *Christian Observer,* prospectus and

preface to 1; 1, no. 3 (March 1802): 176–80; John D. Walsh, "Origins of the Evangelical Revival," *Essays in Modern English Church History in Memory of Norman Sykes,* ed. G. V. Bennett and J. D. Walsh (New York: Oxford University Press, 1966), 132–62; "The Anglican Evangelicals in the Eighteenth Century," *Aspects de L'Anglicanisme* (Paris: Presse Universitaire de France, 1974), 87–102; G. F. A. Best, "The Evangelicals and the Established Church in the Early Nineteenth Century," *Journal of Theological Studies,* n.s., pt. 1 (April 1959): 63–78. Even church hierarchy initially hostile came to appreciate Evangelicalism; see Richard Allen Soloway, "Episcopal Perspectives and Religious Revivalism in England, 1784–1851," *Historical Magazine of the Protestant Episcopal Church* 40 (1971): 27–61. I am grateful to Professor Walsh for his encouragement in this project.

39. Chatterton, *Memorials of Admiral Lord Gambier,* 1:307, 304, 227 (see also Roberts, *Memoirs of More,* 2:465–66), 262–63; Roberts, 3:107; Chatterton, 1:263, 291.

40. For the latter view, see Charles Smyth, "The Evangelical Movement in Perspective," *Cambridge Historical Journal* 7, no. 3 (1943): 160–74; Michael Hennell, "A Little-Known Social Revolution," *Church Quarterly Review* 143 (January–March 1947): 189–207; Ernest Marshall Howse, *Saints in Politics: The "Clapham Sect" and the Growth of Freedom* (London: George Allen and Unwin, 1953); V. Kiernan, "Evangelicalism and the French Revolution," *Past and Present,* no. 1 (February 1952): 44–56; Gerald Newman, "Anti-French Propaganda and British Liberal Nationalism in the Early Nineteenth Century," *Victorian Studies* 18, no. 4 (June 1975): 385–418, and Newman's *The Rise of English Nationalism: A Cultural History, 1740–1830* (New York: St. Martin's Press, 1987), 233–44. More appropriately terms the Evangelical position "that state of *between-ity*" (Chatterton, *Memorials of Admiral Lord Gambier,* 1:287), and I have tried to situate her along a continuum of women writers in "Reform or Ruin."

41. *Memoirs of the Life and Correspondence of Mrs. Hannah More,* ed. William Roberts, 3d ed., 4 vols. (London: R. B. Seeley and W. Burnside, 1835), 3:160. "Mac Sarcasm" (see note 29 above) was the Reverend William Shaw, like More a friend of Samuel Johnson; Mary Alden Hopkins, *Hannah More and Her Circle* (New York: Longmans, Green, 1947), 192, traces the nom de plume to Charles Macklin's Sir Archy M'Sarcasm in *Love à la Mode.*

42. *AJRM* 12 (May 1802): 112.

43. *Mendip Annals,* 46, 14, 17.

44. Roberts, *Memoirs of More,* 3:108; the bishop's generosity aroused hostility among his canons, Roberts, 3:102; and others, *AJRM* 13 (October 1802), 200n. For livings and influence, see Roberts, 3:122n; Wickham, *Journals and Correspondence of Whalley,* 2:161; *Mendip Annals,* 44, 184, 191, 225; Spencer,

Truths 41n, 64. Some attributed Bere's hostility to disappointed hopes of preferment through More's influence (*The Autobiography of William Jay,* ed. George Redford and John Angell James [1854; reprint, Edinburgh: Banner of Truth Trust, 1974], 335).

45. *AJRM* 12 (May 1802): 105; 9 (August 1801): 392; Spencer, *Truths,* 6; Mac Sarcasm, *Life of More,* 179; *AJRM* 9 (August 1801): 394; Spencer, 8, 10; *AJRM* 11 (April 1802): 425; Spencer, 64, 62, 48, 41n.

46. *Cobbett's Weekly Political Register* 42, no. 3 (April 20, 1822): col. 188; Brown, *Fathers of the Victorians,* 201, 222, 217.

47. Mac Sarcasm, *Life of More,* vii; More, *Strictures on the Modern System of Female Education, with a View of the Principles and Conduct prevalent among Women of Rank and Fortune,* 2 vols. (1799; reprint, New York: Garland, 1974), 1:6; *AJRM* 9 (July 1801): 294.

48. Roberts, *Memoirs of More,* 3:121; Thompson, *Life of More,* 190. For summaries of contradictory charges, see Thompson, 212–13 (also in Roberts, 3:132–33); Roberts, 3:253–54.

49. Roberts, *Memoirs of More,* 3:174, 221, 183; More, *Practical Piety, or the Influence of the Religion of the Heart on the Conduct of the Life,* in *The Works of Hannah More* (New York: Harper, 1854), 1:445; Roberts, 3:183, 149. See also Roberts, 3:254; Thompson, *Life of More,* 219 (also in Roberts, 3:137); Chatterton, *Memorials of Admiral Lord Gambier,* 1:230, 389–90; Roberts, 3d ed., 3:161–62, for More's obsession with nonretaliation.

50. Brown leans heavily on these revelatory artifacts to substantiate his thesis of Evangelical conspiracy, but he fails to note the key role that gender issues played in their production.

51. Wickham, *Journals and Correspondence of Whalley,* 2:152, 170–71, 149–50, 187; Spencer, *Truths,* 35; Wickham, 2:156–58, 194; *Mendip Annals,* 228; Roberts, *Memoirs of More,* 3:103. More's critics had great fun with Sir Abraham Elton's allusion, because they found a female Scipio intrinsically hilarious, and his fulsome compliments. See Bere (*An Appeal,* 6, 31) on Elton, *A Letter to the Rev. Thomas Bere, Rector of Butcombe, occasioned by His Late Unwarrantable Attack on Mrs. Hannah More. With an Appendix, containing Letters and Other Documents relative to the Extraordinary Proceedings at Blagdon* (London: Cadell and Davies, 1801), 2, 29–30, 46. Whalley was equally adulatory, occasioning more attack.

52. A. E. Snodgrass, "Dr. Johnson's Petted Lady," *Cornhill Magazine* 148 (September 1933): 342; Roberts, *Memoirs of More,* 3:144, 62.

53. Thompson, *Life of More,* 205–6 (also in Roberts, 3:126–27); Roberts, *Memoirs of More,* 3:175; *The Correspondence of William Wilberforce,* 1:235.

54. Wickham, *Journals and Correspondence of Whalley,* 2:179; Dr. Richard Valpy describes More's "perpetually recurring" to this " 'thorn in the flesh,' "

Christian Observer 34, no. 3 (March 1835): 167; Thompson, *Life of More,* 200, 221 (also in Roberts, *Memoirs of More,* 3:123, 138; because Roberts's censored version deletes sections and changes wording, Thompson's printing is cited throughout). Thompson (199) rightly calls this letter to Beadon "the most important single document in existence for the illustration of Mrs. More's character and opinions"; with her usual flair for befriending bishops, More promptly made a supporter of Beadon, "the only person to whom I think myself accountable" (Chatterton, *Memorials of Admiral Lord Gambier,* 1:389). Roberts misdates this 1802 letter as 1801.

55. Wickham, *Journals and Correspondence of Whalley,* 2:212–13, 179, 210, 172, 213.

56. Roberts, *Memoirs of More,* 4:313; "A Cure for Melancholy. Showing the Way to Do Much Good with Little Money," in *The Works of Hannah More,* 1:171; *Strictures,* 1:97–98, 117; *Coelebs in Search of a Wife, Comprehending Observations on Domestic Habits and Manners, Religion and Morals,* in *The Complete Works of Hannah More* (New York: J. C. Derby, 1856), 2:372. I have considered More's Cheap Repository Tracts such as "A Cure" and female philanthropy in "Hannah More's Tracts for the Times: Social Fiction and Female Ideology," in *Fetter'd or Free? British Women Novelists, 1670–1815,* ed. Mary Anne Schofield and Cecilia Macheski (Athens: Ohio University Press, 1986), 264–84. For other perspectives on More's endeavor, see Susan Pedersen, "Hannah More Meets 'Simple Simon': Tracts, Chapbooks, and Popular Culture in Late Eighteenth-Century England," *Journal of British Studies* 25, no. 1 (January 1986): 84–113; and Gary Kelly, "Revolution, Reaction, and the Expropriation of Popular Culture: Hannah More's Cheap Repository," *Man and Nature* 6 (1987): 147–59.

57. Carolyn Walker Bynum's study of an earlier period has much to offer those interested in later women's appropriation of religion as a feminine specialty; see *Jesus as Mother: Studies in the Spirituality of the High Middle Ages* (Berkeley and Los Angeles: University of California Press, 1982).

58. Lawrence Stone, *The Family, Sex and Marriage in England, 1500–1800* (New York: Harper and Row, 1977), 352, 668.

59. The precise linkages between "feminine" domesticity and local philanthropy and women's intervention in national affairs naturally vary by period and country. American affairs have received most attention: for examples of good recent work, see Lori D. Ginzberg, *Women and the Work of Benevolence: Morality, Politics, and Class in the Nineteenth-Century United States* (New Haven: Yale University Press, 1990); and Kathleen D. McCarthy, *Lady Bountiful Revisited: Women, Philanthropy, and Power* (New Brunswick: Rutgers University Press, 1990). For the cultural intervention of late eighteenth- and nineteenth-century British women, see Leslie Howsam, *Cheap Bibles: Nineteenth-Century*

Publishing and the British and Foreign Bible Society (Cambridge: Cambridge University Press, 1991); and Linda Colley, *Britons: Forging the Nation, 1707–1837* (New Haven: Yale University Press, 1992), chapter 6, "Womanpower." For recent general discussion of these issues, see Mary De Jong, "Introduction: Protestantism and Its Discontents in the Eighteenth and Nineteenth Centuries," *Women's Studies* 19 (1991): 260–69; and Cécile Dauphin et al., "Women's Culture and Women's Power: An Attempt at Historiography," *Journal of Women's History* 1, no. 1 (Spring 1989): 64–88.

  60. Spencer, *Truths,* 4, 61; Mac Sarcasm, *Life of More,* 130–31, 27.

Jane Austen: Tensions Between Security and Marginality

𝒬𝒜𝒬 *Jan Fergus*

Jane Austen's class is difficult to identify precisely. David Spring has proposed a term for the Austens' position borrowed from Alan Everitt: the "pseudo-gentry." He specifies that "this group comprised the nonlanded: the professional and rentier families, first and foremost the Anglican clergy; second, other professions like the law—preferably barristers rather than solicitors—and the fighting services; and last, the rentiers recently or long retired from business." [1] Initially, Spring's term for this group may seem appropriate, and certainly Austen herself belongs within it. As an unmarried woman, she derived her position from her father, George Austen, who was a clergyman without land but with landed relatives. Similarly, Austen's mother Cassandra Leigh possessed wealthy relatives but virtually no private fortune. Mr. Austen's income depended almost entirely upon his wealthy cousin Thomas Knight, who presented him with two livings worth about £210 altogether, and who permitted him to farm certain lands. [2] Mr. Austen had also a little property that, together with that of his wife, produced from £120 to £140 a year. [3]

But the group as outlined by Spring is rather miscellaneous. It ignores also the important question of family connections. And to apply the term "pseudo-gentry" to the Austens and to other families whose income came primarily from the professions carries too many connotations of fraudulence to be acceptable. Terry Lovell's phrase "lesser gentry" to describe the Austens' class avoids any implication of imposture, but it suggests perhaps too much security. As Lovell himself points out, the lesser gentry was particularly threatened: "Squeezed between the rising capitalist tenant-farmer and the upper gentry." [4]

258

What seems central to the Austens' position is a sense both of threat, as Lovell outlines, and of security. Their connections to the landed gentry, especially after the wealthy Knights adopted Edward Austen, Jane Austen's brother, offered some security. But only some. The Austens had to draw upon their richer relatives to obtain positions and incomes for their sons; their daughters, as is well known, would face dispossession and a narrow income once their father died. This position, dependent upon the resources of the gentry network, was built into the elite social structure, as all Austen's novels witness. Thanks to the practices of entail and primogeniture, the English landed gentry were always producing unlanded sons and daughters who nevertheless retained gentry status for a generation or two, and for whom their wealthy relatives would solicit whatever places, pensions, offices, livings, or other sources of income they could obtain through their "interest." In this world, everything depended upon "interest," from obtaining a bed in a lunatic asylum to achieving promotion from midshipman to lieutenant—as William Price found in *Mansfield Park*.

I locate the Austens' class, then, as lying on the fringes of the gentry. Jane Austen grew up within a large, happy, entertaining, and loving family, one that provided strong mutual support and encouragement, but the family's actual position in their world was marginal. I would argue that Austen's position within the class structure of her society forced her to experience increasing tension between security and marginality.

The best way to appreciate how deeply and widely the tension between security and marginality was felt within the Austen family is to look at *The Loiterer*, the periodical published by Austen's brothers in 1789–90, when she was thirteen and fourteen. While most Austen critics have examined this publication for early influences on Austen's themes and burlesque style, and for examples of Austen's first published writing,[5] in fact *The Loiterer*'s treatment of class and money offers a more revealing study. When they began *The Loiterer*, both James and Henry Austen were supported by their father at Oxford, and both were intended to support themselves as clergymen. They certainly did not have the money as students to live in the extravagant style deplored by an anonymous pamphlet of 1788, *Remarks on the Enormous Expense of the Education of many young men in the University of Cambridge, with a plan . . . &c.*[6] Even prosperous parents could have difficulty keeping sons at the universities. Contemporary accounts indicate that university expenses could range from £80 to £200 a year.[7] In 1785, it cost Robert Thornton more than £56 for fees and furnishings when he entered Clare Hall, Cambridge; he soon found his allowance of £67 a year inadequate, and even one of his trustees agreed that it was "rather too little."[8] Later, the poet George Crabbe claimed to have spent £1300 educating his first son at Cambridge and his second son there for one term; he wrote to an attorney that "keeping two young men at an University in these times is, I find, beyond my ability."[9]

James and Henry were excused tuition fees at St. John's as founder's kin but must have had to live very cheaply, for their father could not possibly have supported two sons at Oxford at what appears to be the usual rate. Not surprisingly, they make problems of money and class central to many of their essays in *The Loiterer.* They address several times in their papers the horrible fate of, as Henry puts it, "sinking into Country Curates, [growing] old on fifty pounds a year."[10] For example, James adopts the persona of an Oxford scholar who enjoys a college living of £200 a year. He has made his own son a grazier and has taken his grandson away from Oxford "to breed him up an honest and ignorant farmer," asserting that "he will be a richer, and I think a happier man in his present situation, than if starving on a country Curacy of forty pounds a year." The scholar notes too that Oxford extravagance "deprives men of moderate fortune of the power of giving their children a learned education."[11] Characters and anecdotes such as these reappear in other essays.

The emphasis on money and class in *The Loiterer* is ambivalent then. A sense of both threat and security is present. The threat lies in poverty and dispossession, the possible loss of caste, "starving on a country Curacy of forty pounds a year," despite a good education. Security is conveyed by distancing: those facing starvation on poor curacies are usually sons of tradesmen or graziers, with no connections to the landed gentry like those that the Austens enjoyed. The Austen brothers tend to focus their criticism on the circumstances of the class below them, the sons of prosperous or near-prosperous tradesmen, a stance that reinforces their own sense of belonging to the gentry. At the same time, this choice also betrays the insecurities of marginality: extreme awareness or ridicule of the class below one is the hallmark of the arriviste, as Mrs. Elton's attitude to the Tupmans from Birmingham amply demonstrates.[12] Both

James and Henry clearly entertained some anxieties about their future as members of the gentry, and in fact both spent some part of their lives as curates on £50 a year.[13]

This ambivalent sense that one's class and income are both secure and threatened is visible too in all Austen's writing, from the juvenilia to the last novels and *Sanditon*. It is especially evident, however, in the novels that remained unfinished during her lifetime. In two of these, "Catharine, or the Bower" and *The Watsons*, tensions between security and marginality tend to be expressed more directly than in the completed novels. Austen apparently found it necessary to displace or undercut such tensions before she was prepared to publish. But examples from the novels will certainly occur to every reader, and I will briefly consider how these tensions are accommodated in them, particularly in *Emma* and *Sanditon*.

Unlike her brothers, Austen explores marginality from a woman's doubly threatened perspective. Men like her brothers could pursue professions as well as prosperous marriages; women could aspire only to marriage. Single women were marginal even if they apparently enjoyed secure positions within the gentry. A good example is evident in a draft statement written in 1810 concerning the coming of age of a very distant connection of Austen's, Caroline Elizabeth Dryden, the second daughter of Sir John Dryden of Canons Ashby who had died in 1797. According to the draft, Caroline, born in 1789, could purchase with her £800 fortune an annuity of £80, a sum that seems rather inflated. Her mother, Lady Dryden, who had remarried, suggested that this £80 a year would be "quite sufficient" to support her if she agreed to continue where she was as a "parlour Boarder" in London for eight months of the year, visiting her mother at Canons Ashby during the summer and Christmas vacations: "Lady D: does not mean her [Caroline] to be in any manner in the School she merely proposes it as a most respectable Asylum for Miss D: when Lady D. cannot have her with her, or in case of her death, as a single young Lady cannot live upon a small income with credit or comfort by herself, but would be liable to every inconvenience & probably distress & censure."[14] Even a baronet's daughter can evidently sink close to the level of Harriet Smith in *Emma*, left to shift for herself as a "parlour boarder" at Mrs. Goddard's in Highbury.[15]

As an undowered woman, Austen's place on the fringes of the gentry was far more marginal than that of her brothers or Caroline Dryden.

Unless she married, Austen would have an assured home and social position only during her father's lifetime, and perhaps not even then: if he resigned his living or if he retired early, the home would be lost. It was lost, in fact, in 1801, when George Austen turned the rectory and the work of the parish over to James and took his wife and daughters to Bath; Austen is supposed to have fainted when at age twenty-five she first heard of the move.[16]

Austen's intense interest in threatened or dispossessed women certainly predated her own dispossession from Steventon Rectory in 1801. Just five months before copying the unfinished "Catharine, or the Bower" into the third volume of her juvenilia, in August 1792, Austen had been strongly reminded of the marginality of wives or daughters of clergymen. Her friends Mary and Martha Lloyd, also clergyman's daughters, were dispossessed along with their mother from nearby Deane parsonage, which they had rented from George Austen. They had to leave Deane because James Austen married in March 1792, receiving the curacy and parsonage from his father. At this time, the Lloyds (who had already been displaced from their father's rectory when he died three years earlier) moved sixteen miles away,[17] a loss to Austen that may account for some of the uneven tone of "Catharine." The bower of the title was created before the novel opens by the heroine in company with her friends the Wynnes, daughters of a clergyman whose death has forced them—like the Lloyds—to leave the neighborhood. As marginal women, they must depend upon their rich, fashionable, and selfish relatives. As a result, one of them has been forced to seek a rich husband in India, and the other has become an unpaid companion in a relative's family. The fate of Cecilia and Mary Wynne is presented in a somber style that quarrels with the exuberant comedy of Catharine's exchanges with the mischievous Edward Stanley and his inane sister Camilla.

Having money and education but no family, Catharine Percival[18] occupies an ambiguous social position—one that possibly the young Austen, well-connected to the gentry, felt to be the obverse of her own. Austen writes of her heroine, "As an heiress she was certainly of consequence, but her Birth gave her no other claim to it, for her Father had been a Merchant."[19] Catharine is not marginal precisely because no one with enough money can be, but she is not secure either. She is subjected to the snobbery and snubs of the Dudleys and Stanleys, who look down upon her birth, and she is confined by an aunt who (as the first sentence tells us) "watched over her conduct with so scrutinizing a severity, as to make it very doubtful to many people, and to Catharine amongst the rest, whether she loved her or not" (*MW* 192). Mrs. Percival refuses to mix more with her neighborhood lest Catharine encounter ineligible young men (*MW* 196). Catharine is secure in money, education, and values but marginal in every other way—deprived of society, love, and friendship, and threatened at the end with dispossession of the bower that she romantically clings to as "sacred," the one relic of her friends' love (*MW* 195). Tensions between security and marginality here generate an uneasy conflict between seriousness and comedy—one that many critics think Austen failed to resolve.

The Watsons, written some twelve years later, probably in 1804, dwells even more directly on dispossession, poverty, and marginality. Emma Watson is Austen's most marginal heroine. Before the novel opens, she has successively lost her immediate family, then a beloved uncle, and finally an aunt and a fortune. Having the upbringing of a gentry heiress without any means at all, Emma has been thrown back on her father, a poorly beneficed clergyman who has three other unmarried daughters and who is likely to die soon. The eldest daughter, Elizabeth, eloquently expresses the sisters' position: "you know we must marry.—I could do very well single for my own part—A little Company, & a pleasant Ball now & then, would be enough for me, if one could be young forever, but my Father cannot provide for us, & it is very bad to grow old & be poor & laughed at" (*MW* 317).

The argument that follows between Emma and Elizabeth Watson, over single gentlewomen's few ways of avoiding being poor and laughed at, presents a kind of dialog between security and marginality—a more direct one than Austen included in any work that she published. I suspect that she was unwilling to print anything so revealing. The heroine Emma is secure and confident, despite being dispossessed; her sister is not. Emma avers,

> "To be so bent on Marriage—to pursue a Man merely for the sake of
> situation—is a sort of thing that shocks me; I cannot understand it.
> Poverty is a great Evil, but to a woman of Education & feeling it ought
> not, it cannot be the greatest.—I would rather be Teacher at a School
> (and I can think of nothing worse) than marry a Man I did not like."—

"I would rather do any thing than be Teacher at a school—said her sister. *I* have been at school, Emma, & know what a Life they lead; *you*
never have.—I should not like marrying a disagreable Man any more
than yourself,—but I do not think there *are* many very disagreable
Men;—I think I could like any good humoured Man with a comfortable
Income.—I suppose my Aunt brought you up to be rather refined."
(*MW* 318)

Just a year or two before Austen wrote this passage, she had refused to
marry a gentleman whom *she* did not like, although he was from her own
favorite county of Hampshire, the eldest son of a man of fortune, and
the brother of her good friends. Austen herself had acted as Emma Watson dictates—but ambivalently. She first accepted Harris Bigg-Wither,
on December 2, 1802. She then changed her mind overnight and refused him the next day.[20] The dialog that she creates here in *The Watsons*
is also ambivalent. One does not feel that right sits easily on Emma's
side, or that Elizabeth's position is entirely to be despised. By contrast,
the similar conversation in *Pride and Prejudice* between Elizabeth Bennet
and Charlotte Lucas is surrounded by comic irony, and Charlotte's position is undercut by her cynicism in a way that Elizabeth Watson's is not.
Emma Watson's elite upbringing *has* refined her; she does not know the
kind of life that teachers at school live. She is a woman of education and
feeling divorced from the money and class that should support them:
"of importance to no one, a burden on those, whose affection she c^d not
expect, an addition in an House, already overstocked, surrounded by
inferior minds with little chance of domestic comfort, & as little hope
of future support" (*MW* 362). Tension is present between the unsup-
ported security of Emma's values and the marginal position that she
shares with Elizabeth. Interestingly, although most of the manuscript
of *The Watsons,* according to R. W. Chapman's edition, is heavily inter-
lineated, erased, and corrected, Austen seems to have written out the
first two passages here quoted quite freely, without any alterations or
second thoughts.[21] They came easily.

Although such passages came easily to Austen, they apparently did
not agree with the sense of security that she wished to incorporate into
her early novels. She seems to have enjoyed creating marginal positions
for her heroines, but she did not choose to complete works in which
the heroine—and the comedy—become too threatened. The dispos-

sessed Dashwoods of *Sense and Sensibility* nonetheless enjoy a comfortable home and income. The threat of dispossession hangs over the Bennet sisters of *Pride and Prejudice,* but because the only character who takes it seriously is the idiotic Mrs. Bennet, this quite genuine threat is comically undercut—as is Charlotte Lucas's plight, by different means. In the later novels, however, Austen finds ways to introduce somewhat greater tensions between security and marginality without completely destroying comedy. In *Mansfield Park* and *Persuasion,* the heroines' different homes are uncomfortable, even painful, but they do not really face dispossession. Sir Thomas Bertram establishes in the first chapter that if they adopt her, Fanny Price must be secured the provision of a gentlewoman even though she does not marry, and he never actually considers ejecting Fanny permanently from Mansfield. Anne Elliot must leave Kellynch, and finds herself a guest in many houses, but "she might always command a home with Lady Russell" (146).

The later novel that most thoroughly considers the plight of marginal women is in fact the most comic one, *Emma*. There, because her heroine is so secure, nearly as secure as a landed man, Austen is free to explore issues of women's power and marginality more profoundly than she had in earlier novels, without destroying comedy. Accordingly, whenever readers look at almost any woman in *Emma* apart from the heroine, they encounter a sense of threat. They do so even in the first chapter. It is quite surprising, for instance, to notice how much Mr. Knightley insists that Miss Taylor needs to be "settled in a home of her own . . . secure of a comfortable provision" (11). Why is he so insistent? He cannot imagine that the Woodhouses would ever have discarded this "beloved friend" (6). Before her marriage, Miss Taylor is in as secure a position as any unmarried woman without a fortune can be, but Mr. Knightley considers her insecure—as she is. If Mr. Woodhouse were to die and Emma were to marry, Anne Taylor would have to leave Hartfield even if the Woodhouses left her an income. Any home that she could then afford would be much inferior, but no doubt she would be somewhat better off than the other threatened spinsters in the novel—Harriet Smith, Jane Fairfax, or Miss Bates. Jane Fairfax is, of course, the worst off, for although she has for the present a home with the Campbells, who educated her, that home is so insecure that Jane has resolved to renounce it for work as a governess, the only career possible for her: "As long as [the Campbells] lived, no exertions would be necessary, their home might be her's for ever; and for their own comfort they would have retained her wholly; but this would be selfishness:—what must be at last, had better be soon" (165). The prospect for Jane of "penance and mortification for ever" (165) is more immediately threatening than life at Mrs. Goddard's for Harriet Smith or Miss Bates's occupation of the "drawing-room floor" of a house belonging to "people in business" (155). But in the bleak words of Mr. Knightley, Miss Bates "is poor; she has sunk from the comforts she was born to; and, if she live to old age, must probably sink more" (375). "Neither young, handsome, rich, nor married," she lost her home when her father, a former vicar of Highbury, died (21). By contrast, the very first sentence of *Emma* assures us that Emma Woodhouse, "handsome, clever, and rich," possesses among other seemingly "best blessings of existence," "a comfortable home." The importance of a home for a single woman is insisted upon again and again—but its unlikelihood is made clear.

I would suggest, then, that in *Emma,* Austen achieved her most successful accommodation between the demands of comedy and those tensions between marginality and security that preoccupied her imagination. This accommodation permitted her to take a sharper look at women's position in society than she does in any other completed novel. But a reading of *Sanditon,* the novel left incomplete at her death, indicates that at the end of her career she was prepared to explore women's marginality even more profoundly than in *Emma.* The village of Sanditon seems to be populated mostly by women, from Mrs. Whitby who runs the not very successful circulating library to all the cooks, servants, and washerwomen unnecessarily rounded up by Diana Parker as possible employees for Mrs. Griffiths. The transient population is even more emphatically female. Thirteen women and nine men subscribe to Mrs. Whitby's circulating library (*MW* 389).[22] Diana and Susan Parker are accompanied only by their supine brother Arthur. Mrs. Griffiths brings the West Indian heiress Miss Lambe as well as the two Beaufort girls. And of course the Thomas Parkers have brought the heroine, Charlotte Heywood, to Sanditon.

All the single gentlewomen in *Sanditon* are marginal in some way, even if they have money. Miss Lambe is rich but is also a mulatto. The Miss Beauforts have recently spent too much on dress and are forced to economize. Miss Denham, Sir Edward's sister, has less means to support her position than her brother does. Even Charlotte Heywood is marginal: although her parents are well-off, their fourteen children force economy upon them, and they are unlikely to be able to afford generous dowries for their daughters. The Miss Parkers have genteel incomes but are so marginal within their world that their energies, finding no other outlets, make them ill. As Charlotte concludes, "The Parkers, were no doubt a family of Imagination & quick feelings—and while the eldest Brother found vent for his superfluity of sensation as a Projector, the Sisters were perhaps driven to dissipate theirs in the invention of odd complaints" (*MW* 412). The word "driven" is revealing. Thomas Parker can expend his energy on turning Sanditon into a fashionable spa, but Diana and Susan have no such "vent." This perception has serious implications for women, glanced at in *Persuasion* when Mrs. Croft describes the consequences of being unable to accompany her husband on his ship: she had "all manner of imaginary complaints from not knowing what to do with myself, or when I should hear from him next" (71). Absence of usefulness or power causes debility.

The very wide array of marginal women in *Sanditon* most conspicuously includes the threatened antiheroine Clara Brereton. She is poor and completely dependent on a distant relation, the capricious and selfish Lady Denham. She is also the object of a seductive plot by Sir Edward Denham, who hopes to divert his aunt Lady Denham's money to himself. Although we are told that Clara has not the least intention of being seduced (*MW* 405), Charlotte glimpses her at the end in a clandestine meeting with Sir Edward: "It could not but strike her rather unfavourably with regard to Clara:—but hers was a situation which must not be judged with severity" (*MW* 426). Clara's plight and the presence of so many apparently superfluous women in the fragment suggest that in *Sanditon,* Austen was engaged in a more penetrating study than she had yet attempted of women's limited options within a class system that makes them marginal.

Notes

An earlier version of this essay was read at the American Society for
Eighteenth-Century Studies convention in Minneapolis, 1990. Some of the
arguments have since appeared in abbreviated form in *Jane Austen: The Literary
Career* (New York: Macmillan and St. Martin's Press, 1991).

1. David Spring, "Interpreters of Jane Austen's Social World," *Jane Austen:
New Perspectives, Women and Literature,* n.s. 3 (1983): 59.

2. George Holbert Tucker, *A Goodly Heritage: A History of Jane Austen's
Family* (Manchester: Carcanet New Press, 1983), 27, 30–31; William Austen-
Leigh and Richard Arthur Austen-Leigh, rev. and enlarged by Deirdre Le
Faye, *Jane Austen: A Family Record* (London: British Library, 1989), 14.

3. The Austens' property can be inferred by examining Mrs. Austen's income after her husband's death. She was left with what little property had
been settled on her, which produced only £140 a year by one account, £122 by
another more reliable one. Fanny Catherine Lefroy, in her anonymous article
"Is It Just?" (*Temple Bar* [February 1883]: 275), quotes Mrs. Austen as writing
to "her wealthy sister-in-law" (presumably Mrs. Leigh Perrot): "One hundred
and forty pounds a year . . . is the whole of my own income. My good sons have
done all the rest." Mrs. Austen wrote to Mrs. Leigh Perrot on January 4, 1820,
that the banker Hoare receives her dividends, "amounting to not quite £116
a year; this sum, with a little land at Steventon, which I let for £6 a year, is
the whole of my own property, my good children having supplied all the rest"
(R. A. Austen-Leigh, *Austen Papers, 1704–1856* [London: Spottiswoode, Ballantyne, 1942], 264). The similarity in the two accounts suggests that Lefroy
had seen the letter of January 4, 1820, but remembered it inaccurately. This
meager property had of course made it impossible for the Austens to dower
their daughters.

4. Terry Lovell, "Jane Austen and the Gentry," in *The Sociology of Literature:
Applied Studies,* ed. Diana Laurenson (Keele: Sociological Review Monographs
26, 1978), 21.

5. Recent examples include articles in *Jane Austen's Beginnings: The Juvenilia and Lady Susan,* ed. J. David Grey (Ann Arbor: UMI Research Press,
1989), especially A. Walton Litz, "Jane Austen: The Juvenilia," 4–5, and John
McAleer, "What a Biographer Can Learn About Jane Austen from Her Juve-

nilia," 14. Earlier, Litz explored the influence of *The Loiterer* on Austen in more detail in *Jane Austen: A Study of Her Artistic Development* (New York: Oxford University Press, 1965).

6. Quoted by Christopher Wordsworth, *Social Life at the English Universities in the Eighteenth Century* (Cambridge: Deighton, Bell, and Co., 1874), 149, 168, 491.

7. For accounts of university expenses, see Wordsworth, *Social Life at the English Universities*, 414: he quotes a 1760 source that asserts "that 80*l. per annum* was enough, but a gentleman-commoner spent 200*l,*" and adds with apparent admiration that "Charles Simeon's whole income, when at King's about 1780, was 125*l. per annum:* he used to dispose of one-third of that sum in 'charity.' "

8. Northamptonshire Record Office (hereafter NRO), Thornton 28, 27, 37.

9. Renè Huchon, *George Crabbe and His Times, 1754–1832,* tran. Frederick Clarke (1907; reprint, London: Frank Cass and Co., 1968), 221–22.

10. James Austen and Henry Austen, *The Loiterer,* 2 vols. (Oxford: Prince and Cooke, 1790), no. 8, p. 7.

11. *The Loiterer,* no. 15, p. 12.

12. Jane Austen, *Emma,* vol. 4 of R. W. Chapman's edition of the novels, 3d ed., 5 vols. (London: Oxford University Press, 1933), 310. All subsequent citations from Austen's novels will be taken from this edition and will appear in parentheses in the text.

13. James Austen became curate of Stoke Charity in June 1789, upon taking orders, then curate of Overton, presumably in 1790, and vicar of Sherborne St. John in September 1791 (Tucker, *A Goodly Heritage,* 103, 105). Upon his marriage in 1792, a distant relative presented him to the living of Cubbington, valued at £269 a year (Robert Bearman, "Henry Austen and the Cubbington Living," *Persuasions,* no. 10 [1988]: 23). Clearly, James Austen almost never was restricted to £50 a year. Interestingly, he apparently was content to pay his curates at Cubbington, where he never resided, a mere £45 a year, retaining £225 for himself (Bearman, 24). After his bankruptcy in 1816, Henry Austen obtained the curacy of Chawton on December 26, 1816, at a stipend of £54.12.0 (Winifred Midgley, "The Revd. Henry and Mrs. Eleanor Austen," *Annual Report of the Jane Austen Society* [1978]: 14, 19).

14. NRO D(CA) 364/10, "Statement of Miss Dryden's affairs," draft dated February 9, 1810. After remarrying, Lady Dryden kept the title that she obtained with her first marriage—a common enough practice.

15. Caroline Dryden eventually found what one hopes was a more agreeable "Asylum" with her unmarried brother Lempster, vicar of Ambroseden

(*Northamptonshire Families,* ed. Oswald Barron [London: Constable, 1906], 55). She died in 1872, so if she did purchase an annuity of £80 a year for £800, she got a splendid bargain.

16. Constance Hill, *Jane Austen: Her Homes and Her Friends* (London: John Lane, 1904), 91.

17. See Le Faye, *A Family Record,* 64–65, 67.

18. Although Austen spells her heroine's name "Catharine" in the title and on the first page, in other places she spells it "Catherine" or refers to her as Kitty. Her last name sometimes appears as Peterson, the original version, and more frequently as Percival, the later choice. The change from a plebeian name such as Peterson to Percival is probably significant: Austen is lessening the apparent social distance between her heroine and the Stanleys and Dudleys.

19. "Catharine, or the Bower," in R. W. Chapman's edition of Austen's *Minor Works,* vol. 6 (London: Oxford University Press, 1954), 223–4 (hereafter cited as *MW* in the text).

20. I am grateful to Ruth Perry for making this point about the ambivalence of Austen's own choices in response to an earlier version of this essay.

21. Indications of Austen's manuscript corrections are preserved in the notes to R. W. Chapman's edition of *The Watsons* (Oxford: Clarendon Press, 1927).

22. I have taken this list from the facsimile, *Sanditon: An Unfinished Novel by Jane Austen,* ed. B. C. Southam (Oxford: Clarendon Press, 1975), 50. Chapman's edition prints "Mrs. Davis," but the facsimile seems to read "Mr." If Chapman's reading is accepted, women outnumber men by fourteen to eight.

"That Abominable Traffic": *Mansfield Park* and the Dynamics of Slavery

᜕᜔᜕ Joseph Lew

> The evil in question began in avarice. It was nursed also by worldly interest.
>
> —Thomas Clarkson
>
> I saw in these . . . [slave-owning] provinces so many vices and corruptions, increased by this trade and this way of life, that it appeared to me as a gloom over the land.
>
> —John Woolman

In the summer of 1814, popular opinion in England about the international slave trade rose to a fevered pitch. In June, the Houses of Parliament were deluged by more than eight hundred petitions, with more than a quarter of a million signatures, demanding international abolition.[1] On August 1, 1814, Castlereagh, foreign minister and British plenipotentiary at the Congress of Vienna, wrote to the duke of Wellington: "The nation is bent upon this object . . . and the ministers must make it the basis of their policy."[2] Holland agreed to abolition in June 1814. The restored Bourbon king of France, Louis XVIII, refused immediate abolition, promising only eventual abolition—presumably only after replenishing supplies and clearing uncultivated lands. Napoleon, on his return from Elba, abolished the slave trade in an attempt to curry support from Britain.

That deluge of petitions descended upon Parliament during the month following the advertisement for Jane Austen's third published novel in the *Morning Chronicle* (May 23 and 27, 1814). That novel, *Mansfield Park*, dramatizes what Thomas Clarkson, an author Austen "loved,"[3] called "the Slavery and Commerce of the Human Species." The novel's opening sentences describe "all Huntingdon's" reaction to the attainment, by Miss Maria Ward, of a husband, title, and estate to which "her uncle, the lawyer, himself allowed her to be at least three thousand pounds short of any equitable claim."[4] Two pages later, after being sent "advice and professions," but more important, "money and baby-linen," Lady Bertram's now-impoverished younger sister hands over Fanny, her second child. As Avrom Fleischman, Margaret Kirkham, and Claudia Johnson (among others) have noted, the question of slavery and the slave trade appears obliquely in the novel through references to Sir Thomas's Antigua estate and Fanny's questions about the slave trade (178). More than merely topical, these allusions underscore the larger political context—a context that goes beyond the explicitly gendered issues portrayed. In short, *Mansfield Park* continues debates over slavery and over women's political rights.

By demonstrating how self-interest motivates even the well-meaning Edmund to justify morally questionable behavior, the novel tacitly indicates how the Bertrams think—or refuse to think—of their slave-earned fortune. Historian R. S. Neale notes:

> It was Jane Austen's genius in *Mansfield Park* and in her creation of the character of Fanny Price to suggest that Fanny's moral stance on the performance of *The Lover's Vows*, apparently fundamentally concerned with sexual propriety, was actually an unrecognized defence of property and existing political conditions. And then to show her as a sort of existential heroine refusing to sell herself to property. To suggest, that is, the impropriety of conventional propriety yet all the while, through Fanny's and our own knowledge of the fact that the estate at Mansfield Park was propped up by the exploitation of slave labour in Antigua, to confront us with our own and Fanny's alienation.[5]

As McKenzie observes, the fact that Sir Thomas "absented himself to oversee the work on a plantation . . . casts a slight shadow on the sources of his consequence."[6] Eighteenth-century writers used similar terminology: John Woolman, an antislavery writer quoted in Clarkson's

History, described the effects of such sources as "a gloom over the land," giving rise to both "vices and corruption." Clarkson maintained that the slave trade "began in avarice. It was nursed also by worldly interest."[7] By expanding upon political and theoretical pronouncements common to her day, Austen depicts the society in which "the evil in question began." The slave trade and slavery itself are but the symptoms of the avarice and worldly interest that some critics locate in Mansfield.

Literary critics, however, have traditionally hesitated to grant Austen such political acumen; Johnson complains that "allusions to . . . the slave trade in Antigua . . . are first passed over, then believed not to exist at all."[8] From anything modern criticism has to say about her readings of Goldsmith's *History* or Macartney's *Embassy to China* (alluded to in *Mansfield Park*), one must assume that Austen somehow missed the explicit or implicit political theorizing—that, like the Miss Bertrams, she had gleaned only "the principal rivers of Russia," "the chronological order of the kings of England, with the dates of their accession, and most of the principal events of their reigns," or "the Roman emperors as low as Severus" (15, 16). Honan's mis-citation of Austen's reading is typical: "Jane herself read a book by Thomas Clarkson on African slavery in which the most villainous figure was named Norris, and in her *Mansfield Park* she would allude to slavery."[9]

This paper builds upon and combines the pioneering historical work of Fleischman with the recent feminist insights of Johnson and Mellor.[10] In the first section, I establish the parlimentary and literary background Austen drew upon, focusing upon the contributions of women writers. The second section discusses the dynamics and politics of slaveholding in the years after the French Revolution. The last two sections discuss *Mansfield Park* in terms of contemporary political theory, especially as embodied in the works of Montesquieu, Brougham, and Macartney.

When Austen began her new novel during the final years of the long struggle against Napoleon, the title she chose suggested the great moral issue of contemporary politics: the slave trade. The novel's title and central location alludes to Lord Chief Justice Mansfield, who, in the case of James Somerset, ruled that, once transported into England, a slave could not be forcibly removed from the country. In that same year, 1772, Burke considered drafting a scheme for gradual emancipation.[11] That this plan never reached the House floor stemmed from

Burke's "conviction that the strength of the West Indian body"—to which Sir Thomas Bertram, Baronet and M.P., belonged, "would defeat the utmost efforts of his powerful party, and cover them with ruinous unpopularity." [12] Abolition was later taken up by the Evangelicals, particularly by members of the Clapham Sect; its eventual triumph was aided ideologically by the establishment of Bonaparte's military despotism in France; earlier, abolitionists—including William Wilberforce and Hannah More—were suspected of Jacobinical leanings. [13] Abolition had been made possible by British command of the seas, especially after Nelson's overwhelming victory at Trafalgar in 1805. With the slave trade closed off to European nations under Napoleon's continental system and the United States's movements toward abolition (achieved in 1808), the threat that Britain should be superseded in this commerce by its rivals disappeared. For several years, only Britain's allies, Portugal and Spain, could import slaves into their American colonies. In the meantime, Britain had captured and held the overseas colonies of France and Holland.

As the long war drew to its slow yet inevitable close after Napoleon's disastrous retreat from Moscow, British men and women considered the fates of the overseas conquests. It seemed likely that most of the former Dutch and French colonies would be returned. In fact, after more than two decades of almost uninterrupted warfare and a final, resounding victory, Britain returned all but Mauritius, Tobago, and St. Lucia to the French, and the Cape (South Africa) and three small Guiana settlements to the Dutch. In exchange, the British government and people wanted only three things: the assurance that the Scheldt Valley and Antwerp should go to a strengthened Holland; that British views on maritime rights should be accepted internationally; and that the France, Spain, and Portugal should abolish their slave trades. Hence, the relevance of the name of William Price's ship, the *Antwerp,* a ship named after the famous low-country port indissolubly linked (in the public's mind) with the question of international abolition. Thus, during the two years (1811–13) Austen worked upon *Mansfield Park,* and even after its 1814 publication, what Mr. Bertram had to say about the slave trade became topical again, as William Wilberforce and his Evangelical and Tory Radical supporters pressed for international sanctions.

Mansfield Park is the first novel Austen wrote with an awareness of an audience outside her family—the first one to be written largely after the publication of *Sense and Sensibility* in 1811. Austen could hope to exert at least some small influence on public opinion. *Sense and Sensibility* had been read and admired, not merely by people of the "middling sorts," but by the highest reaches of the aristocracy (e.g., Lady Bessborough, mother-in-law of a future prime minister) and even by members of the royal family itself (the duke of York and the princess of Wales)— precisely those people best able to influence public and foreign policy.

The novel's title participates in a network of references to the slave trade or to related issues. Fanny's (and Austen's) favorite poet, William Cowper, vehemently opposed the trade and published a series of anti-slavery poems: "The Negroe's Complaint," "Pity for Poor Africans," and "The Morning Dream" (1788), and "Epigram" (1792).[14] Fanny's often-noted Evangelical character traits link her both to the Clapham Sect and to "methodists," many of whom were active in the propaganda campaign surrounding abolition; a few years before his death, Wesley published his *Thoughts upon Slavery* (1787). Even Fanny's hometown, Portsmouth, fits into the novel's web of slave-trade references, if only negatively. Bristol and Liverpool (the former especially) dominated the British share of the trade, distantly followed by other ports on the west coast of England. Portsmouth was largely untainted by the slavers' interest; what Johnson calls Fanny's lack of "uncomfortableness" about Sir Thomas's involvement in the trade is explicable partially through her early years in Portsmouth (107). Sir Thomas is similarly "marked" by his traveling from Antigua via the notoriously anti-abolitionist port of Liverpool.[15]

From the very inception of the English novel, writers were intrigued by the dynamics of slavery.[16] Aphra Behn's *Oroonoko* draws parallels between the condition of English women and of African slaves in Surinam.[17] When abolition of the slave trade reached the national political stage in the 1780s, women entered the public debate.[18] Anna Letitia Barbauld campaigned not merely for abolition, but for the repeal of the Corporation and the Test acts.[19] Hannah More nicknamed her own social and religious circle "the Anti-Slavery Junta."[20] Her 1788 poem, *Slavery,* was later retitled *The Black Slave Trade.*[21]

Sarah Scott, in her popular *Description of Millenium Hall* (1762; fourth edition by 1778), described an estate owned and operated by a female.[22] The narrator, a relative of one of the Hall's founders, has been touring England in order "to cure the ill effects" of "a long abode in the

hot and unwholesome climate of Jamaica," which has increased his fortune but "impaired" his "constitution." Implicitly, the narrator learns
the proper and humane methods of running an estate as he perforce
compares the profits of benevolence and gratitude with those of despotism and forced labor. Charlotte Smith's novel, *Desmond,* provided
yet another model for incorporating "political" issues into aspects of a
"domestic" plot. Smith asks her reader to make explicit comparisons
between West Indian slavery, marriage, and other types of property:
"The romantic action of *Desmond* draws the institution of marriage into
a, by then, carefully ordered 'grouping' of opinions about the ownership
and government of property and invites readers to compare analogues—
that is, to consider wives, too, as a kind of property—and themselves
make inferences about the moral implications of such comparisons." [23]

The innovatory multi-generational plot of Elizabeth Inchbald's first
novel, *A Simple Story,*[24] influenced not merely *Wuthering Heights* as Castle
claims but also, as Doody notes, *Mansfield Park.*[25] *Mansfield Park,* of
course, is a kind of family saga. In a sense, it begins precisely where
Pride and Prejudice (published as Austen was working on this new novel)
leaves off—with the marriages of three sisters. The story of this first
generation is truncated—in the early novels we have learned about the
Charlotte Lucas–like Miss Ward, who has married a sycophantic clergyman, and the Lydia Bennet–like Miss Frances, who has married "to
disoblige her family" (2). *Mansfield Park* collapses these already-written
histories into its first chapter. As with the second half of *A Simple Story,*
the reader gauges the effects of the first generation's actions upon the
lives of their children.

More interesting than this distorted structural similarity, however,
is a similarity in subject matter: the reason that removes the patriarch
(we may also read "despot") from the domestic focus of the narrative,
and that brings about the narrative's climax. After Sandford unites Lord
Elmwood and Miss Milner in marriage, they live together happily for
four years before, like *Mansfield Park*'s Sir Thomas Bertram, Elmwood
leaves "in order to rescue from the depredation of his own steward,
his very large estates in the West Indies" (175). Condemnation of the
Elmwood money remains implicit; however, the events culminating in
Lady Elmwood's adultery occur during her husband's three-year absence. The novel suggests that, had Elmwood remained in England, his
wife's virtue would have remained "intact." A wife and yet no wife, Lady

Elmwood must, like the haremed women in Montesquieu's *Lettres per-sanes,* accept an epistolary substitute for the absent husband. Elmwood falls ill, as did *Millenium Hall*'s narrator and so many others. In 1794, some twelve thousand Englishmen died in the islands; in 1802, yellow fever and other tropical diseases utterly destroyed Napoleon's force of thirty-three thousand veterans in Haiti;[26] Cassandra's fiancé died in the West Indies; Austen's famous contemporary, Matthew Lewis, died re-turning from Jamaica. When Elmwood's letters cease, Lady Elmwood accepts Lord Frederick as her lover in a mixture of pique, confusion, and sheer physical desire. Elmwood's unexpected return strikes his wife like a thunderbolt; she flees to a northern estate, where she devotes herself to repentance and to her daughter's education. Like Lord Elmwood, Sir Thomas Bertram's economic and social status, as well as his political clout and possibly even his parliamentary seat, depend upon the proper management of slave labor. Both novels feature a capricious patriarch. And both novels take advantage of the extreme fluctuations in the price of sugar during the late eighteenth and early nineteenth centuries in order to remove the despot from the scene. In both, the ultimate con-sequence of the vacuum of authority is adultery. *A Simple Story* relegates the emotional and moral vortex to the summary opening of volume 3 (a summary so like *Mansfield Park*'s chapter 1); *Mansfield Park* explores this in often painful detail.

Mary Wollstonecraft's *Vindication* is the *locus classicus* for structural similarities among kinds of oppression, whether political, economic, or gender-based: "Is one half of the human species, like the poor African slaves, to be subject to prejudices that brutalize them?"[27] Wollstone-craft intends "brutalization" to be read etymologically, not metaphori-cally; in her view, both slaves and British women are dehumanized, dressed up and paraded to potential buyers like horses: "What can be more indelicate than a girl's *coming out* in the fashionable world? Which, in other words, is to bring to market a marriageable miss, whose person is taken from one public place to another, richly *caparisoned*."[28] Political, economic, and domestic despotism is a kind of disease, a "corruption" or a "baneful lurking gangrene."[29] The solution, Wollstonecraft argues, involves changing the education of women: "It is likewise proper . . . to make women acquainted with . . . the science of morality, or the study of the political history of mankind."[30]

Wollstonecraft's metaphors of despotism as a form of "disease" also appear in male writers, forming a *topos* of colonial political theory. Clarkson himself declared, "If the unhappy slave is in an unfortunate situation, so is the tyrant who holds him. Action and reaction are equal to each other, as well in the moral as in the natural world. You cannot exercise an improper dominion over a fellow-creature, but by a wise ordering of Providence you must necessarily injure yourself."[31] Montesquieu argued that slave owners developed bad habits from the exercise of absolute power: "Slavery . . . is neither useful to the master nor to the slave. [The master] contracts among his slaves all sorts of bad habits, and accustoms himself to the neglect of the moral virtues. He becomes haughty, passionate, obdurate, vindictive, voluptuous, and cruel."[32] In light of contemporary stereotypes of white West Indian society, Sir Thomas Bertram's decision to have his son and heir accompany him to Antigua, "in the hope of detaching him from bad connections at home," seems ludicrously ill-informed.[33] Resident society was widely believed to be a moral cesspool, and the plantations breeding grounds of literal and metaphorical corruption. In his notorious hatred of the planters, Samuel Johnson went so far as to propose a toast "to the next insurrection of the Negroes in the West Indies."[34] Fictions, whether in prose or in verse, contributed to the propaganda war surrounding abolition; moreover, both sides were aware of this. G. Francklyn accused Clarkson of precisely this manipulation: "I doubt not, you will have had repeatedly acted [*The Tragedy of Oronooko, the Royal Slave,* or the play of *Inkle and Yarico*] to influence the minds of people whom he, and others, have endeavoured to impose upon."[35]

As I have hinted, Austen had an abundance of printed matter containing historical, economic, moral, and theoretical West Indian issues to draw on when she began *Mansfield Park*. At least some of this, particularly Clarkson's definitive *History of Abolition*, she is known to have read and "loved." This is not to claim that *Mansfield Park* is incredibly bookish—although Austen took great pains over detail, as her letters of advice to a would-be novelist, her niece Anna, indicate. Austen derived much knowledge from personal experience: from recollections of her own relatives, who had concerns stretching from Antigua itself (George Austen's trusteeship there) to India.[36] Moreover, the period of composition (1811–13) and date of the novel's appearance determined the way in which most of her readers would react to the Antigua allusions. Having recently abolished the slave trade for themselves, the British public was bent on abolishing that of the rest of Europe as well. Before providing a reading of the novel, I will discuss the most common probable contemporary responses to questions such as: What were the losses Sir Thomas experienced, and how did they come about? What did Sir Thomas have to say about the slave trade? How are these issues thematically important to the novel?

The "losses" Sir Thomas suffers from his Antigua estate must have seemed as mysterious to the Bertrams as to modern readers of *Mansfield Park*. Despite the many cost- and labor-saving devices (including the local growth of food crops such as yams, the introduction of Otaheite or Bourbon cane, and the development of more efficient methods of extracting cane juice), profits declined markedly during the latter part of the eighteenth and early nineteenth centuries. This was due partly to Napoleon's continental system, which prevented the re-exportation of sugar to Europe. More damaging, however, was a steady inflation of estate necessaries; for example, the price of white oak staves used for making sugar hogsheads rose from £3 per thousand in the 1750s to £15 or £20 in the 1820s.[37] Losses were common, especially for absentee land-owners. William Beckford had an income perhaps as high as £70,000 from his Jamaican estates when he inherited them in 1770; in 1797, his total income was perhaps £155,00, but by 1806 was only £30,000.[38] While Beckford was raising debts, however, his agents, the Wildmans, were profiting: Thomas Wildman bought Newstead Abbey from Byron for 90,000 guineas, or £94,300.[39]

Matthew Lewis's journal provides valuable insights into what Sir Thomas Bertram may have experienced on arriving at his Antigua estates. Moreover, as Lewis and Bertram attempt similar supervisory strategies, the journal foregrounds the problems inherent in episto-lary "accounts" important for my later discussion. Lewis first visited his estate, Cornwall, in 1816. He continued to supervise another estate, Hoadley, by letter: "report[s] assured me that Hoadley was the best-managed estate in the island."[40] Upon visiting Hoadley in 1818, how-ever, he was rudely awakened: "I expected to find a perfect paradise, and I found a perfect hell . . . my trustee had assured me that my negroes were the most contented and best-disposed . . . I found them in a perfect uproar."[41] Despite his own prior experience at Cornwall, Lewis trusts the "report" from Hoadley because it is in his interest to do so—his belief absolves him from the knowledge of cruelties for which he is ultimately responsible and allows him to view himself as a model landlord. Gaspar notes that such observations "reflect a ruling class maneuver to make [the slaveowner] feel better about owning slaves." [42] Raymond Williams claims that "absentee landlords . . . are a class who, whatever they say, have always known what is being done, through and for them." [43]

Planters sometimes went to incredible lengths to justify their treatment of slaves. G. Francklyn claimed that the pain caused in branding slaves "cannot be half so considerable as a young lady must feel on having her ears bored" (176). Francklyn, of course, had undergone neither operation. Colonel Phipps argued that such abuses as did occur were rare and not systematic: "There was once a haberdasher's wife who locked up her apprentice girl, and starved her to death; but did any body think of abolishing haberdashery on this account? . . . the Negroes were cheerful and happy." [44] While some of these assertions are not entirely false, they deceive because they deliberately omit salient details, a strategy utilized by Mrs. Norris. On most estates, every Negro did have "a little spot of ground . . . and time to cultivate it"; [45] such cultivation was a brutal necessity, for the planters generally did not import enough food even to sustain their property's lives. Besides saving the planters money on supplies, the policy of keeping slaves in a constant state of malnutrition, it was believed, made them more docile and less likely to revolt. As Fleischman argues, "the task in which Sir Thomas was likely to have been engaged . . . was the elementary one of seeing to it that his slaves did not die *so readily* of malnutrition, overwork, or brutality." [46]

The planters and their allies in England shared an amazing intransigency. Those in Parliament who both owned slaves and supported abolition, such as Sir James Johnstone and Lord Holland, were exceptional. [47] William Beckford, author of *Vathek,* supported slavery his entire life, as did Matthew Lewis. Rather than having his mind changed after a short residence in the West Indies (as Fleischman argues for Bertram), Lewis had many of his preconceptions reinforced. He may have disliked the word "slavery" but not the thing itself: he commanded one of his possessions, "say that you are my negro, but do not call yourself my slave." [48] Even those who recognized the essential inhumanity of trade and slavery (including Gibbon and Montesquieu) believed the slave trade a necessary evil; as one M.P. put it: "it was not an amiable trade, but neither was the trade of the butcher an amiable trade, and yet a mutton chop was, nevertheless, a very good thing." [49] At best, planters might agree to a suspension of the slave trade in order both to maintain their monopoly upon the sugar trade and to prevent an oversupply. In February 1804 (when Sir Thomas was considering making his journey), Wilberforce wrote to Hannah More, "some of the principal West Indian proprietors begin themselves to relish the idea of suspending the Slave Trade for three or five years. They have not the assurance to pretend to be influenced by any principles of justice, but merely by a sense of interest." [50]

Throughout the propaganda over abolition, supporters of the status quo touted the symbolic nature of any tampering with private property. In 1793, the earl of Abingdon postulated a connection between Jacobin-ism and abolition: "For in the very definition of the terms themselves, as descriptive of the thing, what does the abolition of the slave trade mean more or less in effect, than liberty and equality? What more or less than the rights of man? And what is liberty and equality, and what the rights of man, but the foolish fundamental principles of this new philosophy." [51] Wilberforce's sons record a conversation in which a Cabinet member said to Lady Spencer, "Your friend Mr Wilberforce will be very happy any morning to hand your ladyship to the guillotine." [52]

Because a slave was property, the argument went, the continuation of slavery was protected by the British Constitution, which, as Locke had it, guaranteed "life, liberty, and property." Other writers, how-ever, noted the structural similarities between slavery and recognized forms of government and customs. In other words, the slave estate, ruled by fear, was a small despotism. Wollstonecraft began *The Wrongs of Woman* with: "all women everywhere are slaves." In *A Vindication of the Rights of Woman,* Wollstonecraft developed the parallels among slavery, despotism, and the condition of women in England, as my earlier quotes suggest. In *Emma,* Austen herself angrily castigated "the governess trade."

In concentrating on the network of connections among *Mansfield Park,* acrimonious parliamentary debates over the slave trade and the continuance of the institution of slavery itself, I am arguing, essentially, a much broader interpretation than the one usually given to the famous letter to Austen's niece, Anna. In critiquing Anna's novel-in-progress,

Austen suggested: "we think you had better not leave England. Let the Portmans go to Ireland, but as you know nothing of the Manners there, you had better not go with them. You will be in danger of giving false representations. Stick to Bath & the Foresters. There you will be quite at home." [53] As I have shown, Austen knew a great deal about both the "manners" of the West Indies, and the various "representations" of them current, not merely from her reading but from George Austen's trusteeship of an Antigua estate, her brothers' naval stations in the West Indies, and through Cassandra's fiancé and other friends of the family. *Persuasion*'s Mrs. Croft echoes Austen's own knowledge and love of precision, saying: "We do not call Bermuda or Bahama, you know, the West Indies." [54] By sticking to places where she can feel "quite at home," however, Austen devastatingly exposes the contradictions inherent both in absentee landlordism and in the ideologies and realities of family life. This section discusses first, how Austen's contemporaries conceptualized the relationship between family and state, and second, the parallels between Austen's and Montesquieu's depictions of the politics of representations of reality.

That Austen should choose to do so by depicting "3 or 4 Families in a Country Village" should not surprise us, familiar as we are with the feminist equation of the personal and the political. [55] Gary Kelly notes that "throughout Anti-Jacobin fiction there is a tendency not only to reduce large political and public issues to their domestic, everyday, commonplace consequences in individual domestic experience (a tendency found in Burke's *Reflections* and fully developed in the Romantic historical novels), but also actually to translate the political and public issues into private and domestic equivalents." [56] Johnson notes that Burke's *Reflections* "is striking for the degree to which it presents a vast and multifaceted series of events in France as a unitary family drama." [57] Burke was not an anomaly; as J. C. D. Clark argues, the theoretical identification of family and state by no means died after the Glorious Revolution, as the common use of the term "patriarchy" in the period makes clear. [58] Two decades before the publication of *Esprit des lois,* Montesquieu illustrated, in a hybridized novel form, the structure of the despotic state as family in *Lettres persanes.* [59] Family quarrels could still lead to revolution or to civil war, as was feared when King George IV attempted to divorce his wife only three years after Austen's death suggested. Anti-abolitionists used this identification of family and state to support their positions as slaveholders, often finding biblical justifications for owning slaves. Franklyn argued: "But it appears clearly, from the context, that the *elder* brethren of Canaan were involved in the sentence; a sentence pronounced by Noah, the supreme lord of the whole earth, and the only person, since our first parent, who had a right to claim the title of universal monarch."[60]

As Johnson notes of *Pride and Prejudice,* the presence of Lydia Bennet deflects criticism from Elizabeth's behavior; Lydia acts as "a decoy who attracts the disapproval to which Elizabeth herself could otherwise be subject."[61] In *Mansfield Park,* Edmund similarly acts as a decoy for his father. Monaghan indicates the problems inherent in Edmund's acceptance of multiple livings, yet fails to note that this *reflects* his father's possession of multiple estates. Supervision of multiple estates within England itself, or even within the British Isles as a whole, could be maintained through annual peregrinations. Despite Sir Thomas's voyage to Antigua, he remains an absentee landowner, although now of Mansfield Park itself.[62] Sir Thomas Bertram's attempts to regulate affairs at Mansfield fail as miserably as his earlier epistolary supervision of Antigua, and for precisely the same reasons.

Sir Thomas's vision of the familial government he has established at Mansfield Park does not coincide with the life his children experience. In this noncoincidence between what we could call "theory" and "practice" resides a key to the novel's political system; Montesquieu's classic definitions of forms of government help here. Sir Thomas likes to believe his Northampton estate (and we should hear that embedded syllable, "state") is monarchical: a rule by one, true—but a rule by law both founded upon and endeavoring to instill a love of "honor" in its subjects. While he succeeds to a limited degree with Edmund, the Miss Bertrams experience not monarchical law but despotic caprice, a domination based upon fear. Deprived as we are of representations of Sir Thomas's pre-voyage interactions with his daughters, we must reconstruct his relationships with them from Maria's and Julia's reactions to the news of his departure, their responses to his letters and return, and from his subsequent treatment of them.

Sir Thomas, who "had never seemed the friend of [his daughters'] pleasures" (28), has adopted a distant, slightly preoccupied authoritarian stance. Never having been inspired with any "love" for their father, Maria and Julia experience his absence, not as an emotional void but as "welcome," as a "relief," as the negative creation of freedom by the removal of "restraint" (28). Although still subject to the father's word, especially now that that word is written, they paradoxically feel more autonomous, "at their own disposal" (28). Subjected all the same, their condition *feels* different because they are no longer objects of the despot's informing gaze. As if he had been blinded (a metaphor all the more compelling in that it was common knowledge that many Oriental despots, from Gibbon's Byzantine emperors to the Persian shahs of Chardin or Montesquieu, disqualified other claimants to power by blinding them), Sir Thomas must now order and give orders to a reality he can no longer directly observe. And because Mrs. Norris, the Miss Bertrams' great ally, assists in creating the representations of reality sent across the Atlantic to Antigua, Maria's and Julia's euphoria stems in part from the power over reality as text newly "at their disposal."

I have drawn upon Montesquieu's *Esprit des lois* (1748) in order to highlight eighteenth-century distinctions between monarchic and despotic rule. The situation I now describe, however, bears greater resemblance to *Lettres persanes* (1721). In the "seraglio" subplot of that text (the letters exchanged between Usbek and various eunuchs and women in his harem), the reader gradually discovers the horrifying abyss between the represention of idyllic life in the despot's absence and the grim yet equally represented accounts of disorder, deceit, and sexual misconduct in the final letters. As the eunuchs jockey for power, the Persian women take advantage of the fissure formed between rival factions, rewarding those who turn a blind eye to misconduct and who participate in misrepresenting the fictional world. Within the moral system of *Lettres persanes*, Usbek's "honor" resides in the fear-enforced chastity of his women; as time passes and his return to Ispahan is repeatedly postponed, that fear lessens and the harem becomes irremediably corrupt.

Mansfield Park depicts a similar chain of events. Sir Thomas's absence is motivated by epistolary accounts of the Antigua estate's "poor returns" (28). Father and son depart in the fall, intending to return the following September (32–33). Sir Thomas leaves a strange "regency" behind him, dividing his "confidence" between "Mrs. Norris's watchful attention" and Edmund's "judgement" (28). A full year passes almost without incident—indeed, in only two pages. But only Tom returns on time; Sir Thomas is delayed and delayed again, until more than two years have passed. Austen reminds us of the difficulties of long-distance governance: it is "some months" before the inhabitants of the Park receive his consent to Maria's engagement (34).

Although the first year of Sir Thomas's absence passes relatively quietly, it lays the groundwork for the swift moral decay of the second. Most obviously, it introduces Rushworth and the Crawfords (35).[63] The conspiracy between Maria and Mrs. Norris, their manipulations of the texts by which Sir Thomas must order Mansfield, begin with the request for his consent to Maria's engagement. Mrs. Norris seems to have used Edmund as a test case for Sir Thomas's response; Austen notes that "no *respresentation* of [Mrs. Norris's] could induce [Edmund] to find Mr. Rushworth a desirable companion" (35, my emphasis). The text suggests that Aunt Norris, accepting discretion as the better part of valor, decides that "no representation" of Rushworth's obvious personal shortcomings might be the best representation of all. Sir Thomas's response supports this reading, noting Rushworth's economic qualifications and political connections while making no comment upon his character: "Sir Thomas . . . was truly happy in the prospect of an alliance so unquestionably advantageous . . . . It was a connection exactly of the right sort; in the same county, and the same interest" (35).[64] The despot, always subjected to human limitations, cannot obtain omniscience, but must rely upon the often self-interested representations of others. Distorting these representations becomes just one technique by which the relatively powerless subvert power.

Chapters 5 to 20 are punctuated by Sir Thomas's letters home, well-intentioned attempts to run Mansfield. His efforts at long-distance direction parallel those of Usbek. As with his Oriental counterpart, Sir Thomas's letters arrive too late; they address situations already superseded. As communication, they fail utterly, producing effects in their readers entirely different from their author's intentions; even "the day at Sotherton, with all its imperfections, afforded the Miss Bertrams much more agreeable feelings than were derived from the letters from Antigua" (96). Sir Thomas's letters respond to a fictive past, to other letters that rhetorically represent reality (the novel as *we* read it). Mrs. Norris's letters in particular seem to have recreated Rushworth in a flattering light; upon returning, Sir Thomas is surprised by his prospective son-in-law's purely negative personal virtues: his possessing "not more than common sense," his having "nothing disagreeable in . . . figure or address" (33). Because these letters correspond to an alternate reality, they create unresolvable paradoxes for the tenants of Mansfield: because they are the words of the father, and because they are signed with the Name of the Father, they ought to be obeyed, yet cannot be. They add to the instability of the regency government; by their unmeaning, yet imperative significations, they change the mere absence of authority into a vacuum that threatens to suck all the narrative's characters into a moral, social, and economic abyss. Because Sir Thomas corresponds with a partially fictionalized past, his letters legitimize transgression. He leaves behind him subjects already chafing at his restraints; despite the Miss Bertrams' good intentions, never "*aiming* at one gratification that would *probably* have been forbidden by Sir Thomas" (28, my emphases), they move imperceptibly (and at Sotherton, quite literally) down the garden path, recreating at Mansfield the conditions of economic and ethical insolvency that Sir Thomas has attempted to rectify in Antigua. Maria resolves upon a loveless marriage in order to escape restraint; ultimately, she criminally elopes with Henry Crawford from London. This transgression can only be revealed in letters.

The famous theatricals, the abortive preparations for the performance of Inchbald's *Lovers' Vows* (an adaptation and translation for the English stage of Kotzebue's *Das Kind der Liebe*), do not merely strike at the moral system upholding Mansfield Park or blur boundaries between illusion and reality. We can read, in the rehearsals of an Inchbald play in a novel itself modeled in some ways upon Inchbald's fiction, an odd continuation of the tradition of eighteenth-century masquerade that Castle sees culminating in *A Simple Story*. The ecstatic liberation characteristic of earlier masquerades was predicated upon the marked visual disjunction between the carnival and everyday life: the visor covering the face, the costume disguising the body. In *Mansfield Park,* however, even these marks are "internalized."[65] Without the formality of costume, and in the absence of "good hardened real acting" (112), the boundaries between performer and role disappear, as Mary Crawford's playful confusion of pronouns demonstrates: "Who is to be Anhalt? What gentleman among you am I to have the pleasure of making love to?"

Mary Crawford's speech suggests another theme of the carnivalesque: the World Upside Down. Inchbald's play not only brings together social ranks that should be kept separate (in a way reminiscent of Richardson's *Pamela*), but reverses quotidian courtship practices; the play continues the sexual allegory of the Sotherton episode. Now, however, the possibilities of transgression are not limited to the tame "wilderness," but spread like an infection from one Mansfield room to another, even to Fanny's attic. Fanny must first "make love" to Edward herself, helping him to prepare his part—then cede that role to Mary, while paradoxically remaining (as prompter) guardian of the text.

The most severe upheaval, however, occurs in the twin male sanctums of Mansfield, the billiard room and Sir Thomas's bedroom. In these rooms, striking out against a restrictive moral system becomes a striking out of the signs of the father, of patriarchal texts. Yates transforms the billiard room from a locus of ritualized combat between men into an arena for narcissistic self-display: a stage replaces the billiard table. The entire room is feminized, cordoned off with what later become Mrs. Norris's green curtains. Sir Thomas's room is equally transformed, uncharacteristically lit up by candles; its most distinguishing piece of furniture, the bookcase, is removed. As if in revenge for those disagreeable letters from Antigua, the father has been written out, not merely of the play but of his own room. His physical return restores apparent order to the disordered estate, scattering its inhabitants, acting "comme la foudre qui tombe au milieu des éclats et des tempêtes," which Usbek had wished his letters to be. Despite letters announcing that return, it is unexpected and strikes terror into his children's hearts. He appears like a revenant, leaving Julia "aghast." While the written words from Antigua reinforced the false security of absence and enabled the endless speechifying of the theatricals, the spoken word of return leaves all speechless, closing the first volume without authorial comment. Julia's words—"My father is come! He is in the hall at this moment!"—echo in the space between volumes, accenting the caesura-like pause and ringing with the deadly certainty of Judgment.

Sir Thomas's return (as his later mistreatment of Fanny makes abundantly clear) forces all of the women to realize, at least subconsciously, that the apparent "freedom," the absence of "restraint," was illusory. For this freedom can never, in the despotic world, be a freedom to "act" in any way; even by escaping the father's gaze, the objects of that gaze can never become subjects, except in being "subjected." The Antigua trip creates a freedom to desire, a sense that "every indulgence is . . . within reach" (28). But as in *Lettres persanes,* female desire must not be satisfied: to move beyond restraints is to transgress fatally, because sexually. The twin allegories of *Mansfield Park,* volume 1 (the wilderness of Sotherton and the theatricals), play upon this sexual transgression. *Mansfield Park* and female-authored anti-Jacobin novels make clear that both restraints and apparent liberations are constructed by and in the self-interests of men.[66] Literally, walls and gate of the "wilderness" of Sotherton are constructed by men, just as the script of Maria's transgression is written by Henry: "prohibited," "authority," and "protection" are all Crawford's words, as is the suggestion of evading the locked gate. Maria's entrance into The Wilderness and her later elopement, like the sexual fall of Elizabeth Hamilton's Julia Delmond, are engineered by hopeful seducers. The theatricals, and eventually *Lovers' Vows* itself, are suggested by Yates, just as the casting of the major roles is at least nominally determined by men.

The narrator of Sarah Scott's *Millenium Hall* describes his "impaired constitution," explaining why the corrupting climate of Jamaica forced him to return to England. In the eighteenth century, the "corruption" inherent in certain climates increasingly came to be seen as merely the outward manifestation of moral and political corruption. This section discusses a few significant stages in the development of the multifaceted theories concerning corruption, arguing that Sir Thomas needs to be "read" as a modification of the stereotype of the returned planter. By looking at Macartney's debunking of eighteenth-century depictions of China, I claim that Fanny's reading of Macartney prepares her to resist Sir Thomas's demands.

Montesquieu's theories of the impact of climate not merely upon the physical constitution of the individual human body but also upon the political constitution of the state explained why geographical areas prone to diseases such as yellow fever were also prone to despotic forms of government. Cooler climates, such as those of Europe and of the North American colonies, produced healthier individuals and healthier governments. Because the body politic, like the human body, was exposed to agents of "corruption" both within and without, Montesquieu could explain why apparently healthy governments, such as those of late Republican Rome or of seventeenth-century France, could degenerate into despotisms. Material goods, especially luxuries, mysteriously affected both the human body and the body politic.[67]

Scientific advances, such as Harvey's discovery of the circulation of blood, seemed to reinforce and even to suggest improvements upon these theories. An empire, conceived of as a body, relied upon the circulation of goods but also of persons for its continued existence. Novels, the drama, and political treatises document the circulation of individuals (their departure from and return to the mother country) as part of the normal workings of empire.[68] These men, theories and fictions agree, are adversely affected by prolonged residence in a corrupting climate and society.

In *An Inquiry into the Colonial Policy of the European Powers*,[69] first published in 1802, Henry Brougham described how the West Indies affected the physical health and the personal morals of English residents as well as the constitution of the mother country, explicitly counterpointing the various meanings and methods of "corruption." He begins by discussing the degeneration of the Englishman's moral character in the absence of Englishwomen and the development of patterns of promiscuity that encourage the spread of specifically sexual diseases: "The want of modest female society—the necessity of gratifying the desires engendered by a burning climate—the abundance of unhappy women, whose blood boils with still stronger passions, and renders them, in the European's eyes, only an inferior race, formed for the corporeal convenience of their masters—these are other causes of dissolute morals. The want of female society, while it brutalizes the minds and manners of men, necessarily deprives them of all the virtuous pleasures of domestic life, and frees them from those restraints, which the presence of a family always imposes on the conduct of the most profligate men"[70] (i, 70). Worse even than the sexual "brutalization" of the planters are the political "contaminations" they undergo: "Hence arises the most disgusting contamination with which the residence of the new world stains the character of the European—a love of uncontrouled power over individuals—a selfish reference of their situation to his own wants—a disgraceful carelessness about the happiness of a race, with whose enjoyments he cannot sympathize—a detestable indifference to the sufferings of his fellow-creatures—and a habit, no less odious, of indulging, at their expence, every caprice of temper or desire." Could this contamination be subject to quarantine—could the lands "beyond the pale" be cordoned off from the "mother country," the damage to England's "sons" contained? Unfortunately, however, because of the "circulation" of populations, the "character" of the mother country is also damaged:

"Upon their return to their native country, their habits are too deeply rooted, to be shaken off; and their influence is not inconsiderable upon the society in which they mingle. Others find in the West Indies, a station congenial to their former lives; but they return still more depraved in principles and taste, armed with an influence which they did not before possess."[71] By sending a character to the West Indies, novelists implicitly encoded what appears to be a violation of the law of conservation of character. West Indians were particularly known for heartlessness and irascibility: "A correspondent in the *Public Advertiser* (September 29, 1780) records an incident of which Goldsmith had told him, in which 'several cottages were destroyed' near the house of 'a great West Indian.'"[72] While an underling such as St.-Preux returns tamed, perhaps even emasculated, from Anson's punitive expedition against the Spanish Main, Inchbald's Dorriforth returns from his West Indian estate a confirmed tyrant, authoring capricious laws, insisting upon observance of their letter, and pronouncing unjustifiably harsh and woefully inappropriate sentences to witting and unwitting offenders, as the twin banishments of Lady Elmwood and her daughter Matilda illustrate.[73]

In this light, Fleischman's emphasis upon Sir Thomas's new "firmness" is entirely appropriate.[74] That Fanny possesses even a negative will becomes abhorrent to Mrs. Norris and Sir Thomas alike. Her refusal to enter into a loveless marriage with Henry Crawford (and thus promote the system of familial alliances to which he sacrifices his own daughter) produces a crisis qualitatively similar to that caused of the princess of Wales's refusal to marry in 1815. Having accustomed himself to exerting *de facto* absolute power over his Negro chattel (*de facto* in light of the inadmissibility of evidence by coloreds against whites), Sir Thomas expects an identical submission from the inhabitants of Mansfield, females especially. By saying "no," Fanny commits a treasonous act, a crime of *lèse majesté* punishable by exile and even death. For, as Austen makes clear, the very air of Portsmouth undermines Fanny's health and could lead to her demise.[75] Exiling a young woman in already dubious health to a city becomes a judicial murder or a domestic equivalent to the colonial practice of starving slaves into submission. It duplicates the contemporary practice of transportation, which deported those convicted of crimes against property to unhealthy climates—to Botany Bay, where Austen's aunt Perrot would have been sent if she had been convicted after having been accused of stealing twenty shillings worth of lace. Maria Bertram is similarly exiled for adultery, for exerting female will and asserting female sexuality. Mrs. Norris travels with her to an "establishment" in "another country"; both are condemned to an islanded existence, "remote and private," and with "little society" (424). These exiles repeat the sentences imposed upon slaves convicted of participating in the 1736 Antigua uprising.[76]

Fanny's "no" is an act of rebellion, endangering a system based upon the exchange of women between men as surely as a slave's refusal to work. It poses both an economic and an epistemological threat to the patriarchal system: saying no, "by repudiating the principle of submission it struck at the heart of the master's moral self-justification and therefore at his self-esteem."[77] Lady Tremor, a character in Inchbald's *Such Things Are,* expresses this concisely, asking: "Is it true that the Sultan cut off the head of one of his wives the other day because she said 'I won't?' "[78] Throughout *Mansfield Park,* Sir Thomas and Mrs. Norris discuss Fanny's economic value, usually in negative terms. At nine years old, she is as costly and as unwanted as a child slave; the "trouble and expense" she will be to the Bertrams can only be justified in terms of an alternative economy. As a resident of Mansfield Park, the child Fanny will become a visible and above all daily reminder to the neighborhood of a member of Parliament's "benevolence" (3). At the same time, the Bertrams' expense must be minimized; the governess and other instructors employed for the Miss Bertrams become more cost-efficient by being assigned a third pupil. From the very beginning, Mrs. Norris touts the possibility that she may extend the Bertram connections by marrying into a "creditable establishment," in implicit contrast to her mother. Moreover, by seeing Fanny raised as their sister, it will become "morally impossible" that either Tom or Edmund should duplicate Miss Frances's *mésalliance* by marrying not only beneath them but also endogamously.

Fanny improves her position at Mansfield by demonstrating her economic value. David Stalker, an employee on the Stapleton plantations in Nevis, had advised buying slaves young: "they are fully seasoned by 18 and in full as handy as them that is born in the country [Creoles] but them full grown fellers think it hard to work never being brought up to it they take it to heart and dy or is never good for any things."[79] In the early chapters of the novel, we have witnessed Fanny's "seasoning";

from having been merely a debit for almost a decade, a body for which so much clothing and food (but not firewood!) must be set aside every year, Fanny becomes a "credit." After Maria's marriage, Fanny becomes an unpaid companion to Lady Bertram, providing a service *gratis* for which many impoverished young women, including Sydney Owenson, received wages. When she attracts the attentions of the wealthy Henry Crawford, her value rises still further. Doweryless as she is, Crawford's proposal converts her into an extremely marketable commodity. At very little cost to himself, Sir Thomas can gain all the advantages of a connection that, in Maria's case, cost him many thousands of pounds. Fanny's insistent refusal, as absurd and as infuriating as a cargo of sugar (or of slaves) refusing to be sold to the highest bidder, also potentially alienates Henry and the naval interests to which he is so closely connected (through Admiral Crawford)—interests crucial to the continued well-being of the British West Indies.

The text implies Fanny may on some level be aware of the revolutionary potential of her "no." She has been reading, we are told, Macartney's *Travels in China.* In the mid-1790s, Lord Macartney had been sent to the Celestial Empire in an abortive attempt to extend British commercial privileges. Barlow published a biography and extended excerpts from Macartney's journal after the lord's death in 1806; Fanny seems to have read these. Macartney's journal is noteworthy in that it opposes popular eighteenth-century notions of China as a near-utopian benevolent despotism, governed by a bureaucratic meritocracy. Instead of Voltaire's and Goldsmith's visions of a nation of philosophers, Macartney posits a nation whose inhabitants are prone to the same moral failings as those of Europe: "the boasted moral institutes of China are not much better observed than those of some other countries, and that the disciples of Confucius are composed of the same fragile materials as the children of Mammon in the western world." [80] Macartney's China is an absolute patriarchy: "all power and authority . . . derive solely from the sovereign," who, we learn, has sired many sons. The emperor/father's word is immortal; the laws he and his predecessors have made so inviolable that "no consideration could ever induce him to infringe them." [81]

In Great Britain, as my discussion of both pro- and anti-abolition tracts illustrated, the patriarchal family was regarded as both a microcosm of the monarchical state and necessary to the continuance of that state. Macartney indicates that the same is true in China: "A Chinese family is regulated with the same regard to subordination and economy that is observed in the government of a state[;] the paternal authority, though unlimited, is usually exercised with kindness and indulgence." Although "usually" kind and indulgent, the prose suggests, the "paternal authority" can be abusive; a father may even sell his girl-children into slavery. Where this authority is absolute, there are no legitimate means of redress—all demurrals are rebellions. All individual wills are and must be subordinated to that of the father. The child must feel grateful; any child who attempted to claim an "interest" contrary to that of the father "would be unnatural and wicked." Chinese society, Macartney asserts, has so successfully inculcated the virtues of obedience that "an undutiful child is a monster that China does not produce." [82]

Fanny's reading, then, prepares her for her rebellion but also makes that rebellion more difficult. Through his demystification of the eighteenth-century concept of "China," Macartney teaches Fanny to recognize that a "usually" kind and indulgent despot is still a despot, that the "inviolable" word may be inapplicable to changed circumstances. Yet Macartney cannot suggest how one might resist the "unusual" injustices without becoming "unnatural," "wicked," or a "monster." Like his contemporary, Burke, Macartney believes that amelioration of the conditions of the subjected may be achieved gradually: "A sudden transition from slavery to freedom, from dependence to authority, can seldom be borne with moderation or discretion. Every change in the state of man ought to be gentle and gradual, otherwise it is commonly dangerous to himself and intolerable to others." Macartney draws connections among the dangers of reform in China and the atrocities that resulted from revolution in France and, interestingly enough, the West Indian island of Saint Domingue: "the Chinese, if not led to emancipation by degrees, but let loose on a burst of enthusiasm would probably fall into all the excesses of folly, suffer all the paroxysms of madness, and be found as unfit for the enjoyment of freedom as the French and the negroes." [83] We can begin to imagine, then, how Fanny's reading, which suggests analogies not merely between conditions in China and those in the West Indies but also with her own odd status at Mansfield, may have prompted and shaped those unrecorded questions about the slave trade.

Critics as diverse as Halperin and Claudia Johnson share a dissatisfaction with the ending of *Mansfield Park,* especially in comparison to the uplifting endings of *Pride and Prejudice* or *Emma.* Fanny rejects Henry Crawford in order to marry a younger son, a clergyman, almost incestuously. Yet the Crawfords inhabit a realm vicious enough to corrupt young women, as Mary's shamelessly open reference to homosexual sodomy, to *"Rears* and *Vices,"* makes abundantly clear. After Fanny's marriage to her first cousin Edmund, Austen relegates them first to Thornton Lacey, then to the parsonage at Mansfield. Yet this less-than-euphoric ending is necessary to the novel's, and particularly Fanny's, integrity. *This* Pemberley is tainted. We have seen enough of Edmund's casuistry (especially where Mary Crawford or acting are concerned) to postulate that, should his elder brother Tom die childless, he could have reconciled himself to absentee landlordism or slaveholding as easily as he reconciles himself to holding plural livings.

At the conclusion of *Mansfield Park,* Austen leaves us not in the fairytale-like atmosphere of *Emma* or *Pride and Prejudice* but in one resembling the world and family she knew. The errors of Elizabeth Bennett or Emma Woodhouse have no lasting effects on the societies around them; the moral effects of slaveowning and absenteeism come close to destroying the circle at Mansfield, which is a microcosm of Great Britain itself. Literature by women in the early nineteenth century often, as I have argued elsewhere, explored the ethical dimensions of empire building.[84] Like Sydney Owenson before her and Mary Shelley after, Jane Austen depicts the inescapable problems and the moral compromises made inevitable by the power dynamics of Britain's "second" empire: one based not upon settlement but upon subjugation.

Notes

1. John Pollock, *Wilberforce* (London: Constable, 1977), 245.
2. Cited in Wendy Hinde, *Castlereagh* (London: Collins, 1981).
3. Jane Austen, *Letters,* ed. R. W. Chapman (Oxford: Clarendon Press, 1932), 292.

4. Jane Austen, *Mansfield Park* (Oxford: Oxford University Press, 1970), 1.

5. R. S. Neale, *Class in English History, 1680–1850* (Oxford: Basil Blackwell, 1981), 200.

6. T. McKenzie, "Derivation and Use of 'Consequence' in *Mansfield Park*," *Nineteenth-Century Fiction* 40 (1985): 281–96.

7. Thomas Clarkson, *The History of the Rise, Progress, and Accomplishment of the Abolition of the African Slave-Trade by the British Parliament*, 2 vols. (London: Longman, Hurst, Rees, and Orme, 1808), 1:24. Throughout this paper, I will indicate information available to Austen from her reading of Clarkson by providing citations from his *History of Abolition* in lieu of the original citations.

8. Claudia Johnson, *Jane Austen* (Chicago: University of Chicago Press, 1988), xvii, 107.

9. Park Honan, *Jane Austen: Her Life* (London: Weidenfeld and Nicolson, 1987), 334. The book *A History of the Abolition of the Slave Trade* only peripherally concerned African slavery. Chapman argues that, in referring to Clarkson in the letter dated January 24, 1813, Austen is "more probably" referring to Clarkson's 1813 *Life of William Penn*. The edition of the *Edinburgh Review* in which the *Life* was reviewed appeared five months after Austen's letter—it is highly unlikely that Austen would have attained and read this work in the first three weeks of the year. Moreover, the context of the letter—its use of the preterite—indicates that Austen is referring to an earlier work by Clarkson.

10. See especially Avrom Fleischman, "*Mansfield Park* in Its Time," *Nineteenth-Century Fiction* 22 (1966): 1–18, and *A Reading of "Mansfield Park"* (Minneapolis: University of Minnesota Press, 1967). For a reappraisal of Austen's commitment to feminism, see Margaret Kirkham, *Jane Austen: Feminism and Fiction* (Totowa, N.J.: Barnes and Noble, 1983), and Anne K. Mellor, "Why Women Didn't Like Romanticism: The Views of Jane Austen and Mary Shelley," *The Romantics and Us,* ed. Gene W. Ruoff (New Brunswick: Rutgers University Press, 1990).

11. Roger Anstey, *The Atlantic Slave Trade and British Abolition, 1760–1810* (Atlantic Highlands, N.J.: Humanities Press, 1975), 241. Also referred to in Clarkson, *History of Abolition*, 2:335.

12. Robert Isaac and Samuel Wilberforce, *The Life of William Wilberforce,* 2 vols. (1840), 1:152.

13. Clarkson wrote that anti-Abolitionists "represented" Abolitionists "as a nest of Jacobins; and they held up the cause . . . as affording an opportunity of meeting for the purpose of overthrowing the state" (*History of Abolition,* 2:209).

14. In "Table Talk," Cowper suggested that the American Revolt was an action by Providence in punishing Britain's sins, hinting at the toleration of slavery and the slave trade, while in *The Task,* book 5, he exploited the meta-

phoric links between, on the one hand, salvation and liberty, and on the other, sin and slavery.

15. The early stages of the anti-Abolition campaign were led by two members of Parliament for Liverpool, Bamber Gascoyne and Colonel Tarleton. Wilberforce sometimes traveled accompanied by a bodyguard; he and other members of the "Anti-Slavery Junta" were threatened with bodily harm, especially in the 1790s.

16. Wylie Sypher, *Guinea's Captive Kings* (Chapel Hill: University of North Carolina Press, 1942), is the standard source for literature in English about slavery. An excellent reappraisal of this material can be found in Gordon K. Lewis, *Slavery, Imperialism, and Freedom: Studies in English Radical Thought* (New York: Monthly Review Press, 1978). While these authors do note the contributions of Behn and More, they generally neglect the work of other women—especially those who, like Sarah Scott and Charlotte Smith, embed their comments within apparently nonslavery-related material.

17. Laura Brown, "The Romance of Empire: *Oroonoko* and the Trade in Slaves," in *The New Eighteenth Century* (New York: Methuen, 1987), 41–61, provides an interesting reading of the conjunction of women and slavery in Behn's novel.

18. Clara Reeve, author of *The Old English Baron,* campaigned actively for West Indian interests. Her *Plan of Education* (1792), despite its claim to "have heard and read all the arguments," sides openly with the interested party, the vocal planters, against the mute slaves: "I have been assured, both by natives of the West Indies, and by those occasionally resident there, that the accounts given by the patrons of the negroes are in some instances false, and in most of the others highly exaggerated." She accepts the rosy pictures painted by slaveowners and traders and, by implicitly contrasting Negro slavery with the conditions of the English poor, she anticipates the arguments of Cobbett: "if these things be true, and they have not been yet disproved, surely it would be better if the gentlemen engaged in the negro cause would turn the current of their charity into another channel, and leave this matter as they found it." Clara Reeve, *Plans of Education; with Remarks on the Systems of Other Writers. In a Series of Letters Between Mrs. Darnford and her Friends* (London: T. Hookham, 1792), 82.

19. Catherine E. Moore, " 'Ladies . . . Taking the Pen in Hand': Mrs. Barbauld's Criticism of Eighteenth-Century Women Novelists," in *Fetter'd or Free? British Women Novelists, 1670–1815,* ed. Mary Anne Schofield and Cecilia Macheski (Athens: Ohio University Press, 1986), 388.

20. Pollock, *Wilberforce,* 88.

21. For a discussion of More's influence on Austen, see Kenneth L. Moler, *Jane Austen's Art of Allusion* (Lincoln: University of Nebraska Press, 1968).

22. Sarah Scott, *A Description of Millenium Hall* (New York: Viking Press, 1986).

23. Diana Bowstead, "Charlotte Smith's *Desmond:* The Epistolary Novel as Ideological Argument," in *Fetter'd or Free,* ed. Schofield and Macheski, 237–63.

24. Elizabeth Inchbald, *A Simple Story* (London: Frowde, 1908).

25. Terry Castle, *Masquerade and Civilization* (Stanford: Stanford University Press, 1986), 346. Margaret Anne Doody, "Frances Sheridan: Morality and Annihilated Time," in *Fetter'd or Free,* ed. Schofield and Macheski, 324–58.

26. Sir Alan Burns, *History of the British West Indies,* rev. 2d ed. (London: George Allen and Unwin, 1965), 32. For more information concerning contagious diseases and the West Indies, see William H. McNeill, *Plagues and Peoples* (New York: Anchor Press, 1976), 266ff.

27. Mary Wollstonecraft, *A Vindication of the Rights of Woman* (New York: Norton, 1967), 218.

28. Ibid., 253, my emphasis.

29. Ibid., 47.

30. Ibid., 263–64.

31. Clarkson, *History of Abolition,* 1:20–21.

32. Ibid., 1:49.

33. Considering Tom's status as eldest son and heir, Austen may be suggesting a possible marital mésalliance—Austen's novels are populated by fortune-hunting young women, including Mary Crawford and Tom's own sister Maria. In this maritime voyage, one may perhaps even read a rewriting of Austen's own affair with another Tom, Tom Lefroy, who was shipped off to Ireland by his mother in order to detach him from the young novelist. The best discussion of this affair occurs in Honan, *Austen: Her Life,* especially 105–13.

34. James Boswell, *Life of Johnson,* ed. George Birkbech Hill, 2 vols. (Oxford: Clarendon Press, 1934), 2:200. Pages 200–206 provide a discussion and even a partial bibliography for the antislavery debate.

35. G. Francklyn, *An Answer to the Rev. Mr. Clarkson's Essay* (London: Logographic Press, 1789), 2.

36. Through Warren Hastings, whose son was apparently the ward of Austen's aunt Hancock.

37. J. R. Ward, *British West Indian Slavery, 1750–1834: The Process of Amelioration* (Oxford: Clarendon Press, 1988), 44.

38. James Lee-Milne, *William Beckford* (Wiltshire: Compton Russell, 1976), 11, 70. Estimates of Beckford's income from its component sources in Jamaica, from land in England, and from the funds vary greatly—due partly to his inherited propensity to exaggerate his wealth.

39. Lee-Milne, *Beckford,* 73.

40. Mathew Lewis, *Journal of a Residence Among the Negroes in the West Indies* (London: John Murray, 1845), 164.

41. Ibid.

42. David Barry Gaspar, *Bondmen and Rebels: A Study of Master-Slave Relations in Antigua* (Baltimore: Johns Hopkins University Press, 1985), 188.

43. Raymond Williams, *The Country and the City* (New York: Oxford University Press, 1973), 82.

44. Clarkson, *History of Abolition,* 1:304.

45. Reeve, *Plans,* 79.

46. Fleischman, *A Reading of "Mansfield Park,"* 17, my emphasis.

47. Clarkson, *History of Abolition,* 1:458, 2:551.

48. Lewis, *Journal,* 31.

49. United Kingdom, *Parliamentary History,* vol. 29, col. 28; paraphrased in Clarkson.

50. Clarkson, *History of Abolition,* 1:224.

51. Anstey, *Atlantic Slave Trade,* 317–18.

52. Isaac and Wilberforce, *Wilberforce,* 2:72.

53. Austen, *Letters,* 395.

54. Jane Austen, *The Novels of Jane Austen,* ed. R. W. Chapman, 6 vols. (London: Oxford University Press), vol. 5, 70.

55. Austen, *Letters,* 401.

56. Gary Kelly, "Jane Austen and the English Novel of the 1790s," in *Fetter'd or Free,* ed. Schofield and Macheski, 285–306.

57. Johnson, *Austen,* 4.

58. J. C. D. Clark, *English Society: 1688–1832* (Cambridge: Cambridge University Press, 1985).

59. Montesquieu, *Esprit des lois* (Paris: Didot Frères, 1849); *Lettres persanes* (Paris: Garnier-Flammarion, 1964).

60. Franklyn, *An Answer,* 31.

61. Johnson, *Austen,* 76–77.

62. Moreover, until the introduction of steamships, a planter could, for surprisingly long periods of time, be an "absentee" of both West Indian and British estates. Having left London November 5, 1817, Lewis's arrival in Jamaica was delayed by adverse weather until January 20, 1818—a period just short of eleven weeks.

63. Rushworth's name recalls the name of a character in *A Simple Story:* Rushbrook.

64. It is even possible that Rushworth is himself an absentee planter or an investor in the slave trade, as the West Indian planters and slave traders were powerful enough in Parliament to be called an "interest."

65. Castle, *Masquerade and Civilization,* 341.

66. Here, I depart from Johnson's interpretations of such "conservative" novels as Hamilton's *Memoirs of Modern Philosophers,* arguing instead in a line parallel to that of Mellor's "Female Romantic Ideology."

67. In *Journal of the Plague Year,* for example, Defoe reported beliefs that the plague had been brought first to Europe, then to England, in cloths. Montesquieu and Gibbon suggested that "corrupt" Oriental manners were imported into Greece and Rome along with luxury goods; individual and political morals depended upon the material conditions of life.

68. Moll Flanders goes to Virginia, Dorriforth and Sir Thomas Bertram go to the West Indies and St.-Preux circumnavigates the globe during the War of Jenkins' Ear (1740–48); Antony Harlowe suggests for James Jr. a bride whose name, d'Oyley, associates her with the Jamaican plutocracy; Antony Harlowe and Samuel Foote's Nabob (in the play named after him) exert power gained through commerce with and residence in India; William Beckford, Jr. (the novelist), was the son of a returned Jamaican who retained his colonial accent throughout life, and Matthew Lewis died returning home from his second voyage to his Jamaican estates.

69. Lord Brougham, *An Inquiry into the Colonial Policy of the European Powers,* 2 vols. (New York: Augustus M. Kelley, 1970).

70. Ibid., 1:72.

71. Ibid., 1:77.

72. Williams, *Country,* 75.

73. The despotism and irascibility of both the returning planter or returning Nabob became commonplace in late eighteenth-century fiction and theater. Examples include characters in Frances Sheridan's *Sidney Bidulph* (which Doody believes to be another model for *Mansfield Park*); in Foote's *The Nabob;* and throughout Inchbald's dramatic works, especially *The Wise Man of the East.*

74. Fleischman, *A Reading of "Mansfield Park,"* 17.

75. Recent critics, used to the improved sanitary conditions of modern cities, tend to pooh-pooh Austen's direct assertions; epidemiology and modern statistical studies, however, assert that, well into the nineteenth century, even Paris and London were remarkably unhealthy places. Their unprecedented eighteenth- and nineteenth-century growth were due not to natural increase but to migration from the healthier countryside.

76. Gaspar, *Bondmen,* 8.

77. Eugene Genovese, cited in Gaspar, *Bondmen,* 131.

78. Elizabeth Inchbald, *Such Things Are,* in *The Complete Plays* (London: Garland, 1980), act I, scene i.

79. Cited in Gaspar, *Bondmen,* 88.

80. George Macartney, *An Embassy to China,* ed. J. L. Cranmer-Byng (Hamden, Conn.: Archon Books, 1963), 161.

81. Ibid., 238, 168.

82. Ibid., 224.

83. Ibid., 239, 239–40.

84. See especially Joseph W. Lew, "Sidney Owenson and the Fate of Empire," *Keats-Shelley Journal* 39 (1990): 39–65; and "The Deceptive Other: Mary Shelley's Critique of Orientalism in *Frankenstein,*" *Studies in Romanticism* 30 (Summer 1991): 255–83.

✨ Contributors

Jill Campbell teaches English at Yale University. She is the author of *Natural Masques: Gender and Identity in Fielding's Plays and Novels,* and is at work on a book about Lady Mary Wortley Montagu, Lord Hervey, Alexander Pope, and the construction of gender in eighteenth-century England.

Dianne Dugaw, associate professor of English at the University of Oregon, has written *Warrior Women and Popular Balladry, 1650–1850.* She has published essays on literature, folklore, music, and women's history and has written a book on the satire of John Gay.

Jan Fergus is professor of English at Lehigh University. She is the author of *Jane Austen and the Didactic Novel* and *Jane Austen: A Literary Life,* and has been at work on a study of the reading public in the eighteenth century.

Kathryn Kirkpatrick is assistant professor of English at Appalachian State University in North Carolina, where she teaches courses in feminist theory and women's studies. She is the editor of an edition of Maria Edgeworth's *Belinda* and is

at work on a study of Edgeworth's novels.

Beth Kowaleski-Wallace, editor-in-chief of the *Feminist Literary Theory: A Dictionary,* is the author of *Their Fathers' Daughters: Hannah More, Maria Edgeworth, and Patriarchal Complicity* and coeditor of *Refiguring the Father: New Feminist Readings of Patriarchy.* She teaches in the English department at Boston College.

Joseph Lew teaches English at the Univerity of Hawaii at Manoa. His articles have appeared in *Studies in Romanticism, Keats-Shelley Journal, Eighteenth-Century Studies,* and *The Other Mary Shelley.* He is at work on a book on romantic global narratives.

Shawn Lisa Maurer, a former graduate fellow at the University of Michigan's Institute for the Humanities, teaches English and women's studies at Texas A&M University. She has published articles on Mary Wollstonecraft and early periodical literature and is at work on a study of gender and class in the eighteenth-century English periodical.

Mitzi Myers teaches at UCLA and writes about late eighteenth-century women writers, education, autobiography, and children's literature. She has published numerous essays on Hannah More, Mary Wollstonecraft, and Maria Edgeworth. She has received grants for her book on Edgeworth from ACLS and the Guggenheim Foundation.

Ruth Perry, a utopian projector, founded the women's studies program at MIT, where she is a professor of literature, and the graduate consortium of women's studies at Radcliffe. Her books include *Women, Letters, and the Novel, The Celebrated Mary Astell,* an edition of George Ballard's 1752 *Memoirs of Several Ladies of Great Britain,* and a volume of essays about nurturing creativity, *Mothering the Mind.*

Susan Staves is Paul Proswimmer Professor of the Humanities at Brandeis University. She is the author of *Players' Scepters: Fictions of Authority in the Restoration* and *Married Women's Separate Property in England,* as well as many articles on a variety of eighteenth-century subjects, literary and legal. With John Brewer, she has edited and contributed to a collection of essays, *Early Modern Conceptions of Property.*

Janice Farrar Thaddeus, who is head tutor of the history and literature program of Harvard University, has published a number of articles on eighteenth-century women writers and has been at work on a book-length critical study of Frances Burney.

Beth Fowkes Tobin teaches Engish at the University of Hawaii at Manoa. She has published articles on Jane Austen, Maria Edgeworth, and Henry Fielding as well as on the concept of motherhood in eighteeth-century women's magazines. Interested in issues of poverty and property, she is the author of *Superintending the Poor: Charitable Ladies and Paternal Landlords in British Fiction, 1770–1860.*

🙢 Index

303

Philanthropy, 161, 162, 167, 175. *See also* Benevolence; Women: and charity
Piety, 113, 230, 245
Pilkington, Laetitia, 121
Pinchbeck, Ivy, 203
Poaching, 205–6
Pocock, J. G. A., 187
Poovey, Mary, 5, 143, 198, 199
Pope, Alexander, 64, 65, 73, 74, 143, 156 (n. 6)
Poverty, 260, 263
Pratt, Samuel Jackson, 160, 166–69
Primogeniture, 25, 258
Private sphere, 114, 118, 120, 134, 205, 231, 232, 239, 241, 248 (n. 9)
Productivity, 159
Profession, 154–55, 157, 180–84, 191
Profit, 161, 169, 171, 176, 181, 182, 185, 186, 207
Property, 114, 180, 186, 188, 195 (n. 11), 196 (n. 18), 198–205, 219; private, 201–3, 205, 206, 222–23, 281; slaves as, 280, 281; women's access to, 203–7, 221, 222
Propriety, 117, 198–207, 241, 244, 245
Public sphere, 7, 15, 19, 21, 33 (n. 5), 84 (n. 15), 142, 148, 154, 230–32, 239, 242, 248 (n. 9)

Quinlan, Maurice, 199

Race, 5, 6, 175. *See also* Native Americans; Empire; Slavery; Slave Trade; West Indies
Racism, 49
Rack-renting, 189
Radcliffe, Mary Ann, 211

Rake, 56
Rape, 114; attempted, 7, 87, 91, 95, 102, 103, 104; and class, 89, 109 (n. 8), 205–6; false charges of, 91, 96, 97, 102, 106; and female desirability, 8, 90, 91; in Fielding's novels, 86, 87, 89, 90; history of, 88–89, 93, 99, 102–4; legal history of, 8, 88–89, 93, 95, 96, 97, 100–108; trials, 93, 96, 100–108; as violence against women, 88, 109 (n. 8)
Reeve, Clara, 171, 296 (n. 18)
Richardson, Samuel, 114, 124, 125
Robinson, Lillian, 4

Schweickart, Patrocinio, 2–3
Science, 170, 173, 174, 176, 183
Scott, Joan, 9, 10
Scott, Sarah, 128, 139 (n. 40), 159–63, 170, 175–76, 177 (n. 1), 275–76, 288
Scott, Sir Walter, 172
Separate spheres, 17, 19, 35 (n. 27), 118, 119
Sheridan, Richard, 45
Shevelow, Kathryn, 14
Simpson, Antony, 88, 89, 98, 103, 111 (n. 27)
Simpson, Catharine, 3
Slave, 7, 147, 275, 277, 278, 280, 291–92
Slavery, 49, 50, 51, 54, 62 (n. 19), 271–300 passim; domestic, 228–29; sexual, 39, 46, 47. *See also* Empire; West Indies
Slave trade, 272–74, 280, 296 (n. 18); abolition of, 271, 274, 279. *See also* Empire; West Indies
Smallwood, Angela, 89
Smith, Charlotte, 276
Smollett, Tobias, 143, 156 (n. 6)